Second Edition

Public Affairs Reporting:

The Citizen's News

Second Edition

Public Affairs Reporting:

The Citizen's News

Ralph S. Izard • Marilyn S. Greenwald

 Wm. C. Brown Publishers

Book Team

Editor *Stan Stoga*
Developmental Editor *Jane F. Lambert*
Production Coordinator *Kay Driscoll*

 Wm. C. Brown Publishers

President *G. Franklin Lewis*
Vice President, Publisher *George Wm. Bergquist*
Vice President, Publisher *Thomas E. Doran*
Vice President, Operations and Production *Beverly Kolz*
National Sales Manager *Virginia S. Moffat*
Senior Marketing Manager *Kathy Law Laube*
Marketing Manager *Kathleen Nietzke*
Executive Editor *Edgar J. Laube*
Managing Editor, Production *Colleen A. Yonda*
Production Editorial Manager *Julie A. Kennedy*
Production Editorial Manager *Ann Fuerste*
Publishing Services Manager *Karen J. Slaght*
Manager of Visuals and Design *Faye M. Schilling*

Cover design by Benoit & Associates

Library of Congress Catalog Card Number: 90–81595

ISBN 0–697–08615–1

Printed in the United States of America by Wm. C. Brown Publishers, 2460 Kerper Boulevard, Dubuque, IA 52001

10 9 8 7 6 5 4 3 2 1

Contents

Preface

The approaching twenty-first century will bring with it expanded public and journalistic expectations about the role of news organizations in society. Journalism always has been expected to provide citizens with accounts of important events and discussions of what those events mean. It may be impossible that any individual journalist or news agency will achieve all the excellence such attitudes may be construed to mean. But the effort is a significant fact, and even slight progress represents a step toward journalistic maturity.

The expanded journalistic roles apply to reporters in whatever news medium—radio, television, newspapers, magazines or even newsletters. Of course, presentation techniques differ from one medium to another, and these techniques have impact upon methods of gathering information. But whatever the technique, it's inescapable that reporters through the remainder of the twentieth century and into the twenty-first century will have to know more about the subjects with which they are dealing. It's inescapable that news organizations will have to dedicate more funds and time for reporters to do the job expected of them.

This does not signal the death of general-assignment reporters. The necessary diversity of news media content requires aggressive individuals, strong in interviewing and writing skills, who tackle any assignment and rapidly produce understandable, meaningful, and interesting copy. Today's news events are important. Democratic society requires that citizens know what happens in their communities on a day-to-day basis. The talent to handle that diversity makes general-assignment reporters the very backbone of American journalism.

But, as the Commission on Freedom of the Press said in 1947, "It is no longer enough to report the fact truthfully. It is now necessary to report the truth about the fact." The journalistic response to this challenge has been impressive. More and more reporters, usually those with general-assignment backgrounds, have been ticketed to step into expanded roles. These are journalistic specialists—or, as they are called in this book, expert reporters—who concentrate their attention on specific types of subject matter. Augmented by additional college training, continuing education and/or intensive on-the-job training, their special skills are designed to provide depth to coverage of single areas of journalistic and social concern.

It will be the combination of efforts by the expert reporters and the general-assignment reporters that will move the news media closer to the new ideals being set by themselves and by the public they serve.

This book is an effort to chronicle the development and role of the specialist, or expert reporter, in American journalism. It seeks to blend subject-matter description, performance analysis, and discussion of techniques. Even though only two authors are listed, this book in many ways is produced by a "committee." Let us hope that it is without the usual dreary results of a committee report. That committee is composed of those journalistic professionals who were willing to devote their time to being interviewed and to share their knowledge and experience with others. Many journalists are cited in the text; others were used in general background ways. But all were valuable.

We are grateful to be involved in a profession that thrives on the exchange of ideas and on the willingness to share. We express our debt and thanks to many of those people who so capably represented that kind of dedication. Most of those people are listed here as representatives of the organization for which they worked at the time they were interviewed.

Akron Beacon Journal: Richard Metchen, Doug Oplinger.

Arkansas Gazette: Ernie Dumas, Carol Griffee.

Arkansas Times: Bob Lancaster.

Associated Press: Dolores Barclay, Alton Blakeslee, Richard Carelli, Louise Cook, George Cornell, Linda Deutsch, Keith Fuller, Howard Graves, Jules Loh, Kevin McKean, Walter Mears, Brian Sullivan, and Jonathan Wolman.

Athens Messenger: Herb Amey, Bob Ekey.

Atlanta Journal: Mike Kautsch, Selby McCash, Charl Seabrook, and Tom Walker.

Arizona Republic: Ira Fine.

Baltimore Sun: Lyle Denniston.

Boston Globe: Robert Turner.

Bridgeport Post: Frank Decerbo.

CBS News: Bill Plante, Eric Ober.

Charleston News and Courier: Jeff Watkins.

Chicago Tribune: William Barnhart, Casey Bukro, Bruce Buursma, Manuel Galvin, Ron Kotulak, Michele Norris, Meg O'Connor, and Clarence Page.

Cincinnati Enquirer: Jim Delaney, George Hahn, John Kiesewetter, John Morris, and James B. Smith.

Cincinnati Post: John Leach.

Cleveland Plain Dealer: Steve Adams, Tom Diemer.

Cleveland Press: Brent Larkin, Bud Weidenthal.

Columbia State: Maureen Schurr.

Columbus Dispatch: Catherine Candisky, Debra Mason, David Lore, and Robert McMunn.

Cox Newspapers: Andrew Alexander, Doug Lowenstein.

Dallas Morning News: Tom Bayer, Tom Belden, Bill Choyke, Carl Freund, Dotty Griffith, Bill Kenyon, Linda Little, and Rita Rubin.

Dayton Daily News: Dave Allbaugh, Michael Frisbee, and Wes Hills.

Dayton Journal Herald: Cilla Bosnak, Fred Lawson, Cathy Martindale, and Tom Price.

Denver Post: Gay Cook, Virginia Culver, Jim Diffy, Todd Engdahl, Carol Green, Chuck Green, Carl Miller, Dan Russel, Peggy Strain, Bob Threlkeld, John Toohey, and Max Woodfin.

Detroit Free Press: Scott Bosley.

Fairchild Publications: John Byrne.

Florida Times-Union: Margo Pope.

Fort Worth Star-Telegram: Anita Baker, Charlotte Guest, Glen Guzzo, Herb Owens, Phil Record, Z. Joe Thornton, Nancy Webman, and Gerald Zenick.

Fredericksburg Free Lance-Star: Ed Jones.

Freelance writers: Jon Conroy, Jean McCann, and Dan Cordtz.

Freemont News Messenger: Roy Wilhelm.

Gannett News Service: Anne Saker.

Group W. Television: Val Hymes.

Hartford Courant: Robert Lamagdeleine.

Houston Post: Arthur Weise.

Jackson Clarion Ledger: Frederic Tulsky, David Phelps.

Knight-Ridder: Steven Dornfeld.

KIRO, Seattle: Herb Weisbaum.

KOOL-TV, Phoenix: Burt Kennedy.

KOY, Phoenix: Paul McGonigle.

KPIX-TV, San Francisco: George Foulder.

Lexington Herald-Leader: John Carroll.

Los Angeles Times: Erwin Baker, Al Belugach, Dick Bergholz, John

Dart, Frank del Olmo, Bruce Keppel, Claudia Luther, Jack McCurdy, Larry Pryor, Bob Rawitch, Carl Redburn, David Shaw, Gaylor Shaw, and Don Speich.

Louisville Times: Dick Kaukas.

Louisville Courier-Journal: John Crocker, Phil Moeller, and Bob Pierce.

Michigan State University: Mary Gardner.

Milwaukee Journal: Frank Aukofer, Paul Hayes, Larry Lohmann, Sam Martino, Joel McNally, Marie Rohde, and Neil Rosenberg.

Minneapolis Star: Joe Rigert.

University of Missouri: Byron Scott.

Mother Jones: Adam Hochschild.

National Public Radio: John Felton.

New Haven Journal-Courier: John Mongillo.

Newsday: Rita Ciolli, B. D. Colen.

News Election Service: Janyce Katz.

New York Times: Sheldon Binn, Kenneth Briggs, Jane Brody, Jerry Flint, Glenn Fowler, Henry Lieberman, and Louis Uchitelle.

Newport, R.I., Daily News: David Offer.

Norfolk Virginian-Pilot: Margaret Edds, Michael Hardy.

Ohio University: Hugh Culbertson, Richard Vedder.

Philadelphia Inquirer: James Detjen.

Pittsburgh Post-Gazette: Stuart Brown, Dick Fontana, Susan Manella, Henry Pierce, and Regis Stefanik.

Pittsburgh Press: Bob Karlovits.

Peoria Journal Star: Shelley Epstein.

Religious News Service: Darrell Turner.

Reuters: Ingo Hertel.

Richmond Times-Dispatch: Bill Miller.

St. Louis Post-Dispatch: Gerald Boyd, Pamela Meyer, Jon Sawyer, Dana Spitzer, Susan Thomson, Victor Volland, and Ron Willnow.

Sarasota Herald Tribune: Bill Steiden.

Seattle Times: Paul Andrews, Dean Katz, and Hill Williams.

States News Service: Geoff O'Gara.

The Tennessean, Nashville: Frank Sutherland.

Topeka Capital Journal: Mary Ericson, Stephen Munro, and Gene Smith.

Troy Daily News: Howard Wilkinson.

United Press International: Wesley Pippert.

U.S. News & World Report: David Pike.

Wall Street Journal: Walt Bogdanich, Tim Metz, Priscilla Meyer, and Jeffrey Tannenbaum.

Washington Post: John Berry, Warren Brown, William Greider, Rudy

Maxa, Bill Richards, Charles Seib, Frank Swoboda, and Anne
Swardson.

WOSU, Columbus: Maria Vitale.

WRC-TV, Washington, D.C.: Leah Thompson.

Weatherford Democrat: Jim Golding.

WSGN, Birmingham: Les Coleman.

WSOL-TV, Charlotte: Doug Caldwell.

WTOP, Washington: Rich Adams.

Non-Journalists: Ralph Abernathy, civil rights leader; Dick
Anderson, Battelle Memorial Institute; Ralph Derickson, Council of
State Governments; Lou Fabro, Nationwide Insurance Co.; Barbara
Haas, Quaker Valley Schools, Pennsylvania; Thomas Hodson, attorney,
Athens, Ohio; Ken Klein of the press office of U.S. Sen. Bob Graham;
Richard Lamm, governor of Colorado; Elliot L. Lewis, Sanford R.
Goodkin Research Corp.; Gene Maeroff, Carnegie Foundation for the
Advancement of Teaching; U.S. Rep. Clarence Miller of Ohio; Ralph
Nader, consumer advocate; Franklin Parisi, Getty Oil Co.; Debra
Phillips, Harvard University; James Rogers, Consolidated Coal Co.;
Rozanne Weissman, National Education Association.

In writing a book of this nature, one accumulates a long list of
individuals who have earned special gratitude. Among those to whom
we offer special thanks are: Halina Czerniejewski, whose inquiring
mind and editing skills helped to make this book what it is; Jeff
Brehm, Diane Campbell, Karen Cappone, Chris Celek, Mary Jo
Crowley, Debbie DePeel, Mary Beth Egland, Deena Ferguson, Cindy
Fodor, Tom Hodson, Jim Jennings, Barbara Kaufmann, Peter King,
John Kiesewetter, Sue Kiesewetter, Ed Miller, Stephen Munro, Randall
Murray of California Polytechnic State University in San Luis Obispo,
Mike Prager, Mary Quinn, Anne Saker, Patsy Smith, and the Ohio
University chapter of the Society of Professional Journalists.

We also want to thank the following reviewers of the first edition
and of the manuscript for the second edition for their insightful and
useful suggestions: Raymond Anderson, University of Wisconsin,
Madison; Frank Deaver, University of Alabama; Greg Hoffman,
University of Wisconsin, Milwaukee; Marian Huttenstine, University of
Alabama; June O. Nicholson, Virginia Commonwealth University;
Edward Weston, University of Florida.

And, finally, we remain grateful for financial support for the first
edition through a Chairman's Discretionary Grant from the Ohio
University Research Committee.

RIZ, MG

The Expert Reporter

In journalism education, students are advised consistently—and usually required—to develop academic programs based on a solid core of the traditional liberal arts. Professional journalism skills classes, while obviously important, are given less emphasis in favor of broader knowledge of the society. The reason for this, the students are told, is that a journalist must know more than how to communicate; a journalist must also have something to communicate.

That advice is crucial to those who are journalists, as well as to those who want to become journalists. The exponential increase of knowledge and the growing complexity of social life are placing major burdens on the shoulders of those whose task it is to inform and to explain. The ability to communicate in a meaningful way depends first on having the initial understanding that provides the foundation of the message.

This concept certainly is not new, but it achieved increasing significance in the latter half of the twentieth century. As the Commission on Freedom of the Press said as early as 1947, "It is no longer enough to report *the fact* truthfully. It is now necessary to report *the truth about the fact.*"

Thus, while journalists have always covered the experts, more journalists now are being called upon to be experts themselves.

Explain the trend by whatever means appropriate: an effort to cope with increasing social complexity, acceptance of more journalistic responsibility, or a means of better informing citizens in democratic society. News organizations have added to the traditional general-assignment reporter a cadre of individuals who, by virtue of extensive on-the-job learning or academic training, may reasonably be considered authorities on a particular area of coverage. They get there by different routes, and they express different attitudes about what they are doing. Yet they share a common purpose of providing deeper and broader coverage of citizen needs and of social efforts to meet those needs.

Linda Deutsch, at age 26, was writing about movie stars for The Associated Press in Hollywood. She was doing what she had prepared for as an English major at Monmouth College. When movie star Sharon Tate was brutally murdered, Deutsch was called upon to write that story.

Linda Deutsch
of The Associated Press (Associated
Press photo)

"As a result of that, I wound up writing about the (Charles) Manson trial, which was the most incredible form of theater I had ever covered," she says. "The Manson trial began as a brief assignment and wound up being almost a lifetime. When I finished the Manson trial, I figured if I could survive that, I could survive anything. And I was suddenly a trial specialist."

Caren Marcus didn't quite realize it at the time, but she used every available opportunity at Northwestern University to prepare herself for a career as an education writer.

Caren Marcus
of Pittsburgh Press (Pittsburgh Press
photo by Thomas Ondrey)

"Every time I had to do a paper I always seemed to lean toward children or education. You really don't realize why you do that type of thing except you have an interest in it," she says. "When I came to the (Pittsburgh) *Press*, I did obits and everything, and whenever I had time to do a feature, I just happened to lean toward education. When the opening came up here, I think the Press realized it, and we just matched up. I wish I had more time to go to graduate school and get a master's in education."

Frank del Olmo, who now works as a columnist for *The Los Angeles Times*, originally defined himself as a "specialist by default" or a "specialist by neglect" for his newspaper. He says candidly that he took Chicano affairs out of a concern that his paper would not otherwise devote adequate attention to the Latin population of the area.

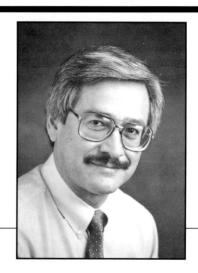

Frank del Olmo
of The Los Angeles Times (Los
Angeles Times photo)

"I semivolunteered, semiagreed with the desk, to take on this area of coverage, but I've consciously made an effort not to get myself too deeply into specialty because I don't really think it's a valid specialty. It's the kind of thing the paper should cover as a whole. I don't think I got it because I am a Chicano, but because I could speak Spanish."

Lyle Denniston's career, which has brought him to his current position as U.S. Supreme Court reporter for the *Baltimore Sun,* has been a combination of persistence on his part, solid educational background and continued learning.

"I began in journalism as a 17-year-old boy at the Nebraska City, Nebraska, *News-Press.* I had multiple responsibilities, one of which was to cover the county courthouse. I had a broad exposure to news of all types, but for reasons I don't know any more, I found myself fascinated by the courts."

He later attended the University of Nebraska and worked for the local paper, where one of his beats was the county courthouse. Because of his developing interest in constitutional law, he eventually went to graduate school at Georgetown University, where he majored in political science, with an emphasis on constitutional law. Subsequent positions at the *Wall Street Journal* in Washington and the *Washington Star* found him lobbying internally for the U.S. Supreme Court job. In both cases, he succeeded. When the *Star* folded, he moved to the *Baltimore Sun.*

Lyle Denniston
of the Baltimore Sun (Baltimore Sun photo)

"My career has been a process of having a very centered kind of aspiration from a very young age," he says. "I have maneuvered, angled, and manipulated to wind up on the legal beat. I have become largely a legal specialist for the *Sun.* I also write about Supreme Court arguments for the *American Lawyer,* and most of my freelance work is on the same type of subjects. I teach law at the Georgetown Law Center, even though I've never been to law school."

The careers of Deutsch, Marcus, del Olmo and Denniston clearly indicate the difference between what authorities consider to be the difference between persons who may be considered experts and those who merely are competent. Robert J. Trotter, senior editor of *Psychology Today,* for example, says experts develop the ability to perceive large meaningful patterns and do so with such speed that it appears almost intuitive.

He quotes Robert Glaser and Michelene Chi of the University of Pittsburgh's Learning Research and Development Center as saying the most important principle of skill performance depends on how much people know.

"In general," they say, "the more practice one has had in some domain, the better the performance, and from all indications, this increase in expertise is due to improvements in the knowledge base."[1]

THE SPREAD OF SPECIALIZATION

Specialization is not a new concept. Today's expert reporter represents an intensified application of an old idea—that the importance of the news media to democratic society lies in its ability to provide information upon which citizens make decisions. One might be tempted, especially in this age of skepticism about big government, big business, and big news media, to conclude that the process has become distorted. But the very faults of the media that feed such a conclusion also represent the reasons that the news media hungrily adopted the idea that they needed journalistic experts to report on the social experts.

In his classic essay, "The World Outside and the Picture in Our Heads," famed syndicated columnist Walter Lippmann, as early as 1922, pointed out the need. Lippmann argued "that representative government, either in what is ordinarily called politics, or in industry, cannot be worked successfully, no matter what the basis of election, unless there is an independent, expert organization for making the unseen facts intelligible to those who have to make decisions."[2]

Years later, in 1965, Lippmann expressed unbridled enthusiasm for the journalistic response—a trend toward greater use of specialized, more expert, reporters. He called it "the most radical innovation since the press became free of government control and censorship. For it introduces into the conscience of the working journalist a commitment to seek the truth which is independent of and superior to all his other commitments."[3]

This is not an isolated trend. Granted, specialists are more numerous and more conspicuous in large news organizations, but even small newspapers and broadcast stations may have individuals who, because of their special knowledge, cover specific assignments. Thus, the huge

Los Angeles Times may label as much as 50 percent of its staff as specialists and devote thousands of dollars to their support, and this may represent the corporate extreme.

But consider the Spokane, Washington, *Chronicle,* which has a circulation of about 62,000 and a total reporting staff of fifteen. In addition to such standard assignments as police and city hall, the paper has three reporters who devote most of their time to stories about medicine, environment, and education from kindergarten through higher education.

Although examples are not as numerous and the trend is not as pronounced, a parallel exists in broadcasting. At the network level, it's relatively common to hear specialized reports, for example, from NBC's Irving R. Levine and Mike Jensen on business; ABC's Tim O'Brien on law, Dr. Tim Johnson on medicine and Jim Slade on space and science; and CBS's Fred Graham on law.

Larger local stations in metropolitan markets also designate several specialists on their news staffs as providing more comprehensive coverage of some social areas. Most frequent among these areas, says Eric Ober, formerly of WBBM-TV in Chicago and now president of CBS News, are consumer affairs, health and medicine, business and economics, politics and the arts. The smaller the station, of course, the less likely that it will be able to afford the luxury of specialist reporters.

The fact that smaller newspapers and broadcast stations do not emphasize the use of specialists should not be surprising. To provide an individual with the time and financial resources to work for days, weeks, or even months on a single story or to concentrate exclusively on specific subject matter is out of the reach of smaller news organizations. It's not a matter of philosophy. The degree to which one person on a staff of six people (or fewer) devotes time to a specialty is the degree to which coverage of important local activities must be reduced. Given the choice, it perhaps is better that smaller organizations concentrate on local news coverage and rely on news agencies and networks to discuss the major social issues of the day.

This is not to say that smaller organizations don't have a responsibility for comprehensive coverage of issues as well as events. The two simply cannot be done on the same level. The wise editor or news director, spotting issues which have particular local impact, occasionally will juggle the schedule to release a reporter to provide special coverage. And many do.

WHAT MAKES A SPECIALIST?

Who, then, are the specialists? How does the job they do differ from traditional expectations of reporters? Keith Fuller, former president and general manager of The Associated Press, provides the most basic answer:

"When you define specialization, it's really more of a continuity of subject—just staying within the confines of a general subject. Your attention is not diverted to other things, and you get to know all the sources in that field, not only in a business sense but at their conventions and other activities. You win their confidence. They start opening up some really good material. You get to the point at which you can sense the slightest changes, the nuances that would be lost on the general reporter."

That provides one easy distinction between the specialist and the general-assignment reporter. The generalist covers many subjects and usually does not enjoy such a continuity of sources. But Fuller's statement does not explain how the specialist differs from the traditional beat reporter. The terms often are used interchangeably. But there is a difference, based on some fine lines, and often it is only a matter of individual performance.

For one thing, specialists tend to have more time and flexibility. Beat reporters more often function under specific expectations of type and quantity of coverage. Specialists tend to have greater control over how they spend their time.

A beat typically is expressed in geographic or jurisdictional terms: city hall, county government, the school system, federal court, hospitals, and police. Specialists deal with a broad subject matter such as urban affairs, education, legal affairs, medicine, or law enforcement. The implications are more than semantic. They represent coverage philosophy. There's a big difference, for example, between covering activities at city hall—mayoral news conference, city council meetings, specific service programs, and the budget—and relating those activities to the broad problems and directions of the community and to other communities.

That emphasis on broader perspective constitutes a third general distinction. Frequently, the specialist reporter is more likely to concentrate on process rather than on activities. In journalistic terms, this leads reporters more into trend stories than into spot news stories. This does not mean that the specialist never covers spot news. Nothing could be further from the truth, and nothing, in the long run, could be more detrimental.

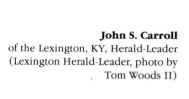

John S. Carroll
of the Lexington, KY, Herald-Leader
(Lexington Herald-Leader, photo by
Tom Woods II)

Says John Carroll, editor of the *Lexington,* Kentucky, *Herald-Leader,* "Our feeling is that covering daily events provides good material for trend stories. If you just sit in the office and sort of abstractly try to think up trends without getting out and meeting people and covering events, pretty soon your stories are going to get pretty ethereal and aren't going to have much grounding in reality."

Most specialist reporters, therefore, will cover spot news and, when the need arises, they may be pressed into general service. However, this tends to occur less frequently for them. And the specialist usually controls spot news coverage, gaining more opportunities to concentrate on stories that relate the specifics to the general trends and help citizens better understand the implications of that spot news.

The distinction between the specialist and the beat reporter depends most on how reporters and their employers handle the assignments. It depends on the expectations and the approach. For example, city hall typically is considered a beat. But a thoughtful and knowledgeable reporter, given employer support, will be able to expand the focus. City hall may be a beat in which citizens are told what local government did today, or it may be a specialty in which the orientation is toward citizen understanding. Or it may fall somewhere in between.

Whatever the organizational label, the expert reporter is in a position to function effectively if given the opportunity. In practical terms, specialists have more opportunities; beat reporters may create their opportunities; and even general-assignment reporters occasionally find themselves dealing with familiar material in a situation that makes such coverage possible. It's partly a matter of individual drive and desire, and it's partly a matter of knowledge and understanding gained through some combination of education and on-the-job training.

Education is a valuable component in the making of the expert reporter. Although an increasing number of journalists are seeking advanced academic degrees, it is not necessarily a requirement. Many specialists emphasize that on-the-job learning may produce a person with the kind of knowledge needed to function effectively as an expert reporter. Some very frequent advice is to obtain a broad liberal arts background, perhaps with a concentration of coursework in a specialized field (e.g., several survey courses in different scientific or business disciplines). Often, specialists have opportunities to participate in mid-career programs sponsored by professional organizations or colleges to improve their content backgrounds.

While a journalism education is accepted as a valuable means of gaining entry positions, it is assumed that the expert reporter will have supplemented that education or gained journalistic know-how through practical experience. Seldom will new graduates move into specialty slots. The route to finding one's place as a specialized expert is general-assignment experience. The *Denver Post*, for example, hires as specialists individuals with four to six years of reporting experience, most of which is in general assignment.

The idea is that, aside from simply having proven themselves and paid their dues before moving into a specialty, reporters benefit from the general experience by having the chance to develop basic skills and journalistic maturity. It helps young reporters develop tenacity, aggressiveness, and interview technique. This is common advice, typified by the experience of Georgie Anne Geyer, columnist for the Universal Press Syndicate:

"I have five years on society and local news, and I can't say how much I feel that slow, sort of everyday, repetition really trains in news judgment. But we talk about truth, and we are the ones who really can approximate more of the truth because we see it in front of us. It's not philosophical. It's the truth of what's going on around you. In order to do that, you have to sharpen your abilities to observe, and I think you do that in everyday work as a reporter."[4]

This on-the-job development of expertise—along with various forms of formal education—provides the reporter with knowledge needed to both understand and be able to explain specialized subjects. While it's not always a substitute, the value of personal experience should not be underestimated. For example, Charlotte Anne Smith, a freelance writer for twenty years, says that she has learned the value to her writing of experiences she had, things she has observed, and what she has learned from different persons with whom she has been associated.

"Are you active in a sport, craft or organization?" she asks. "Do you have a hobby? Do you enjoy reading in a certain field? Are you or members of your family or close friends engaged in an unusual occupation? You may be far more of an expert than you think, and the answers to these questions will help you recognize potential stories and markets and give your writing that extra something that makes the reader think, 'Now this person really knows what she's talking about.' "[5]

THE ADVANTAGES

So, the expert reporter must have the basic skills of the general-assignment reporter; that is writing skills, reporting skills, and understanding of subject matter. The difference between the two lies in the specialist's emphasis on the latter and the opportunities the reporter gets to develop and use that content understanding.

The specialist, or expert reporter, often tells the desk what stories he or she will cover, while the opposite applies to the generalist. This has strong implications.

First, it means that story topics coming from a reporter are more likely to be oriented toward the practical problems of citizens or those who work within that subject area. Editors sitting in the office may lose touch with their readers and make assignments on the basis of long-standing personal prejudices. The field reporter daily confronts real life.

Second, it means greater diversity and depth of coverage. The expert reporter is in constant contact with sources and with the literature of the field, usually attends meetings (both for coverage and informational purposes), and thus knows the issues and developments. Many stories that percolate from this process involve topics that otherwise would have gone unnoticed. The expert reporter will find stories not obvious to the editor or the general-assignment reporter.

Third, relative autonomy allows the expert reporter to concentrate on stories that he or she considers most appropriate. Any good reporter must be able to handle almost any assignment and often will work on uninteresting ones. That's the nature of journalism. But common sense says that human beings do the best job on tasks that interest them.

Fourth, it means greater journalistic competition, the force that drives news organizations to the twin peaks of more and better. A specialist seeking the bigger picture should have a perspective that goes beyond the local community. While the point of coverage remains local, the processes of comparison and contrast force an outward orientation on area, state, or national subject matter. Specialists tend to know each other and to know that others across the country may be working on their own versions of the same story.

THE POTENTIAL PROBLEMS

Specializaton is not new. Political, sports, business, education, and government reporters have been around for a long time. What is new is the application of the concept to important fields of social inquiry (e.g., medicine, environment, consumer affairs). And what is new is the overall emphasis and shifting of resources to support such specialized coverage. Yet in terms of its development, specialization is in no more than its adolescent stage. News organizations have seen how the expert reporter contributes diversity and depth in response to modern requirements. But they don't yet know the full potential, and they are at best only vaguely aware of the potential problems. Even in this early stage, at least three important questions have arisen to haunt those responsible for running newsrooms.

First, could specialists become too expert, too close to their subjects and sources and lose the journalistic edge of being outside observers? Second, could reporters fall into the trap of an arrogance of knowledge that diminishes their ability to approach a story with fresh curiosity? Third, could reporters tire of day-in-and-day-out dealings with the same subjects and sources and become "burned out" on a subject?

Whether an individual reporter's expertise leads to conflicting interests, of course, depends upon the individual. Some with formal legal training, for example, find their education to be a valuable tool in their efforts to report comprehensively on the nation's criminal justice system. Others lose the ability to communicate with lay citizens and to think independently.

The reporter conceivably may become so much a part of the system that he or she identifies with sources and begins to communicate sources' specialized jargon or espouse their concepts. What is perfectly clear to a source and reporter may be gobbledygook to readers, to viewers, or to listeners. To the petroleum engineer, 64 billion barrels of oil is a meaningful concept. To the public it means nothing. In education, implications of "educating the whole child," perhaps apparent on the surface, have ramifications that escape all but the professional educator.

From the journalistic perspective, other problems arise when reporters become too secure in their knowledge about a coverage specialty and lose the ability to approach a story with a searching and questioning perspective. This is not an uncommon problem in all fields of endeavor. Physicist Richard Feynman, for example, criticizes the arrogance that causes people to overvalue their own intelligence and to lose the ability to accept the fact that their knowledge is limited. He uses government as one example.

"We all know that they don't know what they're doing in Washington," he says. "It's not that they're fools; it's just that nobody knows how to handle many of the problems. A lot of experts have studied these subjects. But they know much less than they will admit. If somebody ran for office saying that they didn't have answers, nobody would pay attention to him. Everybody wants answers."[6]

Another specific version of the problem exists—reporters becoming what social scientists call "co-opted" by their sources. At its worse, co-opting results in the loss of stories because a reporter commiserates with sources and is too easily convinced, for example, that timing is wrong for publication or that publication would be detrimental. Those are valid decisions when made on journalistic grounds; they're not necessarily so when made according to the criteria of sources.

Such distortions are not going to happen in all cases, but news organizations have seen examples of individuals who stay in one subject area so long that they grow tired of it. They share the perceptions of their sources or the industry those sources represent. They become opinionated or prejudiced. They overly enjoy a sense of power and prestige within the field.

Editors' solutions to many of these problems have been to transfer individuals from one specialty to another. On the surface, that is contradictory and distorts the concept of specialization. But the attitude is that, given sound writing and reporting skills and an opportunity for study, good reporters may in a limited time pick up enough background knowledge for a new specialty.

One caution, however, is that the transfer works best when it is accomplished between related disciplines. For example, it's quite easy to slide from writing about the environment to writing about energy because these topics are so intertwined and sources are frequently tuned to the same wavelengths. Likewise, to shift from science to medicine or among various levels of government is not overly difficult. But it's difficult to take someone from religion and put that person into a completely different specialty, such as science.

Within certain reasonable boundaries, transferring specialists is accomplished smoothly and with a minimum of lag time. It generally is expected that such actions will result in a fresher journalistic perspective and that it possibly will rejuvenate individual reporters by providing them with new challenges. But, of course, exceptions abound. Some reporters are so thoroughly professional and so journalistically fascinated with their subjects they never tire of them.

WHAT THE BOSS OWES THE SPECIALIST

Assignment transfer is one institutional action designed to make the system work more effectively, but it is not the only responsibility of the news organization that is serious about specialists. The organization must create an environment for its experts' effectiveness. This includes time, financial support, guidance, coordination, and opportunities for professional improvement and stimulation.

Predictably, one of the keys to effectively managing the expert reporter is good leadership. If specialists are selected with care, if they have the right training, if they have the right attitude, and if their relationships with editors or news directors are sound, most of the potential problems will never materialize. But editors must agree that time and money will be available, and they must place special emphasis on their functions of coordination and communication.

If a reporter does in fact use specialized jargon or concepts, it is an editor who remembers that the lay audience is being forgotten. When specialties such as energy and environment are related, it is an editor who keeps tabs on what is being done and encourages communication to avoid duplication or even contradiction. It is also an editor who assures that what specialists produce is journalistically sound and within news organization policy.

Editors integrate specialists into the operation to achieve what sociologist Emile Durkheim called "organic solidarity" within the organization.[7] The components of news production depend upon each other, and the total impact depends upon the interrelationships of the individual parts. When an organization functions with division of labor, fine tuning is necessary to achieve the balance that provides the greatest efficiency and maximum effect. That balance comes through artful coordination.

For one thing, editors must ensure a proper balance between specialists and general-assignment reporters. The day-to-day spot news content provides much of the information citizens seek when they come to their newspaper or broadcast program. While emphasis on spot news and human interest coverage may become excessive, as may emphasis on specialty material, careful orchestration will achieve the blend suited to community needs and desires.

CONCLUSION: THE EXPERT REPORTER

Is it possible that by so wholeheartedly accepting the concept of the specialist or expert reporter, journalism is sowing the seeds of doubt among its audience? After all, these are times of public distrust of experts. They are times in which citizens are concluding that answers are not the exclusive domain of a small elite. They are times of enormous public debate worldwide on matters previously left to those in official positions (e.g., abortion and governmental reforms in Eastern Europe).

The answer could be frightening, except that the journalistic expert exists not as part of the problem but as part of the rescue force. The expert reporter does not create new bodies of contradictory theory or new social programs or products that may go astray. The expert reporter exists as a means of helping the citizen understand what is being done and said by social and scientific experts.

The ability to understand and communicate remains the goal of journalists of all types. Coping with specialized, highly technical, or complex information is the challenge of the expert reporter. The effect represents a desire by journalism to dig deeper, to be more comprehensive, and to broaden the scope of public knowledge and understanding. To accomplish those goals, reporters themselves must know and understand.

That's why American journalism and American citizens need the expert reporter.

NOTES

1. Robert J. Trotter, "The Mystery of Mastery," *Psychology Today,* July 1986, p. 34.

2. Walter Lippmann, *Public Opinion* (New York: Free Press, 1922), p. 19.

3. As quoted in Jeremy Tunstall, *Journalists at Work* (Beverly Hills, Calif.: Sage Publications, 1971), p. 1.

4. Georgie Anne Geyer, panel discussion, Region 11 Conference, Society of Professional Journalists, Costa Mesa, Calif., April 22, 1978.

5. Charlotte Anne Smith, "You May Be an Expert and Not Know It," *The Writer,* January 1989, p. 26.

6. Alvin P. Sanoff, "Most Experts Don't Know More Than the Average Person," *U.S. News and World Report,* March 18, 1985, p. 79.

7. Emile Durkeim, *The Division of Labor in Society* (New York: Free Press, 1933), p. 131.

Fundamentals of Covering Local Government

2

One of the first assignments given to a young, newly hired reporter on any newspaper or broadcast outlet is usually a meeting of a government body. That's because despite the beat that they are assigned, most reporters will be required to attend countless meetings—meetings of councils, boards, commissions, committees, departments, and agencies.

Local government news may be the major contribution by newspapers and broadcast news departments to the life of the average person. Citizens can get news from networks and national newspapers like *USA Today;* but nearly all the information they get about local governments must come from local media.

In spite of greater impact by state and federal governments, the most immediate governmental effect comes through local programs. The news media, as the principal source of public information, play an important role in local decision making. It isn't exactly a mutual admiration society—the relationship between local officials and reporters—but both groups know they rely on each other and, more than that, they know the public benefits from both their working together and their moments of discord.

But the media are criticized because they too often simply funnel through what government officials say or what happened at last night's council meeting. They give little evaluation, little bigger meaning, and little explanation of the impact of a statement or action upon citizens.

A frequent topic of examination for newspaper and journalism researchers is the content of the news—in this case the actual amount of meeting coverage found in newspapers. But the *Oakland Press* in Pontiac, Michigan, once did a survey of its own. The paper's content showed that 45 percent of its news hole consisted of "dry, factual accounts of local government and school board actions and nonactions," while general features made up less than 5 percent and school features under 2 percent.

"That isn't an ideal balance," the *Press* concluded. "There is nothing wrong with local government news, and it is not the intent . . . to phase it out of the newspaper. But there is something wrong when who-what-where stories from little meetings devour nearly half of our local news hole.

"What it all means is that all too often—for instance, all the time—we write news in the form of a resume of a boring meeting. It is accurate. It is factual. And it is pitifully dull." In a policy booklet, the *Press* told its staff, "If we look at the newspaper with the reader's critical eye, we ought to see two things: A lot of what we're writing doesn't belong in print at all, or should be there in barebones, short-as-possible form; a lot of what survives that test has to be written from a different slant. Where the subject is complex and inherently dull, it's not enough to tell the reader what happened. Tell him—and show him—why it happened and what differences it can make to him."[1]

Providing this additional twist is a burden to readers.

First, it means they must provide more news from the reader's perspective. Presenting the viewpoint of government officials is not all bad, but in many instances it fails to satisfy readers who have a different perspective. It is not enough to report that a local tax increase will add so many thousands of dollars to the treasury. How much will it cost the individual reader? What will the reader, as a citizen, gain from government as a result?

Second, it means reporters must reduce their dependence upon news releases, handouts, news conference statements, and prepared remarks. Few will complain about the use of such material, but it should not be the reporter's sole source.

The more efficient local government, the more influence it tends to exert on the media. It regularly presents in writing a wide variety of materials: memos, staff studies, inter-office staff communications, background materials, and detailed explanations. Officials volunteer selected comments. As a result, some lazy reporters wait for the information to come to them rather than do the digging themselves. Some reporters will take all the paperwork or official comment without carefully evaluating it and perhaps will not discover an important, unmentioned angle of the story.

Third, it means reporters need to take a more evaluative attitude, based on their knowledge of the structure, functions, and organization of local government. If a reporter simply reports what happened at the meeting, or what the mayor said, there is little need for a full understanding of the complexities of governing even a small town. But if the goal is to place governmental activities into a fuller perspective, reporters need a more aggressive and knowledgeable approach.

Some reporters believe that many government reporters approach their job passively—in part because they feel that's what their editors and publishers want, and in part because they are rarely given the opportunity to develop expertise in a specific area and to question the experts.[2]

Providing comprehensive coverage of the complicated maneuverings of even a small local government is difficult because reporters require quick access to so many resources. It doesn't make any difference whether it is a city, county, state, or national government. Reporters need an expert's grasp on the power structure, the process, and the wide range of governmental subject matter. Even though government reporters may be defined as journalistic specialists, they actually must serve a generalist function. One day they may be writing about airports, the next day about a poverty or welfare program. Or dog licenses. Or housing, highways, or hospital rates.

The frequency of meetings, governmental style, amount of material to be covered, available time, and editor's attitudes all are factors in what reporters can do on a given assignment. The challenge is to know the system so well that daily happenings may be placed into a larger meaning.

OFFICIAL AUTHORITY COMES FROM THE STRUCTURE

The name of the game in the American system of local government is power. Who controls? Who influences? Who decides? A citizen or a reporter who can answer these questions is in a position to understand the forces that provide the flavor of any community. Textbooks say, correctly, that the American system is based on negotiation and compromise, resulting in complete satisfaction for no one, but also complete dissatisfaction for a few. At the same time, one does not have to be a political scientist to know that some people get more from the system because either they help make the decisions or their opinions reach those who make the decisions.

Getting a share of that power depends upon several things, including politics, personality, wealth, and social status. But official authority grows out of one's place in the governmental structure of the city, village, town, borough, or county. It's here that reporters have to start in their quest to understand local issues, policies, and directions. Government is not a static entity; it's a process that depends upon interplay among those people in authority.

Although some forms of governmental organization vary according to state laws and local traditions, governmental textbooks list three traditional types.

The *mayor-council* type is characterized by an elected executive and an elected legislative body. In practice, this type takes two forms, with administrative authority providing the basis for the difference. One is the *strong mayor* structure, in which the mayor dominates administratively and the mayor and council share in policy making. The mayor carries out established policy, usually prepares the budget, proposes new programs, and supervises department heads whom he or she may have appointed. The council's major duties are budget approval and working with the mayor in setting policy.

The *weak mayor* form, the older of the two forms and generally popular in smaller cities, gives the executive limited and frequently only ceremonial authority. This person usually presides over the city council, but the council itself retains most of the power. Members sometimes serve in city departments, often prepare the budget, and may have the final word in municipal appointments.

A most interesting feature of the *commission* form of government is that it violates the tradition of separation of powers. A small number of elected commissioners, usually five or seven, retains all legislative and executive authority. One of the commissioners usually serves as mayor, but he or she has limited additional powers, frequently only ceremonial. At times, especially in larger county governments, this form may feature an appointed administrative officer.

Council-manager governments consist of an elected council that appoints a professional administrator to guide the operations of city departments. Council members are responsible to the public for establishing policy and, ultimately, for the overall operation of the government. The administrator, usually called city manager, is responsible for seeing that programs are carried out. Managers usually have authority to hire and fire, prepare the budget for council approval, and serve at the will of the council. This form has tended to put municipal operation in the hands of trained, career professionals. If there is a mayor, his or her authority is limited.

The reporter's relationship with officials in any of these systems depends upon the official's structural authority and actual power. From a practical standpoint, the reporter's concern is getting good information from that person over a period of time. The system of professional managers tends to be an advantage because professional managers often are more comfortable dealing with reporters and usually are sensitive to journalistic requirements.

However, dealing with professional managers may provide reporters with some challenges because a professional who understands how to cooperate with the press also knows how to control the flow of news. Most professional managers are ambitious and therefore careful. They are concerned about what image is conveyed.

A contrast is most apparent in the weak mayor and commission forms, termed "amateur governments" by some political scientists. Their approach often is secretive and distrustful. Officials react in either of two ways. They try to become close to the reporter in the hope that by establishing some sort of friendship that they can understand and deal trustingly with each other. Failing that, or as an alternative, the officials try to keep reporters at a distance.

The commission—the most common form of county government—can be difficult to cover because it lacks a central figure with whom reporters can work regularly. They must deal with the commissioners as a group and develop diplomatic working relationships with all of them. If a county commissioner or administrator emerges as a spokesperson, the reporter may have some sort of centralized source. But, fundamentally, it is up to the reporter to do the necessary legwork, to fit the pieces together, and to provide the analysis.

A commission gives reporters a real challenge because of the lack of dividing lines between administrative and legislative authority. Commissioners can do almost anything with three or four votes on a given day. That can be efficient, but the absence of checks and balances offers the opportunity to conduct business out of the public's eye. It also can mean less open conflict.

"This is a challenge to a reporter because it's difficult to write interestingly and clearly about noncontroversial stuff," says Bruce Keppel of *The Los Angeles Times.* "Well, they're controversial, but they're not the epithet-tossing sort of controversy. The controversy is in the method of resolving the problem, and it really is hard to write about."

Whatever the form of government, the job of the reporter is to provide readers, viewers and listeners with an understanding of what Keppel calls the "delivery end of government services—what the local problems are, how they're resolved, or why they're not resolved."

Much of the reporter's preparation for this assignment will involve lower-echelon individuals who perform the specific tasks of local government. The journalistic value of these officials will vary. Some are elected and thus are in a position to be independent in their comments unless controlled by political leaders. Appointees, however, may be cautious in dealing with reporters because of their dependence on top officials for their jobs. These are not hard-and-fast rules, though. In both cases, local political structure and personality factors may override the traditional expectations.

Bruce Keppel
of The Los Angeles Times (Los
Angeles Times photo)

In any event, reporters have to deal with the following local officials:

Chief Legal Officer (city or county attorney, counselor, solicitor, counsel, or law director), who gives legal advice to city officials and represents the government
in court. As adviser, this person has an impact upon policy decisions through
helping establish legal boundaries on what a local government is permitted to
do.

Clerk (clerk of council), who functions as the official caretaker of local records and
often keeps formal minutes of council meetings. But, especially in smaller cities,
clerks may be of greater journalistic assistance. Often, because they remain
in their positions for long periods, they know more about the specifics of local
government operation than anyone else, at times even being called upon for
advice by officials.

Treasurer, although essentially a bookkeeper with no authority, may be an excellent
source, as custodian of local funds. Treasurers account for every dollar, make
deposits, pay bills on order, and without doubt, are the most knowledgeable
persons on the specifics of local finances.

Controller (comptroller) works in relative obscurity, but serves as the chief fiscal
assistant to city officials. Controllers often actually prepare the administrative
budget and, once it is approved, assume internal responsibility for adminis-
tering it.

Assessor (board of assessors) has responsibility for determining valuation of property, which dictates the amount of property tax to be collected. Although assessors seldom have a direct role in establishing local policy, their
responsibilities for making funds available may position them to influence that
policy directly.

Auditor, the watchdog of the budget, generally serves as agent for the council in
determining if administrative expenditures were made according to appropriation.

Planner (planning commission) may be an individual or a group or may consist of
public officials or lay citizens. But, in any event, city and county planners are
responsible for converting long-range goals into local policy. Planning is an
effort to make most efficient and progressive use of available land and, as such,
may have significant impact upon lifestyles.

Even in smaller communities the responsibilities incorporated into
these offices do not cover the range of services local government attempts to provide. Reporters will spend varying amounts of time with
the heads of specific departments. These contacts not only reduce dependency upon government's higher officials, but they also have additional value because department heads usually have more specific
knowledge about the "delivery end" of local government. It is at the
departmental level that citizens have their direct contact with their local
government.

That contact is made when citizens have needs or problems with local
government services, which may include any of the following:

Police and fire protection

Construction and maintenance of streets, bridges, sidewalks

Medical care and/or promotion of good health practices

Public parks and recreation

Supply and distribution of water, electricity or natural gas

Public transportation

Libraries, museums and art galleries

Sanitation services, including sewage and solid-waste disposal

Noise pollution

Public education

How many of these functions will be included in the reporter's responsibilities depends upon news organization preference. Education,
for example, usually is a separate entity and a separate beat. Law enforcement frequently is a separate journalistic assignment. But the degree
to which the services are covered may well be the greatest determinant
of quality in local government reporting, at least in terms of journalism's
responsibility to report what is most significant to the citizens.

The magnitude of local government coverage explains why many reporters are tempted to limit the number of sources with whom they deal. It is that magnitude that highlights the need for a broad base of sources and an issue orientation, not to the exclusion of spot news, but as a means of helping citizens understand their governments.

THEY'LL ALWAYS HAVE MEETINGS

The effort to find time and sources to provide information on local public trends is being applied by more reporters to the legislative side of government as well as the administrative side. Most news media tend to use some combination of three approaches to cover meetings of council, commission, or committee.

One, which may be labeled the *paper-of-record* approach, is characteristic of smaller communities where the relationship of local governments to their citizens is closer. Here the reporter makes a point to include practically all business conducted, not just highlights. The idea is that even a relatively insignificant item is worthy of mention because some reader will have both an interest and a need for that information.

Of course, detailed discussion is not provided for all agenda items. Often, a rather standardized "in-other-action" list at the end of a story summarizes lesser points.

The second major philosophy of meeting coverage grows out of consideration of space and time and geographic area. The *major-business* approach rules broadcasting reporters, for example, who do not have the air time to discuss items of limited interest. It often is followed by newspapers whose reporters cover wide geographic areas involving numerous local governments, as well as specialized publications whose readers are interested only in certain parts of government business.

Partly, the major-business approach grows out of the notion that much of what governments do is routine, repetitive, and therefore boring. Reporters see little public value in writing about a routine transfer of funds from one budget category to another or about an item significant to a limited number of citizens. The approach is partly a function of what can be accomplished given journalism's natural limitations. Simply put, ignoring many of the smaller news items gives reporters more time and space to devote to major business.

From the reader's perspective, this approach can result in valuable—if not comprehensive—coverage of a meeting or other local government activity. Handled improperly, however, it can result in coverage that suggests that governmental decisions are too big to be directly related to individual readers. Such coverage may reinforce a general attitude that government is impersonal and distant.

Issue Orientation—in which the function is more explanatory than a blow-by-blow account of a given meeting—is the third approach. The idea is to present the *meaning* of meetings and actions. This is the advice given to local government reporters at the *Oakland Press*:

Our story should not be a summary of what went on there. If participants babble about trivia while the real news is hiding nearby, we must find that news and ignore that babble. If the city council debates three hours about some fire truck bids, and five minutes about a contract with the mayor's brother-in-law, we are not obligated to give news space to each in proportion as the council gave each its time.

"Forget the smoke, forget the babble. Write the news. And write it for the guy who's worked hard all day, given most of what's left of it to his family, and hasn't the time, the background or the inclination to wade through a long dull governmental-handout type of story and try to guess what it means to him."[2]

The issue approach may mean holding the story until more research broadens the discussion, or it may mean talking after the meeting with participants or presenting some of the floor debate rather than simply recording the decision.

Many reporters regularly broaden a story by talking with council members, public representatives who participate in meetings, and individuals who may be affected by a decision. Of course, the extent of this broadening may well be a function of deadline pressure, but reporters who make this questioning a practice, even if it is necessarily limited, find their stories improved.

At times, legislation is so complicated that council members themselves may not know what action they took. Sometimes the reporter may have to speak with the city attorney to get an interpretation of what happened.

Reporters often have to deal with local officials who, although perhaps efficient and honest in their operation of government, are tight-lipped and reluctant to be quoted. Perhaps discussion is limited at council meetings. A resolution or ordinance is introduced and approved. Debate may have been private. Some officials believe open discussion hampers their effectiveness and, in spite of sunshine laws, they conduct a rather quiet, behind-the-scenes operation.

At the other extreme, perhaps, are governmental bodies that deal with a bewildering array of alternative points of view, changes of mind, backtracking, and amendments from officials committed to public debate. Deciding how much of this discussion to present is a headache for the reporter. It's one thing to show openness; it's another to indicate confusion. It takes a reporter who fully understands what is happening to find the proper blend that shows citizens how their government functions as well as how it informs them of specific actions.

A similar type of difficulty for reporters, especially in smaller and rural towns and counties, is the informality in meetings of councils and commissions. Reporters expect an agenda, formal business sessions, and periodic background materials. Often, agenda items will be discussed, people will walk in and out of hallways, pop in to say hello to commissioners or councilpersons, or shake hands and talk for a while. Then they'll go about their agenda until something else happens.

Catherine Candisky, who covered suburbs for *The Columbus Dispatch,* believes the meetings of small-town councils and school boards are, in some ways, tougher to cover than those of larger cities. "It's very folksy—there's certainly no press table where all the reporters sit. You might be the only reporter there," she said.

Consequently, it's easy to become, as she puts it, "one of them." That is, it's easy in a setting like this for reporters to take sides in an issue or become subjective. "Just make sure you don't become part of the news," she advises. "Maintain a distance."

Reporters usually have many opportunities to report on particular pieces of legislation. The legislative process is deliberately repetitious, with each step designed to give the public and officials a chance to comment. Reporters can write about a particular proposal as it goes through committee meetings, public meetings, and the lawmaking process.

Reporters have to decide at what stage of this process they should intensify their journalistic attention and when they are overcovering an event or issue. The initial determination is based on newsworthiness when an issue first comes to the reporter's attention. The amount of follow-up depends on the controversy or reaction the first story may have stimulated. A particularly important or controversial issue may require constant and detailed coverage of the formal proceedings, supplemented by additional interview material.

An important part of this legislative process is committee meetings. Reporters will differ on how many committee meetings should be attended regularly, but they will argue that some meetings require the reporter to be on the scene. Often it is in committee session that disagreements are settled and final forms of proposals worked out. Whether such meetings require a reporter's presence depends on the importance of the issue and what is expected to occur during the meeting.

The practical problem with committee meetings is that there are simply too many that usually cover such topics as finances, safety, environment, transportation and others. Also, much of the testimony at committee sessions will be repeated when the full council or commission convenes. Reporter attention to committee meetings is increased, of course, when the issue is important to the community. And, if it's not possible to attend a meeting, reporters often will pick up much of it by talking with the committee clerk or committee members.

If the reporter determines that the issue does not merit continued coverage, he or she will make a note to be sure to provide later coverage on the matter's resolution. Too many stories are never followed through, and the steady reader often is disappointed in efforts to follow an item of business to its conclusion. It's much too easy to let that follow-up slide, especially if the item is not controversial, in the pace of day-to-day activities.

SOMETIMES THEY WON'T COOPERATE

Information doesn't always come easily. Governmental officials have a long list of reasons—some good, some bad—for not wanting to comment or to cooperate with reporters. They may feel the information is too sensitive to be made public. They may not trust a reporter's ability to understand or report accurately. They may want to withhold information until it is to their political advantage to release it. They may not like the reporter. They may be seeking to protect negotiations that they think are best conducted quietly. They may be attempting to hide a wrongdoing.

Although not usually the case, some reporters will agree at times that it's best not to make certain information public. But, for the most part, reporters feel that *they*, not government officials, should make that decision.

In many ways, control of information is the ultimate political tool, and both reporters and officials will continue to guard jealously what they consider to be their right. They will always be in conflict, and therefore it is in a reporter's best interest to know how to do more than scream when public information becomes private.

Going to court is an obvious choice. Almost all states have open-meeting and open-record laws. Although content varies, they do give the news media the right in certain situations to sue for public access to governmental information. The federal Freedom of Information Act gives the public, including reporters, the right of access to public records of the executive branch of the federal government.

But more reporters and editors these days are urging that news organizations not be too quick to jump into court. A lawsuit plays into the hands of a legal system that would like to think it should make the decisions in journalistic-governmental conflicts. Reporters are not attorneys. They must understand the law, and they must know how to make it work for them. But going to court should be the last resort. They must first attempt to gain information through more informal methods in time for the next deadline.

Part of the answer lies in good journalistic technique, specifically in developing additional sources who will provide information that the reporter will then confirm or, in special instances, use on an unattributed basis. Use of unidentified sources, however, should be restricted to unusual cases. Many reporters feel strongly that it is not often necessary.

There also is the argument that the audience should receive enough information, including the name and background of the source, that *it* can determine the validity of information. Of course, that also doesn't relieve the journalist of evaluating the source's credibility.

Former *The New York Times* reporter David Burnham classifies all governmental employees according to usefulness as sources:

"The head of an agency, because of his position, must offer self-serving, overly optimistic portraits of his operations. The second and by far the largest group of government employees are so filled with bureaucratic fears that they never tell you anything—honestly or dishonestly. The third group, comprised of individuals I actively seek out, can be called the malcontents. These are the people who for varying motives, sometimes good, sometimes bad, sometimes a mixture of both good and bad, provide the reporters with leads, information, and documents that the head of the agency usually does not want a reporter to see."[4]

Journalists must, of course, work to discourage the withholding of information. But the media must also share in the blame for governmental secrecy because of superficial or inaccurate reporting. As most government officials, editors, and reporters would agree, public trust for journalists will grow only out of professional reporting.

NOTES

1. "Covering Government: A New Testament to Newswriting," *Oakland Press,* Pontiac, Mich., 1976, p. 5.

2. "Covering Government," p. 13.

3. David Burnham, *The Role of Media in Controlling Corruption* (New York: Criminal Justice Center, John Jay College of Criminal Justice), pp. 2–3. Reprinted with permission from the John Jay Press.

The Heart of Local Government Coverage   3

To many reporters, following the day-to-day announcements, meetings, press conferences and other official "reports" by local government officials is more than enough to fill their day. After all, reporters may believe, if they miss one of these formal announcements, the competition is sure to get it and beat them.

But following the formal announcements is only a small part of the reporter's job, according to one former reporter who is now a communication researcher. Lewis Wolfson summarizes his view of why reporters do not always give readers and viewers their "money's worth" when it comes to covering local government:

> The press is at its best when it shows how government actually affects people, and local government reporters have a unique opportunity to do this. They report not just about dry bills, budgets and hearings, but also what is on the minds of neighbors. They see issues firsthand. They also see the consequences of government's actions or neglect—whether it is a honky-tonk commercial strip eating away at neighborhood pride, a scenic river turned stagnant, or a much-publicized superhighway that could become tomorrow's eyesore.
>
> How well does the press explain local government and what it does for, or to, us? It may be rash to generalize, but newspapers, and to a lesser extent TV and radio, probably deserve a B for telling us about government's most visible activities: a battle over taxes, a key council or school board meeting, or the exposure of corruption. They do a much better job of keeping on top of the performance of a mayor or council member than watching a congressman or state legislator. But most get no better than a C when it comes to explaining how the system really works. They don't consistently tell us what local government can and cannot be expected to accomplish, how effective it is, and what its impact is on the community.[1]

Wolfson, and other critics of the media's coverage of local government, believe that reporters focus too much on personalities and spot news. Further, news releases and press conferences may be a convenient way to get the news, but many reporters simply do not make the effort to get the *other* side of the story from the person who does *not* issue the release. Or, as Wolfson writes, "We may learn more about a mayor's skill at winning elections than about how effective he or she is at developing policy, brokering diverse community interests, and keeping city hall's bureaucracy responsible."[2]

MONEY: THE NITTY AND THE GRITTY

"Follow the money." That's the most basic, yet comprehensive, advice veteran reporters give about covering government at any level. Strictly speaking, not all stories are financial stories. But the monetary path leads reporters into all sorts of interesting and important places. The presence or lack of funds, demands by citizens for satisfaction of certain needs, and governmental response to those demands are indicators of the degree to which citizen and governmental priorities mesh.

The heart of local government coverage is comprised of reports of official efforts to improve quality of the lives of its citizens. It's people stories—where they live, the problems they face, their attitudes about each other, and their attitudes about their community and its leadership. An integral part of all this is the question of whether money is available.

The news media and textbooks devote countless columns, minutes, and pages to the fact that the American city is in trouble. The demand for services is not matched by funds to provide those services. Movement to suburbs, both by individuals and by industries, has reduced the likelihood of local governments meeting their financial needs. There is an increasing problem of the homeless in large, sprawling urban areas as well as in smaller cities.

These are important stories. They are mandatory. The public must know of deteriorating cities, of the poor distribution of wealth between core cities and suburbs, of diminishing opportunities to fund special or even regular services. The U.S. government is based on the accountability of government officials. They may or may not have caused the disease of cities because circumstances cannot always be controlled. But, regardless, the nature of government is that its officials answer to the public. In most instances they answer only if reporters ask the right questions at the right time.

Sources of Local Government Revenue

That, of course, means more than crisis reporting. It also means paying close attention to local government finances on a daily basis. It's a difficult ideal to achieve, but citizens should not be surprised when crises occur.

The story of funds for the future will be based on the problems with traditional sources: tax limitations that restrict local revenues, decreasing ability of property taxes to meet local needs, and fluctuating trends of state and federal funds coming into the community. The story starts with the revenue sources: local taxes, intergovernmental revenue, nontax fees and service charges, and borrowing.

With few exceptions, local governments are restricted by state law in both the type of taxes that they may impose and the levels of that taxation. The practical effect is that property taxes have been the major source of local money for local needs.

Several states permit local government to impose (among others) income or sales taxes, taxes on automobiles, taxes on use of hotel and motel rooms, or special taxes such as those on cigarettes. In most cases, however, state limitations are such that income received does not solve the local financial problems. Since state and federal governments make extensive use of sales and income taxes, local areas have been forced mainly to rely on and struggle with administration of property taxes. These may apply to *real* property (buildings and land), *personal* property (possessions such as furniture, jewelry, and clothing), and *intangible* property (bank accounts, stocks, and bonds). The problem with such dependence is that property taxes are assessed on the value of a person's real estate rather than that person's ability to pay, and much of the property tax revenue comes from relatively low-income persons, especially retirees who own property but have fixed incomes.

In addition, any adjustments in the property tax formula must be submitted to the voters in the form of levies. But, in recent years, voters have become more reluctant to accept local governmental requests for maintenance or increases in property tax formulas.

Partial relief has come from programs that funnel state and federal funds into the local communities. Generally these funds consist of grants-in-aid to finance specific community efforts such as crime control, housing, or special education programs.

Through grants-in-aid, aggressive local governments can provide citizens with many opportunities they would otherwise not be able to afford. Basically competitive, the system requires that the community develop a specific program and submit a grant proposal to the appropriate state or federal agency. These funds are meant to redistribute wealth, assist communities with large low-income populations, or help solve particular problems. Some may stimulate local efforts to raise funds by including a matching requirement, often on a percentage basis.

Governmental grants, of course, come with strings attached and herein lies the basis for some considerable criticism. At the worse, critics charge, the grants threaten local self-government because external authority determines local policy and how and for what purposes certain funds will be spent. It can be broader than that since federal officials at times will threaten to withhold funds to achieve some unrelated goal (e.g., the national 55-mile-an-hour speed limit, or raising the minimum legal age to drink alcoholic beverages).

Critics also say that at best the availability of grant funds changes priorities of local communities. Instead of emphasizing what their citizens feel are the most important issues, local officials often are inclined to attend to those programs for which they have some chance of securing external funding.

On the local scene, governments have numerous opportunities to raise funds by charging fees for services they provide. The idea is that in many instances (e.g., water, hospitals, and public housing) certain individuals or groups benefit more from a service. Thus, they should pay for that service. This concept has come to be applied to other areas such as sewage, garbage collection, street lighting and cleaning, snow removal, and weed cutting.

In some instances when municipalities operate gas, water, or electrical facilities, they can make a profit. But utilities seldom are important sources of revenue because they are very expensive to operate. Few public transportation systems, for example, meet operating expenses because they must serve all the people in the entire area. Thus, they often run nonrevenue routes in poorer parts of the city or offer reduced fares to senior citizens or low-income individuals.

Some communities may levy service charges for services provided as a means of making the tax level appear lower. For example, a sewage charge added to the water bill will produce funds that otherwise would have been raised through taxes. Such charges may also be used to equalize local taxation or to reach local industries that are, for example, discharging a disproportionate amount of waste into the sewage system. Or they may be a means for the local government to gain some funds from tax-exempt property.

Special assessments represent yet another means of charging citizens according to the benefit they receive from a city or village service. The most common of these is assessing persons in a neighborhood for all or part of the cost of new street paving, installation of water lines, construction of off-street parking areas, and street lighting.

Local governments, like individuals, often find they have needs or desires, but they don't have the cash. Then they face the same decision: Do they wait until enough cash is available or do they borrow? While some officials believe even governments should operate on a cash-only basis, the dominant attitude is that it is most desirable to have the facility or program now and pay for it over time.

Despite some exceptions arising from emergencies, it generally is accepted that local governments should not borrow to meet current operating expenses. When they borrow to pay for long-term local improvements or emergencies, it is in anticipation of future incoming funds.

Borrowing for a local government generally takes the form of issuing bonds, which are little more than loan arrangements in which the local government agrees that the money will be paid back with interest. They are purchased by banks or other financial institutions. Since interest received on a municipal bond is not taxable, local governments usually pay less than the standard rate of interest. In general, municipalities issue three types of bonds:

General-obligation Bonds are supported by the full credit of the local government. In effect, they carry a promise that the resources of the community are available to pay them off and that the tax rate will be sufficient to pay the interest and eventually pay off ("retire") the bonds.

Mortgage Bonds, like mortgages on an individual's home, normally are used when the community wants to purchase or construct a utility, and the security for the loan is a mortgage or utility.

Revenue Bonds are issued when a community wants to construct a revenue-producing facility such as a toll bridge, tunnel, or electricity or water system. Revenue bonds stipulate that the funds to be obtained from operation of these facilities will be used to pay off the bond. Sometimes, bondholders, in addition, will get mortgages on the utilities.

Financial Planning: The Budget

Other than in times of crisis, the occasion most likely to attract reporters' attention to governmental finances is the often long process of preparing and approving the budget. The complexity of the process will vary, of course, but the path toward budget approval involves a number of rather standardized steps, each of which gives reporters opportunities to weigh local priorities.

Often the budget is prepared by the budget officer or controller under supervision of the chief executive. In consultation with department heads, the executive estimates revenues and determines priorities that influence allocation of those funds. This report usually contains a summary and a detailed breakdown of the anticipated revenues and expenditures. The spending pattern is divided into various funds, starting with

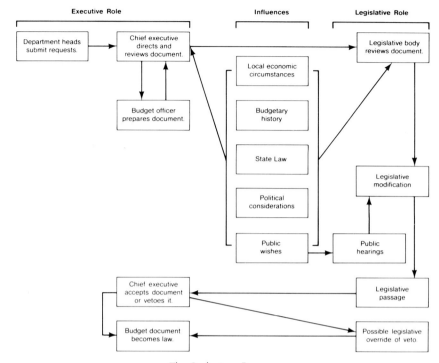

The Budgetary Process

the general fund and then listing others designed to meet special needs such as streets and highways. Often a separate capital improvements budget and perhaps special arrangements to pay off debts will be presented at a different time.

The document contains specific allocations of funds for specific purposes. Generally called a *line item budget,* it restricts the administration in rather precise ways depending upon the philosophy of the local government. Modern trends lean toward what may be called a *performance budget* or the *project approach,* in which the budget contains allocations of specific amounts for individual programs, but leaves room for administrative flexibility within those categories.

Once completed, this executive budget goes to the council or commission for discussion, modification, and approval. Included in the process at this stage are committee meetings and full-council discussion. Public hearings often will be held to allow citizens the opportunity to object to specific provisions or make special requests for funding of programs not included. Usually, persons who appear before the council represent interest groups rather than a cross-section of citizens. If the chief executive is weak administratively, department heads may appear before the council with requests for modifications.

The legislative body has the authority, then, to increase, reduce, delete, or add any specific item or amount. The document it ultimately approves returns to the chief executive, who often has the authority to veto any specific item. It then becomes a question of whether the council or commission has the desire and the votes to override a veto.

The process is designed to gain maximum input from all persons or groups who would be affected by funds spent on programs. The fact that such input usually comes from only a few who have strong interests and seldom involves the public at large is an accident of democracy that adds to the responsibilities of reporters covering the deliberations.

"How a governmental entity gets and spends its money is the nitty and the gritty of local news," says the *Oakland Press* of Pontiac, Michigan, in a booklet prepared for its staff. "But that doesn't mean the budget interests the reader, who long ago faced the fact that there's no way he can control what's in it. Who goes to public hearings on the budget anymore? No one, you say? An occasional eccentric, you say? You are right. Neither will the reader's interest be trapped by a newspaper story that is a rewrite of the budget book. These always come out as long lists of dollar signs and numbers that mean nothing to him and he won't, and shouldn't, remember."[3]

But the reporter who remembers that those dollar signs and numbers do mean something and who concentrates on that meaning instead of the numbers can produce story after story that will catch the reader's attention. A budget is, after all, a planning document, a statement of philosophy that sets the priorities for the coming year.

How much money will be spent on recreation and how does that compare with previous years and with facilities and programs now available? The answer tells the readers more about government's interest in providing community recreation than hundreds of official declarations. Specific appropriations may determine the treatment your dog will receive if picked up by the local dog catcher, whether you will be able to ride the city bus to work, whether the potholes on your street will be fixed, and what the likely political arguments will be in the next election.

Throughout the process, the story is not in the numbers. The story is in how those numbers relate to people. The story is in local priorities. Why does a department head so strongly support a new bond issue? Why

does the mayor oppose it? Is the city manager more interested in con-
structing buildings or supporting social service programs? Why don't officials support a citizen request that a new street be built on the south
side of town? Discussion of why certain groups or individuals make certain recommendations often is of greater significance than amounts of
money. The behind-the-scenes negotiations or public debates probably
are more political than financial, and that's the essence of good journalistic copy.

The good stories don't come only from the expenditure side of the
budget. The estimates of revenue are full of possibilities. Where does
the city or county get its money? Is it simply milking the citizens through
taxes? Or does it take advantage of numerous opportunities to get
funding? Do city services pay for themselves, or is there likely to be an
increase in water rates next year?

The soul of any funding story will be people, and it should be couched
in people terms. The reporter should be alert to the possibilities. A good
first place to look is for dramatic increases or decreases in any of the
major revenue categories: taxes; income from fines, permits, licenses,
parking meters, and so forth; federal and state grants; and payment for
services. Potential tax increases are the most obvious, of course, but at
times the suggestions may be more subtle. For example, an expected
increase in revenue from contracting out fire department services could
signal a major improvement in fire protection for residents of a nearby
community.

SUBURBS POSE SPECIAL PROBLEMS

Look at any metropolitan newspaper and you'll find traditional beat
reporters who are the backbone of the city staff—the city hall reporter
who spends all day in city hall; the police reporter stationed at the police
department pressroom; the court reporter who walks the halls of the
courthouse, not the newsroom.

But if you look at any metropolitan area, you'll see that most of the
population since World War II has shifted from the aging central city to
the suburbs. These are rapidly developing cities and villages that are
independent residential, recreational and education centers, and regional economic centers. Around the large shopping malls will be acres
of homes, fast-food restaurants, and new-car dealers.

To a degree, the 1980s brought a move to the "gentrification" of old
and deteriorating housing near the downtown area; that is, some
people—particularly young people who grew up in the suburbs—decided to invest in the rehabilitation and renovation of housing near

downtown. But while downtown areas around the country have experienced this gentrification, most of the 6,500 suburbs in the United States continue to grow rapidly.

Consequently, reporters assigned to a metro desk find themselves dealing with not only just one city hall or city school board, but also with many cities, each with its own mayor, city administrator or clerk, elected city council, city services, fire/police chief, zoning and health codes, and sometimes a judicial system (mayor's court). Often, newspapers and television stations can have as many as thirty city, county, or township jurisdictions within their viewing or circulation areas.

Who lives in the suburbs? These are the people who shop at those regional shopping malls, have children in one of the suburban school districts, and probably work in a suburban office or industrial park near the interstate highway. They go to movies in regional cinemas and to dentists and doctors near the regional hospitals. In fact, many people who live in the suburbs have all the goods and services they need within driving range, and they seldom have a reason to go into the central city. They aren't touched by the decisions made in city hall or by the city's board of education.

Because of the growth of the suburbs and outlying areas, many large newspapers have established "zoned editions"—editions of a newspaper that are tailored specifically for certain areas of the county. Editorial content and advertising in each of these editions cater specifically to that one region.

A startling number of big-city problems (crime, labor disputes, hazardous wastes or working conditions), like the population, have drifted from the central city. The metro reporter also will have a share of major news stories. Airplanes crash in suburbs because airports are built at the edge of the metropolitan area. Hazardous chemical wastes are hauled from city plants to rural, isolated landfills.

Cathy Candisky, who used to cover the eastern suburbs of Columbus for *Neighbor News* of the *Columbus Dispatch,* believes the issue of annexation of suburbs into major cities will be a major one in the 1990s. Because of the rapid growth of suburbs, many large central cities are losing their population base; as a result, many cities are "annexing" suburban land in an attempt to expand the central-city tax base. Predictably, these annexation attempts often are the center of dispute between suburban and central-city residents. These disputes usually focus on use of school districts and city services of the central city and the suburbs.

Often, to get the nitty-gritty on annexation stories, reporters must be familiar with actions of local zoning boards and commissions, where those types of decisions are discussed.

A thorough understanding of the physical and economic traits of a community is vital to finding regional story ideas. The old mill towns are concerned with accommodating expanding, aging plants; redevel-

Cathy Candisky
of *The Columbus Dispatch* (Columbus
Dispatch photo)

oping their decaying central business districts; and attracting young people. The new cities are suffering as variety of growing pains—battles usually found over zoning and development—as developers plan apartments and shopping centers near expensive homes, as superhighways dump traffic into inadequate two-lane roads, or as folks petition for a zone change to convert an old house into a shop for a butcher, baker, or candlestick maker.

People in the suburbs care about the same things city residents care about. They care about zoning, sewers, water rates, crime, fire protection, traffic, and development of nearby land.

But getting that suburban news poses problems, says John Kiesewetter of the *Cincinnati Enquirer.* Of course, a reporter can't be stationed in every city hall every day. The reporter must develop good contacts in each suburb, and make those contacts feel important. Key sources of information will be police chief, fire chief, mayor, city manager, council clerk, and safety-service director. Often, the service director is the full-time administrator. It's important that reporters can reach these people at work and at home, because most elected suburban officials work daytime jobs and do their politicking at night.

Bob Karlovits, who heads the neighborhood zoned editions at *The Pittsburgh Press,* believes his suburban reporters must be "experts" in a variety of fields—that is, they usually must, to a degree, be familiar with city hall, education, business, and all other facets of the suburbs they cover.

Just like the city hall reporter, the suburban reporter will find that covering meetings is a staple of the suburban beat. Periodic visits to council meetings show an interest in the community and help maintain contacts. At the council meetings, reporters will get a spot news story or two. Also, citizens will talk about problems that could become topics of regional suburban stories, and reporters will hear about people and their business or other interests that could make good feature stories.

Attending meetings also gives reporters a firsthand look at the operation of the city. The potential for corruption or ineptitude is so much greater in the suburbs because the people running the city and its police/fire departments and other services often are making considerably less money than major metropolitan officials. The suburban official, who has just as much power to run a city or its departments, *could* be much less qualified for that position than in the larger cities. Reporters also should watch for signs of overaggressive police who could be violating civil rights during arrests, of mayors who could conveniently change dispositions of cases during or after mayor's court sessions, of council members who pack city hall with friends and relatives, and of ineptitude in city finances.

But as Candisky notes, it might be impossible for a suburban reporter to cover *all* the meetings on his or her beat. Often, she said, actual meetings simply give elected officials a chance to "rubber stamp" agenda items without thoroughly discussing them. The discussions usually come at more informal meetings held a day or two before the group actually meets formally. Often the discussion is heated during these informal meetings; a reporter who wants a more in-depth story on an issue or topic should cover these meetings, Candisky said. The formal meetings—such as a council meeting—need not always be covered to get the story, she believes.

The suburban reporter must be alert to two distinct levels of story possibilities: regional, countywide trend stories and spot news stories pertaining to a single community. Most news organizations do both. They not only discuss the lack of low-income subsidized housing in the suburbs, but they also discuss the story on an individual basis. If a suburban council votes Monday night to allow a low-income housing project to be built, the people expect to read about the council meeting on Tuesday morning. News organizations not only discuss dwindling school enrollments and closing schools, but they also discuss a specific school board meeting and report the next day on the board's decision to close two neighborhood schools and change attendance districts.

By talking to contacts and keeping an eye on suburban weeklies, reporters will know which meeting to attend and which not to attend. They'll also see which topics are discussed by various cities, which will provide the news peg for a regional story.

Another staple of suburban coverage tends to be profiles. Reporters write about mayors, trying to use the story as an effort to describe the person as well as the characteristics of each community. They write about the people who run shops in the suburban business districts, people who are seen and heard often by fellow suburban residents. To Candisky of the *Columbus Dispatch,* the suburbs of even the biggest cities in the country often offer a glimpse of "small-town" America. That is, the atmosphere of small towns can often be captured by the reporter.

The suburbs are filled with people, and that has to be an important focus of the reporter. Those rows of houses are filled with people. The regional shopping malls and traffic congestion are people stories. They can't be covered by telephone. The suburban or metro reporter must be a foot soldier by getting out of the office, by talking to people, and by listening.

POINTING THE JOURNALISTIC FINGER

David Poole of the *Times & World News* in Roanoke, Virginia, documented illegal purchasing practices by the town of Rocky Mount, including the award of a dozen lucrative tax-supported contracts to favored local businesses without competitive bidding.

WSMC-TV in Nashville and reporters Erin Hayes and Paul Slattery aired a series of reports showing how the city's sewer department dumped sludge into creeks and rivers used by the public.

"Everyone knew" that many New York City police officers were sleeping on the job, but David Burnham documented the practice for *The New York Times.*

Things do go wrong in local government. Some individuals take advantage of their official positions. Some seek financial or other personal gain. Some simply seek ways to avoid doing the job for which they receive public funds. Shouldn't someone point an accusing finger?

"An examination of the problem of corruption—whether within a police department, the Central Intelligence Agency, or a major corporation such as ITT—shows that major, sustained efforts to control the problem have almost always required an outside stimulus," says Burnham in a booklet called *The Role of the Media in Controlling Corruption.* That stimulus frequently has been the mass media. But despite the numerous examples of media reporting about corruption, including the whole Watergate incident, Burnham feels reporters have not been doing the job adequately.

Covering or uncovering corruption in a local government cannot be accomplished, he says, by doing what too many reporters do best; that is, reporting what the politicians or administrators say. It requires energy and legwork. It requires hours of observation, of reading through documents, and of interviewing persons other than those in the highly placed official positions.

Town prepares to become city's next suburb

By June Cavarretta

There's no gas station or grocery store in Gilberts, and the Village Hall, which has no full-time employees, is open only four hours a day.

But the country town of less than 1,000 people 45 miles northwest of Chicago is likely to become the metropolitan area's next suburb.

What makes Gilberts almost unique is that it is quietly preparing itself for the expected growth in the 1990s with a degree of foresight rarely seen in communities its size. It is making big plans.

"We're sleeping dogs. We're in a unique position in that we have a lot of opportunity for expansion. Things are happening out here that will have a major effect on Gilberts, and a lot of people are looking [at us]," said Mayor Ronald Lammers.

Like people in many old towns in the rural expanse of Kane County west of the Fox River Valley, the residents of Gilberts, which was incorporated in 1858, are beginning to see evidence of urban sprawl on the horizon.

Although the Northwest Tollway skirted the southern edge of town in 1958, Gilberts remained relatively isolated because no interchange was built there. Ill. Hwy. 72 still bridges the tollway with no connection.

But a tollway interchange is now under construction at Randall Road a few miles to the east. That and the relocation of the Sears, Roebuck & Co. Merchandise Group to Hoffman Estates farther east are expected to cause a boom in north-central Kane County.

The interchange, scheduled for completion next summer, is already opening up Randall Road for development. Two developments, for a credit card center and a consumer electronics company, are under construction near the interchange.

For now, Gilberts is surrounded by farms, and officials want to preserve the town's rural character even when urban sprawl finally hits.

But they also want to expand in order to control the type of development that comes in, which means the town may have to get involved in an annexation war with larger Elgin to the southeast. Elgin's comprehensive plan calls for annexations as far north as possible, bringing its city limits to Gilberts' back door.

"Under whose government Randall Road develops is still up in the air, but whoever controls the infrastructure will control [the corridor]," Lammers said.

In that respect, Gilberts is far behind its larger neighbor. The village doesn't have a sanitary sewer system and all houses have septic fields.

If the town wants to compete for development it will have to look at building a sewage treatment plant and expanding its water system, the mayor said.

According to Kitty Masek, who was recently hired as the town's first village administrator, officials are now looking for ways to finance the expansion of those utilities.

"We're hoping that by bringing in sewers we'll be able to attract development," Masek said.

Gilberts is also preparing for growth by expanding its Village Hall and updating its comprehensive plan, which has been done twice in the last six years.

"We want to control our destiny, and our comprehensive plan is our marketing tool. It's telling developers what we feel should happen in Gilberts and how they could fit in," Lammers said.

The prospect of growth is hard for some residents to swallow, he said, but landowners have the right to sell their property and the town must be prepared when the growth comes.

Masek said the town's planning is progressive considering its size. The town began putting aside money for the Village Hall expansion some time ago, and like an Amish barn raising, residents are pitching in with donated labor to complete it. Alongside its computers, the new hall is furnished with hand-me-down furniture, which helps contain costs.

"This town has an amazing amount of foresight, but even so, the theme is the same. You still have that old against the new faction, and you see that in the elections and in the issues," Masek said.

"But ours is the next stop west [of the Fox River Valley communities], and all of a sudden people know we're here. And we have to be ready."

Small towns and suburbs throughout the nation are experiencing expansion and growth. This story, from the *Chicago Tribune,* November 16, 1989, describes the situation in one tiny town, and how expansion is affecting citizens, services and attitudes. (Reprinted by permission.)

Burnham's story about "coping," the New York City Police Department's time-honored expression for sleeping on duty, was documented between 2 and 6 A.M. on those occasions when he and a photographer prowled the docks, alleys, and parks of New York City. In another story, he determined that a large proportion of those arrested for robbery won almost immediate dismissal, that only a tiny fraction was brought to trial, and that those who pleaded guilty received sentences of under one year. He gained this insight by pouring for many weeks over the "sloppily maintained filing system of the New York courts."

On another occasion, Burnham says, he decided to test the hypothesis that corruption and its easy tolerance profoundly influenced the performance of the police.

"I began interviewing literally hundreds of New Yorkers from all over the city and from all walks of life," he says. "I interviewed—usually with a promise that they would not be quoted by name—bartenders, restaurant owners, liquor store owners, delicatessen operators, tow-truck drivers, building contractors, parking attendants, supermarket managers, numbers game operators, bookmakers, policemen, detectives, prosecutors, lawyers, judges, blacks, whites, and Spanish-speaking people."

These interviews consumed more than a year of evenings and free moments during the day. Combining them with an examination of the handful of corruption cases being prosecuted at that time, Burnham concluded that corruption did in fact dominate many of the activities of the New York City Police Department; and corruption had significantly decreased the effectiveness of the police.

The reactions to his stories about corruption, especially the coping story, have led Burnham to what he terms "a fundamental truth about journalism": Most important stories concern widely known and generally accepted practices.

In this day of mass cynicism, too many reporters have learned to live with the existence of corruption. But the question, Burnham stresses, is not whether there always will be corruption, but why there seems to be more in one place than another, or at one time than another, and what steps can be taken to reduce it. Such considerations have led him to what he considers to be his job as a reporter: "to devote most of my energy to trying to describe those practices and procedures that stop a particular agency from achieving its stated goals."[4]

Most local government officials are honest and dedicated. But reporters owe it to themselves and to their public to be alert to the possibility that some are not. They must be willing to devote the time and effort required to document any story about practices and procedures that hamper the official effectiveness of an individual or an agency. Corruption stories are not written simply for their readership value; they are not written as an assertion of a journalist's power. They are written because it is the public that pays the financial, psychological, and sometimes physical price when government goes wrong. Whether it's corruption, incompetence, or simply faulty judgment makes little difference. Reporters are watchdogs, not lapdogs, of government.

COVERING THE CITY, NOT JUST THE HALL

Reporters have for years been covering city halls and county courthouses, and they have kept citizens at least relatively informed. But city hall and the county courthouse are more complicated now. Officials have greater responsibilities; they handle more money, and they often are tied together in cooperative programs, not only with each other, but also with the state and federal governments. News coverage is difficult. And talented as they may be, individual reporters simply do not have the time and sometimes the resources to do the whole job. Therefore, a new approach is needed.

As a result several trends have emerged. Some newspapers and television stations have labeled their city hall coverage *urban affairs* reporting. Urban affairs reporters cover not just city hall and council, but also community development—the growth of cities and suburbs, including newly developed subdivisions, offices, and retail space.

Some media outlets have expanded the team or cluster concept of reporting. Team makeup varies, of course, but usually includes reporter responsibility for city hall, county government, local politics, local courts, and sometimes police.

The move is partly one of efficiency; team members will cover for a fellow staffer on vacation or on special assignment. But, more important, it's a move designed to enterprise and to improve investigative work. Because team members can work together and cover for each other on the day-to-day breaking news requirements, they then can be free to concentrate on broader stories that the normal city or county government reporter could seldom find the time to do.

Another side of the urban affairs reporting, one most frequently found at the nation's largest newspapers and wire services, is the reporter with no day-to-day breaking news responsibilities who looks only at the big trends. This includes getting the broad picture of community problems that affect all residents, regardless of where they live or how much wealth they have accumulated. For example, the effort to solve the significant urban problems of poverty, poor education, crime and slums is costing billions of taxpayer dollars.

Other issues that will demand coverage in the 1990s are the growing problem of the homeless and the poor in large urban areas and suburbs; the increasing demand for police and fire coverage and other services in rapidly expanding suburbs; and, consequently, what city officials and citizens will do to revitalize sometimes deteriorating inner-city neighborhoods.

NOTES

1. Lewis W. Wolfson, *The Untapped Power of the Press* (New York: Praeger Publishers, 1985) pp. 153–154.

2. Wolfson, p. 154.

3. "Covering Government: A New Testament to Newswriting," *Oakland Press,* Pontiac, Mich., 1976, p. 14.

4. David Burnham, *The Role of Media in Controlling Corruption* (New York: Criminal Justice Center, John Jay College of Criminal Justice), pp. 1–14. Reprinted with permission from the John Jay Press.

Covering Law Enforcement

4

Based on their exposure to it in films, on television, in books, and in newspapers, the American people should certainly know about crime. They should know that more crimes are being committed each day and that they should be careful when walking the streets at night.

But most Americans have never witnessed or been involved in a major crime, although that fact is hard to believe, considering the coverage it is given in the media. Crime has always been a subject of interest to editors; consequently, it is of interest to reporters and prominently written about in newspapers and on news broadcasts.

Reporters have always been in the police stations and will continue to be there as long as law enforcement remains a necessary social activity. In short, they will be there for as long as there is crime. The public is interested in crime and law enforcement, perhaps because of curiosity or because of a fear of what might happen to them someday. In either case, information about crime is essential to their understanding of their own community.

That's why journalistic interest in law enforcement is most likely to concentrate on local crime and local police. But jurisdictions of such agencies overlap, and from time to time reporters find themselves seeking information from various types of law enforcement officials.

For information on efforts to maintain the peace in rural areas and small communities, the focus may be on activities of a *township constable* or *village marshal*. Larger communities have professional or *city police* whose efforts to enforce municipal ordinances and state statutes within city limits provide reams of journalistic copy.

At the county level, the principal official is the *sheriff,* and there may be *county police* who serve under the sheriff or who are an independent agency with full powers. Sheriffs' authority has been declining nationally, but reporters follow their work in unincorporated areas and as caretaker of the county jail.

Called by varying names, *state police* may be restricted to highway patrol duties or to serve general police functions, particularly in rural areas. Most states have an agency to investigate state crimes, keep records, and compile statistics. Generally known as the Bureau of Criminal Investigation, these agencies can provide a wealth of information for enterprising reporters.

The federal government has numerous law enforcement agencies, but reporters have most encounters with the Federal Bureau of Investigation, which has responsibility for looking into violations of federal laws.

SOURCES, TRUST AND CONFIDENTIALITY

Veteran reporters know and young reporters learn very quickly that working with law enforcement officials at all levels and of all types can be very difficult. Stories of conflict, usually ideological but sometimes physical, are legion. History may have never recorded the hour in which some police official somewhere was not refusing to give information to reporters. Under many circumstances, that official was citing reporters' lack of dependability as the reason for the refusal.

One study of twenty-five police chiefs in cities of more than 100,000 people said their lower-ranking officers view media as "carping critics seeking out 'warts' that did not really exist."[1] A major complaint of police officers in this study was also that police spend too much time briefing young, inexperienced reporters.

Still, police officers realize that good relations with the media can help them. Typical of this is a journal article in which a Michigan police administrator called for a "concentrated public relations effort" through the media.[2]

Most police reporters find if they are polite and persistent, they can get the information they want. Amy Geisel, a police reporter for the *Knoxville News-Sentinel*, calls sources her "lifeblood." In that way, she believes, the police beat is no different from any other beat because it is often necessary to "cultivate" sources even before a big story breaks. "Simply be nice and courteous; it makes the difference between having a person help you when you need it and getting no help," she believes. "Talk to sources even when you don't need information. Get to know them."

Personality plays an important role, but it's also an atmosphere of trust, of knowing each other. It's building good relationships with the sources used day in and day out. Without such sources, there will be no tips and few stories beyond the commonplace. Reporters who don't care about relationships with their sources will get maybe one good story. In some types of reporting, it may be possible to "burn" sources and not have to encounter them again. But in police reporting, the journalist who burns an officer will have to see the officer tomorrow and the day after that and after that.

The desire for trust based on continuity of relationship was emphasized in a survey conducted by The Associated Press Managing Editors. Eighty-one percent of police chiefs indicated they felt frequent changes in news media personnel are not beneficial. They want to work with reporters they know. Editors apparently share the attitude because 82 percent of them indicated they do not shift police reporters frequently.[3]

If reporters stay on the job long enough, they develop contacts among people who move up the ranks. Today's officer is yesterday's beat cop. Experienced reporters have learned which officers are trusting and will permit a few liberties and which officers insist on a strict, according-to-policy relationship.

Developing sources is like making friends; it's a long process that involves a lot of trial and error. For example, the reporter goes to the local police department and seeks out the desk officer. Introductions come first. Then a few exploratory questions and a little self-revelation. Over time, the reporter and source get to know each other's jobs and styles fairly well, and the relationship comes close to being a friendship. But a friendship it is not.

The reporter must walk the tightrope between understanding the police officer and beginning able to think too much like that officer. As in any professional situation, the reporter must keep a distance so that it will not be difficult for coverage to involve officers' mistakes as well as their successes.

Reporters must keep their function clear in their minds. Police gather information for successful prosecution of violaters of the law. Reporters gather information to allow the public to judge the fairness and effectiveness of its government. To lose sight of the distinction is to erode the profession.

At times, the police and reporters work together to help solve a crime and provide information to listeners and viewers; but the difference in the roles of the two can cause clashes—just ask Jeff Stalk of the Ventura County (California) *Star-Free Press.*

After a series of terrorist attacks against local narcotics officers, police in Ventura County asked the local newspaper if they could work with reporters. The terrorists had been sending letters to the newspaper, claiming responsibility for the attacks. The letters were important clues, and law enforcement officials wanted permission to intercept them and open them under laboratory conditions. The request was granted with the understanding that a reporter be present when the letters were opened and that he or she be given copies.

But the effort was far from harmonious, and it wasn't long before both parties began to grumble about their "partners." Editors and reporters expected police to be candid about the progress of the investigation, and police expected the newspaper to be discreet about the operation. Both sides were disappointed, even though they each tried to understand the job of the other.[4]

Who Needs to Know?

Even under the best of circumstances, one of the realities of journalistic and legal life is frequent disagreement over what information should be made public and under what circumstances. For example:

> More than three years after a 1983 shootout in which a police officer and seven civilians were killed in Memphis, Tenn., the Supreme Court of Tennessee granted *The (Memphis) Commercial Appeal* the right to public findings of an internal police investigation which had been closed by state and city officials until the ruling.[5]

> The Oregon Legislative Assembly passed a law prohibiting official public disclosure of criminal records, including records of "arrest, detention, indictments, information or other criminal charges . . . sentencing, correctional supervision, and release." The law created chaos, not only for reporters, but also for state government officials and police themselves. It was repealed four days later in a special session of the assembly.[6]

The roots of such instances grow from three attitudes of public law enforcement and legislative officials. One, of course, is the distrust and resentment many officials hold for reporters whom they consider to be meddling and obnoxious. The second is the arrogant sense of power held by some law enforcement officials. The third, especially in recent years, is rooted in growing feelings about the need to protect individual privacy and resulting federal and state actions that cause local police to put a lid on enforcement.

In fact, a President's Task Force on Victims of Crime in 1983 recommended that the home addresses and telephone numbers of crime victims and witnesses be kept secret unless a court ruled otherwise. The task force, which was set up to tell public and private agencies what they could do to help crime victims, strongly recommended that laws be enacted to ensure the privacy of victims and witnesses. The 144-page report stated in part that "if jurisdictions require that certain police reports be open to the public, they should either amend their statutes or redesign their forms so that some information (like home addresses or telephone numbers) is not available for publication."[7]

Locally, reporters and law enforcement agencies collide over the document known by various names but generally called the "police blotter," a law enforcement agency's record of its actions. Police departments use different forms, sometimes a chronological listing, sometimes a card file, but included in the police blotter is a mixture of serious and not-so-serious complaints and subsequent police actions.

Depending on the policy of the individual agency, however, it may include less official information, such as speculation by an investigating officer. It may also have information which departmental policy dictates should be kept confidential, such as the name of an undercover agent. Among the most controversial pieces of information frequently on the blotter are the names of rape victims or juvenile offenders. It is general practice as well as police policy to avoid publicly naming rape victims on the grounds that they have innocently suffered enough, or to avoid naming juveniles on the grounds that publicity may reduce the chances for a return to a normal life. Often, the law solidifies the policy regarding juveniles.

However, journalists insist that even in these cases the information is public record, and journalists should decide whether to use it. Reporters have for years scanned these records daily, noted which items they wanted to pursue, and then gathered more complete information for their stories by looking at other records or interviewing appropriate officers.

Reporters traditionally have analyzed and ignored much of what has appeared in police records. In many instances, this continues to be the standard practice, but as the use of computers by law enforcement agencies increases, some officials are becoming even more difficult. Modern technology has increased the dangers of using the information, according to an official of the New York Fair Trial Free Press Conference.

As these governmental-computerized information storage and retrieval systems are linked, it becomes possible for the same system to hold records of arrests, convictions, and dropped charges along with other records on the same individual that do not necessarily have any relationship to criminal activity. Consequently, the records can be factually inaccurate, be incomplete, or be taken out of context.

Bugs within the system itself can haunt reporters, who argue that such inefficiency is not the reason to deny access. They say a person's criminal history, for example, is public record because it is part of a public arrest or public trial, because it is kept at taxpayer expense, and because it is kept at the mandate of the legislature or courts. If the government orders such record keeping, they say, it must be available for public access.

Story is repeated, in big towns and small

By Robin Yocum,
David Jacobs and Jim Woods
Dispatch Staff Reporters

Crack not only has taken up residence in Ohio's largest metropolitan areas, it has sent offspring to populate the small cities and rural areas.

In Newark, a city of 45,000 east of Columbus, crack and cocaine use is "growing by leaps and bounds," police say. They attribute the growth to increasing involvement of Columbus and Detroit drug dealers.

Usage and dealing have been rising since late last year and culminated in Newark's first crack-related arrest in June, Detective R. A. Villinger said.

"This is a two-faced problem," Deputy Chief Al Zellner said last week, just days after a five-month investigation led to the arrests of eight people on drug charges. Users "are a drain on our resources because they spend money that leaves the city, and they eventually require services that taxpayers must pay for."

Villinger said the recent drug-related arrests are "just the tip of the iceberg." He expects more because there is a profit to be made.

He said a person can go to Columbus and buy a rock of crack fo $20, and then sell it in Newark for $25 to $35. Some Newark dealers will break the rock into several parts and sell them for $5 to $10 each, he added.

Villinger has also documented instances of people driving to Detroit and purchasing crack or cocaine for sale in Newark.

The Detroit connection also has turned up in Mansfield, a rust-belt city of 52,000 about 70 miles north of Columbus that has small town charms and some big city problems.

"Per capita, we have just as bad a crack problem as Columbus and Cleveland have," Police Lt. Philip Messer said.

Earlier this month, police arrested two boys, ages 16 and 17, who had moved from Detroit into Mansfield for a summer business venture—dealing crack.

They were staked by their mentor with bags of crack, $250 apiece and handguns, police say. The boys set up shop at a house on a back alley near downtown.

Their business raked in an estimated $10,000 a week for five weeks before police raided the house. It was the 12th suspected crack house raided by Mansfield police this year, Messer said. Police raided 27 houses in 1988.

"I think it's just so competitive in the major cities, like Detroit, that a gang thinks it can come in and make a killing," Messer said.

Geron Tate, a counselor at Serenity Hall in Mansfield, said crack use is reaching epidemic proportions among the young in Mansfield's black community.

Crack raids also have been conducted this year in Lima, Fostoria, Defiance and Fremont.

Predictably, the large cities have been hardest hit:

● A Cleveland narcotics officer called the problem "monumental." Cleveland police made 1,700 arrests in 1986. This year they are expected to make 6,000 arrests, the majority of which will be for crimes related to crack use.

● Crack houses open with such frequency in Toledo that police can't keep up. "As soon as we close one, another opens," said Narcotics Lt. Ralph Kuyoth.

● Prostitutes working for a dealer took over a Dayton apartment and set up an elaborate crack and cocaine distribution center. A police officer said it was "second to none. McDonald's could have learned from those people."

● In Akron, the Los Angeles-based Crips youth gang contributed to escalation of the problem, said Lt. Victor Norman, who heads the Akron police drug bureau.

The Crips began to move into Akron in late 1987 and set up an intricate network that brought in crack and cocaine from Los Angeles. The number of cocaine cases handled by Akron police jumped from 111 in 1987 to 189 through the first six months of 1989.

"The Crips targeted Akron because the profit margin was double or triple what they could make in Los Angeles," said Ken McHargh, an assistant U.S. attorney in Cleveland.

Norman said Akron's biggest crack problem "still comes from Detroit. We probably get four or five crack dealers from Detroit for every one we get from California, and that's a low estimate."

Law enforcement of drug abusers will no doubt be an important story in small towns and big cities throughout the 1990s. This story appeared in the *Columbus Dispatch,* August 20, 1989, as part of a week-long series on crack-cocaine in Ohio. Note how it describes simply and clearly the scope of the problem in one state. (Reprinted with permission from the *Columbus Dispatch.*)

Reporters frequently use three methods to gain information from governmental records. One method is the informal route of developing sources who will provide information, perhaps on an unattributed basis. While at times effective and necessary, this method carries with it the usual potential danger of using secondary sources of information. Another method is establishing trust, confidentiality, and professional respect—an atmosphere in which officials are much more likely to be cooperative. A third method is taking legal action when state or federal freedom of information laws apply.

THE MATTER OF PUBLIC ACCOUNTABILITY

But there's another reason for maximum access to criminal records besides those records being public record. Those people involved in law enforcement recognize that they are accountable to the public, and many argue in favor of the media's watchdog role in enforcing this accountability.

But it isn't really that simple when reporters do try to fill that void. Ask reporters from KABC-TV in Los Angeles who staged a determined battle with the Los Angeles Police Department to get details of police shootings of civilians. It took more than a year of dedicated reporting and the support of a city council member and the *Los Angeles Times* before the police finally released the requested statistics. And the statistics showed that of 223 shootings of civilians over two years, 35 were judged to be below department standards.[8]

The difficulty of getting official information on police activities is further demonstrated by a report from the Chicago Law Enforcement Study Group, a joint research project of Northwestern University's Center for Urban Affairs in cooperation with a number of community groups. The report underscores the lack of accountability under which many police departments function.

It recommends establishment of a Police Information Center that could collect and distribute information (especially statistical information) to provide an overview of police activities, accomplishments, and weaknesses. It specifically calls for statistics on incidence of crime in various parts of the city; a statistical breakdown of complaints, arrests, referrals to social welfare agencies, prosecutions and convictions; complete statistics on juvenile crime; the disposition of cases in which calls to the police did not lead to arrests; number of complaints made against police officers; awards presented; promotions granted; deaths resulting from police operations; weapon usage; and data on race involved in each circumstance.[9]

The justification for these requests was simply stated: "The Chicago Law Enforcement Study Group, from its inception, has been a consistent advocate of the public's right to know what its officials are doing."[10]

GETTING OUT ON THE STREET

Covering police activities is more than analysis of statistics and police records. It is—or should be—getting out on the street to capture the drama of police activities and, more important, to keep in contact with citizens.

Amy Geisel of *The Knoxville News-Sentinel* believes getting on the street—including being on the scene in hostage takeovers—is vital, in part because reporters can talk directly to police and to those involved in the incident. "It's best to talk to police and not PIOs (public information officers)," she said. "The cop is a firsthand source. I view PIOs as an avenue of last resort." When she started covering the police beat, Geisel rode with police officers for several shifts as they covered their beats; that way, she became familiar with their jobs and them, as well as learned firsthand about the difficulty of their jobs.

Reporters on the scene also must rely on their own abilities to observe and to make judgments about what is happening. They use their own sight and their own senses. They have to discover quickly whose word to accept because often there's no way to verify it. They do not use rumors as information, however, but as tips to be checked out.

Good reporters are aware and wary of the tendency to isolate some part of the action or some especially moving human component and to emphasize that as if it were the total story.

The on-the-scene problems for reporters are compounded, of course, in those situations involving hostages, especially if the major point of the whole incident is to gain publicity. The situation places journalists in two very awkward positions that force them to make difficult decisions. First, how do they avoid becoming the "captives" of terrorists; that is, how do they distinguish between covering an event and being used? Second, how do they cover such an event without informing terrorists of police strategy or without providing information that may place hostages in even more jeopardy?

Law enforcement authorities tend to argue that journalists hamper efforts in several ways. They can inadvertently give intelligence and tactical information to terrorists and dilute police authority by talking directly to hostages. In addition, they can create traffic problems at the scene or tie up telephone lines. Some law enforcement officials also believe that reporters can reinforce the terrorists' sense of power, or (perhaps) worse raise their anxiety level by printing or broadcasting inaccurate or premature reports.

It's unlikely that journalists and officials will agree on everything in terrorist situations. But police and the news media can work, if not together, at least side by side, especially if they can gain understanding of how each must function.

One of the answers is training, with reporters sharing sessions with police officers. Another answer is experience. Some news organizations have sought a third answer by developing internal guidelines to blunt the impact of the media on such stories, while at the same time stressing that the reporter must cover the event independently.

Drug Abuse Deserves Attention

Another kind of street crime story in which participants are not seeking publicity involves drugs: their use and abuse, their sale, their impact, the extent of their usage, and the efforts of law enforcement and other governmental and private agencies to control them. More individuals are using illicit drugs now than at any other time. The drug abuse treatment industry employs more than 54,000 persons (by most responsible estimates), and governments at all levels spend millions of dollars on drug law enforcement.

Throughout the 1990s, federal efforts at drug prevention is likely to be a major story, especially with President Bush's war on drugs. Throughout the nation, hundreds of newspapers and television stations have localized the federal crackdown on drugs by airing and publishing stories on the effect of drugs in their communities.

Local clinics and treatment centers may be willing to help reporters gain an understanding of the medical and psychological problems related to drug abuse, as well as provide assistance in developing source inroads to users and sellers.

In addition, drug historians and researchers are tucked away in laboratories, frequently on university campuses, and may be consulted by an enterprising reporter. Pharmaceutical companies are also a source, although they may be somewhat defensive if they manufacture a drug that is being abused.

But regardless of the source, reporters must be especially cautious with any statistics or figures provided, especially about the "street value" of drugs. As a rule, police have not been willing or able to assess accurately the value of what they have received, and news media have tended to pass along unverified police figures. The answer, of course, is in multiple sources—even, if necessary, consulting drug users about current street values.

One drug story that will always require solid coverage is drug treatment. But reporters should be skeptical of treatment program operators and look past statistical statements of success—particularly if treatment officials imply that one type of treatment is suitable for everyone.

THE TIGHT-LIPPED FBI

In a public program in which he discussed his coverage of an Arizona hostage situation, Paul McGonigle of KOY Radio in Phoenix drew laughter from his audience of fellow journalists when he told them of the arrival of FBI agents.

"That meant nothing was happening because when the FBI gets there, they like to pretend: 'What bank? What hostage? What gun?' But the FBI actually was, I thought, quite efficient."

That's a good summary. The FBI perhaps is the most tight-lipped, of-ficial-sources-only law enforcement agency with which most reporters will ever deal. Field agents know the policy, and at least on the surface, they live by it.

"The only person authorized to release information concerning an investigation is the agent in charge of the major field division or his au-thorized representative," says one agent who, true to form, would not speak at all unless it was agreed that his name would not be used.

In this country 8,500 FBI agents are organized into 59 field offices and sprinkled in resident agencies that sometimes consist of one agent. Many cities and towns have no local agent. The reporter, then, must deal with field agents or media liaison officers hundreds of miles away.

More importantly, it's difficult to get anything other than minimal facts.

"Even in criminal cases, if you contact the liaison officer, you do not get much of the color that you might be interested in because they're pretty restricted in what they can hand out: 'Yes, this individual by name and descriptive data was arrested on this charge pursuant to some in-dictment return,' and it's pretty much the technical description of what he was arrested for," an agent says. "It will not include anything con-cerning the evidence backing up the charge."

In a small town with a field office hundreds of miles away, the standard practice is for the local investigating agent to write a press release, which would be approved by the field office and made available locally.

That's officially. Unofficially, reporters and agents know that, like most other situations, it's possible to gain information from the FBI if trust has been built up. "Trust," an agent stresses, "is the entire basis of my relationship with a given reporter." That trust, as always, is built up as reporters demonstrate their accuracy and their dependability to main-tain a confidence.

However, that's not the only means available to reporters. "As a prac-tical matter," the agent says, "in almost all of these instances, we work very closely with the local (law enforcement) agency because we have concurrent jurisdiction. A bank robbery still is an armed robbery from the state perspective, and I work much more closely with police de-partment officers and detectives than I work with our own agency."

Local police sources, therefore, should have the same information, and the reporter who has developed these sources in most instances will experience little difficulty.

IT IS NOT ALL MURDER AND RAPE

Public speakers seem to like the old line about the martians who base all their knowledge about life on Earth on what they read and view in the mass media. Here's another variation: If those martians—or indeed the American public—depend on the media for an understanding of local crime, the attitudes thus formed are likely distorted. Many critics charge that crime reporting in general does not distinguish journalism because of its overemphasis on the sensational, the bizarre, or the latest journalistic fad.

It's a fact of life that accounts of more dramatic crimes will always be a staple of American journalism. The problem is one of emphasis. Other kinds of less exciting crimes also affect citizens and impact the quality of their community life. They merit attention. Journalists have done this through a variety of approaches.

To Amy Geisel, the quality of police protection is a big issue. "Look into things like response time, how the quality of police protection varies in different parts of the city." Geisel believes that business scams and "flim-flams" are also of interest to readers and that they fall into the category of crime prevention.

To some police reporters, crime statistics provide many different kinds of stories. Pamela Zekman, a reporter with WBBM-TV in Chicago, was one of those rare reporters who didn't simply accept crime statistics distributed by that city's police department. In 1982, city officials reported that Chicago was "the second safest city" in the United States, based on FBI crime statistics.

With a little digging, Zekman and an investigative team found that "thousands of crimes (are) routinely wiped off the books as though they never happened." Using this accounting technique, more than one-half of the rapes and one-third of the robbery and burglary reports examined had been "killed" by detectives. Zekman's five-part series showed that the credibility of some police statistics are in doubt, as well as illustrated flaws in the coverage of police departments and crime.[11]

LOOKING TO THE FUTURE: CRIME PREVENTION

Some journalistic organizations have focused a portion of their efforts on crime prevention. Such crime-watch programs often are joint efforts of broadcast outlets and newspapers. Other crime prevention "how-to" stories may include step-by-step procedures on how to label goods with an engraving pencil and other consumer tips.

Media outlets are doing more stories on white-collar crime and "trend analysis"—not simply on the reporting of single crimes. Trend analysis is the interpretation of crime statistics to tell viewers and readers where and when crimes are likely to happen.[12]

Organizations and publications for police reporters

Journalists interested in covering the politics of policing may find the following organizations and publications useful.[13]

Organizations

Bureau of Justice Statistics, U.S. Department of Justice, 633 Indiana Ave., N.W., Washington, D.C. 20531. (202) 724–7777. Contact: Julie A. Ferguson. Sponsors the National Crime Survey, a random sample of Americans interviewed about crimes against them. Publishes an annual *Sourcebook of Criminal Justice Statistics.* Summaries of latest data on topics such as violence between strangers, interpreting crime statistics, and demographic data on victims are included in free monthly *BJS Bulletin* series. Also publishes occasional in-depth special reports.

Federal Bureau of Investigation, Uniform Crime Reporting Section, J. Edgar Hoover Bldg., Washington, D.C. 20535. (202) 324–5015. Contact: Vicki Major. Publishes *Crime in The United States,* annual compilation of crime reports taken by local police agencies.

International Association of Chiefs of Police, 13 Firstfield Rd., Gaithersburg, Md. 20878. (301) 948–0922. Contact: Robert Angrisani. Studies issues affecting its members, 14,000 police executives, most in small cities and towns. Free list of publications.

National Criminal Justice Reference Service, P.O. Box 6000, Rockville, Md. 20850. (301) 251–5500. Central repository of published research on crime and criminal-justice issues. Index of 70,000 documents ($65) and monthly list of data-base additions (free). Prepackaged data searches (some free) and custom searches ($48 and up) can be ordered by telephone.

National Organization of Black Law Enforcement Executives, 8401 Corporate Dr., Suite 360, Landover, Md. 20785. (301) 459-8344. Contact: William Mathews. Represents views of 700 black police executives.

National Sheriffs Association, 1250 Connecticut Ave., N.W., Suite 320, Washington, D.C. 20036. (202) 872-0422. Contact: Cary Bittick. Represents views of nation's elected sheriffs.

Police Executive Research Forum, 1909 K St., N.W., Suite 400, Washington, D.C. 20006. (202) 466-7820. Contact: Gary Hayes. Studies issues such as effectiveness of 911 emergency numbers, robbery and burglary investigations, and deployment of officers for chiefs of large police agencies. Free list of publications.

Police Foundation, 1909 K St., N.W., Suite 400, Washington, D.C. 20006. (202) 833-1460. Contact: Tom Brady. Conducts research on police practices such as use of deadly force and foot patrol. Free list of publications.

Vera Institute of Justice, 30 E. 39th St., New York, N.Y. 10016. (212) 986-6910. Contact: Michael E. Smith. Conducts research and runs pilot programs with New York City and London (England) police testing effectiveness of policing techniques. Free list of publications.

Books and pamphlets

Crime and Public Policy, edited by James Q. Wilson, 1983. Institute for Contemporary Studies, 260 California St., Suite 811, San Francisco, Calif. 94111. Provocative ideas on crime and the police from 13 experts. $22.95 cloth/$8.95 paper.

Crime Statistics: How Not to be Abused, by David Burnham, 1977. Investigative Reporters & Editors, P.O. Box 838, Columbia, Mo. 65205. Pamphlet explaining limitations of police statistics on crime. $1.25.

Criminal Violence, Criminal Justice, by Charles Silberman, 1978. Random House. Broad examination of the nature of violent crime and government response. $15.00 cloth/$4.95 paper.

How to Rate Your Local Police, by David C. Couper, 1983. Police Executive Research Forum, 1909 K St., N.W., Suite 400, Washington, D.C. 20006. Pamphlet by the police chief of Madison, Wis., proposing criteria for evaluation of police agencies. $5.

Know Your Local Police, by Mae Churchill, 1981. Urban Policy Research Institute, 185 Pier St., Santa Monica, Calif. 90450. Pamphlet outlining ideas about examining the police as protectors, agents of justice, and intelligence-gatherers. $2.50.

Readings on Police Use of Deadly Force, edited by James M. Fyfe, 1982. The Police Foundation (see Organizations). Examines officer-involved shootings, their impact on police and the community, and legal issues. Also of note: The Police Foundation's 1977 study, *Police Use of Deadly Force.*

Periodicals

Law Enforcement News, published at John Jay College of Criminal Justice, 444 W. 56th St., New York, N.Y. 10019. Twenty-two issues annually; $18/yr. Peter Dodenhoff, editor. Newspaper covering latest trends in police practices, research, and law.

Police Magazine. Subsidized by the Ford Foundation until the magazine closed earlier this year; copies can be found in libraries and through police officers. Thoughtful examinations of such subjects as affirmative action, police use of computers, internal affairs divisions, and weapons policies.

Reprinted from the COLUMBIA JOURNALISM REVIEW, September/October, 1983.

NOTES

1. Jerome Skolnik and Candace McCoy, "Police Accountability and the Media," *American Bar Association Research Journal,* 542, Summer 1984.

2. James B. Bolger, "Marketing Techniques and Media Relations," *The Police Chief,* 50, December, 1983, p. 36.

3. "Police and the Press," *News Research for Better Newspapers,* Vol. VI (Washington: American Newspaper Publishers Foundation), pp. 94–95.

4. Jeff Stalk, "Police and the Press," *Editor & Publisher,* Dec. 21, 1985, p. 12.

5. See "Police Records: An Open and Shut Case," *The Commercial Appeal,* Memphis, Tenn., Feb. 23, 1986, p. E1.

6. Barry Mitzman, "Too Much Privacy," *Columbia Journalism Review,* January/February 1976, p. 36.

7. James E. Roper, "Stop Printing Victims' Addresses: Crime Panel," *Editor & Publisher,* Feb. 12, 1983, p. 11.

8. Glenn Easterly, "It's the Reporters Against the Cops," *TV Guide,* Nov. 12, 1977, p. 44.

9. Ralph Knoohuizen, *Public Access to Police Information in Chicago,* (Evanston, Ill.: Chicago Law Enforcement Study Group, 1974), pp. 52–55.

10. Knoohuizen, p. i.

11. David Johnston, "The Cop Watch," *Columbia Journalism Review,* September/October 1983, p. 51.

12. Johnston, p. 53.

13. Johnston, p. 54.

Covering Courts: The Issues

5

It was the biggest show in Cleveland during the latter part of 1954 when Dr. Sam Sheppard was being tried on a charge of killing his pregnant wife. The trial had all the elements: murder, society, sex, and suspense.

It's an old example, but it's classic. The trial judge, a candidate for reelection, simply lost control of his courtroom. Reporters and photographers took advantage of the opportunity. They roamed the corridors, hounding participants. When the judge and attorney went into the judge's chambers, they had to fight their way back out again through the crowd of reporters jammed into the judge's anteroom.

At the trial, twenty reporters got an up-close look from a table inside the bar within three feet of the jury box. Others occupied the first three rows. They used every room on the floor. One radio station set up broadcasting facilities in a room next to the jury room. The judge permitted himself to be interviewed on the courthouse steps. As they dashed in and out of the courtroom, reporters created so much confusion that it was difficult to hear even though a special loudspeaker system had been installed. Sheppard and his attorney had to leave the room if they wanted to talk privately.

All three Cleveland newspapers published the names and addresses of prospective jury members, and many received anonymous letters and telephone calls. The court permitted photographers to take group pictures in the jury box and individual pictures of the members in the jury room. During the trial, pictures of the jury appeared more than forty times in Cleveland newspapers.[1]

Twelve years later, the U.S. Supreme Court, in *Sheppard v. Maxwell,* overturned the conviction, citing conduct at and outside the trial, including that of the news media. That decision, said Jack Landau then of the Reporters Committee for Freedom of the Press, enshrined a legal and political crisis in the relationship between the news media and the courts.[2]

The continuing debate has its basis in two constitutional amendments, the first, which guarantees freedom of the press, and the sixth, which assures a defendant the right to a public trial by an impartial jury. No one disagrees with either of these high principles. The problem arises over the question of how these amendments can coexist.

Doesn't publicity prejudice jurors and thus destroy the chances for a fair trial? Shouldn't judges have the power to control such publicity? But isn't the presence of the media the most effective means of protecting the accused from an arbitrary decision?

Attorneys express concern over "trial by newspaper" or "trial by television." They fear jurors will base their decisions on information gained from the news media, not from the controlled courtroom.

While they generally accept and in some cases defend the right of the news media to report the facts of a criminal case, judges, lawyers, and even some reporters list at least six types of information that could be prejudicial.

Two of these stand out: confessions and a defendant's previous criminal record. Justice officials argue that publicity that an individual has admitted guilt or has been convicted before, especially on a similar charge, is very damaging. The court might not admit a confession as evidence. Officials first must determine whether it was voluntary, whether the accused had access to an attorney, and, in general, whether the confession was given according to proper legal procedures. Individuals have been known to confess to crimes they did not commit. Likewise, information about the past misconduct of an individual usually is not admissible as evidence because it implies a predisposition toward criminal acts that should not be considered in the present case.

Also potentially prejudicial to the defendant is publicizing opinions about the accused's character or results of tests such as fingerprints or lie detector.[3]

Attorneys say jurors must apply the standard that the accused is innocent until proven guilty beyond a reasonable doubt. So they contend that the courtroom scene is structured to carefully screen facts and comments, giving the prosecution full responsibility for proving its case without the help of media-inspired prejudice.

Nevertheless, most journalists would argue that the potential for prejudicial publicity does not argue for the restriction of press coverage of trials. The arguments they offer claim news coverage ensures a defendant's Sixth Amendment right to a speedy trial by an impartial jury and protects the openness of investigations, arrests, and imprisonment.

In a democracy, journalists serve as the public's representative. It is not the right of journalists that's at stake; rather it's the public's right to know the activities of government.

On the question of prejudicial publicity, journalists argue that those in the justice system are underestimating the abilities of jurors to make a fair decision. After all, the system was established on the idea that a jury of peers that's knowledgeable about the community and personal circumstances would be in the best position to judge fellow human beings.

Jack Landau, for example, notes many instances in which the impact of massive publicity seemed to have been negligible; at least three of those instances came out of the Watergate affair. Former Attorney General John N. Mitchell was acquitted in his home city of New York in spite of publicity. And, in the face of claims of prejudicial publicity, U.S. courts of appeals affirmed the convictions of Watergate break-in defendant G. Gordon Liddy and Watergate coverup defendant Dwight Chapin.[4]

Landau and others point to the responsibility of trial judges to control their courts. They urge that before judges step on First Amendment rights by closing trials or resticting coverage, they should apply several other well-known remedies to the impact of prejudicial publicity:

Change of venue: moving the trial to another area where pretrial publicity has not been so great.

Continuances: delaying the trial until possible impact has been reduced.

Venire from another area: bringing in jurors from another area where publicity has been less.

Voir dire: careful questioning of prospective jurors and excusing those who have developed attitudes.

Admonition: a judge's instructions to jurors that they should not read or listen to media reports about the trial.

Sequestering: keeping members of the jury out of public circulation while the trial is in progress.

Severance: conducting separate trials for codefendants in a trial if one has received considerable publicity.

Attorneys note that these remedies may be effective at times, but that many of these remedies are time consuming, expensive, and not as easily accomplished or as effective as journalists seem to think.

The result of this disagreement has been the refusal of more judges to allow reporters access to certain information and the closing of portions of the trial process. News organizations often win appeals in these situations, but only long after the timeliness of the story has diminished.

One courtroom controversy that emerged in the 1980s (and is likely to continue through the 1990s) is whether cameras should be allowed in courtrooms. Long banned from all courtrooms, many judges are now allowing cameras in their courtrooms; but most impose limits on their use. Ronald Solove, a juvenile/domestic relations judge in Franklin County, Ohio, believes the physical size of most courtrooms makes it difficult for them to accommodate a multitude of cameras—particularly television cameras. He advocates the use of a "pool" camera for news organizations who want footage of court proceedings. (One photographer from one news organization operates a pool camera, and the footage is distributed to all reporters requesting it.)[5]

Some television and radio reporters, naturally, resent limitations on the use of cameras and recording devices in courtrooms, offering the same argument as Maria Vitale, a reporter for WOSU Radio in Columbus. Without the "tools" of recording devices and cameras, Vitale claims, broadcast reporters cannot do their jobs. "Would a judge keep a newspaper reporter from taking a notebook and pen into the courtroom?" she asks.[6]

THE HUMAN SIDE OF CRIME COVERAGE

Reporters covering the criminal justice system face these issues daily. Their goal is to provide journalistically sound coverage of a specific case, but at the same time they are not unaware of the need for sensitivity. Thus, they often temper their journalistic decisions with considerations for the human impact of what they are doing. They know they are dealing with serious problems. They know their coverage can have an impact on individual lives, and they know that specific decisions cannot be made automatically. They must be based on careful consideration of a given case and balanced between journalistic values and human considerations.

Drama Without the Sensational Overplay

Court reporters face a built-in dilemma. They, like any other reporter, do not have the time or the space to cover everything. In consultation with their editors, they decide, first of all, the significance of public interest in a case. Perhaps it is true that journalists overestimate at times the audience's attraction to the bizarre or the sensational. But even the most responsible news judgment will lead reporters to those cases that are inherently interesting.

"The kinds of cases that the press has time to cover in detail are going to be those that involve either a notorious defendant, a particularly ghastly crime or some other element of a bizarre set of facts," says Lyle Denniston of the *Baltimore Sun.* "The press is not going to cover the routine case of a traffic court."[7]

But this situation has two edges. The very circumstances that attract attention offer the greatest temptation for the reporter to overwrite.

"One of the principal problems in covering cases that merely by themselves are going to be sensational is that the press does tend to exaggerate the use of words and descriptions that do arouse emotions in covering the criminal law," Denniston explains. "These cases are inherently interesting. They are inherently emotional, and the press gets caught up in them the same way that spectators do in the courtroom. I suppose the answer to that is simply that the press has to be more disciplined. If a case is sensational, if it is inherently fascinating to the public, it is not at all necessary to overwrite it, to use buzz words, to use highly selective material in order to create that fascination. It is there already."

One of the main causes of overwriting (and curiously, also the cause of dull writing) is the trap of limiting court coverage to the immediate. Such stories emphasize only what happened in the courtroom today, stressing the process rather than the human participants, the specific case rather than the issue. This is not to say day-to-day coverage should not be provided; it is necessary. But today's testimony is not an end in itself. The strongest reporting seeks a context, then zeroes in on the problem involved rather than on plodding through the actual details of the court system. What happens today has its maximum meaning when related to what happens outside the courtroom, the backgrounds of the participants, and the importance of the case to the community.

This is part of another valuable saving grace available in dealing with a dramatic case—the traditional journalistic goal of serving as an observer regardless of one's attitudes about the trial.

"Reporters need to stand away more and be a good deal more neutral in dealing with these cases than perhaps reporters or individuals as human beings are able to do," Denniston says. He suggests that failure to stand back with a basic reason for the news media's problems in the celebrated Sheppard case.

"It wasn't that the press was fascinated, as was the public, with the bizarre crime itself," he says. "It was that the press suddenly acted as if it were an arm of the prosecution. I have no basic ethical objection to crusading journalism as such, but I do have a very fundamental, basic, and pervasive objection to the press in any way becoming a part of the state, certainly the prosecutorial arm."

When Not to Tell All

Simply because a fact is available does not mean that it will be included automatically in a story or, indeed, that a story will be written. Journalistic tradition has it, for example, that there are times when the identity of a source may be withheld to protect the source. Many journalists will agree to withhold information about a police investigation if publication is likely to endanger the lives of undercover officers. In times of war, it is conventionally accepted that publication of information about troop movements could result in disaster.

But even those decisions are not always automatic. Responsible and sensitive journalists will agonize over them, remembering their responsibility to inform the public. Some journalists argue, with some justification, that news organizations should not practice censorship; that is, should not make value judgments. The reporter, they say, presents information without consideration as to whether it be good, bad, harmful, or beneficial.To do otherwise is to violate the principle of journalistic neutrality. And, they say, the policy of making information public in the long run will be more beneficial than harmful.

But that is rather naive. Journalists do make value judgments by the mere fact that a news story has space and time limitations. Journalists do withhold information, sometimes even information of potentially high readership. When covering the criminal system, it's possible to identify at least six broad reasons why some reporters would consider not publishing specific information about a case:

The information is irrelevant to the specific case.

It is premature and therefore subject to change.

It is an unnecessary invasion of individual privacy.

Publication would place individuals' lives in jeopardy.

Publication is possibly libelous.

Individual human beings deserve compassion.

Sentencing guidelines endorsed
Va. judges hail plan to curb disparities

By Patricia Davis
Washington Post Staff Writer

Virginia's circuit judges have voted overwhelmingly to establish statewide sentencing guidelines after a one-year experimental program significantly reduced sharp fluctuations in sentences in comparable cases.

The proposed change, which would include Virginia in a small but growing number of states that use some form of sentencing guidelines, will be put before the General Assembly for approval when it convenes in January.

The guidelines grew out of a study, based on more than 30,000 cases, that showed a kind of luck-of-the-draw system in which sentences could be influenced by a defendant's sex, race and socioeconomic status or, most significant, by whichever judge happened to be sitting behind the bench.

In one of the most extreme cases, offenders with similar criminal backgrounds who committed almost identical burglaries received prison sentences ranging from one to 20 years.

Organizers said such discrepancies all but disappeared during a recent 12-month pilot program involving six of the state's 31 judicial circuits. The guidelines for each crime reflect the middle range of sentences actually issued by Virginia circuit judges in recent years.

"They're just extremely helpful," said Lewis H. Griffith, chief judge of the Fairfax County Circuit Court, the only circuit in Northern Virginia to participate in the experiment. "It's comforting to know you're in the range of what other judges are doing in similar cases."

Fairfax Circuit Judge F. Bruce Bach, one of six judges on a statewide sentencing guidelines committee, said, "It's just not right to have two people in the penitentiary, one of them doing one year and one doing 20 years for the same thing."

Although the guidelines are voluntary, judges in the six pilot circuits complied with them 78 percent of the time, according to Richard P. Kern, director of the sentencing project with the Department of Criminal Justice Services. In four meetings held since the pilot program ended in June, judges voted 95 to 3 in favor of the guidelines.

If the General Assembly approves funding for the sentencing project, which is expected to cost about $800,000 during the first two years, the guidelines could be in every courthouse by next summer, Kern said. A panel of judges would continue to review sentencing patterns as the state's data continue to grow to determine if any guidelines need changing in the future.

Although the federal government and about 15 states, including Maryland, are using sentencing guidelines in some capacity, Virginia's proposal differs in several key respects, Kern said.

Unlike federal sentencing standards, Virginia's guidelines—which were overseen by a committee of judges—allow circuit judges to ignore the guidelines when they choose. Virginia's guidelines also are not intended to raise or lower sentences, for either reducing prison populations or altering the severity of sentences, Kern said.

The guidelines, based on an analysis of 33,573 felony sentencings that has grown to more than 60,000 cases, were designed strictly to reduce unwarranted sentencing disparities, he said.

"In a way they're kind of a model," said Michael Sabath, director of the Center for Criminal Justice Research and Information in Indianapolis, who traveled to Richmond to take a look. "Their methodology is very sound."

Evidence of unwarranted sentencing disparities began accumulating in 1982 when then-Governor Charles S. Robb appointed a task force on sentencing. In 1983, the task force concluded that inequities existed, partly because of race and other circumstances. It called for the development of historically based sentencing guidelines.

In 1986, Harry L. Carrico, chief justice of the Virginia Supreme Court, commissioned a comprehensive analysis of sentencing practices. A panel of judges confirmed the Robb Commission's findings, and a second judicial committee began devising the new guidelines.

The guidelines were designed to be simple. They are organized into eight offense groups: assault, burglary, drug violations, fraud, homicide, larceny, robbery and sexual assault. Points are assigned to various factors within a group, such as a defendant's criminal history, whether a weapon was used, and whether anyone was injured. The point total is checked against a table to determine recommended sentence ranges.

Although Virginia law already mandates ranges of penalties for specific offenses, such as five to 40 years for drug distribution, it does not spell out which factors should be considered in sentencing or how much weight they should be given.

Virginia is also one of only a few states in the nation in which both judges and juries determine sentences. Jurors are not allowed access to the same background and other testimony as judges in determining sentences, and they would not have access to the sentencing guidelines. However, judges are allowed by law to decrease jury sentences that they consider excessively severe.

Fairfax Public Defender R. Dean Kidwell said that judges were generally reluctant to tamper with jury sentences even if the guidelines called for shorter sentences, a phenomenon also found in the other pilot circuits. Other than that, Kidwell had only praise for the guidelines.

"They're helpful to the defense because you can tell your client up front, fairly early on, the range of penalties faced if convicted," Kidwell said, "They allow for early decisions" on whether to plead guilty.

Fairfax Commonwealth's Attorney Robert F. Horan Jr. also praised the guidelines, pointing out that they are voluntary— "there's an exception to every rule"—and that they are historically based, unlike the federal guidelines.

Kidwell and Horan questioned one aspect of the sentencing guidelines: The rules do not differentiate between drug dealers caught with large quantities and smaller dealers. Because so many judges stated that void as a reason for not allowing the guidelines, the state is reanalyzing drug cases to determine how judges have sentenced dealers with different quantities, Kern said.

This reporter wrote an interpretive report on an issue long plaguing the justice system: sentencing disparities. The story appeared in the *Washington Post,* November 19, 1989. (Reprinted with permission.)

One common point of disagreement between journalists and law enforcement officials is whether to print or air a previous criminal record. Often, many arrests are made and charges are dropped; or a person on the stand for one crime (e.g., bank robbery) has had unrelated convictions. In those cases, reporters and editors often choose not to print previous criminal records. But if previous convictions are found for the same crime, they may choose to print such information.

Another circumstance in which reporters might withhold information—even at the risk of losing a good story—is when such information is premature. For example, suppose a reporter gets a clue or outright information from a judge or law clerk on the outcome of a civil case. The judge or clerk, working on an opinion to be released later, will say, "Yeah, I'm leaning toward A rather than B for this reason." Few reporters would jump in with a story at that point. It's too risky. The judge could change his or her mind, or the law clerk could discover a new case that bears on the decision.

Reporters also are exercising more professional judgment about how far they will invade someone else's privacy. This is particularly true with regard to domestic relations court or probate court; that is, courts that involve emotion and deeply personal feelings. This also is true in juvenile court, where decisions can influence a youngster's future, or in cases that involve innocent victims, such as in sexual assaults.

Much of the consideration is not over whether a story is presented, but whether the individuals involved will be named. It is generally (not universally) accepted that the names of juveniles charged with crimes will not be used, although there is greater likelihood the name will appear if the juvenile is close to the legal age of adulthood, especially if the offense is not the first and if the crime is particularly serious.

Identification of the victim of a sexual assault, likewise, often is not used in news accounts. Many journalists have concluded that sensitivity is necessary because of the potential harm publicity could bring to the innocent victim. For that reason, many news organizations have policies that prohibit airing or publishing the names of victims of sexual assault.

There is, of course, another side to the issue, one noted by Rita Ciolli, who covered an attempted murder-rape case for *Newsday:*

"I think you have to take these one case at a time, depending on the victim," she says. "I had an attempted murder-rape case in which the victim was a 58-year-old woman. I talked with her before the trial and she said she would not be troubled at all by use of her name or anything else because she was able to reveal her life, and she felt she wanted just to talk about it. She had no problems because she felt it was so important for people to know that victims, especially of sex crimes, have to come to court and have to testify."

Protection of other individuals involved in the justice process prompted *Newsday* to take a different tack; however, the paper holds back some identifying facts about jurors in cases involving violent crime.

"It's a big problem when you know that the two people who are on trial are part of a group of dangerous people who are free," Ciolli says. "So now we're leaving out jurors' addresses, even in their own towns, just to make the jurors more comfortable."

Such compassion, under certain circumstances, may even be extended to the person accused of a crime, although that decision must be balanced by other community considerations. For example, a reporter may hear a number of police reports of an exhibitionist. At that point, without knowing who it is, the reporter probably would write the story as a community warning. The reporter then must pursue the story to its conclusion, using the accused person's name. Likewise, if such a case were well known in the community and had become a subject of popular conversation, there would be a duty to provide coverage to ensure that the information traded among citizens would be as factual as possible.

But in the absence of rumors and especially if it is the individual's first offense and he or she cooperates by taking psychological treatment, many reporters will agree there is no story.

"Where the press learns about an incident of that kind, where there are no victims other than the individuals whose sensory sensitivities have been invaded, I think that the press might just as well forget those stories," Denniston says.

The distinction is thin, however, between omitting stories out of human compassion and becoming part of the system or of going too far in protecting individuals from their own mistakes. Human considerations must be cautiously weighed in journalism. Reporters should be compassionate, but only while recognizing their ultimate responsibility to keep the public informed about important public matters.

SOFT ON THE JUDICIARY?

When city councils schedule executive sessions, reporters pound on the doors and demand admittance. When mayors avoid questions about sensitive public issues, reporters insist on explanations. When county commissioners spend federal funds on a special program, reporters want evidence the money was properly spent.

But when judges hold private hearings, too many reporters wait for information to come out of those hearings. Sometimes they wait impatiently. But they usually wait.

Furthermore, when a decision by an appellate judge is unclear or contradictory, some reporters will write unclear or contradictory stories rather than seek explanations. There is a tendency in journalism to permit the judicial branch privileges not usually afforded (fortunately) to other branches of government. This may be true in part because the public doesn't really understand the judicial system well enough to open some of its traditional windows.

As for the news media, tradition has bound reporters. Judges have created a forbidding atmosphere, and they've reinforced the assumption that it would be undignified or unethical for them to work closely with reporters. Compounding this is a lack of reporter training and a lack of time to give courts the same scrutiny other governmental agencies have received. The average reporter assigned to "the courthouse" often covers a large part of local government as well.

The belief that these are not really adequate excuses, however, is reflected in growing efforts in some of the larger news organizations to bring about a new journalistic specialty—legal affairs reporting. This new generation of reporters, many of whom have legal training or degrees themselves, is giving the same kind of attention to the judiciary that the news media traditionally have given executives and legislators. They're absorbed in getting the bigger picture. They want to chronicle the trends, the policies, the injustices, and the overall impact of courts on the average citizen.

These reporters look at courts as their readers and viewers would— as "consumers." They report on court operations, problems within the legal profession, and so forth.

An increasing professionalism about covering legal affairs is imperative. There is, of course, the potential long-range impact that this coverage could have in opening up the judicial system itself. But there is also the fact that many persons these days are going to court for one reason or another, particularly for reasons involving civil cases. Disputes that used to be settled in the family, in the neighborhood, or in the church are now being settled in court.

And the reach of the courts' arm often extends beyond the participants themselves. Legal scholars have noted a greater tendency by courts, in effect, to write laws through powers to interpret constitutional issues. Two of the most far-reaching social issues of the twentieth century— desegregation of schools and the right to an abortion—gained their impetus not from legislative or administrative action, but from decisions of the U.S. Supreme Court.

To know when judges are moving in new legal directions or how the system fails certain defendants requires a level of expertise that few reporters have achieved. An increasing number of reporters are responding to that challenge through legal training.

Of course, such training has its advantages and disadvantages. Reporters with legal training are no longer mystified by legal jargon and proceedings, and they can give them a full understanding of legal procedure. But reporters must boil down abstract and often lengthy thoughts to a few sentences, while the law teaches them to pursue different paths and alternatives.

Reporters who can maintain the balance between these two perspectives can function wth a "foot in each world," probably to the benefit of both. However, if they are unable to separate the functions, then they will fall into the very trap that leads many journalists to be suspicious of both the necessity and the value of formal legal training.

They are skeptical of the necessity of legal training because they feel strongly that a person with an inquiring mind and a reporter's curiosity can learn enough on the job. Through personal study and an occasional special seminar, they feel that they can cope with the mystique and the complexity of the legal process. They are skeptical of the value of legal training because they fear that it may lead reporters into thinking like attorneys and into becoming too much a part of the system.

This is another journalistic debate that will never be settled. Perhaps it's enough to say that providing consumer-oriented coverage of the judicial process requires more of reporters. It requires a level of understanding that only a few reporters in the past have been able to attain on their own. As in other coverage categories, a growing number of reporters will seek formal training as the basis of their efforts to go beyond being just reporters of events.

NOTES

1. All descriptive facts of the Sheppard case are drawn from the U.S. Supreme Court decisions; 384 U.S. 333 (1966).
2. Jack C. Landau, "The Challenge of the Communications Media," *American Bar Association Journal,* January 1976, p. 56.
3. Thomas Hodson, remarks made during "Law and the Media" conference, sponsored by the American Bar Association, Columbus, Ohio, July 8, 1989.
4. Landau, p. 60.
5. Ronald Solove, "Law and the Media" conference.
6. Maria Vitale, "Law and the Media" conference.
7. Denniston has written a detailed and excellent book about court coverage: Lyle Denniston, *The Reporter and the Law,* (New York: Hastings House, 1980).

The Where and Who of Court Reporting

6

Most journalists will probably acknowledge that they learn while covering a beat; that is, they can research it before they start covering a new beat, but much of the education comes from actually doing it.

Expecting to learn while on the job can be dangerous to those reporters covering the criminal justice system. It usually pays to know the system before stepping onto the beat: Just ask Shelley Epstein of the Peoria, Illinois, *Journal Star.* Epstein remembers the time he covered a trial and the verdict came back "not guilty." He asked the prosecutor if he was going to appeal. "Well, the prosecutor has no right to appeal in that instance," he remembers.

Shelley Epstein
of the Peoria Journal Star (Journal Star
photo)

STATE SYSTEMS: COURTS
AND COURT ACTIONS

Courts serve two broad purposes: to facilitate criminal justice by providing decisions when individuals are accused of violating laws and to provide a forum for the settlement of civil rights disputes between individuals and/or groups within the society. To accomplish this, courts are organized first into trial courts that have original jurisdiction because they provide the first (and usually the last) hearing of evidence and decision in a case. Individuals who feel that an improper decision has been made or that improper procedures have been followed can take the case to one of several appellate courts that evaluate the basic fairness of the trial court decision.

In addition to the normal criminal and civil functions, courts handle other special duties that concern reporters. Depending on the size of the system, these other duties may involve special departments or temporary renaming of the court to perform the special duty. In either event, these special functions would include juvenile, probate, domestic relations, small claims and equity.

Reporters, therefore, first need to know the purview of a given court, in terms of both its authority to handle certain types of cases and to handle its geographic area. This must include the distinction between serious crimes (felonies) and crimes of a lesser nature (misdemeanors). The distinction is based on the severity of the offense, which also determines the penalty allowed—the maximum fine or maximum imprisonment, and whether that separation from society is in a penitentiary or a local jail.

State and federal courts are organized into hierarchies with the extent of the authority of each level carefully defined by their geography and type of case (jurisdiction). Although states have differing systems, a number of common strains run through the functions designated to particular courts.

Justice and Municipal Court

The lowest rung on the judicial ladder is occupied by elected justices of the peace, municipal court judges, or police court judges. Although not a feature of all state systems, justices of the peace generally preside over rural areas and have limited jurisdiction. In metropolitan areas, municipal courts or police courts are similar although they may have slightly broader jurisdiction. These courts usually deal with both civil and criminal cases.

In civil cases, a court will handle those cases whose claims fall below a specific maximum amount. In criminal cases, all three courts deal with misdemeanors and matters such as traffic offenses. They also conduct the initial hearing in which individuals arrested on felony charges are informed of the specific charges against them, of their right to counsel, of whether they may post bond, and of their right to either request or waive a preliminary hearing. The same official also may conduct the preliminary hearing, in which the magistrate determines whether a crime was committed and if there is "probable cause" to believe the accused committed that crime. If so, the magistrate will bind the defendant over to the proper court for trial or to the grand jury for further proceedings.

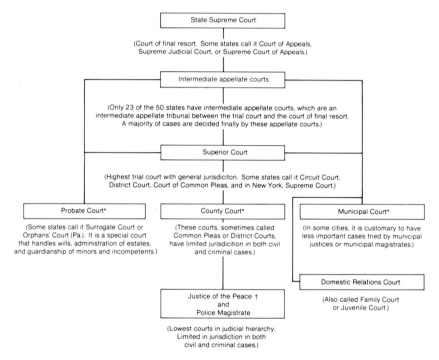

* Courts of special jurisdiction, such as Probate, Family or Juvenile, and the so-called inferior courts, such as Common Pleas or Municipal courts, may be separate courts or may be part of the trial court of general jurisdiction.

† Justices of the Peace do not exist in all states. Their jurisdictions vary greatly from state to state where they do exist.

The State Judicial System

(Chart courtesy of West Publishing Co., St. Paul, Minn.)

Small Claims Court

Another function of many municipal and justice courts is to provide an informal civil hearing that involves small sums of money. Designed to reduce the expense and delay of a normal trial, small claims courts are limited to suits under a state maximum. The system does not usually involve attorneys. Instead both parties may represent themselves in suits for personal injury, property damage, labor, goods sold, money lent, a bad check, or a dented fender. No jury is involved; the judge or referee makes the decision and transcripts usually are not kept.

Courts of Original Jurisdiction

Journalists will have most of their dealings with the trial courts in the judicial districts. These courts have varying names, including superior court, circuit court, district court, court of common pleas, and (in New York) supreme court. The jurisdiction of these courts varies little from state to state.

Juvenile Court

Usually not a separate court, but a division of the court of original jurisdiction, the juvenile court is perhaps the most functional example of the philosophy behind the whole court system; namely, that it should be rehabilitative rather than punitive. Not that it works in all cases, of course, but when dealing with individuals under legal age (usually 18), the courts have demonstrated a greater awareness of the impact of court action and of the need to give an offender the opportunity to start a new life.

In general, juvenile courts deal with persons under legal age and some adults who are charged with contributing to the legal problems of juveniles. Three types of juveniles fall under their domain: those who do not have a proper home or parental guidance or who are dangerous to the community because of a mental or physical problem; those who commit any felony or misdemeanor that would be a crime if the perpetrator were an adult (generally charged with delinquency); and those who behave in a way that could be harmful to themselves or to the community, which involves such actions as truancy, disobedience toward parent or guardian or custodian, and associating with disreputable people.

Probate Court

Usually a department of the court of original jurisdiction, probate courts supervise the administration of wills. They seek to ensure payment of debts and distribution of property to beneficiaries. In many states, probate courts also have the responsibility for guardianships and for commitment of individuals to mental health institutions.

Domestic Relations Court

Efforts to settle domestic disputes usually first involve attempts at conciliation. If that fails, the court processes such matters as annulment, dissolution or divorce, child custody, visitation rights, division of property, and child and spouse support.

Appellate Court

Courts of appeal exist to ensure the basic fairness of the decisions made in trial courts, either in the application of specific laws or in the procedures used in considering evidence and reaching decisions. To cut back on heavy case loads, thirteen states have established intermediate appellate courts, and in all states a state supreme court stands at the top of the court of last resort.

Jurisdiction of intermediate appeals courts varies from state to state, but it usually includes the review of decisions of courts of original jurisdiction and at times the consideration of appeals from municipal courts or justice courts. Intermediate courts usually have authority to issue writs of habeas corpus and writs of mandamus, certiorari, and prohibition.

The state supreme court has appellate jurisdiction over appeals from intermediate courts and judges disputes involving state constitutional interpretation. Its decisions bind courts within its state and in only one instance is there any avenue for further appeal—when federal law is involved. In such an instance, the proceedings leave the state level.

THE FEDERAL SYSTEM

There's meaning to the common advice, "Don't make a federal case out of it." Federal courts function more stringently and formally than state courts, perhaps because these judges are selected with greater care, because they are appointed for life, or because of tradition.

"A federal judge is a king," says David B. Offer of the Newport (R.I.) *Daily News.* "A federal judge is so powerful and so important. He's got two or three full-time lawyers as clerks and assistants, and the little people insulate the judge more often than not."

David B. Offer
of the Newport, RI, Daily News
(Newport Daily News photo)

The U.S. Constitution established the federal court system. It called for the Supreme Court and gave Congress the authority to set up other courts. The result is a three-part federal system with functions similar to those of the state systems; namely, trial courts, appeals courts, and special courts.

In the federal system, reporters deal most frequently with district courts in the country's ninety-one judicial districts. These are the federal trial courts. As courts of original jurisdiction, district courts handle most federal cases. They conduct the first hearing of almost all federal cases and the last hearing of a large majority of such cases.

Federal court jurisdiction is outlined in the Constitution (Article III, Section 2) and covers two types of cases that the state courts are not equipped to handle. The first type involves the interpretation of the U.S. Constitution, as well as federal laws and treaties. The second type includes cases involving ambassadors, cases in which the United States is a party, and the so-called "diversity-of-citizenship" cases in which the dispute involves the U.S. government, different states, or individuals living in different states or countries.

"There are criteria for jurisdiction that have to be met before a federal court will take a case," Offer explains. "For example, if it's a criminal matter, it has to be a violation of a specific federal law. Shoplifting is not a federal crime. Neither, generally, is murder. On the other hand, kidnapping is, bank robbery is, extortion can be depending on the elements of the crime, various kinds of mail fraud are, any crime committed on an Indian reservation is, and so on."

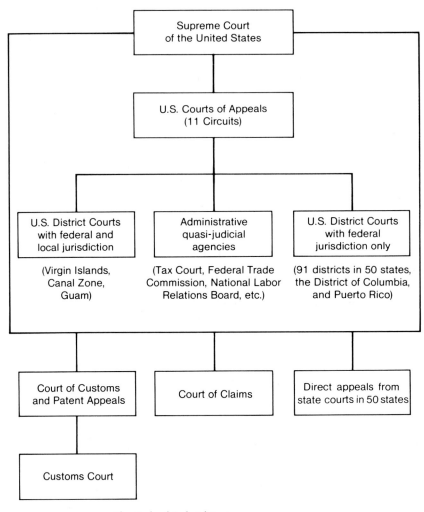

The Federal Judicial System

(Chart courtesy of West Publishing Co., St. Paul, Minn.)

However, federal judicial officials can expand the list of criminal actions with which they may deal. If a murder is a state crime, for example, and it was committed by an individual acting in an official capacity (a police officer, for instance), but the state doesn't choose to prosecute, federal officials can go in and investigate because it would be a possible violation of civil rights.

Federal civil jurisdiction follows a similar pattern because the cases tend to involve constitutional interpretation, interstate matters, or federal law. Thus, for example, the federal courts would consider questions of interstate commerce, a labor-management question covered under the National Labor Relations Act, civil rights, or freedom of the press.

Like some state systems, federal courts provide two levels for appeal, an intermediate level consisting of eleven circuits of the U.S. Court of Appeals and, at the top, the U.S. Supreme Court.

The courts of appeals have appellate jurisdiction only in cases that already have been tried in a lower court. An appeal might question either facts or law, but more appeals are brought on grounds that the law is unconstitutional or that it was incorrectly applied. A court of appeals usually doesn't retry the case; it reviews court records to decide whether the lower court judge has applied the law properly.

The Supreme Court has both original and appellate jurisdiction, but the bulk of its work involves appeals from a federal district court, court of appeals, or a state supreme court. Supreme Court justices select the cases they want to consider, and these usually fall into two classes: violations of federal constitutional rights or of federal law, and cases in which a state law or clause in a state constitution is believed to violate some federal law or the U.S. Constitution.

In Supreme Court cases, both parties submit written briefs, and each side then has one hour for oral argument and questions from the justices. After the case has been heard, the justices confer privately and cast their votes. The majority rules. Written explanations accompany each decision. If the decision is not unanimous, dissenting opinions may be written. Concurring opinions may be written by justices who agree with the majority or the minority, but for differing reasons.

Special Courts

Political scientists call the federal courts "constitutional courts" because they were created under authority granted by the constitution. Congress also has established a number of special courts that exercise jurisdiction only in certain cases. Labeled "legislative courts," they have only the jurisdiction granted to them by Congress.

Territorial courts function in the Virgin Islands, the Canal Zone, and Guam. They are defined as U.S. District Courts and have the same jurisdiction.

Court of claims hears suits for damages filed against the U.S. government. These suits are typical of those found in civil law, involving chiefly breaches of contract and torts (civil wrongs such as trespassing).

Customs courts hear complaints from foreign importers who maintain the tariff they pay is excessive.

Court of military appeals reviews in all cases of court martial in which a general or admiral has been found guilty, or in which any member of the armed forces has been sentenced to death.

Reporters have few dealings with these special courts. They more often cover those quasi-judicial administrative agencies such as the tax court, Federal Trade Commission, and the National Labor Relations Board. These agencies conduct hearings and make decisions within their special area of concentration.

U.S. Commissioner

In effect, the U.S. Commissioner is a justice of the peace for the federal court system. U.S. commissioners provide a source of frequent contact for reporters. They are appointed by each district court, and their duties are to issue arrest warrants, take bail, and determine whether probability of guilt is sufficient to hold an accused person.

SOURCES OF INFORMATION

The barrage of discussion in journalistic trade publications about court secrecy prompts the belief that the reporter's life is filled with constant battles to gain information. The battles are there, but the average local reporter who understands how the court system works can find pertinent information easily and, with a little effort, can find even controversial information.

Information is gathered in three general ways. The first way is by using the documents of the court, which are public records. The second way is by using what reporters see by sitting in a courtroom and watching the hearing or trial. The third way is by using what reporters hear outside of the court.

That out-of-court information, of course, comes through interviews. In spite of professional codes, attorneys especially tend to be willing, even anxious at times, to talk about a case with reporters. The same applies to judges, who in most cases are facing re-election.

As important as documents are to the reporter, talking with people who work in and around the courthouse may be even more important to a reporter, says Bill Steiden of the Sarasota, Florida, *Herald Tribune.* "Documents are important, but don't rely on them solely," he says. "Talk to people. If you don't understand something, don't pass it off as meaningless. Try to find out what it is about."

He also suggests getting to know clerks in the clerk's office, bailiff, court stenographers and lawyers. "Don't guess what arcane legal terminology means—ask attorneys. They'll appreciate that you got it right," Steiden adds.

Judges Can Be Cooperative

"For some reason, and I don't really understand it, a lot of reporters seem to be afraid of judges," says David Offer. "I don't mean to demean judges when I suggest this, but all a judge is is a successful politician who wears a black robe. The same reporter who wouldn't stand for any kind of garbage from the mayor and would just demand accurate answers is absolutely terrified to go up and ask a judge if he is going to have court tomorrow."

Offer suggests that it isn't proper to ask judges about what their decision will be in a particular case, but the reporter may get information on scheduling, explanations about completed court proceedings, or, importantly, information about some of the legal issues involved in a complex case.

"At the very worst," he adds, "they'll tell you that they won't talk to you, but that doesn't hurt very much. The rudest that anyone has ever been to me is to tell me to get lost. But they can be exceptionally helpful. In lower courts, the judges are politicians. They usually are elected. They know the reporters who frequent the courts and they like to see their names in print. There's a camaraderie there that's not true of a federal court. Those judges are appointed by the president, they serve for life and they tend to be, for the most part, pretty unapproachable."

"Renting" a Judge

Because of the backlog of caseloads in most courts nationwide, two states—and probably more in the future—are permitting parties in a dispute to "hire" a judge and solve their disputes outside the courtroom. This process, known as *alternative dispute resolution,* is now legal in Ohio and California, but will probably become more popular in the 1990s, says Richard M. Markus, an attorney with Porter, Wright, Morris & Arthur in Cleveland, Ohio, and chief executive officer of Private Judicial Services.

Markus explained that under the system, two parties agree to use the services of a retired state judge, whose decision is binding. The parties involved must pay for the service, as well as for the space for proceedings, the physical staff, and most other expenses. The public pays only for the parties' use of the clerk of courts.

This privatization of the legal system certainly has its advantages for clients and the public. It is convenient for clients and helps save taxpayer money. Markus warned, however, that it gives the public aspect of court proceedings a new dimension. Because these proceedings are private, the media need not be notified, and, in many cases, never know the proceedings are taking place. This, obviously, can lead to less access to such proceedings, and is an issue that reporters may have to deal with more in the future.[1]

Attorneys Like to Talk

Lawyers, by definition, are advocates. It's the basis of their training, the basis of the system in which they work, and fundamentally, the basis of their relationship with reporters. They can be friendly, helpful, and valuable, but only to the reporter who exercises caution and who understands that a lawyer's adversarial background means he or she will be trying to use the media as another weapon in achieving a goal.

"My most trusted lawyer source I would only believe about 40 percent of the time," says Marie Rohde of the *Milwaukee Journal.* "Lawyers have so much to gain, and it is obvious that you have to be very, very careful with them. Also, attorneys, I think, because of their training, can take virtually any concept and justify it, which I find very irritating. They don't have to believe what they are saying, but they're trying to convince you that you should believe it."

But reporters can't do without attorneys. Given natural journalistic caution, they know lawyers can help in a wealth of ways. They are, first of all, principal sources for stories on the facts, the issues, and the approaches to the case.

Perhaps the best way to learn about the intricacies of the judicial process is to spend a great deal of time covering the courts or simply observing them. In the absence of this, however, reporters can get a crash course by finding attorneys who will take the time to sit down and discuss the issues in generally off-the-record terms. "OK, I think the strategy in this case is this, and I think Attorney X did this because he was trying to do that, and I think the judge's ruling was because. . . ."

Although most lawyers are happy to deal with reporters, it is only the reporter who builds a reputation of trust who will continue to get this type of help from attorneys. As Steiden says, "Be honest with clerks, attorneys, those you work with. You have to get to know them, prove to them you're accurate and fair before you go running around trying to get information."

For specific on-the-record information, however, reporters find prosecuting attorneys more cooperative than defense attorneys. They are more used to the media than defense attorneys, and they usually are elected by voters.

Actually, defense attorneys seldom speak at all, unless they think it is to their advantage. Clearly, they have enough problems taking care of a client who is fighting for his or her freedom. They don't need to take chances with potentially negative or derogatory publicity that suggests their client may have committed a crime.

The relationship with defense attorneys is double-edged. On one hand, they need journalists to be watchdogs in order to carefully scrutinize the prosecutor, the police, and the judge to ensure that they're doing their job and doing it fairly. On the other hand, they don't want to cooperate too much. They don't want to breach the confidence of their clients or disclose something that should not be disclosed until the trial.

Prosecutors, however, because they are elected officials and because many are politically ambitious, are more likely to answer specific questions with some candor and to be more open to publicity.

Exceptions abound, of course. Individual personalities defy pigeon-holing. Some prosecutors won't say anything beyond a recitation of the facts of a case. Some defense attorneys, such as Melvin Belli or F. Lee Bailey, enjoy national reputations because of their flamboyant personalities, their well-known clients, and the fact that they skillfully orchestrate their dealings with the media.

It's all in the Clerk of Courts' Office

Without question, the clerk of courts can be the journalist's most valuable source. Because many court reporters cover county government and are often responsible for fifteen to twenty full-time judges, they simply cannot be everywhere at all times. They must choose the several meetings or trials that they will attend, and they must find some way to cover the rest of the day's activities. This process starts and sometimes ends at the office of the clerk of courts, who maintains public records of all judicial proceedings.

If for no other reason, the clerk is significant because he or she prepares the daily court calendar, which must be religiously checked by the journalist to determine the schedule of court activities. And, for the reporter who is unable to cover everything in person, the clerk's office contains all the written documents on which coverage may be based: applications, motions, petitions, pleadings, answers, and historic materials. Any routine news may be picked up here, and the enterprising journalist with time to review the records can uncover a treasure chest of information.

The clerk's office, in fact, contains more than any reporter can read carefully on a regular basis, even in metropolitan areas where several checks are made daily. That's why reporters work hard to ensure the cooperation of the clerk, deputy clerks, and other office staff. This is one place where the hurried reporter makes it a point to slow down and chat.

Bailiff Keeps Tabs on Everything

Technically, a bailiff is a court attendant whose duties are to keep order in the courtrooms and to have custody of the jury. But to a reporter, the bailiff is much more. He or she may be a better source for the whole system than anyone, including the judge. The bailiff knows such things as who is in chambers with the judge, and what they are discussing.

Reporters make a point to check regularly with bailiffs because they generally know not only what is going on in their courts, but also in everyone else's court, too. It's a kind of intelligence system that develops in the courthouse, and bailiffs seem to be most willing to discuss courthouse politics. Because of their constant contact with lawyers, bailiffs often know what is going to happen before judges do.

Court Reporter Has the Quotes

The most quiet, and perhaps the busiest, person in the courtroom is the court reporter. This is the person in the movies who sits at the front of the room, looks uninspired, never glances around, and just taps away with both hands on a machine. The court recorder's function is to record and to transcribe all court testimony, objections, and rulings made during the court proceeding. For the journalist that spells potential value in confirming direct quotes or covering missed material.

"It happens with all too much frequency, maybe once a week," Offer says, "there are two things going on simultaneously. I have to choose one. I'll go to the court reporter later for the other one, and he or she will almost invariably agree to read the pertinent parts, even though there really is no obligation to do it."

The detail of the court reporter's tape recording or transcript at times can prove a real blessing for reporters looking for something more than the legal facts of a case. Offer provides an example: "I had one case in which I couldn't attend the sentencing. So I stopped by to see the bailiff just to find out what the sentence was, and he said, 'You should have been there. That woman stood up and screamed and cried for her children and begged the judge not to send her to prison. The judge sentenced her to 120 days, and she fainted.'

"I went to the court reporter who had all those screams down, as best you can transcribe a scream in a stenographer's notebook, and she read back everything the judge had said, everything the woman had said. And I got a helluva story because the court reporter was willing to read it to me."

Interview the Defendant?

Often, a reporter will have the opportunity to interview a defendant outside the courtroom, on a one-on-one basis. Should he or she take advantage of this opportunity? Some judges say no, citing that the publicity that such an interview might generate could prejudice the trial.

Publication of such interviews raises several questions. Should a newspaper judge a story by its newsworthiness or by its potential harmful effect on the criminal justice system? Also, does a defendant have a right to tell his or her side of the story outside the courtoom?

As usual, there are several sides to the issue. And journalists are not unanimous in their attitudes about whether statements outside the courtroom from the defendant should be made public. Some believe they should remain as detached as possible, confining their stories to reports of official statements and actions. To publicize confessions, for instance, is playing into the hands of law enforcement officials, and to publicize private statements from the defense is becoming part of the defendant's strategy.

But, particularly if they believe that their job is to tell the human story instead of simply to provide the official facts, most journalists would use statements, though cautiously.

Information Officer May Be Helpful

Like other government offices, courts in some states and at the national level often have public information officers available to assist reporters. Journalists evaluate the assistance provided by these individuals much as they would any source.

Reporters stress strongly that information officers are not an adequate substitute for contacts with other court officials. But they can be helpful by providing—as is the case with the U.S. Supreme Court—synopses of each decision tailored to fit the needs of the news media, background information on complicated legal issues, or suggestions for stories (especially feature stories).

NOTES

1. Richard Markus, remarks made during 1989 Law and the Media Conference, July 8, 1989, Columbus, Ohio.

Most of the Action Precedes the Trial

7

Despite the unexpected confessions and surprise witnesses that characterize many courtroom dramas on television and in the movies, anyone who spends a lot of time in courts and deals with the criminal justice system will tell you such drama is unusual. Matters often are settled before the players—judges, lawyers, plaintiffs and defendants—take to the field, the courtroom. That's how the system is structured.

One of the ways the system disposes of cases before they get to the trial stage is plea bargaining. It happens very frequently. A defendant is charged with selling cocaine and suddenly that charge is dropped, and he or she pleads guilty to possession of marijuana. It's a legitimate legal procedure, but it's an understatement to say that it appears strange to the public.

There's a natural suspicion: Somebody is getting off easy. Somebody has been bought. Somebody didn't do the job. Such suspicions often are incorrect, but attorneys are nervous enough about plea bargaining that few really want to talk about it, especially if their comments are likely to reach the public.

From the prosecution's standpoint, the discussion of a plea bargain for a defendant may suggest that the attorney does not have a strong case against the defendant. And while it's true that building of a case may depend more on activities at the time of the arrest than on any subsequent prosecutor investigation, attorneys know the public doesn't look at the situation that way. The prosecutor is held responsible, and it's a source of embarrassment to be forced by a reporter into detailed discussions. On the other side, when the defense discusses plea bargaining, it almost forces admission of guilt. The common feeling is, if innocent, why is the defendant willing to plead to anything, even a minor charge that may bring little more than a suspended sentence.

Such attitudes ignore at least two good reasons for the existence of plea bargaining. One is related to the fact that the whole concept of American justice places the burden on the state to prove "beyond a reasonable doubt" that the defendant is guilty. Prosecutors know that's difficult at times, and they would rather be assured that an individual be found guilty of something—even a relatively minor offense—than to get off.

Attorneys also stress that most instances of plea bargaining occur in cases of relatively minor offenses. It would be impossible, they say, for a municipal court to go through the whole trial process for every drunken driving charge. So prosecutors carefully select the cases that they want to try and then seek to reduce the volume of the remaining cases through plea bargaining.

But attorneys still don't want to discuss it very much, and the reporter must understand the means that they will use to avoid publicity, such as arranging for a judicial hearing before a judge at an unusual time. The whole process takes five minutes, the reporter doesn't know it's happening, and the page one story still says this trial will open tomorrow.

Unless the reporter is in the courtroom at the time of this process, the chances are slim he or she will get the parties to say much about it. The result and perhaps the legal reasons can be discovered through open court documents, but those don't always get to the heart of the situation. It's possible, for example, that plea bargaining may be used to keep facts of a situation from becoming public because only the decision may be announced, not the process or reasoning leading to it. A reporter needs sources and court documents, and he or she needs to do legwork and needs to know the law and court personnel well enough to predict when plea bargaining is likely.

COVERING THE CRIMINAL PRETRIAL PROCESS

Similar drive is needed to overcome problems created by the complexity of the judicial system. Certainly, many of the decisions are made during the pretrial process, but reporters do not have the time (or, sometimes, the interest) to give each step full attention. It is physically impossible and generally undesirable for every reporter to cover every hearing of every case.

Court reporters, especially those who work for smaller news organizations and have responsibilities for more than the courtrooms, are faced daily with decisions about which of the numerous activities to cover. They base their decisions by using standard news-judgment values, by trying to determine whether the people or the legal issues are of interest

to the public and by trying to determine whether there are novel interpretations of the law, a seldom used legal strategy, or a great deal of
money involved. In general, they're trying to determine whether people
are going to be either interested or affected by the judgment.

Reporters know, however, that because they must limit their coverage
to certain cases they are missing a significant part of the judicial process
for which they are responsible. This results in a great deal of legal activity conducted without public scrutiny. They know that they would
better understand a specific trial or indeed the whole system if they could
be more intimately involved with the pretrial process of more cases, even
if they didn't get a daily story out of it.

The pretrial process provides a rehearsal of the witnesses and strategy
of the case. It gives the reporter a better background and results in richer
trial coverage. One reason for this is that participants in pretrial hearings
generally are more open in what they say.

COMPLAINT

The undersigned complainant, being duly sworn, states that on or
about _____, 19____, within _____ Ohio, _____
                                  (county/city)   (defendant's
_____ did _____[1] in violation of _____.
name)   (ordinance/statute)

The complaint is based on _____[2]

_____
(Complainant's signature)

Sworn to and signed in my presence this _____ day of _____,
19____, at _____, Ohio.

_____
(Magistrate, Clerk, etc.)

[1]Recite essential facts constituting the offense, e.g., "failed to yield ... " *[or]* "assault
(victim's name) ... "

[2]Here put "facts and circumstances known to Complainant," if there are no affidavits of
persons other than Complainant. If there are other affidavits, put "the attached affidavit(s)."

Comment: A complaint is a written statement of the essential facts constituting the
offense charged. It must state the numerical designation of the applicable statute or
ordinance and be made upon oath before any person authorized by law to administer
oaths.

Source: All court documents are courtesy of Anderson Publishing Co., Cincinnati, Ohio.

If there are procedural problems in the case against a defendant, they tend to be discovered early and, with some exceptions, are not likely to come up during a trial. Thus, covering pretrial hearings helps reporters to let the public know why many cases are dismissed. Perhaps there was questionable police behavior such as an improper search or a wiretap without a warrant.

Publicity on cases that are dismissed because of improper police behavior is a sensitive issue to prosecutors. As elected officials, they don't like publicity that (in their opinion) overstates their role.

They point out that the most vulnerable part of a criminal case is the time immediately surrounding the arrest, and the prosecuting attorney may not be involved at that time. Perhaps the prosecutor's only alternative is to dismiss. Yet, when the story is reported, they say, it reads, "prosecutor dismisses case."

They're partly right. In other instances, though, the prosecutor controls the means through which charges are brought against an individual. For example, if police learn of the whereabouts of a suspect, the prosecutor often specifically coordinates efforts to check out information and to make an arrest.

WARRANT

To any law enforcement officer of _____.

(this city / this county)

WHEREAS, there has been filed with me a complaint stating that

_____ did _____

(defendant's name or description allowing reasonably certain identification)

_____ [1] in   violation   of   _____

(ordinance / statute)

_____, a copy of which is incorporated or attached hereto.

YOU ARE COMMANDED to arrest the above described person in this or any adjoining county you shall find him and bring him without necessary delay before this issuing Court to answer unto the charge set forth herein, or, if he be found in any other than this or any adjoining county, to arrest and take him before a court of record therein having jurisdiction of this offense, to be dealt with according to law.

Given under my hand this _____ day of _____, 19____.

_____

Judge / Clerk of Courts / etc.

[1] Give a description of the offense charged in the complaint.

Comment: The warrant must contain: (1) the name of the defendant or, if that is unknown, any name or description by which he can be identified with reasonable certainty; (2) a description of the offense charged in the complaint; and (3) the numerical designation of the applicable statute or ordinance. The warrant shall command that the defendant be arrested and brought before the court issuing it without unnecessary delay. A copy of the complaint shall be attached to the warrant.

The normal stimulus for an arrest is provided by either of two procedures, both of which are controlled by the prosecutor: an indictment returned by a grand jury or what is called a bill of information filed in court by the prosecutor. In either instance, the legal requirements are rather simple. The charge must set forth the time, date, and place of the alleged criminal act as well as the nature of the charge.

Initial Appearance

Once arrested, an individual generally first appears in municipal or justice court (in federal cases, before a U.S. commissioner), regardless of whether the crime is a misdemeanor or a felony. The first appearance has three functions: (1) to decide whether the accused gets his or her own attorney or whether the court needs to appoint one, (2) to decide whether the accused wants a preliminary hearing, and (3) to decide whether the accused is a good risk for bond.

News from this initial appearance concerns whether the accused is released and the amount of bond. In most states, a person charged with murder is not eligible for release on a bail bond. In other cases, the judge sets a figure in accordance with the severity of the crime. The idea is that rather than forfeit the bail amount, the individual will return for further proceedings. Practices vary, but generally the person is permitted to post 10 percent of the face amount. Often individuals may engage professionals who for a fee will assume the financial obligation. Persons who cannot afford to post bail themselves or to borrow it will remain in jail until their cases are decided.

Alternatively, the magistrate may decide that an accused person is likely to appear in court for the trial. The judge can release such persons on their own recognizance, that is, on their own promise to appear.

Preliminary Hearing

Some states have both an initial appearance and a preliminary hearing; others combine all the functions in a single appearance, usually called the preliminary hearing. But in either event, the functions tend to be the same.

At the preliminary hearing, which may be requested or waived by the accused, the state presents evidence to convince the magistrate that there is sufficient reason to believe the accused probably committed the crime, so that a grand jury or trial court should consider the case. The role of defendants will vary from case to case, but they must be present at the preliminary hearing and may give evidence. However, many defense at-

WARRANT

To any law enforcement officer of _____.
(this city/this county)

WHEREAS, there has been filed with me a complaint stating that

_____ did _____
(defendant's name or description allowing reasonably certain identification)

_____[1] in violation of _____
(ordinance/statute)

_____, a copy of which is incorporated or attached hereto.

YOU ARE COMMANDED to arrest the above described person in this or any adjoining county you shall find him and bring him without necessary delay before this issuing Court to answer unto the charge set forth herein, or, if he be found in any other than this or any adjoining county, to arrest and take him before a court of record therein having jurisdiction of this offense, to be dealt with according to law.

Given under my hand this _____ day of _____, 19____.

_____
Judge/Clerk of Courts/etc.

[1]Give a description of the offense charged in the complaint.

Comment: The warrant must contain: 1. the name of the defendant or, if that is unknown, any name or description by which he can be identified with reasonable certainty; 2. a description of the offense charged in the complaint; and, 3. the numerical designation of the applicable statute or ordinance. The warrant shall command that the defendant be arrested and brought before the court issuing it without unnecessary delay. A copy of the complaint shall be attached to the warrant.

torneys present no evidence, preferring instead to place the burden on the prosecution to show probable cause and not (at that time) to reveal their case.

This one-sided nature of the preliminary hearing makes it the core of the pretrial publicity controversy. News organizations continue to challenge such exclusions. In the meantime, most reporters advise continued efforts at coverage, under the assumption the hearings are open.

Depending on a state's system, the result of the preliminary hearing may be any of three possibilities. If magistrates decide the prosecution's evidence is inadequate, they may dismiss the case. If they conclude that the evidence merits further consideration, they may order the defendant bound over to the grand jury. Or, in some instances, they may send the case to the proper trial court.

FINDINGS ON PRELIMINARY HEARING

Preliminary hearing was conducted this ____ day of _____,
19____, on the charge of _____[1] wherein the State by the
Prosecutor of _____[2] offered its evidence in support of the
charge in the presence of

(circle applicable statement)
1. defendant and his counsel
2. defendant, unrepresented by counsel who
(circle applicable statement)
1. likewise offered countervailing evidence
2. after being advised according to Crim. R. 5(B)(3), likewise
    offered countervailing evidence
3. elected not to offer evidence at this time
and the Court having considered all of the foregoing,
FINDS:
(circle proper finding)
(a) That there is probable cause to believe the felony alleged has
     been committed and that the defendant committed it.

(b) That there is probable cause to believe that the felony ____

     _____ and not that alleged has been committed and that
     (title and statute)
     defendant committed it.

(c) That there is probable cause to believe that the misdemeanor

     _____ and not the felony alleged, has been
     (title and statute or ordinance)
     committed and that defendant committed it.

(d) That there is no substantial credible evidence showing probable
     cause as to any offense.
WHEREFORE
(circle proper orders)
(a) Defendant is bound over to the Court of Common Pleas,
     _____, Ohio, whose venue appears, and bail or the condi-
     tions of release here and before prescribed are continued and
     transferred to the Court of Common Pleas.
(b) Defendant is bound over to the Court of Common Pleas of
     _____ County, whose venue appears; the Prosecutor is in-
     structed to prepare and file a Complaint reflecting this finding;
     and bail or the conditions of release here and before prescribed
     are continued and transferred to the Court of Common Pleas.
(c) The prosecutor is instructed to prepare a new Complaint reflect-
     ing this Finding and the matter is retained for trial (or) _____
     Court of _____, Ohio for trial.

_____
                          Judge

[1]State the title of offense.

[2]"the City of _____, Ohio" [or] "_____ County."

The Grand Jury

The function of a grand jury, stated simply, is to look into crimes committed in the district and determine whether available evidence is adequate to bring an accused person to trial. If grand jurors decide it is probable that the accused did commit the crime, they will indict that individual by returning a "true bill." If they decide on the basis of evidence presented that such probability was not established, they will return a "no bill."

Although on some occasions a grand jury may undertake inquiries on its own, it most generally represents a forum for the prosecution. Members consider cases presented by the prosecutor and hear witnesses provided by the prosecutor. The defense has no opportunity to make statements, present witnesses, or cross-examine prosecution witnesses. The accused appears only if called as a witness.

To protect the rights of the accused, grand jury deliberations are secret. Reporters tend to show respect for this secrecy although there are many examples to the contrary, usually under very special circumstances. Former *Washington Post* reporters Carl Bernstein and Bob Woodward honored it when they were preparing to track down a member of the federal grand jury looking into the Watergate incident. In their book, *All the President's Men,* they said:

"Bernstein and Woodward consulted the *Post*'s library copy of the Federal Rules of Criminal Procedure. Grand jurors took an oath to keep secret their deliberations and the testimony before them; but the burden of secrecy, it appeared, was on the juror. There seemed to be nothing in the law that forbade anyone to ask questions. The lawyers agreed, but urged extreme caution in making any approaches. They recommended that the reporters simply ask the woman if she wanted to talk.

"(*Post* managing editor Ben) Bradlee was nervous. 'No beating anyone over the head, no pressure, none of that cajoling,' he instructed Woodward and Bernstein. He got up from behind his desk and pointed his finger. 'I'm serious about that. Particularly you, Bernstein, be subtle for once in your life.' "[1]

This respect does not mean that reporters ignore grand juries when they are in session, but it does mean they place special rigor on the usual journalistic cautions when information becomes available.

One type of grand jury information that requires a conservative stance is the fact that an individual has been called before a grand jury. Too often reporters want to write, "So-and-so was hauled in before the grand jury and questioned," which implies that this person is guilty of something. The truth is that often when a grand jury is in a preliminary stage of its investigation it calls in anyone who might have any information. A person might come in and have none and be dismissed.

Decisions on when to use stories about grand jury activities must be made on a case-by-case basis. Reporters should be considerate of an individual's reputation before they write a general story. They should do more legwork to gain more specific information and verification.

Witnesses also can be sources of information. Bob Rawitch of the *Los Angeles Times* points out that, while not so in most state grand-jury proceedings, a witness before a federal grand jury is not bound to secrecy.

Bob Rawitch
of The Los Angeles Times (Los
Angeles Times photo)

"But you have to treat that information very carefully because you may be getting a distorted picture from one witness as to who a potential target of the grand jury may be and who is a witness," he says. "It's very easy for someone to leak something from a grand jury, but you have to evaluate it very carefully. A prosecutor or a defense attorney or grand juror may be willing to tell you something off the record so that you can determine whether you should write the story on what you got from this one witness, or to keep it in the proper perspective."

The potential cooperation of court officials is always in the minds of reporters. This can come in the form of corroboration, or it may come as a direct leak, perhaps even in the form of actual grand jury documents. Even then, depending on the specific situation, many reporters are cautious.

"Maybe I shouldn't say this but I am privy to indictments before they are presented to the grand jury," one says, "although I have been sworn that I can't print them until they are passed by the grand jury. It took a while to build up trust. Only recently was I allowed to read a proposed indictment, and I was told in no uncertain terms that to print that ahead of time would be disastrous.''

The reporter uses this advance knowledge to prepare background so that when the indictments are officially returned, he or she is ready with a detailed, well-researched report.

If the person indicted by a grand jury is not already in custody, the clerk of courts issues a warrant, and the arrest is made. Often, when the grand jury indicts, no preliminary hearing is held because their purposes are the same.

INDICTMENT

The grand jurors of this County, in the name and by the authority of the State of Ohio, upon their oath do find and present that:

Count One

_____² on or about _____, 19____, did violate _____³ by _____⁴ and that

Count Two¹

_____² on or about _____, 19____, did violate _____³ by _____⁴

_____
(Prosecutor, _____ County [or] in his name by Asst. Prosecutor)

ALL WITHIN THIS COUNTY

A TRUE BILL:

_____
Foreman

¹May be omitted if only one count

²name of defendant(s)

³Statute

⁴Brief description in terms of statute

Arraignment

Of major interest to reporters during the arraignment is the plea of the defendant and the fact that, in many instances, this represents the end of the pretrial process. In some states, the arraignment and the plea are separate proceedings, but in all cases the specific charges and rights are explained to defendants, who are then asked for their plea. Defendants have options that differ from state to state, but four are most standard.

If the defendant pleads *guilty* to a felony charge, the court will set a date for sentencing. For a misdemeanor, sentencing probably will occur at that time, although the judge has the option of delaying it for additional study.

If the defendant pleads *no contest,* meaning no defense to the charge will be presented, he or she is at the mercy of the court, and a sentence usually will be handed down by the judge. This is a practical equivalent to a guilty plea except it cannot be used against the defendant in later court actions.

If the defendant pleads *not guilty,* the case is set for later trial.

If the defendant pleads *not guilty by reason of insanity,* the judge usually orders a series of psychiatric examinations before determining whether a trial should proceed. Most frequently used in homicide cases, this plea centers on a defendant's ability, either temporary or permanent, to distinguish between right and wrong.

BILL OF INFORMATION

_____[1] the Prosecutor of this County, says by way of information that _____[2] the defendant, on or about _____ ____, 19____, did in this County violate _____[3] by _____

_____[4]

_____
(Prosecutor's signature by himself
or by an Asst. Prosecutor)

[1]Prosecutor's name.

[2]Defendant's name.

[3]Statute.

[4]Brief description in terms of statute, e.g., "assaulting _____ with intent to kill," etc.

Comment: The requirements of a bill of information are identical to those of an indictment. It must be signed by the prosecuting attorney or signed in his name by an assistant prosecuting attorney, and contain a statement that the accused has committed some public offense specified therein. Each count of the information shall also state the numerical designation of the statute which the defendant is alleged to have violated.

Motion Hearings

Defense attorneys have a wide variety of special actions that they may request of the court. Their strategic success in using these could have significant impact upon the outcome of the case. At times, these motions are considered as part of a regular pretrial hearing, but such considerations frequently come at a special hearing scheduled by the trial judge (often at the request of the defense) or in an appellate court.

Perhaps the most significant of these is a *motion to suppress evidence* in the case. Usually presented on technical grounds, this motion questions acceptability of a law enforcement action. If the court accepts the motion, the evidence in question will not be used in court, thus possibly reducing—and sometimes destroying—the chances for a guilty verdict.

Often, if their case is thus severely damaged, prosecutors will either drop their charges or be willing to plea bargain.

A major issue for journalists is whether they should report the evidence under consideration. An unanswered question is whether prospective jurors who know of the evidence will be able to dismiss it from their consideration. This was the issue of a 1979 U.S. Supreme Court decision, and the answer was that judges may indeed exclude the public, including reporters, from the sensitive motion hearing.

Given the availability of information, however, most reporters do present it with the thought that any prospective juror likely to be influenced by such information will be excused from service for that particular trial.

Among other motions available to the defense are:

Motion to strike prior convictions: This would remove any consideration by the judge of prior convictions in the determination of the sentence.

Motion to set side: This motion applies to any information presented by a prosecutor or a grand jury indictment for procedural or factual deficiencies. The defense attorney may charge that the district attorney's complaint, based on evidence taken at the preliminary hearing, is not sufficient to prove what it charges.

Motion to dismiss due to lack of speedy trial: This usually is made by the defense when the prosecution or the court delays the start of the trial while preparing its case.

Motion to dismiss due to denial of due process: This may be made when the defendant did not receive the proper explanation of his or her rights at the time of the arrest.

Motion for severance: This is presented when one of several jointly accused individuals believes the best defense would be separate from the trials of the other defendants. It is a request for a separate trial.

COVERING THE CIVIL PRETRIAL PROCESS

A clue to the nature of the criminal justice system is in the titles given to individual cases: *State v. John Jones.* The state, which represents the citizens, is taking action against an individual or group accused of violating a law. Civil actions, on the other hand, usually are labeled with the names of individuals or groups, *Smith v. Jones.* Thus a civil case is one in which an individual, business, or agency of government seeks payment for losses or injuries (damages) or asks that another party be forced by the court to do something or stop some action which is causing problems (relief).[2]

With notable exceptions, journalists do not pay as much attention to civil cases, and this means they are missing much that could be important to their communities. Not only do civil cases constitute the majority of court activity, but they also establish—to put it broadly—the rules of society.

Claudia Luther of the *Los Angeles Times* has extensive experience covering civil activities.

"Civil courts are becoming more and more of a forum for a wide variety of issues that are confronting society today," she says. "People are becoming more judicious. They are finding out that they can go to court and get some relief. The thing I like about civil cases is that the issues are a lot more complex, and they ultimately have much more effect on your life than the razzle-dazzle criminal case."

Claudia Luther
of The Los Angeles Times (Los Angeles Times photo)

It's probably that very complexity that results in poorer coverage, along with news judgment that fails to see the ramifications of what superficially is a simple dispute between two individuals or organizations.

In civil cases, reporters may need to wade through vast piles of discovery motions. They may encounter appraisals in cases involving government purchasing, and the appraisals are very difficult to understand. The civil procedure is more complex in some ways because it's less familiar, and it's more apt to revert to Latin terminology.

It's also more difficult from a reporter's standpoint because a civil judge will see many different lawyers in a month. A criminal judge sees the same set of lawyers. Reporters who cover criminal court also see those same lawyers regularly. They can build relationships that result in their ability to get information. In civil court, reporters may see on Tuesday a lawyer they have never seen before, and then see another new lawyer on Wednesday. Unless they build a relationship with the judge and staff, they are less likely to have someone who is constantly around to act as a translator.

Another problem that makes civil case coverage difficult is the length of the proceedings. It often takes years before the full story of a civil proceeding develops.

Despite problems of covering civil cases, reporters like Luther stress the need for giving more consideration to the potential long-term impact of civil decisions. She functions on advice written to her by her predecessor at the *Los Angeles Times* to look for rulings that change law, cost taxpayers, and affect large numbers of people.

Types of Civil Actions

Generally, civil cases may be categorized into three broad groups according to the request. In the first group, one citizen seeks monetary damages from another; the second group involves an effort to prevent or compel action (equity); and the third group is a catch-all category for a whole group of special court responsibilities.

Termed cases "at law," civil actions in the first group result when one individual believes he or she has suffered damages when a second individual has committed a wrong. Examples are claims made by persons injured in accidents, disputes over property, breach of contact, and such individual offenses as trespass, assault and defamation.

Individuals filing suit may ask the court to require payment of certain sums for three specific purposes: compensation for actual money or property lost, funds to help alleviate physical or psychological sufferings caused by the alleged action, and payment that serves as punishment for the action. If the suit gets to the trial stage, the decision is made by a jury.

Equity proceedings, on the other hand, do not always involve demands for money. In addition to resulting from a wrong already committed, these cases also are efforts to prevent wrongs. For example, a company may ask the court for an injunction to limit picketing by a striking labor union, or an individual or firm may request the court to require another party to live up to the terms of a contract. Equity decisions usually are made by a judge, not a jury.

In addition, courts have been given the responsibility to supervise a number of other actions. These frequently differ in their procedures. Included in these other actions, for example, are dissolution of marriage suits, in which the major journalistic attention often is only a periodic listing, and probate action. Separate stories may be written if prominent individuals, or large sums of money are involved, or if the case contains some other unusual or significant circumstances.

Two other types of cases provide business news: bankruptcy proceedings and corporate reorganizations, both of which fall under the jurisdiction of the U.S. District Court. Reporters seldom attend the hearings themselves, preferring to get information from documents filed in the clerk of court's office, unless large numbers of persons are involved or the actions are contested.

Reporters are unanimous in their advice that the first requirement for anyone assigned to cover civil cases is to learn the system; talk to both sides and talk to the judge.

Focus of Civil Pretrial Coverage

Civil cases are like criminal cases in one important respect. Most never get to the trial stage, partly because judges make special efforts to accomplish as much as possible out of the courtroom and because going to court can be very time consuming and expensive.

Given this, reporters try to be especially alert in the early stages to anticipate an early settlement, so they won't be caught unaware if it occurs and so they can provide readers with the full perspective. Such coverage is accomplished through a combination of three methods: following the documents filed with the clerk of courts, interviewing parties in the case, and attending hearings.

Turnstile justice

By Pete Szilagyi
American-Statesman Staff

A revolving door at the county booking jail and crowded state prisons are quickly sending arrested drug dealers back to the streets, taking the punch out of Austin's war on drugs, while frustrating police and prosecutors and wasting tax dollars going to fight drugs.

The cumbersome and strained criminal justice system assures that crack dealers jailed in raids by the Austin Police Department and other agencies last week will not be off the streets long if they are sent to state prisons.

More than 20 percent of the 131 suspects arrested on felony state drug dealing charges from October 1988 to October 1989 were released on personal bond by Municipal Court judges, according to a survey of court records by the *Austin American-Statesman.*

The rest were given cash bonds ranging from $1,500 to $20,000, but court officials say the majority of prisoners able to post bond were required to pay just 10 percent of the bond amount.

In last week's roundup of crack dealers, most suspects were charged under federal law, so they weren't processed through Municipal Court nor will they serve time in the state prison system. In federal prisons, it is likely they will serve more time than they would in state prisons, according to law enforcement officials.

A closer look at some of the Municipal Court bond cases showed that several suspects had prior drug arrests or had served prison time for drugs. Most had arrests for other crimes such as theft, obstructing police, forgery, assault and parole violations.

In one case, a suspect was still out on bond awaiting trial on another drug charge—in another case, personal bond was granted to a woman arrested near the Drag for selling LSD and who slipped out of handcuffs and escaped police custody for several hours until giving herself up.

Getting out of state prison after conviction may not be as easy as release from Austin's jail after arrest, but convicts with drug offenses can generally count on a relatively brief time behind bars. Bob Perkins, a state district judge who hears Travis County drug cases, calls the system that allows early release of drug dealers a farce.

The result is that police and prosecutors "spend 80 percent of our time chasing the same people" in drug cases, said Terry Keel, an assistant Travis County district attorney who specializes in prosecuting habitual criminals.

Keel offered these cases as examples of how arrests may not deter career drug dealers:

☐ Police obtained a search warrant for a crack cocaine dealer who was selling drugs across the street from an elementary school. The suspect—who had been to state prison three times, once for 30 years for aggravated robbery—was arrested after a large cache of drugs, cash and drug paraphernalia were found in his home, according to Keel.

The suspect was released from Municipal Court on a personal bond and three days later was back in business selling drugs, Keel said.

☐ Another drug dealer, who Keel said had six prior felony convictions and had escaped from an Iowa prison, gunned his car and attempted to run over a police officer who was trying to arrest him. The car then sped out into rush hour traffic on U.S. 183 and was involved in a wreck.

Keel said the suspect was arrested after a struggle with police, and charged with possession of a firearm and aggravated possession of methamphetamine.

The man was released on a cash deposit bond, which requires that just a percentage of the actual bond amount be paid, and he failed to show up for trial. The suspect was arrested again, convicted of six felonies and sentenced to 38 years, which Keel said probably will result in a jail time of just 3½ to five years.

The fact that Municipal Court judges occasionally have released hardened criminals on personal bond has been a point of friction this year between some prosecutors and the judges.

Lt. Dell Shaw, president of the Austin Police Association, said police were also angered earlier this year when Municipal Court judges released a murder suspect on personal bond before he had been charged. Also, Shaw said, a judge gave a car theft suspect from San Antonio personal bond before the police investigation of the case was complete. "The guy was released and he stole another car the next day," he said.

Presiding Judge Harriet Murphy said in an interview last week that she and other judges on the court are aware of the public's negative view of drug dealing and wouldn't knowingly make it easy for drug dealers to return to the streets.

However, Murphy said judges often don't have full knowledge of suspects' criminal backgrounds before they set bonds or are not able to give each case much attention because they may set bond for dozens of suspects on a busy night.

The six permanent Municipal Court judges and several relief judges, who are appointed by the Austin City Council, set bond for most suspects booked into the Travis County Central Booking Facility jail, 700 East Seventh St.

However, suspects or their attorneys can apply for personal recognizance bond, which allows the suspected drug dealer to leave jail by just promising to show up for trial.

Jim Rust, director of the county's personal bond office, said most applications for personal bond are researched by his office, and a recommendation is made to the judge. Several factors are taken into consideration, including the suspect's roots in the community, the presence of relatives in town, whether the suspect is employed and if he or she has a previous criminal record.

Personal bond is offered to assure that suspects who are poor have the same chance of getting out on bond as those who have money or whose family and friends can put up a cash bond. Personal bond assures "there are not two forms of justice, one for the rich and one for the poor," Rust said.

Sometimes, a suspect lies to the personal bond office about his or her criminal record, or the police computerized "rap sheet" on the suspect is not complete, he said.

Despite the public sentiment against drug dealers, many dealers arrested on Austin streets and released on a low bond or personal bond are "not big time dealers, they're just people standing on the street corners getting $10 or $20 for each packet (of drugs) they sell," Murphy said. She added that the purpose of bonding is not to punish suspects but to assure that they appear for trial.

Moreover, she said, large cash bonds often are not a deterrent to drug dealers who often have access to large amounts of cash or who can hire a bail bondsman.

"The ones I don't like getting (personal) bonds are the ones with extensive (criminal) histories and the ones who go right back out and do it again," said Jim Doty, an assistant Travis County district attrorney who works with the police department's Repeat Offender Program.

David Garza, a Municipal Court judge who has been an assistant district attorney, said some factors that cause a judge to give drug dealers personal bond are not readily apparent.

"Sometimes the police officer will say, 'This guy's a first- or second-time offender and he's going to help us make some other cases. Can you give him a low cash bond or a personal bond?' " Garza said.

"I was frustrated when I was a prosecutor and saw these people get in and get out (of jail) very quickly and it made you mad, but I'm wearing a different hat now . . . I can't keep them in jail if there's no basis for it other than they're bad guys, and there are some cases where I would like to," Garza said.

Perkins, whose 331st District Court handles numerous drug cases, said the severe state prison overcrowding allows drug dealers to manipulate the legal system to their advantage. A key element is the state's Prison Management Act, which allows the governor to grant up to 90 days of good time for some prisoners when Texas Department of Corrections prisons are at 95 percent capacity or more, he said.

"A lot of drug dealers will ask for TDC time, because they know they're not going to have to spend any time there," he said. "Ironically, the prisons are acting as magnets. (Some dealers) have been around a long time and they know the practicality of the situation, it's been de-mystified for them, so they'll take the TDC time."

Perkins said, for example, that a dealer may have a choice between a five-year state prison sentence and 10 years probation. "Say he gets a five-year sentence, he can get paroled in five or six months, then for four and half years after that he will have to go to a parole officer," the judge said.

"That parole officer probably has 300 people in his case load and he doesn't have time to see anybody," he said.

On probation, however, the convict will "have to see his probation officer once a month and give a urine sample once a month, and he'll have to pay a $40 a month administrative charge," Perkins said.

"It is a farce, it really has become that," he said.

"Every juror (I) talk to will ask, 'Why is this guy out on the streets?' The answer to that is we just have so many guys in prison that a lot of them get turned out too quickly," Perkins said.

This story from the *Austin* (Texas) *American-Statesman,* November 16, 1989, deals with an issue common to nearly every urban area in the country: overcrowded jails and what to do with inmates. Note how the reporter mixes statistics with comments from local authorities to build a comprehensive story. Reprinted with permission.

"Everything that goes on in court goes on in writing. Almost everything goes on in writing before it goes on out loud," says David Offer of the Newport, Rhode Island, *Daily News.* "That's not true at the final trial level, but a trial is the last thing that happens in court, and about 95 percent of all legal cases—criminal and civil—never get to a trial. So much of the coverage of courts is coverage of paperwork—covering lawsuits that are filed, answers, responses, interrogatories (written questions). I tend to spend much more time writing about paperwork than I do about trials."

It is important, therefore, that reporters know what documents are available and that they almost always are public record. Any member of the public—including reporters—has only to walk into the clerk of court's office and ask for them.

It would be quite possible in most cases for a reporter to use the documents alone to produce readable and accurate stories about civil cases. But it's often desirable to supplement documentary material with conversations and attendance at hearings. The documents give the superficial, but not the undercurrent (the mood) in the courtroom. Attendance at selected hearings may facilitate putting legal points into simpler language. Lawyers will write in legalized style in their briefs, but they speak more plainly in the courtroom.

The Civil Pretrial Process

A civil case begins with a complaint in which a person charges he or she has suffered damage from a wrong action committed by another person. That petitioner is the plaintiff. After explaining what resulted from the alleged action, the plaintiff makes a specific request for damages, judgment, or other relief. Also requested is a summons to notify defendants of the allegations against them and to require that they appear in court.

It may not be in time for a reporter's deadline, but the defendant's answer, called a "pleading," is the next step in the process. It must be filed within a stipulated period, and if it is not, the plaintiff may then request a default judgment. If the answer is filed on time, the defendant has a number of alternative pleadings, which may include one or more of the following:

Motion to strike: Asks the court to rule that the plantiff's petition contains irrelevant, prejudicial, or other improper matter.

Motion to make more definite and certain: Requires the plaintiff to set out the facts of the complaint more specifically or to describe the injury or damages in greater detail so that the defendant can answer more precisely.

Demurrer or motion to dismiss: Questions whether the plaintiff's petition states a legally sound cause of action against the defendant, even admitting for the purpose of the pleading that all of the facts set out by the plaintiff in the petition are true.

CIVIL COMPLAINT; Negligence, Automobile Accident

IN THE COURT OF COMMON PLEAS
OF FRANKLIN COUNTY, OHIO

Paul P. Patton
150 N. High Street
Columbus, Ohio 43214

Plaintiff

vs.   Case No. 13,875

David D. Doe
2861 Summit Avenue
Columbus, Ohio 43228

Defendant

Complaint
Jury Demand Endorsed Hereon

1. On February 16, 1970 at the intersection of East Main Street and College Avenue in Bexley, Ohio, the defendant negligently operated his motor vehicle into the motor vehicle owned and operated by plaintiff.

2. As a result plaintiff suffered injuries of the neck, back, shoulders and other parts of his body, causing pain and permanent damage.

3. Plaintiff has incurred medical and hospital expenses in the sum of $300.00 and expects to incur further such expenses.

4. Plaintiff has lost $600.00 earnings and expects to lose further earnings. His earning capacity has been permanently impaired.

5. Plaintiff's 1969 Chevrolet was damaged in the amount of $800.00.

WHEREFORE, plaintiff demands judgment against defendant in the sum of $16,500.00 and costs.

/s/ Alan Able
_____

Able and Ready
100 E. Broad Street
Columbus, Ohio 43215
Phone 221-4500
Attorney for Plaintiff

Jury Demand

Plaintiff demands trial by a jury in this action.

/s/ Alan Able
_____

Attorney for Plaintiff

Comment: This form can be used for all routine automobile accidents involving negligence. It is not important for the purpose of pleading whether the negligence is assured clear distance ahead, speed or any other cause as conclusionary allegations of negligence are the same in each case under the Civil Rules. Specific facts are to be ascertained through the discovery or pre-trial process.

Special damages are required to be set forth with particularity. The issue of what constitutes special damages is unchanged by the Civil Rules and includes specific injuries, medical expense, loss of earnings, permanency of injury, impairment of earning capacity and property damage. It is recommended that all applicable types of special damages be pleaded briefly as in this form. No technical form of allegation is required although the method of proof remains unchanged.

Answer: This statement by the defendant denies the allegations in the plaintiff's petition, or admits some and denies others and pleads an excuse.

Cross-petition or cross-complaint: May be filed by the defendant either separately or as part of the answer. It asks for relief or damages against the original plaintiff, and perhaps others. When a cross-petition is filed, the plaintiff may then file any of these same motions to the cross-petition, except a motion to quash service of summons.[3]

Most of these motions may be appealed, usually to a higher court, and that's part of the reason why civil cases can take years. Each appeal sets off a whole new series of hearings and additional motions that must be resolved before a trial date is set. It is often at this stage that reporters lose contact with a case unless it happens to be a very big one or involves prominent community individuals.

Reporters' attempts to deal with civil cases often include a personal filing system in which they keep notes and clips of cases that they are attempting to follow. And, of course, the other part is helpful sources.

"There are hundreds and hundreds of documents filed here, and there's no way I can keep up with all of them," says Bob Rawitch of the *Los Angeles Times*. "So I have to rely a great deal on the attorneys and the other people who have contact with the case. I'll tell them in advance of a case I'm interested in and say, 'Hey, let me know when you file a trial memorandum or the defense plea in this case.' For the most part, they're willing to call and tell me."

Good stories also are found in the rather freewheeling and potentially time-consuming process called "discovery," which essentially is the paperwork of asking and answering questions. It's obviously valuable to attorneys to know as much as they can about the other side's case, and it is through discovery that they obtain much of this information.

An important part of discovery is known as an "interrogatory," which is a list of written questions presented by an attorney to the other side that must be answered under oath. The questions may be of a background nature. For example, in a personal injury case resulting from an

ANSWER; General Form Combining a Denial Defense with Other Defenses and Objections

IN THE COURT OF COMMON PLEAS OF FRANKLIN COUNTY, OHIO

Paul P. Patton
Plaintiff

vs.   Case No. 14,264

David D. Doe
Defendant

Answer

First Defense
1. Defendant admits the allegations contained in paragraphs 1 and 2 of the complaint.
2. Defendant admits the allegations contained in paragraph 3 of the complaint except he denies that he was negligent.
3. Defendant alleges that he is without knowledge or information sufficient to form a belief as to the truth of the allegations contained in paragraphs 4 and 5 of the complaint.
4. Defendant denies all of the allegations contained in paragraph 6 of the complaint.
Second Defense
Plaintiff has failed to join the ABC Insurance Company as a plaintiff in this action. ABC Insurance Company has an interest or claim arising out of the same act for property damages subrogated to the aforesaid company.
Third Defense
If defendant is found to be negligent, which he expressly denies, plaintiff was contributorily negligent proximately resulting in his injuries.

/s/ John Jones

Jones and Smith
50 W. Broad Street
Columbus, Ohio 43215
Phone 228-2800
Attorney for Defendant

---

automobile accident, an attorney may ask for the driving record of the defendant, whether glasses are required, whether the defendant had been drinking, or what the defendant had done for the twenty-four hours prior to the accident.

Answering questions may involve the expression of opinion, even if the opinion would not be allowed as evidence during the trial. Or the questions may be strategic in nature, such as a request for the amount of insurance the defendant carries so that the plaintiff's attorney can be guided in the amount of damages to request.

PLEADINGS; Motion for Definite Statement

**IN THE COURT OF COMMON PLEAS
OF FRANKLIN COUNTY, OHIO**

Paul P. Patton
Plaintiff

vs.   Case No. 14,264

David D. Doe
Defendant

Motion for Definite Statement

Defendant moves the court for an order requiring plaintiff to provide a definite statement concerning the following particulars in his complaint as it is so vague and ambiguous that defendant is unable to frame an answer thereto:

1. By setting forth the date on which the accident alleged in the second paragraph of the first claim in the complaint occurred as time is material to the affirmative defense of the statute of limitations.

2. By setting forth items of special damage specially in the fifth paragraph of the first claim as required by Civil Rule 9 (G).

3. By setting forth the circumstances constituting mistake with particularity in the third paragraph of the second claim as required by Civil Rule 9 (B).

/s/ John Jones _____

Jones and Smith
50 W. Broad Street
Columbus, Ohio 43215
Phone 228-2800
Attorney for Defendant

Attorneys even are permitted to ask for a list of witnesses who will appear with the stipulation that such a list be updated until the time of the trial.

In preparation for the trial or as part of pretrial activities, either side in a case has the right to take sworn out-of-court statements from the other party or from any witness. Called "depositions," these statements often are needed because a court cannot require the appearance at a civil trial of a person who lives outside the county. If a person who has given a deposition also testifies at the trial, attorneys may use that deposition to attack his or her credibility.

Depositions may consist of answers to written questions or of an oral examination conducted before an authorized person. In any event, a transcript is made, although some courts permit recordings or even videotapes. And attorneys may cross-examine. Some reporters have found it possible in some jurisdictions to attend the session at which depositions are being taken, but generally they are not considered public record until made public by court order or introduced as evidence in the trial.

INTERROGATORIES: General Form to Corporation

IN THE COURT OF COMMON PLEAS
OF FRANKLIN COUNTY, OHIO

Paul P. Patton
Plaintiff

vs.   Case No. 28,253

ABC Corporation
Defendant

Interrogatories

To the ABC Corporation:

The following interrogatories are submitted herewith to you to be answered in writing under oath within 28 days after the date of service thereof upon you.

Instructions for answering:

1. You are required to choose one or more of your proper employees, officers or agents to answer the interrogatories, and the employer, officer or agent shall furnish such information as is known or available to the organization.

2. Where the word "accident" is used it refers to the incident which is the basis of this law suit unless otherwise specified.

3. Where an interrogatory calls for an answer in more than one part, the parts should be separated in the answer so that they are clearly understandable.

4. "Medical practitioner" as used herein includes any medical doctor, osteopathic physician, chiropractor or any other person who performs any type of healing art.

5. You are reminded that all answers must be made separately and fully and that an incomplete or evasive answer is a failure to answer.

6. You are under a continuing duty seasonably to supplement your response with respect to any question directly addressed to the identity and location of persons having knowledge of discoverable matters, the identity of any person expected to be called as an expert witness at trial, and the subject matter on which he is expected to testify and to correct any response which you know or later learn is incorrect.

QUESTIONS:

(Insert herein questions directed to the particular case)

1. . . . . . .
2. . . . . . .
3. . . . . . .
4. . . . . . .

/s/ John Jones _____

Jones and Smith
50 W. Broad Street
Columbus, Ohio 43215
Phone 228-2800

In addition to interrogatories and depositions, attorneys have other methods of discovery that are used in special instances. Three used most frequently are requiring that documents, records, and books be presented or permission be given to enter someone's property for an inspection; requiring that a person involved in the case take a physical or mental examination; and requiring that the other side admit or deny the validity of documents.

Once all of the various motions and discovery techniques have been used and the case is ready for trial, many states require one final step—a pretrial hearing. Basically an effort to reduce trial time, the pretrial hearing is designed to determine points of agreement (stipulations) among the parties. Participants usually are the attorneys and the judge. Generally, these agreements center on many of the facts of the case, although points of law may be included.

NOTES

1. Carl Bernstein and Bob Woodward, *All the President's Men* (New York: Simon and Schuster, 1974), p. 207.

2. Standing Committee on Association Communications, American Bar Association, *Law and the Courts* (Chicago: American Bar Association, 1974), p. 7.

3. *Law and the Courts*, p. 8.

A Trial is Real-Life Drama

To many reporters, covering a trial is like covering a sporting event, a political campaign, or even a play. As serious as it is, participants take their positions on cue, function within the game plan, and play according to the rules.

Most trials do involve considerable drama. First, they are serious; usually they involve the well-being and even the life of many of those involved. Second, they involve strategy and persuasion by an attorney, who must make certain "constituents" "vote" in a certain way.

In so doing, attorneys—indeed, the whole criminal justice system—are not deliberately trying to protect an individual who is guilty of a crime. They are not saying that laws should be violated. They are seeking to protect a system that maintains that an accused person is innocent until he or she is proven guilty and that the accused has a right to due process and a fair trial.

It is also the job of the reporter to protect that system. The Sixth Amendment of the Constitution guarantees a speedy, public trial with the idea that full exposure to public view provides the best insurance that the system will function as intended. Reporters represent the public in that system. They take full advantage of the fact that court documents, for the most part, are public records and that court proceedings usually are open. They observe what happens in the courtroom, provide the public with descriptions of those events, relate individual and institutional actions to public expectations, and, at times, are critical when some aspect of the system strays from the norm.

Reporters, however, differ about how to cover the courtroom. For example, David Offer of the Newport, Rhode Island, *Daily News* says he spends very little time in it.

"Most trials are deadly dull," he says. "None of them is the Perry Mason type. I must have covered, off and on, hundreds of cases, and I have yet to be at an exciting trial. Most witnesses don't sparkle. Most lawyers don't do a great job of examination. I have yet to see anybody break down and confess on the stand. The way to cover trials is to be sure you've talked to all the lawyers, to be there for the opening and closing statements, and, if you can, skip an awful lot of the testimony in between.''

Offer stresses, however, that reporters can be this free only if they understand the system, religiously read documents, and keep in close touch with attorneys to be assured of knowing what is going to happen in their absence from the courtroom.

That's the general, day-to-day approach, but there are times when a trial will be of such substantial community concern or legal importance that it merits full-time coverage. The reporter then simply has to adjust priorities or get help to be there.

Covering a trial, either full time or on a spot basis, involves knowing what kinds of stories are likely to occur during the various parts of the proceedings. Every step can make news. Every step may provide clues to future developments. Reporting these from a trial that may last days or months can help readers, listeners, or viewers to understand what is happening in an individual case and, more importantly, to know more about the criminal justice system.

JURY SELECTION

The specific jurors who comprise the trial (or petit) jury for a civil or criminal trial are selected from a list of prospects compiled from voter registration lists, from tax assessment lists, or from some other official listing of citizens. The selection process (voir dire) consists of questions from attorneys and/or judges to determine a prospect's suitability. These questions may seek to determine if the prospect has biases that may affect the decision. They may examine the individual's background or knowledge, which could have a bearing on the decision.

Attorneys, naturally, will seek to eliminate jurors who might be biased against their side. In so doing, they may ask the court to dismiss prospective juror "for cause" when they discover evidence of an opinion or prejudice that might influence the decision. Or they may use "peremptory challenges," which permit them to excuse a specific number of prospective jurors without stating a reason.

Reporters ordinarily do not cover the jury selection; instead, they choose to report simply on the results, usually giving a demographic breakdown of the twelve jurors (and, in some states, the alternates). They would report, for example, that a jury was comprised of seven women and five men or that it included four blacks. The basic effort is to provide any information that might be pertinent to the representativeness of the jury. Otherwise the selection process can be time consuming and can result in very little solid information for the reader, viewer, or listener. But there are at least two kinds of situations in which being on the scene may be of value.

A good story could result from the answers or lack of answers given by prospective jurors, especially when there is difficulty in seating the jury for a particularly noteworthy trial. Or the story could be broader, perhaps even only indirectly related to the specific trial.

OPENING STATEMENTS

Attorneys have two opportunities during a trial to move to the center of the stage, command the attention of the whole courtroom, and try to invoke the sympathy of the jurors. In both the opening and closing statements, attorneys may relate more emotionally the facts and law of a case.

The purpose of the opening statements—given first by the plaintiff's attorney in a civil case or the prosecution in a criminal case—is to establish what attorneys feel are the facts of the case. This phase sets the scene. It's like reading a program before a play. Reporters learn the characters and the lines of argument.

PRESENTING THE EVIDENCE

As usually happens during the trial process, attorneys for the plaintiff or the prosecution present their evidence first. Some evidence is in the form of documents or physical objects (e.g., the murder weapon), but most usually comes from witnesses who respond to questions from the attorneys, or, in a few instances, the judge.

Reporters take differing points of view about such testimony. Some, like Offer, tend to remain unimpressed with witnesses, preferring to concentrate on documents and out-of-court comments from attorneys. Others, like Shelley Epstein of the Peoria, (Illinois) *Journal Star,* feel strongly about the journalistic value of reporting testimony directly from the courtroom, especially in an important case.

"It's my feeling that the copy reads best, and you get the best information by sitting through the testimony," he says. "However, that's the most time consuming, and you have a lot of dead time while doing it. But I really don't see any way of doing it fully and properly without listening to the testimony. On occasion, I have skipped witnesses and gone in for the closing arguments and gotten somewhat of a synopsis of what was going on. But I find that what the attorneys are saying in the closing arguments is not always what the witnesses are saying from the stand."

That testimony comes in four ways, as attorneys tug away at the witnesses to make points for their sides. In direct examination, the attorney who calls the witness seeks to present that person's direct experience or expert knowledge about the circumstances or subject matter of the case. The opposing attorney, through cross-examination, then asks questions that seek to lead the jury to doubt the credibility of the witness. Back comes the original attorney, in a redirect examination, to try to repair the damage. The opposing attorney may then conclude the questioning with re-cross-examination.

M.D. disputes Cohen on time of the murder

By Joan Fleischman
Herald Staff Writer

Dade's deputy chief medical examiner made a startling announcement in court Friday: Millionaire Stanley Cohen was probably killed about 3 A.M.—a good 2 ½ hours before his wife reported the murder to police.

The testimony—out of earshot of jurors—incensed lawyers for the defendant, Joyce Cohen. They accused prosecutors of prompting Dr. Charles Wetli to change his opinion mid-trial, sandbagging the widow's defense.

In a pretrial deposition, Wetli said he could not pinpoint the time of death, except to say that Cohen, shot four times in the head, died between midnight and 6 A.M. on March 7, 1986.

Defense attorney Alan Ross told Dade Circuit Judge Fredricka Smith that Wetli should not be permitted to render his new opinion when he testifies before the jury next week.

Ross said he relied on Wetli's earlier statements about the time of Stanley Cohen's death when building Joyce Cohen's defense, and will not have sufficient time to consult his own experts to challenge Wetli's opinion.

Ross also said he might have selected different jurors had he known about Wetli's new testimony. He specifically mentioned one juror he might not have chosen: a physician.

After the judge ruled Wetli can testify about his findings in front of the jury, Ross asked for a mistrial. No, the judge said.

Wetli told Judge Smith that no one prompted him to change his opinion. He said he decided on the eve of trial to review the deposition of Dr. Michael Baden, former medical examiner for the city of New York, whom Cohen's lawyers hired as an expert defense witness.

After reading the deposition, Wetli said, he decided to look at his original photographs of Cohen's body.

He said he projected the slides on a screen in a darkened auditorium. That was when he made the discovery: "It lit up like a neon sign."

Wetli said he saw a "striped" pattern of lividity—a discoloration of the skin caused by the settling of blood after death—that indicated Cohen had been lying on his right side on bed sheets for a couple of hours after death.

He said the pattern of lividity was not visible on photo blowups, only on the original slides.

"It was . . . without coaching by anybody that I made that observation," Wetli said.

Joyce Cohen, 39, has said that her 52-year-old husband was killed by intruders about 5:20 A.M. She said she was talking on the phone to friends from Colorado when she heard a noise, investigated, and found her husband's body.

Although she had deliberately left her alarm system off that night, she said she immediately tripped a panic button and called police.

A neighbor testified earlier in the week that he was awake between 3:30 and 5:30 A.M., but heard no gunshots. He did say he heard the sound of glass breaking and the alarm ringing at about 5 A.M.

Prosecutors and police say Joyce Cohen wanted out of the marriage but feared she would get no money if they divorced. They said she hired hit men to kill her husband.

Thursday, prosecution witness Frank Zuccarello, 25, said he was one of the hired killers. He said Joyce Cohen let him and two friends into her Coconut Grove home the night of the murder. The time, he said, was around 2 A.M.

Unlike fictionalized trials in television and movies, few real-life trials are characterized by shocking announcements or confessions. But here, such an announcement brought the story onto page one. Note how the reporter weaves background information and current testimony for an interesting, readable story. The story appeared in *The Miami Herald,* October 28, 1989, and it is reprinted with permission of *The Miami Herald.*

Most witnesses are restricted to fact in their testimony. They may tell what they experienced directly, or they may identify documents or other physical evidence presented in the trial. They are not permitted to state opinions about those facts, and they often are not allowed to tell what they have heard others say (hearsay).

But one type of witness who may express an opinion is the person with special knowledge, defined as an "expert." Because expert testimony often is technical, some reporters tend to gloss over the testimony of the expert witnesses, presenting little more than a quick summary, and to provide readers, viewers, and listeners with an adequate picture of the value of the testimony, either pro or con. Too much emphasis on the term expert, for example, may obscure the fact that the findings are not adequately scientific or do not provide an important element of the prosecution's case.

Journalists do not, however, gloss over those witnesses who were directly involved in the incident that led to charges being filed; namely, the victim and the defendant.

This coverage applies as well to defendants, who are not required to testify in either a criminal or civil trial. Often they do not appear because their attorneys are reluctant to put them on the stand, where they will be subject to cross-examination. But, if they do testify, reporters make a special effort to be on hand. This, of course, is not only a matter of good reading or viewing, but it is also a part of the natural journalistic tendency to provide readers with as much firsthand detail as possible about all sides of an issue.

That leads reporters to pay considerable attention to the cross-examination. The effort by the court to see that the presentation of evidence is fair basically is in the hands of the judge, who determines the admissibility. But the opposing attorneys are expected to help keep the system honest by calling to the judge's attention what they think are improper practices or inadmissible evidence. Attorneys for either side of a case may lodge objections, but the stakes are higher for the defense. Often the success of an appeal, or even at times the right of an appeal, hinges upon whether the objection was appropriately made.

Whether journalists emphasize or even mention objections in their coverage depends upon the specific circumstances. Often, the outcome of the trial itself may depend on a judge's decision about whether particular evidence may be admitted. In those circumstances, naturally, the reporter will provide full details of the evidence, the objection, and the reasons the evidence was admitted or ruled inadmissible.

In all situations the question to ask is: How important is the evidence in terms of the overall guilt or innocence? This applies even to evidence that is excluded. If, for example, the objection concerns whether the jury will be permitted to hear testimony about an incriminating statement made by the defendant, the jury often will be sent from the room during the discussion. Even if the judge rules out the testimony, most reporters would consider it valuable enough to include in the story. Their goal would be to inform readers of the fact that the defendant made the statement even though it is not going to be entered into the evidence.

Sometimes debates are conducted in the courtroom after the jury has been dismissed, or the judge and attorneys may go to the judge's chambers. Here, too, the reporter makes every effort to get the full story.

"If you see the court reporter going into chambers with the judge and the lawyers," Offer advises, "feel free to go in, too. It's part of an open court hearing. You might get thrown out, but you haven't lost a lot by trying. We bounce painlessly. Generally speaking, any time the judge goes into chambers with the lawyers, the press, if it is excluded, should howl."

Once the prosecution has completed its case, attention turns to the defense, which follows pretty much the same routine. In some instances, defense attorneys present no evidence on the grounds that the burden of proof is on the prosecution and that requirement has not been met.

At the conclusion of the defendant's presentation, the plaintiff's or state's attorney may present additional evidence (rebuttal evidence) to refute testimony and evidence offered by the defendant. This is followed by one more opportunity for the defense to refute the rebuttal.

CLOSING ARGUMENTS

This is the last chance for attorneys to present the case as they believe it should be interpreted. First, the attorney for the plaintiff or state, then the defense counsel, will stride to the jury box, summarize from their perspective, sometimes cajole, sometimes plead, and sometimes demand that the decision be in favor of their side. The importance of closing arguments is not lost on attorneys or reporters.

Although closing arguments may be freewheeling, attorneys still function under restrictions. They must confine their comments to the facts—the evidence presented—and properly drawn inferences of the case. They are not allowed to comment on a defendant's failure to testify in a criminal case. If an attorney gets carried away and goes beyond these boundaries, opposing counsel has the right to object, and the judge will rule on that objection. At the extreme, too much improper argument could result in a mistrial.

Once both sides have concluded, the plaintiff or prosecution gets one final time to address the jury to answer defense arguments.

INSTRUCTIONS TO THE JURY

Although there is potential journalistic value in some situations in the instructions given by the judge to the jury, most reporters find that value limited. Because instructions represent the judge's statement of how the law applies to the facts of the case and provide interpretations and definitions, the point is, of course, that the reporter must understand the case to determine whether to hear them. To the reporter with time, however, the instructions, because they are written by the judge for lay jurors, often can help put a focus on the whole trial.

Although the judge decides which to accept and which to refuse, in some states instructions are based on proposals submitted by attorneys for each side. If an attorney feels that improper instructions were given, he or she lodges an objection for the record, in case of a later appeal.

WAITING FOR THE DECISION

Juries, of course, don't always cooperate with reporters facing deadlines. Once their secret deliberations begin, jurors discuss the evidence in detail and relate that evidence to the possible verdicts given them by the court. In criminal cases, their decision usually must be unanimous. In civil cases, some jurisdictions permit a verdict based on the agreement of nine or ten jurors. If they can't achieve the requirements (a hung jury), the whole trial may be repeated before a new jury.

That rather heavy burden may be taken care of in minutes, but more frequently it requires several hours or even days of deliberation. For reporters, long deliberations can create a void during which they must have the knowledge and initiative to fill editor and audience expectations.

The reporter also watches the courtroom in case the jury returns to ask questions of the judge about the instructions. If such an event is missed, a quick check with courtroom personnel, especially court reporters or stenographers, should cover it.

Keeping in touch with courtroom personnel also helps reporters ensure that they will be available when the jury returns with its verdict, which can happen at almost any time. Generally, reporters who cannot wait in the courtroom (and few ever can) will arrange to have an attorney or other courtroom official call when the jury is expected.

INTERVIEWING JURORS

Once the verdict has been announced and the jury members have been dismissed, reporters often will take advantage of the opportunity to get some good inside information.

Whether reporters do talk with them, of course, depends on the type of case it is, how legally important it is, the degree of public interest, or whether the case is out of the ordinary. Reporters will certainly try to speak to jurors in capital cases and in cases in which persons of some popularity, political standing, or prestige have been on trial.

Although there are no longer ramifications in talking to jurors after the verdict, reporters often have to overcome efforts by some judges to make such interviews difficult. Sometimes, after a noteworthy trial, these judges will tell jurors to avoid reporters. Or they may insist that everyone in the courtroom remain until jurors have left the room. But, for a reporter who has determined that juror interviews are necessary, these efforts should represent little more than minor inconveniences.

MOTIONS AFTER VERDICT

The verdict, once announced, is not official until the judge enters the judgment. And, prior to the judgment, the losing attorney may again make motions if he or she thinks some aspect of the process was conducted unfairly. Among the most common of these motions are:

Motion for a new trial: This sets out alleged procedural errors and asks the judge to grant a new trial.

Motion in arrest of judgment: This attacks the sufficiency of the indictment or information in a criminal case.

Motion for judgment non obstante veredicto: This requests the judge to enter a judgment contrary to the jury's verdict.[1]

JUDGMENT AND SENTENCING

The judgment of the court determines action to be taken based upon the jury's verdict, which is subject, of course, to any appellate court decision.

In a civil damage suit, the judgment establishes the amount of damages a guilty defendant must pay. These damages may compensate the plaintiff for losses incurred (compensatory) or be paid as a means of punishment (punitive). In a criminal case, the judge generally will set a time for sentencing of a defendant found guilty. During the interim, the judge will seek to determine whether other factors should be considered in establishing the sentence. This process gives the reporter several story possibilities, the most significant of which is, of course, the sentence itself.

JUDGMENT OF CONVICTION
Judgment

This _____ day of _____, 19___, Defendant came into Court represented by Attorney _____ and the State/City of _____, came represented by _____, defendant having entered a plea of _____ to the charge (s) of _____.

WHEREFORE, the trial began _____, 19___ and on _____ _____, 19___, having heard all the testimony adduced by both parties, the Court/Jury in writing made its
FINDINGS, to wit:

_____ as to _____ (if motions made, so recite, together
guilty/not guilty   charges
with disposition)

Counsel for defendant having been given an opportunity to speak on behalf of defendant, and defendant personally having been given the opportunity to make a statement in his own behalf and present information in mitigation and _____
"no good and sufficient cause" [or] "good and sufficient cause"
being shown to mitigate punishment and nothing said by defendant as to why sentence should not now be imposed, SENTENCE AND JUDGMENT WAS PRONOUNCED AS FOLLOWS:

For the offense(s) of _____, you are sentenced to _____ _____ (etc.)

Again, interviews with the defendant, the lawyers, jurors, family members about their reactions to the sentence can provide good copy in which the human and legal elements come together.

DEALING WITH LEGAL MUMBO JUMBO

The law is complicated. That's enough to make the job of the reporter difficult. But adding to it is the legal profession's use of black-robe, high-ceiling language that few people but law school graduates can understand. The law, perhaps more than any other profession, still clings to Latin phrases and rambling discourse. "Certiorari," says the judge. "No exeat," pleads the attorney. "What?" asks the citizen.

Cutting through all this legal mumbo jumbo may be the major task of court reporters. First, they have to wade through the jargon and the concepts and gain an understanding themselves. Second, they have to communicate with their audiences, and this means avoiding the terminology and seeking lay definitions.

"That's the problem any specialist reporter is going to have to deal with," says Bob Rawitch of the *Los Angeles Times.* "And the longer you cover a specialty, the more you have to guard against letting the terminology slip into your copy. You have to avoid becoming part of the inner circle. You know what they're talking about in the courtroom with the legal jargon flying from one side of the room to another, but I just don't think you can let it slip into your copy."

NOTES

1. Standing Committee on Association Communications, American Bar Association, *Law and the Courts* (Chicago: American Bar Association, 1980), p. 19.

A GLOSSARY OF LEGAL TERMS

A

abstract of record —A complete history of the case as found in the record, in short abbreviated form.

accumulative sentence—A sentence, additional to others, imposed at the same time for several distinct offenses; one sentence to begin at the expiration of another.

acquittal—A determination after a trial that a defendant in a criminal case is not guilty of the crime charged.

action in personam (in per-sō'nam)—An action against the person, founded on a personal liability.

action in rem (in rem)—An action for a thing; an action for the recovery of a thing possessed by another.

adjudication—Giving or pronouncing a judgment or decree; also the judgment given.

adversary system—The system of trial practice in the U.S. and some other countries in which each of the opposing, or adversary, parties has full opportunity to present and establish its opposing contentions before the court.

allegation—The assertion, declaration, or statement of a party to an action, made in a pleading, setting out what he expects to prove.

amicus curiae (a-me̅-kus kur-e̅-i)—A friend of the court; one who interposes and volunteers information upon some matter of law.

ancillary bill or suit (an'si-la-re̅)—One growing out of and auxiliary to another action or suit, such as a proceeding for the enforcement of a judgment, or to set aside fraudulent transfers of property.

answer—A pleading by which defendant endeavors to resist the plaintiff's allegation of facts.

appearance—The formal proceeding by which a defendant submits himself to the jurisdiction of the court.

appellant (a-pel'ant)—The party appealing a decision or judgment to a higher court.

appellate court—A court having jurisdiction of appeal and review; not a "trial court."

appellee (ap-e-le')—The party against whom an appeal is taken.

arraignment—In criminal practice, to bring a prisoner to the bar of the court to answer to a criminal charge.

arrest of judgment—The act of staying the effect of a judgment already entered.

at issue—Whenever the parties to a suit come to a point in the pleadings which is affirmed on one side and denied on the other, that point is said to be "at issue."

attachment—A remedy by which plaintiff is enabled to acquire a lien upon property or effects of defendant for satisfaction of judgment which plaintiff may obtain in the future.

attorney of record—Attorney whose name appears in the permanent records or files of a case.

B

bail —To set at liberty a person arrested or imprisoned, on security being taken, for his appearance on a specified day and place.

bail bond—An obligation signed by the accused, with sureties, to secure his presence in court.

bailiff—A court attendant whose duties are to keep order in the courtroom and to have custody of the jury.

banc (bangk)—Bench; the place where a court permanently or regularly sits. A "sitting" **en banc** is a meeting of all the judges of a court, as distinguished from the sitting of a single judge.

bench warrant—Process issued by the court itself, or "from the bench," for the attachment or arrest of a person.

best evidence—Primary evidence; the best evidence which is available; any evidence which is available. Any evidence falling short of this standard is secondary; i.e., an original letter is best evidence compared to a copy.

binding instruction—One in which jury members are told if they find certain conditions to be true they must find for the plaintiff, or defendant, as case might be.

bind over—To hold on bail for trial.

brief—A written report or printed document prepared by counsel to file in court, usually setting forth both facts and law in support of his case.

burden of proof—In the law of evidence, the necessity or duty of affirmatively proving a fact or facts in dispute.

C

calling the docket —The public calling of the docket or list of causes at commencement of term of court, for setting a time for trial or entering orders.

caption—The caption of a pleading, or other papers connected with a case in court, is the heading or introductory clause which shows the names of the parties, name of the court, numbers of the case, etc.

cause—A suit, litigation or action—civil or criminal.

certiorare (ser-shē-o-ra′rē)—An original writ commanding judges or officers of inferior courts to certify or to return records of proceedings in a cause of judicial review.

challenge to the array—Questioning the qualifications of an entire jury panel, usually on the grounds of partiality or some fault in the process of summoning the panel.

chambers—Private office or room of a judge.

change of venue—The removal of a suit begun in one county or district, to another, for trial, or from one court to another in the same county or district.

circuit courts—Originally, courts whose jurisdiction extended over several counties or districts, and whose sessions were held in such counties or districts alternately; today, a circuit court may hold all its sessions in one county.

circumstantial evidence—All evidence of indirect nature; the process of decision by which court or jury may reason from circumstances known or proved to establish by inference the principal fact.

code—A collection, compendium or revision of laws systematically arranged into chapters, table of contents and index, and promulgated by legislative authority.

codicil (kod′i-sil)—A supplement or an addition to a will.

commit—To send a person to prison, an asylum, or reformatory by lawful authority.

common law—Law which derives its authority solely from usages and customs of immemorial antiquity, or from the judgments and decrees of courts. Also called "case law."

commutation—The changes of a punishment from a greater degree to a lesser degree, as from death to life imprisonment.

comparative negligence—The doctrine by which acts of the opposing parties are compared in the degrees of "slight," "ordinary" and "gross" negligence.

competency—In the law of evidence, the presence of those characteristics which render a witness legally fit and qualified to give testimony.

complainant—Synonymous with "plaintiff."

complaint—The first initiatory pleading on the part of the complainant, or plaintiff, in a civil action.

concurrent sentence—Sentences for more than one crime in which the time of each is to be served concurrently, rather than successively.

condemnation—The legal process by which real estate of a private owner is taken for public use without his consent, but upon the award and payment of just compensation.

contempt of court—Any act calculated to embarrass, hinder, or obstruct a court in the administration of justice, or calculated to lessen its authority or dignity. Contempts are of two kinds: direct and indirect. Direct contempts are those committed in the immediate presence of the court; indirect is the term chiefly used with reference to the failure or refusal to obey a lawful order.

contributory negligence—A legal doctrine that if the plaintiff in a civil action for negligence was also negligent, he cannot recover damages from the defendant for the defendant's negligence.

corpus delicti (kor′pus de-lik′ti)—The body (material substance) upon which a crime has been committed, e.g., the corpse of a murdered man, the charred remains of a burned house.

corroborating evidence—Evidence supplementary to that already given and tending to strengthen or confirm it.

costs—An allowance for expenses in prosecuting or defending a suit. Ordinarily does not include attorney's fees.

counterclaim—A claim presented by a defendant in opposition to the claim of a plaintiff.

court reporter—A person who transcribes by shorthand or stenographically takes down testimony during court proceedings.

courts of record—Those whose proceedings are permanently recorded, and which have the power to fine or imprison for contempt. Courts not of record are those of lesser authority whose proceedings are not permanently recorded.

criminal insanity—Lack of mental capacity to do or abstain from doing a particular act; inability to distinguish right from wrong.

cross-examination—The questioning of a witness in a trial, or in the taking of a deposition, by the party opposed to the one who produced the witness.

cumulative sentence—Separate sentences (each additional to the other) imposed against a person convicted upon an indictment containing several counts, each charging a different offense. (Same as accumulative sentence.)

D

damages—Financial compensation which may be recovered in the courts by any person who has suffered loss, detriment, or injury to his person, property, or rights, through the unlawful act or negligence of another.

declaratory judgment—One which declares the rights of the parties or expresses the opinion of the court on a question of law, without ordering anything to be done.

decree—A decision or order of the court. A final decree is one which fully and finally disposes of the litigation; an interlocutory decree is a provisional or preliminary decree which is not final.

default—A "default" in an action of law occurs when a defendant omits to plead within the time allowed or fails to appear at the trial.

demur (de-mer')—To file a pleading (called "a demurrer") admitting the truth of the facts in the complaint, or answer, but contending they are legally insufficient.

de novo (dē nō′vō)—Anew, afresh. A "trial de novo" is the retrial of a case.

deposition—The testimony of a witness not taken in open court but in pursuance of authority given by statute or rule of court to take testimony elsewhere.

directed verdict—An instruction by the judge to the jury to return a specific verdict.

direct evidence—Proof of facts by witnesses who saw acts done or heard words spoken, as distinguished from circumstantial evidence, which is called indirect.

direct examination—The first interrogation of a witness by the party on whose behalf he or she is called.

discovery—A proceeding whereby one party to an action may be informed as to facts known by other parties or witnesses.

dismissal without prejudice—Permits the complainant to sue again on the same cause of action, while dismissal "with prejudice" bars the right to bring or maintain an action on the same claim or cause.

dissent—A term commonly used to denote the disagreement of one or more judges of a court with the decision of the majority.

domicile—That place where a person has his true and permanent home. A person may have several residences, but only one domicile.

double jeopardy—Common-law and constitutional prohibition against more than one prosecution for the same crime, transaction or omission.

due process—Law in its regular course of administration through the courts of justice. The guarantee of due process requires that every person have the protection of a fair trial.

E

embezzlement —The fraudulent appropriation by a person to his own use or benefit of property or money entrusted to him by another.

eminent domain—The power to take private property for public use by condemnation.

enjoin—To require a person, by writ of injunction from a court of equity, to perform, or to abstain or desist from, some act.

entrapment—The act of officers or agents of a government in inducing a person to commit a crime not contemplated by him, for the purpose of instituting a criminal prosecution against him.

equitable action—An action which may be brought for the purpose of restraining the threatened infliction of wrongs or injuries, and the prevention of threatened illegal action. (Remedies not available at common law.) obligated is not express, but inferred from his conduct or implied in law.

imputed negligence—Negligence which is not directly attributable to the person himself, but which is the negligence of a person who is in privity with him, and with whose fault he is chargeable.

inadmissible—That which, under the established rules of evidence, cannot be admitted or received.

in camera (in kam'e-ra)—In chambers; in private.

incompetent evidence—Evidence which is not admissible under the established rules of evidence.

indeterminate sentence—An indefinite sentence of ''not less than'' and ''not more than'' so many years, the exact term to be served being afterwards determined by parole authorities within the minimum and maximum limits set by the court or by statute.

indictment—An accusation in writing found and presented by a grand jury, charging that a person therein named has done some act, or been guilty of some omission which, by law, is a crime.

inferior court—Any court subordinate to the chief appellate tribunal in a particular judicial system.

information—An accusation for some criminal offense, in the nature of an indictment, but which is presented by a public officer instead of a grand jury.

injunction—A mandatory or prohibitive writ issued by a court.

instruction—A direction given by the judge to the jury concerning the law of the case.

inter alia (in'ter a'lē-a)—Among other things or matters.

inter alios (in'ter a'lē-ōs)—Among other persons; between others.

interlocutory—Provisional; temporary; not final. Refers to orders and decrees of a court.

interrogatories—Written questions propounded by one party and served on an adversary, who must provide written answers thereto under oath.

intervention—A proceeding in a suit or action by which a third person is permitted by the court to make himself a party.

intestate—One who dies without leaving a will.

irrelevant—Evidence not relating or applicable to the matter in issue; not supporting the issue.

J

jurisprudence —The philosophy of law, or the science of the principles of law and legal relations.

jury—A certain number of persons, selected according to law, and sworn to inquire of certain matters of fact, and declare the truth upon evidence laid before them.

grand jury—A jury of inquiry whose duty is to receive complaints and accusations in criminal cases, hear the evidence and find bills of indictment in cases where they are satisfied that there is probable cause that a crime was committed and that a trial ought to be held.

petit jury—The ordinary jury of twelve (or fewer) persons for the trial of a civil or criminal case. So called to distinguish it from the grand jury.

jury commissioner—An officer charged with the duty of selecting the names to be put into a jury wheel, or with selecting the panel of jurors for a particular term of court.

L

leading question —One which instructs a witness how to answer or puts into his mouth words to be echoed back; one which suggests to the witness the answer desired. Prohibited on direct examination.

letters rogatory (rog′a-tō-rē)—A request by one court of another court in an independent jurisdiction that a witness be examined upon interrogatories sent with the request.

levy—A seizure; the obtaining of money by legal process through seizure and sale of property; the raising of the money for which an execution has been issued.

liable—When it is determined that the plaintiff in a civil case has proved his claim against the defendant, the defendant is "liable" (rather than "guilty," as in a criminal case).

libel—A method of defamation expressed by print, writing, pictures, or signs. In its most general sense, any publication that is injurious to the reputation of another.

limitation—A certain time allowed by statute in which litigation must be brought.

lis pendens (lis pen′denz)—A pending suit.

locus delicti (lō′kus de-lik′ti)—The place of the offense.

M

malfeasance (mal-fē′zans)—Evil doing; ill conduct; the commission of some act which is prohibited by law.

malicious prosecution—An action instituted with intention of injuring defendant and without probable cause, and which terminates in favor of the person prosecuted.

mandamus (man-dā′mus)—The name of a writ which issues from a court of superior jurisdiction, directed to an inferior court, commanding the performance of a particular act.

mandate—A judicial command or precept proceeding from a court or judicial officer, directing the proper officer to enforce a judgment, sentence, or decree.

manslaughter—The unlawful killing of another without malice; may be either voluntary, upon a sudden impulse, or involuntary in the commission of some unlawful act.

master in chancery—An officer of a court of chancery who acts as an assistant to the judge.

material evidence—Such as is relevant and goes to the substantial issues in dispute.

mesne (men)—Intermediate; intervening.

misdemeanor—Offenses less than felonies; generally those punishable by fine or imprisonment otherwise than in penitentiaries.

misfeasance—A misdeed or trespass; the improper performance of some act which a person may lawfully do.

mistrial—An erroneous or invalid trial; a trial which cannot stand in law because of lack of jurisdiction, wrong drawing of jurors, or disregard of some other fundamental requisite.

mitigating circumstance—One which does not constitute a justification or excuse for an offense, but which may be considered as reducing the degree of moral culpability.

moot—Unsettled, undecided. A moot point is one not settled by judicial decisions.

moral turpitude—Conduct contrary to honesty, modesty, or good morals.

multiplicity of actions—Numerous and unnecessary attempts to litigate the same right.

municipal courts—In the judicial organization of some states, courts whose territorial authority is confined to the city or community.

murder—The unlawful killing of a human being by another with malice aforethought, either express or implied.

N

ne exeat (nē ek'sē-at)—A writ forbids the person to whom it is addressed to leave the country, the state, or the jurisdiction of the court.

negligence—The failure to do something which a reasonable person, guided by ordinary considerations, would do; or the doing of something which a reasonable and prudent person would not do.

next friend—One acting for the benefit of a minor or other person without being regularly appointed as guardian.

nisi prius (nı' si' prı us)—Courts for the initial trial of issues of fact, as distinguished from appellate courts.

no bill—This phrase, endorsed by a grand jury on the indictment, is equivalent to ''not found'' or ''not a true bill.'' It means that, in the opinion of the jury, evidence was insufficient to warrant the return of a formal charge.

nolle prosequi (nol'e pros'e kwi)—A formal entry upon the record by the plaintiff in a civil suit, or the prosecuting officer in a criminal case, by which he declares that he ''will no further prosecute'' the case.

nolo contendere (no'lo kon-ten'de-rē)—A pleading, usually used by defendants in criminal cases, which literally means ''I will not contest it.''

nominal party—One who is joined as a party or defendant merely because the technical rules of pleading require his presence in the record.

non compos mentis (non kom'pos)—Not of sound mind; insane.

non obstante veredicto (non ob-stan'tē ve-re-dik'tō)—Notwithstanding the verdict. A judgment entered by order of court for one party, although there has been a jury verdict against him.

notice to produce—In practice, a notice in writing requiring the opposite party to produce a certain described paper or document at the trial.

O

objection—The act of taking exception to some statement or procedure in trial. Used to call the court's attention to improper evidence or procedure.

of counsel—A phrase commonly applied to counsel employed to assist in the preparation or management of the case, or its presentation on appeal, but who is not the principal attorney of record.

opinion evidence—Evidence of what the witness thinks, believes, or infers in regard to facts in dispute, as distinguished from his personal knowledge of the facts; not admissible except (under certain limitations) in the case of experts.

ordinary—A judicial officer in several of the states, clothed by statute with powers in regard to wills, probate, administration, guardianship.

out of court—One who has no legal status in court is said to be ''out of court,'' *i.e.*, he is not before the court. For example, when a plaintiff, by some act or failure to act, shows that he is unable to maintain his action, he is frequently said to have put himself ''out of court.''

P

panel—A list of jurors to serve in a particular court, or for the trial of a particular action; denotes either the whole body of persons summoned as jurors for a particular term of court or those selected by the clerk by lot.

parole—The conditional release from prison of a convict before the expiration of his sentence. If he observes the conditions, the parolee need not serve the remainder of his sentence.

parties—The persons who are actively concerned in the prosecution or defense of a legal proceeding.

peremptory challenge—The challenge which the prosecution or defense may use to reject a certain number of prospective jurors without assigning any cause.

plaintiff—A person who brings an action; the party who complains or sues in a personal action and is so named on the record.

plaintiff in error—Appellant party who obtains a writ of error to have a judgment or other proceeding at law reviewed by an appellate court.

pleading—The process by which the parties in a suit or action alternately present written statements of their contentions, each responsive to that which precedes, and each serving to narrow the field of controversy, until there evolves a single point, affirmed on one side and denied on the other, called the "issue" upon which they then go to trial.

polling the jury—A practice whereby the jurors are asked individually whether they assented, and still assent, to the verdict.

power of attorney—An instrument authorizing another to act as one's agent or attorney.

praecipe (pre'si-pe)—An original writ commanding the defendant to do the thing required; also, an order addressed to the clerk of a court, requesting him to issue a particular writ.

prejudicial error—Synonymous with "reversible error"; an error which warrants the appellate court to reverse the judgment before it.

preliminary hearing—Synonymous with "preliminary examination"; the hearing given a person charged with a crime by a magistrate or judge to determine whether he should be held for trial. Since the Constitution states that a person cannot be accused in secret, a preliminary hearing is open to the public unless the defendant requests that it be closed. The accused person must be present at this hearing and must be accompanied by his attorney.

preponderance of evidence—Greater weight of evidence, or evidence which is more credible and convincing to the mind, not necessarily the greater number of witnesses.

presentment—An informal statement in writing by a grand jury to the court that a public offense has been committed, from their own knowledge or observation, without any bill of indictment laid before them.

presumption of fact—An inference as to the truth or falsity of any proposition of fact, drawn by a process of reasoning in the absence of actual certainty of its truth or falsity, or until such certainty can be ascertained.

presumption of law—A rule of law that courts and judges shall draw a particular inference from a particular fact, or from particular evidence.

probate—The act or process of proving a will.

probation—In modern criminal administration, allowing a person convicted of some minor offense (particularly juvenile offenders) to go at large, under a suspension of sentence, during good behavior, and generally under the supervision or guardianship of a probation officer.

prosecutor—One who instigates the prosecution upon which an accused is arrested or one who brings an accusation against the party whom he suspects to be guilty; also, one who takes charge of a case and performs the function of trial lawyer for the state.

Q

quaere (kwe're)—A query; question; doubt.

quash—To overthrow; vacate; to annul to void a summons or indictment.

quasi judicial (kwa'si)—Authority or discretion vested in an officer, wherein his acts partake of a judicial character.

quid pro quo—What for what; a fair return or consideration.

quotient verdict—A money verdict determined by the following process: Each juror writes down the sum he wishes to award by the verdict. These amounts are added together, and the total is divided by twelve (the number of jurors). The quotient stands as the verdict of the jury by their agreement.

quo warranto (kwō wō-ran'tō)—A writ issuable by the state, through which it demands an individual to show by what right he exercises an authority which can only be exercised through grant or franchise emanating from the state.

R

reasonable doubt —An accused person is entitled to acquittal if, in the minds of the jury, his guilt has not been proved beyond a "reasonable doubt"; that state of the minds of jurors in which they cannot say they feel an abiding conviction as to the truth of the charge.

rebuttal—The introduction of rebutting evidence; the showing that statements of witnesses as to what occurred [are] not true; the stage of a trial at which such evidence may be introduced.

redirect examination—Follows cross-examination and is exercised by the party who first examined the witness.

referee—A person to whom a cause pending in a court is referred by the court to take testimony, hear the parties, and report thereon to the court. He is an officer exercising judicial powers and is an arm of the court for a specific purpose.

removal, order of—An order by a court directing the transfer of a cause to another court.

reply—When a case is tried or argued in court, the argument of the plaintiff in answer to that of the defendant. A pleading in response to an answer.

rest—A party is said to "rest" or "rest his case" when he has presented all the evidence he intends to offer.

retainer—Act of client in employing his attorney or counsel; also denotes the fee which the client pays when he retains the attorney to act for him.

rule nisi, or rule to show cause (ni'si)—A court order obtained on motion by either party to show cause why the particular relief sought should not be granted.

rule of court—An order made by a court having competent jurisdiction. Rules of court are either general or special: The former are the regulations by which the practice of the court is governed; the latter are special orders made in particular cases.

S

search and seizure, unreasonable —In general, an examination without authority of law of one's premises or person with a view to discovering contraband or illicit property or some evidence of guilt to be used in prosecuting a crime.

search warrant—An order in writing, issued by a justice or magistrate, in the name of the state, directing an officer to search a specified house or other premises for stolen property. Usually required as a condition precedent to a legal search and seizure.

self-defense—The protection of one's person or property against some injury attempted by another. The law of "self-defense" justifies an act done in the reasonable belief of immediate danger. When acting in justifiable self-defense, a person may not be punished criminally nor held responsible for civil damages.

separate maintenance—Allowance granted for support to a married party, and any children, while the party is living apart from the spouse, but not divorced.

separation of witnesses—An order of the court requiring all witnesses to remain outside the courtroom until each is called to testify, except the plaintiff or defendant.

sheriff—An officer of a county, chosen by popular election, whose principal duties are aid of criminal and civil courts; chief preserver of the peace. He serves processes, summons juries, executes judgments and holds judicial sales.

sine qua non (si′ne kwa non)—An indispensable requisite.

slander—Base and defamatory spoken words tending to harm another's reputation, business or means of livelihood. Both "libel" and "slander" are methods of defamation—the former being expressed by print, writings, pictures or signs; the latter orally.

specific performance—A mandatory order in equity. Where damages would be inadequate compensation for the breach of a contract, the contractor will be compelled to perform specifically what he or she has agreed to do.

stare decisis (stā′rē de-si′sis)—The doctrine that, when a court has once laid down a principle of law as applicable to a certain set of facts, it will adhere to that principle and apply it to future cases where the facts are substantially the same.

state's evidence—Testimony given by an accomplice or participant in a crime, tending to convict others.

statute—The written law in contradistinction to the unwritten law.

stay—A stopping or arresting of a judicial proceeding by order of the court.

stipulation—An agreement by attorneys on opposite sides of a case as to any matter pertaining to the proceedings or trial. It is not binding unless assented to by the parties, and most stipulations must be in writing.

subpoena (su-pē′na)—A process to cause a witness to appear and give testimony before a court or magistrate.

subpoena duces tecum (su-pē′na dū′sez tē′kum)—A process by which the court commands a witness to produce certain documents or records in a trial.

substantive law—The law dealing with rights, duties and liabilities, as distinguished from adjective law, which is the law regulating procedure.

summons—A writ directing the sheriff or other officer to notify the named person that an action has been commenced against him in court and that he is required to appear, on the day named, and answer the complaint in such action.

supersedeas (sū-per-sē′dē-as)—A writ containing a command to stay proceedings at law, such as the enforcement of a judgment pending an appeal.

T

talesman (tālz′man)—A person summoned to act as a juror from among the bystanders in a court.

testimony—Evidence given by a competent witness, under oath; as distinguished from evidence derived from writings and other sources.

tort—An injury or wrong committed, either with or without force, to the person or property of another.

transcript—The official record of proceedings of a trial of hearing.

transitory—Actions are "transitory" when they might have taken place anywhere, and are "local" when they could occur only in some particular place.

traverse—In pleading, traverse signifies a denial. When a defendant denies any material allegation of fact in the plaintiff's declaration, he is said to traverse it.

trial de novo (dē nō′ vō)—A new trial or retrial held in a higher court in which the whole case is gone into as if no trial had been held in a lower court.

true bill—In criminal practice, the endorsement made by a grand jury upon a bill of indictment when it finds sufficient evidence to warrant a criminal charge.

U

undue influence —Whatever destroys free will and causes a person to do something he would not do if left to himself.

unlawful detainer—A withholding of real estate without the consent of the owner or other person entitled to its possession.

usury—The taking of more interest for the use of money than the law allows.

V

venire (ve-ni'rē)—Technically, a writ summoning persons to court to act as jurors; popularly used as meaning the body of names thus summoned.

venire facias de novo (fā'shē-as dē nō'vō)—A fresh or new venire, which the court grants when there has been some impropriety or irregularity in returning the jury or where the verdict is so imperfect or ambiguous that no judgment can be given upon it.

veniremen (ve-nē'rē-men)—Members of a panel of jurors.

venue (ven'ū)—The particular county, city or geographical area in which a court with jurisdiction may hear and determine a case.

verdict—In practice, the formal and unanimous decision or finding made by a jury, reported to the court and accepted by it.

voir dire (vwor dēr)—To speak the truth. The phrase denotes the preliminary examination which the court may make of one presented as a witness or juror, as to his qualifications.

W

waiver of immunity—A means authorized by statutes by which a witness, in advance of giving testimony of producing evidence, may renounce the fundamental right guaranteed by the Constitution that no person shall be compelled to be a witness against himself.

warrant of arrest—A writ issued by a magistrate, justice, or other competent authority, to a sheriff, or other officer, requiring him to arrest a person therein named and bring him before the magistrate or court to answer to a specified charge.

weight of evidence—The balance or preponderance of evidence; the inclination of the greater amount of credible evidence, offered in a trial, to support one side of the issue rather than the other.

willful—A "willful" act is one done intentionally, as distinguished from an act done carelessly or inadvertently.

with prejudice—The term, as applied to judgment of dismissal, is as conclusive of rights of parties as if action had been prosecuted to final adjudication adverse to the plaintiff.

without prejudice—A dismissal "without prejudice" allows a new suit to be brought on the same cause of action.

witness—One who testifies to what he or she has seen, heard, or otherwise observed.

writ—An order issuing from a court of justice and requiring the performance of a specified act, or giving authority and commission to have it done.

writ of error coram nobis (kō'ram nō'bis)—A common-law writ, the purpose of which is to correct a judgment in the same court in which it was rendered, on the ground of error of fact.

Source: Standing Committee on Association Communications, American Bar Association *Law and the Courts.* American Bar Association, Chicago, 1980, pp. 28–36. Reprinted courtesy of the American Bar Association.

Reporting the Complexity of the Statehouse

9

In direct contrast to the stately halls and meeting rooms that characterize most state capitol buildings is the statehouse press room. Seldom quiet, always cluttered, and certainly chaotic, these pressrooms house state government reporters, who, unlike those they cover, seldom have the opportunity to sit in solitude as they consider their next action.

The governor makes a statement, the legislature passes a bill, an agency head announces an investigation, or a special interest group launches a campaign. The reporter gets the information, dashes back to the press room, perhaps getting comments from another official on the way or making a few telephone calls, and keys in the story on a computer. Maybe, just maybe, the reporter will have a chance later for a more detailed follow-up story.

But not now. There's a committee meeting scheduled, the legislature is about to vote, or the editor has insisted on a story from a commission hearing that started fifteen minutes ago.

But sometimes there is a little time. The reporter may work for a larger news organization that has more than one person covering state government. But this usually just creates greater expectations, and all the reporters keep the same pace and produce more copy. Usually the reporter gambles when he or she takes time to do an in-depth story that what he or she misses will be minor.

Consider the near impossibility of covering government in a small state like West Virginia which, exclusive of courts, lists six statewide boards and commissions, thirty-four state senators, and one hundred members of the House of Delegates. Official business generated on these fronts, plus the activities of thousands of employees, is covered for the two capital city newspapers, the *Charleston Gazette* and *Charleston Daily Mail,* by only a few reporters each.

Even granting that most state officials and employees do not provide much news, it's small wonder that statehouse reporters express frustration over their assignment and that they have had to live with considerable criticism.

Lewis Wolfson, a professor of communication at American University, called statehouse coverage the "orphan" of most newspapers. Many editors give it low priority and doubt people will be interested in it, he believes. "It (statehouse coverage) is not like Washington with all those fancy power probes," Wolfson says. "And it's not like local coverage that hits close to home. Usually reporters respond to orchestrated events planned by skilled public relations people."

Because of this, coverage of the legislature is seen as a "duty" by many reporters and editors, Wolfson said, and "coverage" includes simple reporting of what goes on before their eyes, or what is handed to them through press releases or news conferences.[1]

This criticism is common and, in fact, is made by many statehouse reporters themselves. But at the same time, most of these correspondents know the importance of what they are doing. Even if imperfect, their coverage of state government is the only source of public knowledge other than that which comes from officials themselves.

Thus, they go about their demanding business with some considerable satisfaction, checking regularly with those offices or individuals most likely to produce copy and checking with others occasionally. When desirable, they do attend legislative sessions or committee meetings. But more frequently they get those stories by interviewing the person in charge and by concentrating on reporting official actions. While meetings and governmental documents result in considerable news, a more fruitful source of information is interviewing public officials, politicians, individuals such as lobbyists, who have a particular interest in a state action, and other special-interest representatives.

In covering state government, these reporters may occasionally have help. Often a news organization will assign additional personnel during times of peak activity, such as when the legislature is in session. Or reporters on other beats may find their way to the statehouse. That could be an education reporter, a business reporter, a science reporter, or anyone whose responsibilities include state government implications. Some news media will depend on a wire service for some coverage so their reporters may concentrate specifically on selected issues or acts.

However, coverage assistance goes beyond that and often involves more than one building or one city. Many state agencies, commissions, or offices are outside of the capitol building or even outside the state capital. So the statehouse reporter is the cog and other reporters provide the spokes for total government coverage.

The division among these reporters who regularly cover the statehouse tends to be based on traditional government division of authority—the executive, the legislative and the judicial, with the latter often falling to the court reporter. During legislative sessions, some newspapers and broadcast outlets have one reporter in the state senate, another in the house; and a third responsible for the governor, most of the executive branch, and the state budgetary process.

Other news organizations try to organize more on the basis of specialties of the available reporters. Ernie Dumas, who for about twenty years covered the Arkansas statehouse, said three other regular reporters for the *Arkansas Gazette* cover issues on a day-to-day basis that are directly or indirectly "state government" issues.

One reporter, for instance, covers pollution and environment issues, while another may cover education. "But we have tried to avoid just carving all the state government up and saying this is yours, this is mine, and this is somebody else's. Because whoever got the governor's office, for instance, would have a large part of the more interesting news. So we try to share the more exciting side of the capitol beat."

Regardless of the organization, adequate coverage of state government depends most upon the reporter's knowledge of the people in charge, their responsibilities, how they relate to other officials, and how official governmental actions are interwoven with politics. Without such understanding, the reporter will only get trapped in a maze and will accomplish very little.

COVERING THE EXECUTIVE BRANCH

Some reporters may disagree with Ernie Dumas that the more interesting news comes out of the governor's office. Covering a legislative session, with all of its political maneuvering and backroom trade-offs, can be as interesting as any journalistic assignment. But an active governor is involved in every phase of state government, and covering that office can provide a journalistic challenge hard to match. The legislature sets the policy, allocates the funds, and determines the law. But the executive implements the programs and provides year-round, day-in-and-day-out copy for an enterprising reporter.

The Governor Makes News Every Day

A governor wants and needs news coverage. To say "a governor needs us more than we need a governor" is an overstatement. But to say that to be effective, any governor must gain significant news media attention is a truism.

Organization of Ohio State Government

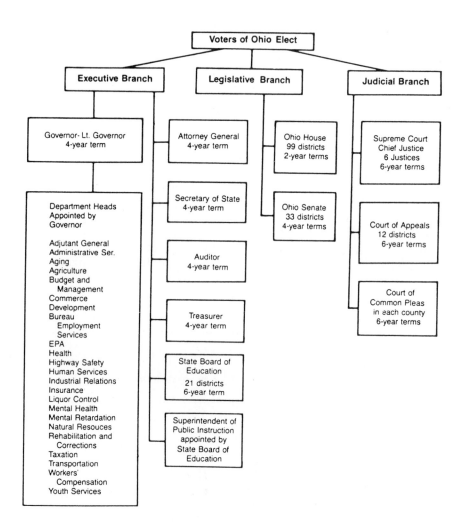

That is not to say, however, that governors will run into the open arms of reporters. Governors and reporters will always have their differences, and that's expected. Even the National Governors' Association admits that any governor will want to earn favorable press coverage, and reporters will see their proper role as informing the public of the facts, whether favorable or unfavorable.

The relationship also depends on individual personalities and experience reporters and governors have had with each other. It is inevitable that at times a governor will be irritated with reporters (and vice versa), and this irritation has been known to reach extremes. Witness the case of former Tennessee Governor Ray Blanton, who once announced that he would no longer answer negative questions by reporters unless they also asked him positive questions.

Whatever the relationship, the governor is news and has to be covered. Reporters may choose to ignore an occasional story, but they have little choice but to persist, and, if necessary, find alternative sources if shut out.

Governors are unusual in American government because their responsibilities cut through traditional separation of powers. While their principal function is executive, they also have legislative and judicial responsibilities that are page-one or top-of-the-newscast candidates.

As executives, governors appoint and remove many state officials. This gives them political clout and often provides them with a means to gain legislative support for programs. They control the overall administration of many of the functions of a long list of state agencies. They are responsible for law enforcement, including the authority over a state police force or highway patrol. They have military powers as commander-in-chief of the National Guard when it is not in federal service. They have significant powers because in most states they draw up and submit a budget to the legislature. Even after the legislature has approved a budget, governors have another means of input through veto power.

Governors also have a wide variety of ceremonial functions that represent vital means of voter relations. Local reporters grumble, but they find themselves following governors to social affairs, dedications of buildings or highways, speeches, welcoming ceremonies for distinguished visitors, and tours to make constituent contact.

The legislative functions of governors are classified under two broad headings: (1) contributing to legislation by proposing or vetoing bills and by delivering special messages to the legislature; (2) calling special sessions of the legislature, sometimes with authority to limit the business of that session to specific matters.

A governor's efforts to obtain legislation are closely watched by reporters because success or failure determines whether the governor lives up to campaign promises or achieves goals set for the administration. The process begins long before specific bills are introduced; it starts when the legislature elects its leaders. A governor's success or failure at influencing political leadership in the legislature is important news. It provides an early assessment of potential success when the governor does make specific legislative proposals.

When governors attempt to gain support by sending or delivering messages to legislators, it is often with the intent that such messages be equally for public consumption. They also meet with legislative leaders and/or members, and they may offer or withhold appointments desired by legislators. If a specific bill has not been passed by the time of adjournment, they may call a special session.

The power, or even the threat, of a veto is an effective weapon of governors in their efforts to control legislation. All governors, except in North Carolina, have the authority to say no to a specific bill and send it back to the legislature. Reporters pay particular attention to the possibility of a veto long before a bill is passed, cover it, and then shift their attention to whether the legislature can muster what is usually a two-thirds vote to override.

In most states, governors may use an item veto to block specific provisions of a bill but allow the remainder to become a law. Often this power is restricted to appropriation bills, although in some states it has broader applications.

Exercise of judicial authorities by governors almost always provides good journalistic copy. Governors serve as a final court of appeal in criminal cases involving state laws, and this may result in the granting of a pardon, reprieve, commutation, or amnesty to convicted criminals.

Normally, governors delegate these powers to a state board, but they will take personal action at times. These actions merit journalistic attention because of their relative infrequency and because the cases tend to be of public interest and frequently involve capital punishment.

The pace of covering a governor's office is cyclical, ranging from frenzy to relative inactivity. Routine stories about minor appointments, state grants, activities of staff members, visits to cities throughout the state, or any of the ceremonial functions almost always are available.

Reporters make it a habit to check with the governor's office early in the day, to get the schedule of activities, and to talk with aides who are assigned as liaisons for state agencies. In general, they try to keep tabs on what is happening and perhaps to get leads on stories to be done then or later.

Major material—developments of state government, activities of state agencies, reaction to legislation, reaction to federal developments, and political activities—generally is obtained through news conferences or interviews with governors, major staff members, or other state officials.

Just how frequently a governor and the reporters should formally get together for specific questions and answers is a source of debate. But even though they want regular gubernatorial news conferences, reporters note that the news conference format has several inherent journalistic problems. It's too easy to control. A governor can structure the content by opening remarks, by giving only friendly reporters an opportunity to ask questions, by informing friendly reporters about which questions would be welcome, by answering (or not answering) specific questions, and by refusing to recognize follow-up questions.

Another problem for competitive reporters is that everyone gets the same information at the same time. The desire for exclusive material is a vital part of reportorial life. And it's a source of considerable irritation to be forced to function in a structure that does not provide individual rewards for individual initiative. In addition to news conferences, reporters also want personal interviews.

Except for an occasional governor who will not cooperate on a consistent basis, governors usually grant these interviews, although a news secretary may first attempt to channel the request to a member of the governor's staff. Governors have their own styles, and reporters quickly learn the basis of how to deal with them. Cleveland *Plain Dealer* reporter Tom Diemer had few problems with James Rhodes, governor of Ohio when Diemer covered the statehouse:

"You couldn't just go right into his office, but if he knew you and if he thought your organization was important to him, it usually was possible to at least get him on the telephone to ask him a question. And usually I could call and get an appointment with him the same day. He understood the media very well."

Press Secretaries May Channel or Block

How much value a press secretary (or news secretary, public information officer, director of public affairs, or whatever the title) is to reporters depends, most of all, upon the individual's relation with the governor and his or her understanding of journalism. Some are integral parts of the decision-making apparatus or at least important advisers. Thus, they know what is going on, and, at times, may even speak officially for the administration. Others have little contact with policy-making, may not know the answer to reporters' questions, or may not be authorized to answer.

Press secretaries, of course, serve two masters: the governor and reporters. In most instances, they serve as a point of contact for reporters who want to see the governor, although as Tom Diemer points out, once a reporter gets to know the governor well, this step often is eliminated. They also arrange news conferences, prepare news releases, and keep the governor informed of news happenings and media reaction to proposed policies. Often they either write governors' speeches or review speech material written by another staff member.

Press secretaries with journalistic background, obviously, are likely to be more helpful. Debra Phillips, former press secretary for Ohio Governor Richard Celeste, spent several years as a reporter on a newspaper before going to work for Celeste. She knew most of the reporters in the Ohio statehouse press corps even before she became press secretary— a fact that made her job both easier and harder.

On one hand, her familiarity with the reporters and their news agencies made her job easier; but, on the other hand, she says, those reporters were quick to blame her if they thought a "friend" was withholding information.

Phillips believes, however, that her years as a reporter gave her an appreciation for the difficulty of the reporters' job, as well as a knowledge of the importance of deadlines and the differing needs of print and broadcast journalists.

A new press secretary very quickly gains a reputation as a knowledgeable straightshooter, as a protective flack, as being removed from policy-making and therefore not authoritative, or as an incompetent. How much reporters will rely on the press secretary for information or comment depends upon their assessment of the person, their professional relationship, and their story. Even if a press secretary is trustworthy and knowledgeable, there are occasions when reporters must still insist on going straight to the governor.

For example, if the governor is in a political struggle with other party leaders or if the reporter is doing a story on outside business activities of the governor, only direct comment is acceptable. If the story involves an assessment of the success of a pet project or, indeed, of the administration, that official assessment must come from the top. If the governor is preparing to move in new program directions, he or she must defend the rationale personally (although it may be possible for a press secretary to provide many of the details of implementation).

In general, if reporters seek specific information, background material, or even a formal statement of policy, a competent secretary may be a reliable source. But the more personal or the more stylistic the information, the more likely the reporters will insist on getting it straight from the person most directly involved.

Other Executive Officials Merit Attention

Governors share executive leadership of a state with several other elected officials who function more or less independently or with appointed officials who serve on a group usually called the governor's cabinet. Journalistic attention given to these individuals depends greatly on their personalities and how they run their offices. But basically, their functions provide the basis for the amount and type of coverage.

As for a *lieutenant governor,* for example, reporters will be interested in stories related to his or her service as presiding officer of the upper house of the legislature; these stories include committee appointments or the progress of specific legislation. Occasionally, news media will notice if the lieutenant governor is acting in the temporary absence of the governor or will report on general political matters that involve the lieutenant governor. However, the position varies in importance from state to state. In states where authority is limited, it tends to gain little public attention unless the individual holding the title has a particularly strong personality or has some special assignment from the governor.

Because the *secretary of state* is the keeper of records and often in charge of state elections and motor vehicle registration, the office can be a source of considerable news material, especially statistical information. In most states, records from the secretary of state provide election results or historic comparisons of the results, provide comparative or up-to-date statistics on motor vehicle registration; or provide invaluable material on corporate ownership, leadership, and operation. Indeed, the material is so varied that reporters other than those regularly at the statehouse often find reason to request information.

The *attorney general* is the state's chief legal officer and principal legal adviser to the governor, to state officials, and to the legislature. The attorney general may get media attention in his or her capacity as the state's chief prosecutor or as the major representative when the state is involved in litigation. Most stories, however, occur when local officials seek an opinion from the attorney general on major legal questions.

Stories involving state financial matters often include information gained from the state *treasurer* or state *auditor.* The treasurer pays the bills and generally maintains all financial records, while the auditor serves as watchdog of state funds. No money may be spent until the auditor certifies that the expenditure is legal in all respects, and this function often results in good journalistic copy. Stories on the financial condition of the state, tax collection figures, tax money use, and efforts to raise additional funds (especially through bond issues) certainly will involve one of these offices, and probably both.

Administrative Agency Coverage is Weak

Maureen Schurr, former senior writer of the government staff of *The State* in Columbia, South Carolina, says coverage of government agencies is often overlooked and seen as boring and overly administrative to many reporters. Nothing can be further from the truth, she believes. "(Agency coverage) is often done by telephone," she says. "Meet the people in these agencies. Find out how they work. Familiarize yourself with what they do. That way, when a crisis develops, you'll know who they are."[2]

In the late 1980s, when a savings-and-loan crisis developed nationwide, many reporters had never before dealt with state agencies and departments regulating the savings-and-loan and banking industries. Consequently, they were at a great disadvantage when trying to describe to their readers the nature of the problem and what could be done about it.

Part of the problem when dealing with state agencies is the complexity of state agency organization. For one thing, there are too many of them. State governments can have as many as 130 separate administrative functions—everything from aging to ethics to natural resources to welfare. And that's only part of the problem. Reporters also face the problem that state governments have outgrown their original capitol buildings, and state agencies are scattered all over the city, and, indeed, all over the state.

For that reason, some people believe that news outlets are becoming more "practical" in covering state government. Wolfson of American University says that many reporters are suggesting to their editors that they shouldn't report extensively on confrontations unless they illuminate an issue. Instead, reporters are examining things like seemingly obscure budget items that, in the long run, can have a great impact on citizens. In short, they are doing more anticipating than reacting.[3]

Maureen Schurr of *The State* advises journalists against what she calls "stenographic" journalism—"they say it, you write it down." Instead, she says, reporters should find out the "why" of legislation and other issues being discussed by lawmakers and agencies.[4]

It is significant that most of the upper echelon officials, even given that they are popularly elected, devote much of their attention to the internal maintenance of state government and have limited contact with the public. At the agency level, specific decisions reach directly into the living rooms and kitchens of the state either through operation of specific programs or through supervision of locally operated programs.

The "people's right to know" is perhaps a cliche, but it's one of truth. They do have a right and a need to know about policies and nitty-gritty operational procedures of statehouse agencies responsible for meeting their needs. Utility regulation, as dull a subject, then hits home. Taxation has become a growing source of public concern and interest. Public education has always been important. What programs provided by the state are of possible benefit to my children? Are we in serious danger because of what the state is or is not doing about environmental protection? Will we have enough energy? Is the state doing anything to protect the consumer? And what about public health? Human rights? Mass transit?

State Administrative Officials, classified by function, 1987

Adjutant General
Administration
Aeronautics
Aging
Agriculture
Air Quality
Alcohol & Drug Abuse
Alcoholic Beverage Control
Archives
Arts Council
Attorney General
Banking
Boating Law Administration
Budget
Building Codes
Chief Justice
Child Labor
Child Welfare
Civil Rights
Clerk of the Court of Last Resort
Coastal Zone Management
Commerce
Community Affairs
Comptroller
Computer Services
Consumer Affairs
Corporate Records
Corrections
Court Administration
Criminal Justice Data
Criminal Justice Planning
Economic Development
Education
Elections Administration
Emergency Management
Emergency Medical Services
Employee Relations
Employment Services
Energy Resources
Environmental Protection

Equal Employment Opportunity
Ethics
Exceptional Children
Federal-State Relations
Finance
Fire Marshal
Fish & Wildlife
Fleet Management
Food Protection
Forestry
General Services
Geology
Governor
Groundwater Management
Hazardous Waste Management
Health
Higher Education
Highway Safety
Highways
Historic Preservation
Horse Racing
Housing Finance
Human Resources
Inspector General
Insurance
International Trade
Juvenile Rehabilitation
Labor
Labor-Arbitration & Mediation
Law Enforcement
Library-Law
Library-Public
Library-State
Licensing (Occupational & Professional)
Lieutenant Governor
Lobby Law Administration
Lotteries
Manpower
Mass Transportation
Medicaid
Mental Health & Retardation
Mining Reclamation
Mining Safety
Motor Vehicle Administration
Natural Resources

Occupational Safety
Oil & Gas Regulation
Ombudsman
Parks & Recreation
Parole & Probation (Adult)
Personnel
Planning
Post Audit
Pre-Audit
Press Secretary
Printing
Public Broadcasting
Public Defender
Public Lands
Public Utility Regulation
Public Water Supply
Public Welfare
Purchasing
Railroads
Records Management
Retirement (State Employees)
Retirement (Teachers)
Revenue
Savings & Loan
Secretary of State
Securities
Small & Minority Business Assistance
Social Services
Soil Conservation
Solid Waste Management
State Fair
State-Local Relations
State Police
Surplus Property
Telecommunications
Textbook Approval
Tourism
Training & Development
Transportation
Treasurer
Unclaimed Property
Underground Storage Tank Program
Unemployment Insurance
Veterans Affairs
Veterinarian

Vital Statistics
Vocational Education
Vocational Rehabilitation
Water Quality
Water Resources
Weights & Measures
Women
Workers Compensation

Source: State Administrative Officials Classified by Function, Council of State Governments, Lexington, Ky., 1987, p. iii.

One aid to reporters when covering agencies is that nearly everyone has an information officer whose job it is to gain coverage. These persons provide the routine news. They send out press releases and call reporters about special programs, qualifications, impending deadlines, application procedures, public hearings, and so forth. Sometimes, the statehouse reporter serves a clerical function and only passes them along, although he or she ordinarily will do some rewriting.

But how a reporter uses the releases depends, of course, on the story, on whether the information officer is trustworthy, on the reporter's competing responsibilities, and on the quality of the releases themselves. Sometimes they should be ignored. Sometimes, on a minor story, the release may be given only a nominal rewriting. Often the reporter will follow up on the release information, will interview the proper authorities, and will write a more comprehensive story, perhaps with a different angle.

But reporters are nervous about depending on information officers. The nature of the information officer's job—to gain favorable publicity for the agency—means reporters have to find the time to make periodic (preferably regular) checks with the agency itself.

That's why Schurr recommends against doing all agency checking by telephone. At least periodically, reporters should visit the agencies and get to know the people who run them, she believes. In addition to finding out what is going on, it also allows the reporter to become acquainted with everyone at the agency—not just the department heads.

Many reporters find out, in fact, that the best sources of information are often individuals at the second and third level. In most instances, these are the people who actually supervise each program, and they tend to know more about the specifics of its implementation. Over a period of time, the reporter will learn who to contact for whatever reason within an agency. The reporter and those sources will develop a sense of understanding and trust. In that way, specific facts and verifications of claims made by a department head literally are at the reporter's fingertips.

Lower level sources also are valuable because they are much more likely to provide the reporter with tips, both on the agency's official activities and on illegal or improper conduct within the agency. Given time constraints and the work load, the statehouse reporter is less likely to uncover a scandal, for example, unless he or she goes looking specifically for something, usually after having received a tip or a leak. It happens sometimes, but that initial information in all probability will not come from the department head. Neither will the document that verifies the information.

In too many instances, a reporter may get very little useful information from department heads, especially those appointed by the governor. Their natural tendency is to shy away from anything but the most positive information, and their job tends to be one of establishing policy rather than implementing a program. The journalistic value of a department head depends upon two things: first, the degree to which the person is secure on the job, which affects how willing he or she will be to speak out; and second, the degree to which the governor's office permits open discussion by department heads.

An elected official is much more likely to be candid than one who owes allegiance to a governor. There are cases, of course, in which the personality of an appointed official is strong enough to override this, but those instances are rare. Many states have administrative policies that stipulate that reporters, especially those with touchy questions, be referred to the governor's office. Many states have policies that reserve announcements of departmental programs and activities to the governor. It takes a stable of ready, willing, and trustworthy sources to overcome these circumstances.

Reporters stress that learning is a combination of formal education and on-the-job experience. Textbooks are helpful in establishing the structure, but only battle scars provide the wisdom to apply that knowledge. Politics functions within a structure, and reporters need both political knowledge and political instinct to give it meaningful perspective.

Combining knowledge and good instinct into political wisdom makes possible the best use of standard journalistic techniques to diminish control by those who would otherwise use the reporter.

Principal among those techniques is the development of a wide variety of sources. The American press was developed originally on the notion that a multiplicity of voices is needed if citizens are to discover truth. Effective political reporters today function on the same notion.

Pressure on Legislators

If the task of reporters were simply to cover legislative debates and votes, the job would be uncomplicated. But it's not. Reporters also must make sense of the very complex pressures placed upon legislators. What individual lawmakers say and how they vote—even what issues come under consideration—may be as much a matter of other forces as the legislators' personal beliefs and ideas. They (and subsequently, reporters) have to cope with demands and efforts to persuade them from a cadre of well-trained and knowledgeable lobbyists from the private world and from agencies within state government. Political interest groups, consumer organizations, the governor, state agencies, the citizens themselves, and local and federal government officials will have access to and hope for impact upon the state legislator.

Many major bills are the products of persons or groups outside of the legislative apparatus, most frequently the governor, who in many states is the dominant force of any legislative session. And most governors will put the total force of their administrative and political leadership behind specific bills or legislative programs.

Closely related is the constant pressure most legislators feel from their political party. While the degree of impact may vary with individual personalities and situations, no legislator is immune. The impact may arise from a particular set of philosophical beliefs; from the practical benefits of patronage, reelection assistance, or committee assignment; or from a strong feeling that members of a minority party must stand together.

Reporters note particularly the impact of a party division in state government. Passing legislation is a simple matter when one party controls both the governorship and both houses of the legislature. When party control is divided, however, the process becomes more complex. Often the intent of legislation is to improve the image of one party or to embarrass the other. For example, a Republican-controlled legislature may pass a bill, knowing that the Democratic governor will be forced to veto it and face public outcry.

The role party politics plays in the legislative process is one that has been criticized by those who forget that it provides the very basis of the American governmental system.

"Almost everything has political implications," says Tom Diemer of the Cleveland *Plain Dealer.* "The reporter has to guard against getting too cynical about that. I guess more than anything since Watergate, the words *political* and *politician* have come to have a negative connotation in many people's minds, and that's bull. Politics is good. Politics is the business of the people. It is true that everything shouldn't be political.

Some things should be done out of ethical motivation. But, at the same time, to approach a news story with a negative attitude because it has a political connection, I think, is a big mistake."

One other important source of influence on the legislator is the constituency he or she represents. The impact, of course, will vary. A number of legislators see themselves more or less bound by desires expressed by a majority of citizens in their district. Others feel that they were elected in a broader sense to vote according to their own intelligence and convictions of what is best for their district. But all will be most interested in passing legislation that has a direct positive impact in their districts, and all will seek local publicity about how well they are serving the interests of their constituents back home.

Legislative Organization

Nowhere is the impact of political parties more evident than in selecting legislative leaders. This is especially true of individuals who will serve as presiding officers of the two houses that make up the legislature in all states except Nebraska, which has one house. In states that have a lieutenant governor, that person usually presides in the senate; otherwise, the senators themselves elect a president pro tempore. All states provide for their lower houses to elect a speaker as presiding officer.

While the specific organization will vary from state to state, like the U.S. Congress, the selection process invariably is political. Often the governor, as leader, is a dominant influence, or the majority party meets in caucus to make the choice. The floor vote is only a formality.

In principle, the presiding officer of each house has authority over discussion and debate on the floor and thus controls the flow of legislation. Equally important, the presiding officer appoints the committee chairperson, committee members, and assigns bills to particular committees.

In addition, each party has its own floor leaders to coordinate activities within each house. Elected by party members, the majority and minority leaders specifically lead the battle for favored bills or against opposed bills. In most states, each is assisted by a party whip.

Another source of some considerable power in the state legislatures, although not as much as in Congress, is those legislators named to chair standing committees. Committees have the responsibility of analyzing bills, of holding public hearings (although these play a much smaller role than at the federal level), of amending them, and of making recommendations to the senate or the house. Committee jurisdiction in most states is defined in terms of its subject matter. Membership (at least in theory) is based on an individual legislator's expertise in that area.

Legislators seek smooth ride for new road taxes and fees

By MARK SILVA and PAUL ANDERSON
Herald Capital Bureau

TALLAHASSEE—Every year more roads clog as Florida's phenomenal growth outstrips the state's ability to pay for it.

The cost is staggering: The average motorist in Florida pays $678 a year in vehicle maintenance and lost work time as a result of deteriorating roads, reports show.

That is what this week's special session in Tallahassee is all about.

With a blend of new fuel taxes, stiff tag fees, rental car surcharges and massive borrowing, legislative leaders hope to pump $5 billion more into Florida's highways, bridges, airports, buses and rail lines during the next five years.

Their success depends on the appeal of a wish list of roads and expressways for lawmakers wary of the price tag. It also depends on Gov. Bob Martinez's flexibility with taxes on the eve of an election year.

Yet even the leaders' ambitious spending plans don't meet half the needs for new roads, bridges and other transportation networks defined by a conservative state Department of Transportation.

"The bad thing about transportation is: When you learn you have a problem, it's too late," says Rep. Mary Figg, D-Lutz, a plan author.

Even as the state builds roads and bridges, existing thoroughfares deteriorate at an accelerating pace. At the DOT's current rate of road work, an agency report shows, one-fifth of the 36,220 lane miles of state highways will be deficient by 1994. And nearly half will be congested by 1998.

With Florida's population growing by 850 people a day, the road situation is worse here than elsewhere:

*Between 1976 and 1986, one national study found, the number of drivers in Florida increased by 33 percent. Nationally, it was 19 percent. The number of vehicles registered here grew 72 percent, nationally 23 percent.

Florida ranks 45th nationally in state and local spending on highways, according to the Florida Chamber of Commerce. The state spends $122 per person on highways, $36 less than the national average, and $2.25 per person on mass transit, $16.16 below the national norm.

Ironically, Florida's rapid development is jeopardizing itself. And business leaders worry about a very real threat of construction bans.

In an attempt to pace growth, the Legislature has required that each county draft rigid rules about where and how much development will be allowed.

The law also demands that counties apply brakes on building wherever roads and other public services are insufficient to serve the development. Feared shutdowns already have appeared on isolated roads in Tampa Bay-area counties, and the state's chief planner expects them in South Florida.

"It could happen in Dade or Broward, where you have particular segments of roads that already are extremely congested, and it's not possible immediately to improve the road," Community Affairs Secretary Tom Pelham says.

Grim prospects

Such bans are a grim prospect for business.

Businesses in Florida already "are losing many millions of dollars in lost productivity and lost time," says Jim Brainerd, spokesman for the Florida Chamber.

Brainerd cites casualities: A Pensacola beer distributor replaces its trucks every five or six years because of added wear and tear on bad roads. The trucks once lasted up to eight years. A Central Florida pest control company bought additional trucks and hired extra crews to meet its schedule because they spend so much time in traffic.

"It's not hard to see what will happen if something's not done," Brainerd says.

Since spring, Democratic legislative leaders and the Republican governor have feuded. Lawmakers have focused on new state taxes and fees. Martinez has promoted more local-option taxation for county road building and multibillion-dollar state borrowing for new toll roads.

Legislators arrive for the three-day session that starts Wednesday with a little of both in mind.

They propose taxes and fees for residents and tourists: A four-cent-per-gallon tax on gas, higher fees for registering all vehicles and additional tag fees for new ones, plus added surcharges on daily car rental.

And they propose at least $850 million and up to $1.2 billion worth of borrowing, issuing bonds for expansion of Florida's Turnpike. That debt must be repaid with already planned increases in turnpike tolls.

State law allows up to 20.7 cents a gallon, 9.7 cents statewide, the rest in local-option levies. The most that motorists pay is 16.7 cents.

Debate over tax

Democratic leaders want the state to collect the extra four cents. Martinez insists that it remain an option only for local governments.

"Unless the tax is a statewide tax, it's not worth having," says Senate Appropriations Chairman Gwen Margolis, D-North Miami.

Breaking this deadlock is the key to success in this week's session because new gas taxes finance nearly half of the new $5 billion road plan.

The portion of the plan financed with new gas taxes and fees, about $3.5 billion, is distributed equitably statewide in a something-for-everyone grab bag of new roads, wider roads and resurfaced roads. It also includes nearly $200 million each for airports, buses and rail lines.

But the turnpike plan remains hard to sell, especially for South Florida lawmakers who see only increasing tolls for their voters.

Turnpike tolls are set to rise statewide until they reach an even six cents per mile on the road, which stretches from South Dade to Wildwood. Tolls now average 4.5 cents per mile.

Several improved South Florida turnpike interchanges are included, but most of the money goes into 75 miles of new toll roads in Central Florida, Tampa and Jacksonville.

The biggest is the Imperial Parkway, a 24-mile beltway around Lakeland. Because it's in the home county of Senate President Bob Crawford and other Polk County lawmakers, it's become known around the Capitol as the Imperial Porkway. In a slip of the tongue, House Speaker Tom Gustafson, D-Fort Lauderdale, recently called the president's home Pork County.

Crawford, D-Winter Haven, defends the parkway as necessary and notes that the county as well as private landowners have donated land to lessen the cost.

For all the new spending envisioned, the DOT recently reported that much more is needed.

This story from *The Miami* (Florida) *Herald,* November 13, 1989, treats two statewide issues that affect nearly every citizen: road repair and taxes. Note how it describes in layman's terms the sources of revenue and the process by which state government works. (Reprinted with permission of *The Miami Herald.*)

It is, of course, to a legislator's advantage to earn appointment as chairperson of any committee, although the importance of committees varies considerably. One that is most significant in all states is the committee given the responsibility of scheduling legislative business. Called by different names—steering committee, calendar committee, rules committee, for example—this group establishes the formal calendars for floor action and determines the rules that govern consideration of bills. Such control of the agenda may be especially important as adjournment draws near.

To assist the committees and the legislature as a whole, many states have established legislative reference services to compensate for the fact that state legislators tend not to have large staffs. Often attached to a state library, such services are available to supply information to legislators on subjects such as possible bills. Some states provide bill-drafting services in which legally trained individuals assist in wording and in ensuring that the bills are not contradictory or incomplete.

The difficulties of conducting all necessary business in the time allocated to a legislative session have prompted many states to establish agencies concerned with planning and advanced preparation of bills. Two types of agencies exist for this purpose, one temporary and one permanent.

In some states, planning is accomplished by interim committees that study proposals on specific subjects and that prepare for the coming session. These committees are bipartisan, are made up of legislators, and are responsible for conducting research on their assigned concerns and for reporting to the legislature when it reconvenes. In this way, members can get a running start on complicated issues.

The other major type of planning body is the legislative council, which is similar to an interim committee except that it is permanent and unrestricted in subject matter. Such councils are more likely to have legislative leaders among their membership. Their primary function is to draft a legislative program for the coming session. Unlike interim committees, they usually have full-time research staff and at times carry their assignments as far as the drafting of specific legislation.

The Legislative Process

Failure by many reporters to understand how state government functions and why it functions that way has resulted in considerable criticism from those who feel the public suffers from bad reporting. Some individuals—particularly those in public relations—believe too many reporters do not understand the nuances of the political process and do not have the energy or ability to learn.

While this attitude may be cynical, a prerequisite to good legislative reporting is first being able to comprehend all of the controls in legislative behavior, the limits of officials' conduct, and the formal and informal rules that establish those norms.

The process through which legislators propose, consider, and pass bills into law is nearly identical in all states and very similar to the federal government. It is a process that is governed by rules with some rules being formal and expressed in writing, and with some being informal and passed along almost as legislative folklore.

The formal regulations, which are as important to reporters as they are to legislators, generally are outlined in published rules of procedure. The 151-page *Rules of Procedure* of the Texas House of Representatives, for example, contains descriptions of the duties and rights of the speaker; it lists employee responsibilities; outlines the jurisdiction of legislative committee; reviews parliamentary rules governing the conduct of debate, amending, and voting; reviews procedures for reconsideration of a bill; reviews requirements for writing and amending bills; discusses procedures for communications from the governor and the Texas Senate; and reviews the work of conference committees.

Understanding such procedural matters, along with standard rules of parliamentary procedure, will get a reporter through some situations that border on the ridiculous. It may not happen frequently, but some reporters will have to cope with the presentation of an amendment that is a substitute for an amendment that is a committee substitute for the original proposed constitutional amendment. Or worse.

It is not really adequate, however, for a reporter to simply refer to a page number in a written manual, for legislatures operate as much by informal rules as formal ones. Tradition plays a large role in the life of state and national legislators, and they must structure their activities according to that tradition. Tradition is much stronger at the national level and at times is a formal rule, but perhaps the best example of such an informal rule is seniority in legislative activities. Likewise, it is often expected in most state legislatures that members will abstain from discussing bills that affect only their sponsor's district, will not criticize or ridicule a member whose constituents are visiting the chamber, and will speak on subjects only when technically or politically informed.

Violation of such traditions by a legislator can result in sanctions, and at times the informal sanctions may be most significant. It is possible, for example, that persistent violators may see their proposed legislation get nowhere or they may not receive a desired committee appointment.

Both formal and informal rules are applied within the larger context of legislative organization and are more or less a standard set of practices through which any bill must pass before it becomes law.

The process begins when any member prepares a proposal in the proper form and submits it to the clerk of his or her house. This may take the form of a bill, which proposes changes in the law, or a resolution, which expresses the feelings of one or both houses. Often such proposals represent more than the desires of a single legislator, and some states have provisions to accommodate joint sponsorship; that is, bills written by committees or bills coming directly from the administration. In an effort to save time, the bill may be introduced simultaneously in both houses. In any event, the clerk assigns a number to the bill, and it is ready for consideration.

Informal considerations enter the picture even at this early stage, giving some bills greater likelihood of passage. A poorly written or incomplete bill immediately begins losing support, and the legislative reputation of the sponsor comes into play. If the bill does not have a direct impact upon their districts, busy legislators will provide more or less automatic support for a proposal from a respected colleague. Even for a significant bill, questioning may be less severe for a bill sponsored by a respected or important legislator.

In some instances, also, a bill that is part of a governor's package or has received the governor's stamp of approval may move more easily through the process. The opposite, of course, is sometimes true within a political context. A Democratic governor will expect Republican criticism of administration bills, and perhaps even real problems if Republicans control one or both houses of the legislature.

As with local governments, a bill or resolution in most states must pass through three readings (two in some instances) before becoming an official legislative action. These readings, however, usually do not involve a full reading of the text. The first often consists of the clerk of the appropriate house reciting the title of the bill and the number assigned to it.

The presiding officer then assigns the bill to the appropriate standing committee. Many political scientists and journalists consider this stage the most important part of the deliberations, and reporters cover committees and subcommittees as closely as time permits. A bill may die right there. But some states have taken away the power of committees to "pigeonhole" legislation by requiring them to report on all bills referred to them or by establishing a rather easy way (generally majority vote) to call a bill out of committee.

Committee deliberations may mean that members simply express their opinions, or they may call for additional research or public hearings. When the deliberations are completed, the committee may recommend to pass or to reject the bill or, in some states, it may amend or rewrite it. The amendment process will vary. Committees of the Texas House of

Representatives, for example, have no power to change a bill. Instead, they recommend amendments to the full house and these become effective only if approved by a majority.[5]

Having survived the standing committee, a bill must then go through one more step before reaching the floor. This is the committee that sets the specific agenda with a legislative calendar. In most circumstances, this is not a serious hurdle. The committee (e.g., Calendar Committee, Rules Committee, Steering Committee) often has the power to kill a bill if it delays placing it on the agenda long enough.

Discussion on the floor of most state legislatures usually is not as complicated as in Congress. Most states do not permit extensive filibustering, although each knowledgeable legislator does have the opportunity to speak. Generally, this discussion and debate is the second reading of the bill, and it is the point at which all members may offer amendments or statements of support or opposition.

As much as possible, reporters will attempt to cover committee meetings and fuller debate on issues of importance. Scheduling often makes this impossible, especially for committee meetings, and reporters simply have to determine their priorities, cover the most significant meetings, and get information on them by talking with the chairperson, committee member or a legislative aide.

With regard to floor debate, reporters know that statements made often are more symbolic than real. The debate often is more for the news media and constituents than for fellow legislators, and it is rare that voting decisions are influenced. To the degree that a legislator does not have a preconceived notion, decisions are much more likely to result from private conversations. That's also how reporters gain their understanding of the prospects of a particular bill.

The major value for reporters in hearing the debate personally is the opportunity it provides for human interest material. Solid information may be rare, but good direct quotes, color, and anecdotes may be abundant.

The vote, of course, is journalistically important, and reporters may make a special effort to be on hand if the issue is significant and if the deadline is near. The voting stage usually is defined as the third reading. Many states require a roll call vote for final passage or, if a voice vote is used, relative ease in insisting that the role be called.

With the exception of Nebraska, a successful bill is then passed on to the other house, where the process is repeated. If the same bill was introduced in both houses, then the one passed will simply be substituted for its counterpart. If the two houses do not agree on the substance and wording of a bill, a conference committee of members from both houses is named to work out the differences. The compromise version is then submitted to both houses and generally is accepted.

Once passed by both houses, a bill will be sent to the governor for his or her signature, and it becomes law after a certain passage of time specified by the state. In the case of a veto, the legislature will enter the picture once more as it considers whether the required number of members (usually two-thirds) will vote to pass the measure over the veto.

Legislative Sources

So where does the information come from? There's nothing unusual about legislative coverage. All of the traditional journalistic methods of collecting information are appropriate. Much comes from observation. Much comes through the journalistic interview. And much—perhaps more than for many other areas of coverage—comes from documents.

For the most part, it's fair to say that legislators want to be interviewed and that they are most likely to cooperate with any request. Of course, there are those who at times will not cooperate, especially if the issue is controversial. But with few exceptions, legislators know that their political careers depend, at least in part, upon keeping their names before their constituents. They know that every mention, every picture, and every television or radio interview may someday be translated into votes. There are times, in fact, when some are so anxious that reporters have to fight them off.

For understandable reasons, the most frequently used sources tend to be the legislative leaders in both houses: the presiding officers, majority and minority leaders, the whips, and the committee chairpersons. After all, these are the individuals who are responsible for guiding legislation through the process. They tend to have a more thorough knowledge and a broader view of the status of a given bill. They tend to be in closer contact with the governor and party leaders. The fact that they have achieved a position of leadership may indicate that they are respected by their colleagues and know how to deal with reporters.

Likewise, administrative leaders who have much at stake in what the legislature does, particularly with regard to funding, are frequent sources of comment. One of the necessities complicating the life of the statehouse reporter is the task of coordinating coverage of the governor's office, for example, with legislative coverage. They are often covered by different reporters who must maintain constant contact with each other to avoid duplication and to ensure coverage of an issue from all important angles.

But, as in all reporting, a problem exists in overemphasizing leadership sources. Statehouse reporters try to develop a diversity of individuals from whom information is gained. For example, it is a mistake to ignore the sponsor of a bill. Presumably, that individual presented the proposal for a reason and has knowledge about the bill's progress and opinions about its importance. Likewise, reporters will seek out legislators whose districts will be directly affected by a bill. If a bill has statewide implications, an effort is (and should be) made to reach a cross section of the legislators, with special effort to avoid overconcentrating on those who simply are most quotable or who have proven themselves dependable in the past.

Legislative aides also may be extremely valuable for factual or background information, particularly for statistics. They are contacted on a formal or informal basis, depending on the confidentiality of the information. Frequently, a legislative aide can provide the reporter with good behind-the-scenes information if mutual trust has been built. Although reporters often go to state agencies for material on a legislative issue, often the same information is more readily available through a legislative aide.

Reporters tend to be cautious in two ways, however, when dealing with legislative aides. After all, those people do work for the legislature and they are in a good position to provide one-sided or otherwise misleading information. First, reporters make sure the original source of the information is clear. They must know if it comes from a state agency, from staff research, or from private research. It must be perfectly clear whether it is legitimate research or whether it is guesswork. Second, reporters are very cautious in selection of persons with whom they deal, especially when information is being provided on a not-for-attribution basis. Confirmation is important always, but especially so until the reporter learns that a source is dependable and trustworthy.

A related information source often is the very group used by legislators for much of their information. Two research-oriented arms of most state legislatures are the legislative reference services and the legislative councils. It is quite possible (and desirable) in many states for a reporter to simply request copies of reports and studies so that he or she can deal with the same sources as the legislators.

Lobbyists provide a controversial, but nonetheless often used, source of information for reporters. Often the most knowledgeable person on a particular bill—perhaps even more than the sponsor—will be the lobbyist who is in the information business. Some lobbyists don't want to talk to reporters. Most lobbyists shy away from public comment. Many define their business as being a private matter between whomever they represent and the legislator.

In spite of that and the fact that information received from lobbyists will be one-sided, most reporters have few problems getting background or technical information from them. But they do so with caution.

Tom Diemer of the Cleveland *Plain Dealer* stresses that his dealings with lobbyists have generally been good and profitable, but they make every effort to check information received.

"Usually I turn to a lobbyist only for technical information," Diemer says. "What's in this bill? And this is something that you can easily check by reading the bill line for line. And I want to know his bias, to know where he's coming from. I want to know why the real estate lobby wants this bill. I expect a bias if he's lobbying for a particular cause. I also want the other side—what they don't want."

Understanding the biases of lobbyists, making those biases clear in news accounts, and accepting the responsibility of checking information can open up a very valuable source of legislative information. Few reporters fear that such information will be inaccurate, although they know it will be one-sided. It's not an unusual journalistic situation, and it's up to the reporters to fill in the gaps by talking to lobbyists with different points of view, by checking with legislators and legislative documents, and by seeking information from state agencies.

FUNCTIONS OF STATE GOVERNMENT COVERAGE

Even though reporters and news organizations will disagree on what their main function might be, few would deny that there are at least three tasks that merit attention. It's easy to express very complicated thoughts in a few words: "To inform the public." "To educate the public." "To serve as a watchdog of government." And it's easy to say reporters should be satisfying all of these important social needs. They should. But reporters face a variety of complications in doing what they feel would be the ideal job of covering state government.

Do they have enough time or space to do it all? No. Even if they could produce the copy, would their editors agree on the importance and give it the play it deserves? Probably not. Does the public want extensive coverage and analysis of everything that is significant about state government? Very doubtful.

That provides the context in which reporters determine their priorities of coverage. They have to make hard decisions about how to compromise on what, in a practical sense, they can do and what, in an idealistic sense, they would like to do.

Most frequently emphasized is the attempt to provide readers with up-to-date information about what government officials or agencies did or said today. News accounts relate the facts: The governor announced this program. The legislature passed that bill. A state department head made this statement. The approach is based on the assumption that readers and viewers can take the individual pieces of information and put them together into an understanding of what state government is doing.

This, of course, involves some selectivity. There's no way any given newspaper or broadcast reporter can cover everything. But stressing an informational approach, news organizations generally paint with a rather wide brush, seeking to cover more than just the most significant issues of the day.

Robert L. Turner, a political columnist for the Boston *Globe,* says that sitting through seemingly boring hearings may not provide a story simply for that day or the next. A reporter who listens closely can get material for possibly another story down the road, or add to project stories he or she is working on.[6]

Similarly, Schurr believes in people-oriented method of coverage: "Let the reader know who is influencing what bill. Are the insurance companies, for instance, pouring money into a senator's 'war chest'?"[7]

In legislative coverage, particularly, many newspapers and the wire services may not spend a lot of time or space on a wide variety of issues, but they will provide a quick summary of the status of legislation being considered. Such a daily roundup of legislative activities in bare bones form gives readers a chance to be at least minimally informed on legislation in which they might be interested.

The information approach to coverage is good, however, only if it is supplemented by broader analyses. Occasionally, information-oriented reporters will seek to assist the readers or viewers by doing a "Sunday piece" in which they put the puzzle together into a more comprehensive package. Many wish they had the time to make the idea behind the "Sunday piece" the norm, to make education a function to which they devote major efforts. They would like to do more on how government works, what role it plays in the lives of the people, and, more specifically, what a given piece of legislation or governmental program is likely to mean to specific individuals.

In spite of the rough pace of statehouse reporters' lives, some time must be found to concentrate not only on what government is doing, but also why it's doing it and how it works. This may take either of two forms: stories on the process of government or stories on how *well* it works. The latter is the watchdog, the adversarial, function of the media. The job of the reporter is to lay out the facts regardless of whether they make government officials look good or bad, effective or bumbling, honest or dishonest.

Reporters are natural adversaries of government officials. At its minimum, the adversary relationship involves a healthy skepticism by reporters in their dealings with government. It means asking the tough questions and persisting. It means asking for proof. It means insisting on getting the answers.

At its maximum, the adversary relationship is a full-blown investigation of possible scandalous behavior by government officials. It means digging out the facts on misuse of public money. It means discussion of an official's personal problem (e.g., alcoholism) that interferes with that person's ability to do the job. It means demonstrating how the governor made a serious mistake that cost the taxpayers money.

But the adversarial relationship must remain constructive. It must be to ensure the proper use of public money, to result in a solution to the alcoholism problem, and to prevent the recurrence of the error.

In short, the adversarial relationship can work to the benefit of the readers, the viewers, the listeners, and the government officials themselves.

NOTES

1. Lewis Wolfson, remarks made during "Covering the Statehouse," annual conference, Society of Professional Journalists, Cincinnati, Ohio, November 18, 1988.

2. Maureen Schurr, "Covering the Statehouse."

3. Wolfson.

4. Schurr.

5. Rules of Procedure, House of Representatives, 66th Texas Legislature, p. 53.

6. Robert L. Turner, "Covering the Statehouse."

7. Schurr.

Getting the Local Story from Washington

10

The impact of the federal government in Washington, D.C., is a major force in the lives of all citizens. It does not matter how far away we live; we can't escape the long arm of the federal bureaucracy on the Potomac River.

How rapidly Americans drive to work depends upon the federal government. The amount they pay in taxes depends largely upon the federal government. The quality of their food, the availability of goods, the location of factories and jobs, the interest paid for loans or received on savings accounts, how well they support themselves in retirement, and the quality of their schools are all influenced by the federal government.

Much of the news from Washington affects every citizen generally. It is national news: The president meets a visiting foreign diplomat, Congress considers a tax program or debates defense spending, or the Supreme Court rules on the right to counsel. There is no doubt about the importance of such events, and news organizations devote attention to these stories. To an increasing degree, they also attempt to get ahead of events by surveying broad policy questions and the underlying issues confronting the country. The bigger newspapers, magazines, and broadcast stations cover such news for themselves; others depend on the wire services and the networks for their copy or feed.

But there's another side of that Washington scene. Much of what happens in Washington has impact on only a particular state, region, or town, and it may be considered just as local as if it were out of the county courthouse or city hall. Since the people in Washington must come from somewhere, they're sometimes hometown people.

THE REGIONAL CORRESPONDENT

The more local these stories, the less likely they will be reported by the news agencies, networks, or big national media. These specific stories are the domain of another type of Washington correspondent, one who seldom gains the celebrity status of his or her national counterparts. Called regional correspondents, or "regionals," these reporters thrive on the Washington story with local importance. They may work in the nation's capital, but their news judgment is based on the wants and needs of Hometown, U.S.A.

While newspapers may provide the most examples of regional reporters, the trend is hardly an exclusively print phenomenon. The structure of broadcasting is analogous to print. The networks (like the "big-gun" print reporters) cover the White House and national/international stories. Most midsized and large TV markets have access to regional broadcast reporters, and the smaller markets seldom have representation.

Television stations often have special arrangements to obtain Washington copy.

Some—particularly those owned by media groups—have their own bureaus. The Gannett bureau in Washington, for example, serves the Gannett-owned TV stations. The Post-Newsweek bureau serves Post-Newsweek stations in Miami, Jacksonville, Detroit, and Hartford.

Others contract for services. Many TV stations make arrangements with Washington-based video news services to provide reports. Video reports are transmitted to clients via satellite, generally in the late afternoon. Some TV markets broadcast several Washington stories a week. For example, the Miami, Florida, market views Washington as an important dateline because top local stories include federal actions regarding immigration, drugs, and relations with Cuba.

Some Washington-based video news services handle several clients, while others—such as Potomac News Service with more than 100 clients nationwide—are huge operations. For both print and broadcast regional correspondents, however, the approaches to cover the stories are similar.

For years, Leo Rennert covered Washington for the McClatchy Newspapers and primarily that chain's *Sacramento* (California) *Bee*. Now as the group's bureau chief, he explains:

"You concentrate on covering the Washington news that is of direct immediate interest to the readers of an area of the country. In our case, it's California, and in particular, northern California. We're not there to do the top story of the day on (the) President . . . or on a Senate filibuster. The wires are going to handle that. What we do go after is the very largely uncovered area of California news which the wires either touch only peripherally or not at all. So 90 percent of our stories are really totally divorced from what's moving on the national lines."

Leo Rennert
of McClatchy Newspapers (McClatchy
Newspapers photo)

Rennert and his McClatchy colleagues focus on the congressional delegation, and this is a prime source of news for any regional correspondent. Such officials are the folks from back home who must return occasionally to talk with voters and gain permission to return to Washington for another term. The regional reporters' task, especially in a large state such as California with two senators and forty-five members of the House of Representatives, can be massive.

The regionals also cover federal agencies, which supervise programs and often distribute money to local areas or regulate local activities. Rennert himself concentrated on the Department of Agriculture and those farm policies that relate especially to cotton and wine production, which are both important products to northern California. When the U.S. Supreme Court makes a decision of particular impact to California, one of the McClatchy reporters is there.

Because of the role Californians play in national politics, Rennert also found himself dealing occasionally with stories of national significance. That diversity is normal. So few of the larger bureaus provide opportunities for reporters to focus on a particular subject or government agency, to become an expert in one narrow area, but most, and certainly the one-person operations, must spread themselves over a wide range.

"A Washington correspondent for an out-of-town paper in a relatively small bureau, a bureau of fewer than five people, is really nothing but a fairly educated general-assignment reporter," says Arthur Wiese of the *Houston Post.* "Because one day you're covering air pollution, then the next day it's the defense budget, and the next day the hometown congressman's re-election problem, and the next day the farm bill."

Lawmaker vows scrutiny of airport spending

By KAREN MacPHERSON
Rocky Mountain News Washington Bureau

WASHINGTON—Congress will scrutinize how each federal dollar is spent on the new Denver airport to ensure the project isn't "gold-plated" at taxpayer expense, a key House member said yesterday.

Rep. Robert Carr, D-Michigan, who is next in line to chair the House transportation appropriations subcommittee, said a compromise approved by House and Senate negotiators Monday makes it clear that the new airport will be built.

But Congress also has "valid concerns about things like the federal contribution, how much money Denver has to cough up . . . and reaching agreement with the airlines," said Carr, who has generally been unsympathetic to the project.

The compromise, worked out in a House-Senate conference committee dealing with transportation funds for fiscal 1990, states that federal funds would pay for up to 30% of the new airport's $1.7 billion first phase—which on paper offers the possibility of as much as $500 million in assistance.

"We've never asked for more than that," said Tom Gougeon, aide to Mayor Federico Peña. "It rules out the possibility that it's going to be very low."

"This is a very definite victory," said John Frew, aide to Sen. Tim Wirth, D-Colo.

The compromise approved by the House-Senate conference committee "begins to lay out a blueprint for how this (sub)committee will treat the new Denver airport over the next few years," Carr said in an interview with the *Rocky Mountain News*. Much will depend on Denver's relationship with its two major airlines, United and Continental.

"If Denver and the airlines cannot come to some agreement, we will have to review the matter very, very carefully. . . . I don't want (the compromise language) to be a signal to my good friends in Colorado that they don't have to deal with the airlines," Carr said.

Denver airport director George Doughty said the city welcomes congressional scrutiny of the project.

"We've got a very lean and mean budget. We've always had that. . . . The airport is going to be anything but gold-plated. But it is going to be functional and it is going to solve the problem," Doughty added.

Rep. David Skaggs, D-Colo., who worked with Carr on the compromise, said he thinks the Michigan Democrat "now has a feeling of some ownership in what we're doing."

"He quite rightly . . . wants to make sure that the project is as careful of public dollars as it can be," Skaggs said.

The compromise also directs the transportation secretary to consider potential cost-savings such as terminal size, the number of runways and gates, airport parking concourses, the use of revenues from the sale of Stapleton and making the state and city financially responsible for cost overruns.

The entire transportation funding bill now must go back for a vote in the House and Senate before being sent to President Bush.

The next step for the new airport is for the federal government to issue a "letter of intent" committing itself to a certain amount of funding for the project.

But Carr noted that the letter only binds the federal government to a "certain level of budget requests"—not actual spending, and said that Congress still can exert considerable leverage over the project from year to year.

Doughty agreed that the letter of intent, which may be issued soon, "is nothing more than a moral commitment—if that," but noted that it is important to the city "as a planning tool and something for the financing community to look at."

Federal dollars are spent on local projects, and important local stories often are developed from Congressional allocations. In this story, the Washington correspondent for the *Rocky Mountain News* discusses congressional plans for expenditures for a new Denver airport. (Reprinted with permission from Scripps Howard News Service.)

The method is similar to that of a city hall or statehouse reporter. It's still a matter of developing sources by maintaining frequent contact, keeping track of what's happening, attending meetings, reviewing documents, and conducting interviews. Even some of the stories themselves may be the same as they were back home.

Part of this may be because the correspondents often determine their own stories. With some exceptions, most get little more than an occasional assignment from editors back home or a request from another reporter for information on the federal component of a story.

Maintaining home contact, of course, is a major advantage to the Washington-based print or broadcast reporter. Problems do arise, however, because knowledge of local markets varies, especially for broadcast operations. In some cases, reporters are promoted to Washington from the hometown operation. In other cases, they are hired because of their Washington knowledge and have little or no knowledge of the home market.

"I witnessed a TV reporter on Capitol Hill assigned to get video 'bites' for three markets—one on the West Coast, one in Tulsa, and the third in Florida," says Ken Klein, Press Secretary to Florida Senator Bob Graham. "News desks from those three markets had forwarded questions to the same Washington-based news service, and the reporter had written the questions on a small piece of paper. With the camera rolling, the reporter asked a senator from Florida the question relating to Tulsa."

But not all problems of connecting Washington with the home base are those of the reporter. The regionals often complain about some editors' attitudes toward their Washington offices. At times, this surfaces in what the reporters consider ridiculous story assignments, but the attitudes are more likely to emerge in the treatment of stories from Washington. The complaint is that some editors view the Washington office as a supplementary wire service, not as an extension of the local staff. This results in downplaying of the regional's Washington copy.

The problem, the correspondents say, is that few editors back home have Washington experience and thus have little understanding of what a regional reporter can and cannot reasonably do. Another complaint is that editors at times are provincial in their approach to news and uninformed about national issues.

But reporters also depend on those editors to help them avoid the Washington trap of losing touch with the rest of the world. It would be very easy, over a period of time, to begin to consider Washington the world and to lose the local perspective.

"I think the selection at the outset of a regional reporter is critical from the newspapers' standpoint," Rennert says. "I think maintaining local interest is almost a direct function of your own background as an individual, your own experiences as an individual, your own ties to that area, and your professional background and experience in the newspaper field. If you have a regional beat in Washington and you have only peripheral ties to the area you cover, then the temptation to drift away and become part of the Washington scene, the chance to catch the (Potomac) fever is going to be greatly enhanced."

Once on the beat, most reporters return to home base occasionally and call frequently to discuss coverage within the organization and with possible local sources—the mayor, the governor, and the heads of state agencies. This helps to retain the local perspective and strengthen understanding of local attitudes and expectations about federal policies and programs.

Maintaining such contacts is particularly important since governments are becoming so much more intertwined. Especially when dealing with federal money for specific purposes, reporters must cope with two or three layers of government. To handle these kinds of stories, they need the full assistance of the home office and contacts with officials in all layers.

PATTERNS OF COVERAGE

Among the guidance needs by the Washington regional reporter is full agreement and understanding of what is expected. One person can cover only so much ground, and it is invaluable that all parties to the arrangement know the approach to be taken, the types of stories to be emphasized, and the people on which to concentrate. At the broadest level, this involves some combination of three types of coverage.

One type of coverage is what may be called the *follow-the-legislation* approach. Stressing the nuts and bolts of congressional action, reporters tell the status of legislation, the positions taken, and the roles and votes of hometown members. This type of coverage may result in perhaps three or four 10-paragraph stories daily.

Proponents of this approach say readers, viewers, and listeners are most interested in the day-to-day activities of Congress. They want to be in touch with what's going on. So reporters spend most of their time picking up specific pieces of information and dutifully passing them along. Only occasionally do they take a somewhat broader, long-range look and write a longer evaluative story or "think piece."

It's rare that any reporter avoids the requirement of doing some event coverage. The breaking news must be provided even if the focus is more issue oriented. This second coverage philosophy may be labeled the *project approach.* In it, the idea is that, given some release from event coverage responsibilities, the reporter has more time to study the issues, perhaps even specializing to a degree. This may give wider perspective and more meaning to the news organization's coverage.

At times this approach may assume the appearance of national coverage, but the key lies in careful selection of topics of local interest or value. The stories often get their local flavor through use of examples or sources from back home. Quantity expectations will vary. Some reporters may be expected to provide a major event story once a week, usually in the form of Sunday stories. Others may be given more time to produce a major piece every two to four weeks.

As a kind of hybrid form (although journalistically standard), some news organizations have particular interest in more *personal* stories about government leaders, that is, variations of the hometown-boy-or-girl-makes-good theme. When Geoff O'Gara was a regional correspondent for States News Service for the Charleston, West Virginia, *Gazette,* he knew a strong focus of his work was expected to be West Virginia Senator Robert C. Byrd, former Senate Democratic leader.

"It (the *Gazette*) is less interested in what Byrd has to say about Panama or his positions on national issues," O'Gara says. "But it is very interested in anything that illustrates his kind of personality and the way he handles his position. So whereas the *Gazette* may not want an issue story on something like the labor law, it does want a Byrd story on how he handles the labor law. He's from the area, and readers like to know how he's doing."

This approach is more than reporting about the personalities of government. It's a methodology that seeks to present federal business in a human way. The stories are about individuals, but they also shine through that individual's role to, say, the legislative process of a particular piece of legislation.

"What I like to do," says Bill Choyke, former regional reporter for the *Dallas Morning News*, "is take a situation in which an individual is involved in legislation, call several others who have been following that legislation for special interest groups and say, 'How is Joe Hovinchrogin doing? How's he been voting? Has he been on the right side or the wrong side of the issue?' Then I would go to a committee meeting, watch him perform and talk with him about what I've learned.

"Too much writing is done, both back at the local level and in Washington, based on just what was said at meetings without making those follow-up phone calls. There's too much ink in terms of what individuals say and not what they do."

SOURCES CLOSE TO CAPITOL HILL

Potomac River water apparently infects people with a fear of being quoted by name, and thus attributing a quote to someone becomes one of the most difficult aspects of dealing with Washington sources. From cabinet secretaries down to the lowest congressional staffer, reporters find individuals who open their conversation with "Don't quote me" or "This is for background only."

Some reporters won't take anything off the record, and others thrive on unattributed quotes and "informed sources" statements. But a reporter just starting to cover Washington, either by phone or in person, must be prepared to deal with the problem. The trouble, of course, is that Washington reporters for too long have let officials dictate interview terms, so that it's difficult for a single reporter to buck the tradition.

The best approach to the problem is the same in Washington as it is back home; reporters make it clear at the outset of the interview that they want to quote the source. If that source objects, they then try to work out the best possible deal. How much the reporter cooperates depends on how desperate he or she is to obtain the information or comments from that particular source.

COVERING THE CONGRESSIONAL DELEGATION

To concentrate on the Washington news of greatest interest back home, it makes sense to key in on those decision makers who are from back home. In Congress, that's the local delegation. This helps make elected officials more answerable to their public, and it provides a hometown flavor to issues of importance.

News from Washington generally is of decisions made and problems attacked rather than events occurring, and that fact highlights development of sources and contacts. Regional reporters seldom have time regularly to attend floor sessions or committee meetings, and few members of Congress are likely to hold regular news conferences. Thus, the reporter must develop a strong list of trustworthy sources of information: who is responsible for what and which persons are most likely to talk under what circumstances.

Part of this is understanding the system. Another part is a deliberate effort to cultivate possible sources of information.

"I probably take somebody to lunch at least three times a month," says Arthur Wiese of the *Houston Post*. "It may be a senator's press secretary. It may be a congressman's administrative assistant. It may be a staff member on a committee. It may be a visiting politician or a congressional candidate. It's a good business investment. You may not get a story, and you usually don't out of the conversation, but the next time you pick up the phone and you need something fast or, more important, you need someone to level with you, that personal relationship just pays off."

Getting to know members of Congress as possible news sources is not difficult because of the obvious: The information process is a two-way street. Members of the House of Representatives who must face election every two years are especially anxious to get publicity.

"Most members—whether they are senators or house members—are going to be interested in what's going back to their people," says Rep. Clarence Miller of Ohio's mostly rural Tenth District. "And there's a limit to how far the *New York Times* and *Wall Street Journal* can help. It's what's in the newspaper locally that conveys a message about our thinking to the people."

That means the welcome mat usually is out for reporters, although the Congress member will attempt to structure the conversation to his or her benefit. Predictably, there will be times when an individual member will be less likely to want to talk, especially in the face of a possible negative story.

As a general rule, however, reporters find staff members cooperative in discussing factual information and the role of the representative or senator in specific matters. Reporters soon learn the bases upon which staff members will cooperate, whether information may be attributed, and the circumstances under which is defined as background or off the record. They learn which staff members are capable and with whom they can effectively work.

"I've learned that there are capable and intelligent people on these staffs who are concerned and really try to do a job," says Frank Aukofer, Washington bureau chief for the *Milwaukee Journal.* "Regardless of their politics, and I don't judge politicians by their politics but by how well they present their viewpoints. They all work hard, and they all have a high degree of integrity and do a good job representing where they are coming from. That's all you can ask. They're a good bunch to work with, to trust (which helps), and you soon learn who the people are you can get information from quickly and usably and the people who will bog you down with all sorts of detail you don't need. So after a while, you get your sources, and people begin to call you."

In effect, every member of the staff of a representative or senator has a public relations function. The goal of every employee is to enhance the boss's image. They're therefore willing, and reporters—especially those in small bureaus without clerical or library help—find themselves taking frequent advantage of the opportunities they provide.

An understanding of the PR function of staff members, however, leads good reporters to a wariness about relying on them too heavily or exclusively. They often have vested interests and can guide a reporter to the wrong source or to a source who will merely confirm one point of view. Given an understanding of that fact, reporters can deal effectively with staff members who function under a variety of titles carrying differing responsibilities but who are of several basic types:

Administrative assistant. As the Congress member's top aide, the administrative assistant is involved in nearly everything, knows what is going on, performs a variety of direct services, and thus usually is the best staff source of information. Almost always empowered to speak for the record, he or she is readily available to provide background information or to see that the member of Congress is available. This is especially true if the information being sought concerns a party political matter. The reporter who develops a working relationship with an administrative assistant stands a much better chance of having direct access to needed information.

News secretary. All members of Congress do not have a staff person with this title. But all have someone who serves as the liaison with reporters and coordinates production of news releases, columns, and other statements. At times this latter responsibility and answering queries cover the job description. Depending on how much authority news secretaries are given, reporters may depend upon them as much as an administrative assistant or may confine their contact to minor points.

Case worker. In general, this is a person assigned to work on a particular type of issue, especially one which provokes constituent mail. Often a specialist in a problem area such as veterans' affairs or Social Security, the case worker is a good source of specific professional information.

Legislative assistant. This job is used in varied ways, but it generally indicates an individual assigned to work with specific pieces of legislation. Thus, a legislative assistant to the sponsor of a bill, for example, would be a strong source of information on that bill.

Committee staff. Aides who work for congressional committees tend to have stronger educational backgrounds than those who make up Congress members' personal staffs. Many recently graduated lawyers, for example, may use a committee staff position as an entry into government work. They may be more professional than political and thus serve well as sources for specific legislation and other committee work.

Staff willingness to cooperate, of course, is both a blessing and a curse for reporters. It is, on the one hand, valuable to have resources for quick responses to questions. It's helpful to receive reports or even news releases from the Congress member's office as background or starting points for stories. That makes it more possible to cover the territory expected. But there is the very real problem of becoming too dependent on the releases, the reports, and the ready-made comments. Like their counterparts at city hall, county courthouse, or school system office, harried Washington correspondents at times do yield to the temptations of making their tasks easier. This, when combined with the fact that most news organizations are not represented in Washington, creates a wide boulevard down which congressional staffs drive with glee.

"Traditionally, political coverage in the district has been a case of self-generated news, the individual candidates or elected representatives going to the news media rather than the news media coming to them," says Bob Reintsema, former staff assistant to Rep. Miller. "Principally this is because of the limited size of most of the media operations in southeastern Ohio. The pattern is changing somewhat, given the increasing affiliation of those media operations with state and national news services, but for many of the smaller operations, it's still the standard operating procedure."

That "self-generated news" comes in three standard packages: the news release—and its modern broadcasting equivalent, film, video, and audio tapes—all of which too often are used without indication that they are less-than-true news presentations; the weekly column, used especially by small papers, under the byline of the Congress member; and the visit to news organization offices when the official is back in the district.

Members of Congress are particularly well equipped to fill any need of both print and broadcast journalists. Recognizing the possibilities created by gaps in local-market coverage, they have developed the staffs and the means of filling those gaps.

Both the House of Representatives and the Senate, for example, have available state-of-the-art TV and radio studios, enabling members of Congress to talk "live" with broadcasters at home. In addition, both political parties offer broadcast services to members of Congress. Video crews employed by the parties cover committee hearings, interview members of Congress, and cover news conferences. These party-sponsored video teams regularly send video reports via satellite and at no charge to local TV stations. Some TV stations, especially in larger markets, decline to broadcast video reports transmitted by political parties, but other stations welcome free video from Washington.

Likewise, both the House and the Senate are equipped with state-of-the-art print facilities, including color presses. Some offices use computer graphics equipment to enhance printed material that is mailed to constituents. It is common for members of Congress to prepare a typeset column for distribution to weekly newspapers and smaller dailies.

Indiscriminate and widespread use of this material across the country worries some people who fear most of the print and broadcast news media have permitted themselves to become "propaganda arms" of Congress.

For example, among the most common stories passed along from congressional offices is that a particular member has sponsored a certain piece of legislation. The fact is that very few members ever sponsor legislation that gets passed, says John Felton of *National Public Radio* who adds: "Except for those who chair committees, the best most members can do is sponsor an amendment in committee or on the floor. Most bills have half a dozen or so 'cosponsors' who usually are fellow committee members of the true sponsor but who have little to do with actual passage."

Yet, when Congress members announce in a news release that they have cosponsored legislation, that message gets passed on with little explanation by news media. That's why the critical comments strike home, particularly with small newspapers and broadcast stations, but larger news organizations are not immune to the problem.

For those who are there, however, it's a constant battle to meet the demands from back home without falling back on unrestricted use of news releases and other staff-prepared material. The most effective use of news releases, of course, assuming the story is valid, is as a beginning. The reporter who understands the Washington scene may make a few telephone calls and expand a one-sided release into a legitimate, balanced story.

COVERING THE FEDERAL BUREAUCRACY

There's nearly universal agreement on one point: The federal bureaucracy—the complex and confusing maze of agencies, bureaus, commissions, divisions, offices, branches, sections, and units—is inadequately covered. Reporters who attempt to do it, government officials themselves, and media critics point to thousands of stories that are important to the public that remain buried somewhere in the bureaucracy.

News attention is most likely to be devoted to an agency during an emergency. The potential disaster at a nuclear power plant will put the journalistic spotlight on the Nuclear Regulatory Commission. The collapse of a cooling tower will vault the Occupational Safety and Health Administration into the headlines.

But the journalistic value of governmental agencies is more than regulation and disaster investigation. They represent an almost inexhaustible source of information on almost any subject. Federal agencies are full of experts who are willing to talk about their special subject. The Department of Commerce has experts on the history and technical details of every industry in the country. The Department of Agriculture has experts on every crop. The Department of Education has people who know about the latest research in teaching methods. They're as close as the telephone. They're listed in the directory. But they're seldom called unless some big event captures the attention of journalists.

Andrew Alexander
of Cox Newspapers (Cox Newspapers photo)

Reporters know the problem, they know the reason for it, and they know that many reporters are trying to do something about it. Take, for example, Andrew Alexander, former regional correspondent and now foreign editor for Cox Newspapers, who attempted to expand the attention he gave to federal agencies. In fact, he said, he reached the point that at least half of his regular checks were with such agencies. He believed such attention was necessary because the bureaucracy continues to grow in size and power, with more and more agency officials making decisions that have a direct impact on local jurisdictions.

In spite of such efforts by Alexander and others, many regional reporters will admit that part of the problem is the desire of some reporters to gain journalistic prominence by covering news that will get front-page or top-of-the-newscast play. They also will list more fundamental journalistic problems. The regional reporters in small bureaus struggle daily with inadequate time to find stories buried in a very complex system. Government bureaucrats, ambitious and concerned with protecting their flanks, often are uncooperative with any but the representatives of the nation's most prestigious news organizations.

Unfortunately for the regional reporter representing a smaller news organization, the mentality in Washington is geared to maybe eight or ten newspapers and the major broadcast networks. Many federal officials have developed specific lists of journalists for whom they are frequently available. Other reporters play constant catch-up and find few opportunities to be among the first to gain access to major stories. Among the few ways smaller news organizations may break this cycle is a situation in which a specific Congressional delegation is active on an issue, and bureaucrats see an internal advantage in dealing with reporters from those delegations' districts.

Alexander suggests that one solution to this problem is persistence—to call the official at home and to keep calling, sometimes until very late at night, or until he or she comes to the phone.

"I once did that to a guy who worked at the White House," he says, "and finally got him about 11:30 P.M. The next day he called me and said: 'Look, I'll return your calls. Just don't call me at home again. It drives my wife crazy.' From that point on, he's always returned my calls. Promptly."

To the regional reporter's problem of inadequate time there is no real answer except, perhaps, a change in priorities. It may be that additional coverage of the federal bureaucracy would be of more benefit back home than many of the stories being written now. Aside from the problem of finding the time, the answer is good basic journalism. It's overcoming the complexity by putting in the kind of effort and study required to understand the agencies' functions and how they work.

"Reporters only cover a particular segment of what has become a vast and particularly impressive bureaucracy," says Gene Smith of the Topeka, Kansas, *Capital Journal.* "No one individual can even hope to do an in-depth or even decent day-in-and-day-out job of covering all of the federal government. So you have to pick and choose. In addition to that, to do a reasonably competent job of covering a particular branch of government, it takes considerable background and understanding in that field. It takes a couple of years of on-the-job training before reporters can expect to become even reasonably competent."

It also takes sources. On the other hand, there's the top person, who often is more open than "those 9 million people who 'know just what the boss wants,' " Smith says. But, on the other hand, it's deliberate cultivation of the middle-level bureaucrats who do the day-to-day work and therefore know more about the specific workings of the agency. Only a relationship of trust and respect can overcome their natural inclination to protect themselves through reluctance to make comments to reporters.

Once that trust is established, however, and the reporter knows individuals who can be called at any time, the job of covering the agencies becomes more manageable. It's not possible, or even necessary, to contact every agency every day. It's regularity of contact that helps ensure that individuals will be willing to provide factual information, tips, or sensitive information.

The more a reporter develops good contacts, the more a reputation for honesty and dependability spreads within an agency. That, in turn, opens up additional avenues. And if the reporter is on good terms with the congressional delegation, a call to a senator or representative also may produce enough pressure on uncooperative agency officials to ensure at least some grudging cooperation.

Sources are more than people. One of the best sources to the federal bureaucracy, at least as a starting point, is the *Federal Register*. Published five days a week, it contains information on regulations, grants, deadlines, hearings, and progress reports on federal agency activities. Reporters who find the time to monitor the *Federal Register* regularly find good local stories about the federal bureaucracy and more than they can handle.

WASHINGTON COVERAGE BY TELEPHONE

No news coverage by telephone equals having a reporter on the scene. Granted, even reporters in Washington get much of their information by calling sources across town, but only as a supplement to face-to-face conversation or witnessing an event. To be wholly dependent on telephone interviews is to run the constant risk of missing stories and information because the source is not available at the proper time or does not return calls.

If the regional reporter in Washington has a problem getting officials to call back, that would be magnified for the unknown reporter from a distant city. It's difficult to develop the kind of personal relationships and the kind of trust that leads to sharing of confidential or sensitive information. If a reporter from afar is suspicious about information received, confirmation by WATS line is not easy.

But that's not the question. It is obvious that most news organizations will not have a correspondent in Washington. One does not have to agree with the decision to recognize that many publishers and editors are unwilling to pay the $30,000 to $60,000 a year required to support a full-time person or even $100 a week to share an individual.

The questions are: What can the reporter back home do to broaden coverage of local news that has federal angles? Why don't reporters provide readers, viewers, and listeners with some federal news? Is it not better to attempt the job, given the alternatives of using wire stories and one-sided news from a Congress member's office?

Using all available resources, including the telephone, simply is good reporting. A story with a federal angle should contain information from federal sources. Stories involving varying points of view should utilize several sources, even if some of these sources are miles away. Evaluation of a public official's performance should not be based exclusively on information from that official.

Even home-based reporters for news organizations that have Washington correspondents should form the habit of making their own calls to Washington for the federal information they need. The regional correspondents can provide that service, of course, but a local reporter usually would be better off talking with an agency official rather than having the questions put to the same official secondhand by the correspondent.

Thus, there are a number of circumstances in which local reporters, however small the news organization, should be on the telephone seeking additional information:

1. When the reporter knows of something scheduled that involves local persons or that could have significant local impact. Such initiation of coverage would be appropriate, for example, if the House of Representatives were scheduled to vote on an important bill or amendment sponsored by the local member or if a federal agency were considering a local application for a grant.

2. When a news release is received and involves anything more than straight factual information such as the schedule of the Congress member's next visit to town. Follow-up telephone interviews to broaden or change the focus of the story should be routine. This may be a call to the Congress member, to congressional leadership, or to a federal agency.

3. When a wire service story makes inadequate reference to the local impact of a federal action. It is, of course, possible to contact AP or UPI for a specific story or additional information, but the success of such a request may be spotty or slow. A reporter who personally makes the federal contact has control over the specific questions asked and knows what and when information is available.

4. When a reporter is writing a local story that has a federal component. This may be spot news or issue oriented. A story on local law enforcement, for example, could be greatly enhanced if the reporter had national statistics with which to make comparisons. A story on local educational expenditures, on the need for a new local sewage treatment plant, or on a new bridge all could be more meaningful with material showing how the local situation fits into the national picture.

As initial steps in accomplishing these goals, a news organization must know who the sources are and get to know those sources well enough to cooperate in telephone coverage. Part of the answer lies in the availability of up-to-date reference material, especially directories. It is quite possible to make a blind call to a federal agency, to ask for "someone" who could provide information and to get a story. But it's at least easier, usually more successful, and certainly quicker to know the right person.

Knox drops 17 rungs
on census ladder
City now 94th; officials cite annex inability

By RICHARD POWELSON
News-Sentinel Washington bureau

WASHINGTON—Knoxville has slipped from the 77th largest
U.S. city in 1980 to 94th largest last year, a U.S. Census Bureau
study says.

The drop is explained by a lack of annexation, said Sue
Adams, executive director of the Metropolitan Planning
Commission.

"Knoxville has been totally stymied in its annexation efforts,"
Adams said.

Current law makes it difficult for Knoxville to annex suburbs
and grow, she said. "I think we need to change the law."

The city of Knoxville recently lost a court battle to annex West
Knoxville residential areas with about 10,000 people, spokesman
George Korda said.

The Census Bureau study estimates that Knoxville's
population was 172,080 as of July 1, 1988, which is less than
census figures in 1980—175,045—and in 1970—174,587.

The study says New York City remains the nation's largest city
with 7,352,700 residents. Los Angeles is second with an
estimated 3,352,710.

The other major Tennessee cities did not show as large a drop
in the Census Bureau's estimated rankings.

Memphis was kicked down from 14th to 15th largest, and
Nashville dipped from 25th to 26th. Chattanooga dropped 12
rungs—from 87th to 99th.

Randy Arndt of the National League of Cities said population
figures are listed as one of several factors in apportioning cities'
federal funding. He said a city with little or no population
increase can expect, over several years' time, to see more and
more of its federal funds going to the growing cities.

In the early 1960s, Adams said, it was easier for Knoxville to annex suburbs to the west, north and south. In more recent years, however, neighborhoods opposing annexation have been able to take the city to court. She said juries routinely reject city efforts to annex over residents' objections.

Adams said a study shows that about 75 percent of those living in Knoxville suburbs proposed for annexation work in Knoxville, but they oppose annexation.

The U.S. Census Bureau provides important information about every town, county and state in the country. National news agencies provide broad summaries, but it is up to local news organizations, in this case the Knoxville (Tenn.) *News-Sentinel,* to apply specific information to the local setting. (Reprinted with permission from Scripps Howard News Service.)

That's a problem. Certainly, over a period of time a reporter can get to know sources by telephone. Many are successful at it. They have to be. But a news organization dedicated to getting the local story from Washington could reap long-term benefits by sending a reporter for a short stay in the capital. The reporter or editor would then have the opportunity to know the individual sources most frequently called and, more important, to have them know of the news organization's interest in getting the federal story.

The major alternative, of course, is taking advantage of periodic visits by the federal officials. The most frequent visits will be by members of Congress and their staffs, and there's no question that they will be interested in taking the time to get to know local reporters. Occasionally, however, other federal officials may get into the area, and news organizations should seek time for conversations beyond normal news coverage.

The congressional delegation provides the key to getting local news out of Washington by telephone. Members may have the information readily available. Beyond that, they are in a position to obtain specific information, tell the reporter who the proper source would be, or (on occasion) intercede for the reporter who is having difficulty with other federal sources. Members of Congress, for example, have direct access to the Legislative Reference Service and the Office of Legislative Counsel, whose function is to provide them with information. And, since Congress supervises federal agencies, those officials are less likely to ignore a specific request for cooperation from representatives or senators.

Though hometown reporters depend a great deal on members of Congress, they also seek to develop other sources. Within the legislative branch itself, the best bets are those persons in leadership roles. Persistence may be required to get assistance from high-ranking Senate or

House leaders, but it's an effort that could pay off. Some special attention, for example, should go toward those who chair committees on which members of the local delegation sit.

While it is unlikely these persons will provide evaluative comments on the role of the local delegates until they know the reporter well, other information may result. Does the bill sponsored by the local senator have any chance of passage? What is the importance of the local representative in obtaining either passage or defeat of a particular bill?

More difficult but certainly worth the effort would be establishing a relationship in which information or comment could be obtained from Senate leaders (president pro tempore, majority leader, minority leader, majority whip, or minority whip) or House leaders (speaker, majority and minority leaders, majority and minority whips).

Perhaps the most willing alternative sources would be lobbyists who represent special interest groups in Washington and throughout the country. In Washington, these persons often track reporters down to present opinions about legislation and other governmental actions. The local reporter, therefore, will have little difficulty finding them.

Many lobbyists are obvious national organizations known to have particular points of view on certain subjects (e.g., the American Petroleum Institute on any legislation dealing with oil or the National Education Association on educational issues). Others may be located with a little library work.

Making contact with the proper organization may involve little more than asking the congressional staff which groups have been working on a particular piece of legislation or contacting local groups that are chapters of national organizations. The National Education Association, for example, has organizations in every state that may provide information or help make contact with its national office. It's certainly helpful to get on the mailing list of such national organizations.

Information obtained from lobbyists tends to be too one-sided to be used alone. But it is precisely the kind of material needed to help balance the equally one-sided information received from a congressional delegation.

One other potentially good source of information, particularly at the agency level, usually is close to home but often forgotten by local reporters. All federal government is not located in Washington. Many federal agencies have regional offices scattered around the country whose function is to facilitate communication and program coordination.

The nation was divided into ten standardized federal regions in 1972, and most federal agencies now conform with this organizational setup. For example, the Department of Health and Human Services has regional offices located in Boston, New York, Philadelphia, Atlanta, Chicago, Dallas, Kansas City, Denver, San Francisco, and Seattle. The

Department of Transportation has offices in the same cities, except that nearby Cambridge, Massachusetts, is substituted for Boston and Fort Worth, Texas, for Dallas.[1]

These offices may not be able to provide the specific answer to a reporter's questions, but they may either get the information or refer the reporter to the proper source. As usual, it's experience with a given regional office through which the reporter learns who is helpful and who is not.

RESOURCES FOR THE FEDERAL GOVERNMENT REPORTER[2]

A host of publications exist that may be found useful by a federal reporter inside or outside of Washington. Some are easy to obtain. The reporter will want to own some, but a substantial number will be available in the local library, especially if it's a Federal Depository Library. Most major university libraries are in this category.

The following is intended to be a list of what is available. Certainly, it is not inclusive of all material a reporter would find helpful, but it is more than most would need.

Never-Be-Without Group

Congressional Quarterly, a weekly news journal primarily on congressional activities. 1414 22nd St., NW, Washington, D.C. 20037.

Congressional Monitor, one of the handiest daily listings of all congressional hearings and meetings on Capitol Hill. Published by *Congressional Quarterly.*

National Journal, a weekly news journal on issues and governmental doings. Expensive, but possibly the best. 1730 M St., NW, Washington, D.C. 20036.

Congressional Record, presumably a complete and verbatim account of words spoken in the two houses, but doesn't fit that description because members may have material removed or inserted. Printed in three forms: the daily *Record,* paperbound biweekly *Record,* and the permanent bound *Record.* Inexpensive and handy. Superintendent of Documents, Government Printing Office, North Capitol St., Washington, D.C. 20402.

Washington Information Directory, published annually by *Congressional Quarterly,* has names, responsibilities and telephone numbers of governmental agencies and associations. 1414 22nd St., NW, Washington, D.C. 20037.

Good-to-Have Group

Federal Register, a publication of what executive agencies are doing. Appearing five days a week, it contains a listing of regulations of all executive agencies. Monthly, quarterly, and annual indexes are issued. May be purchased through Government Printing Office (GPO).

Congressional Record Scanner, a quick summary of all in the previous day's *Congressional Record.* Published by *Congressional Quarterly.*

Congress in Print, a periodic publication that lists all hearings, reports and other documents produced by Congress. Available from GPO.

Democratic Study Group Legislative Digest, published by House Democrats, tells what is going on for the week and breaks down the legislation. May be obtained from congressional offices at minimal cost.

House Republican Digest, published by House Republicans to serve the same purposes. May be obtained from congressional offices at minimal cost.

Environment and Energy Study Conference Report, a publication that chronicles legislation on environmental and energy issues. May be obtained from congressional offices at minimal cost.

Other Valuable Material

Included in this category are magazines published by major lobbies that range in philosophy and issues. You may get newsletters from a wide range of such groups from Common Cause to the National Rifle Association. For names and addresses, see *Encyclopedia of Associations* at any library.

Facts on File, a very helpful listing of chronological news summaries. General Accounting Office monthly publication list. May provide excellent material or at least provide a list of monthly reports that reporters can track down. 441 G St., NW, Washington, D.C. 20548.

In addition, a number of magazines should be available. Some are political, such as the *New Republic* or *Progressive* (left) to the *National Review* and *Human Events* (right). Some trade publications might be good, depending on the news organization's area. For instance, a region rich in defense contracts should follow *Aviation*

Week and Space Technology, a McGraw-Hill publication. A farm area reporter should subscribe to farm publications. Also, news organizations may want to use a service called *Roll Call Report,* published by Rick Thomas of Ohio-Washington News Service, which lists the votes of Congress members.

Congressional Budget Office also does excellent issue papers, called *Background Papers,* not just on budget issues. Available through GPO.

Congressional Research Service, Library of Congress, provides very good reports. Available through the library or GPO.

Monthly Catalog of U.S. Government Publications lists every governmental publication for the month, with index. Available through GPO.

Congressional Information Service, a private firm, has all congressional hearings and reports on microfiche. Indexed and abstracted annually. An extremely useful resource. Available at many libraries.

Every newspaper in the country should subscribe to the *Washington Post, Wall Street Journal,* and *New York Times.*

Reference Materials

The following should be a useful part of any news organization's library and should be on the desk or in the office of any reporter who covers politics and government. The texts will supply both valuable background and information and will give quick phone numbers and other details.

Washington area telephone directories.

Executive directories, published by the federal government.

Available through GPO

Congressional Staff Directory, published semi-annually, most useful for staff names and telephone numbers. P.O. Box 62, Mount Vernon, VA. 22121.

Federal Staff Directory, a listing of major departments, bureaus and key officials (including biographies, addresses and telephone numbers). P.O. Box 62, Mount Vernon, Va. 22121.

Judicial Staff Directory, a listing of major personnel in the federal judicial system, including biographies, addresses and telephone numbers. P.O. Box 62, Mount Vernon, Va. 22121.

Federal Yellow Book and *Congressional Yellow Book,* detailed listings of federal agencies, officials, addresses and telephone numbers. Monitor Publishing Co. 1301 Pennsylvania Ave., NW, Washington, D.C. 20004.

Almanac of American Politics or *Politics in America,* both are published every other year as resource books on legislators, their political histories, and the histories of their districts. *Almanac of American Politics,* published by E. P. Dutton, New York, is stronger in its description of congressional districts. *Politics in America,* published by *Congressional Quarterly,* is stronger in reporting what members of Congress have done during their careers.

Congressional Directory, provides information relating to Congress and all other branches of the government. Biographical data, congressional session information, lists of executive officials, governors, and information on international organizations. Available from GPO.

Braddock's Federal-State-Local Government Directory, compilation of telephone numbers and addresses of the federal government. Published by Braddock Publications, Inc., Washington, D.C.

Washington Representatives, an annual guide to lobbyists and the organizations they represent. Published by Columbia Books, Inc., 1350 New York Ave., NW, Washington, D.C. 20005.

National Trade and Professional Association of U.S. and Canada and Labor Unions, published by Columbia Books, Inc.

U.S. Budget, may be obtained from Office of Management and Budget or GPO.

United States Government Manual, specific reference information about all governmental branches. Available through GPO.

General Material

A number of resource materials are available along with other avenues to obtain information easily. Some of these are:

Congressional mailing lists, from a member of either the House or the Senate.

Think tanks, (e.g., Brookings, American Enterprise Institute). These are excellent organizations to contact for quotable experts on domestic and foreign policy. Most publish directories of people, addresses, telephone numbers, and areas of expertise.

Newsletters and other material provided by special-interest groups. Many are located in Washington and are willing to provide oral and written help. Many monitor public policy and the decision-making process (e.g., the National League of Cities, National Education Association, and the National Governors Conference). It would be worthwhile to subscribe to the newsletters of the public interest groups that monitor the activities of the committee on which the local Congress members sit.

Generally, a reporter may make good use of *federal depository libraries* and regional offices, particularly for grants, investigations and other developments.

Other material that might be helpful may be obtained from the *New York Times Index* and through the Library of Congress Information Service.

NOTES

1. *United States Government Manual, 1979–1980.* Washington, D.C.: Office of the Federal Register, 1979, pp. 274 and 440.

2. With special thanks to John Felton of *National Public Radio,* who compiled most of this listing, with the assistance of Bill Choyke, formerly of the *Dallas Morning News;* Andrew Alexander of Cox Newspapers; and Randy Wynn of Ohio-Washington News Service.

Campaigns and Other Assorted Politics

11

Bob Lancaster has spent more than half his life in journalism. Now senior editor of *The Arkansas Times,* a regional magazine published in Little Rock, he labels his one year of college as "very unsuccessful." But he did spend a successful year as a Nieman Fellow at Harvard University, where he studied American intellectual history.

A novelist and biographer of country music star Kenny Rogers, Lancaster has developed a political philosophy from his educational background and his work as a columnist for three Arkansas newspapers (*Arkansas Gazette, Arkansas Democrat,* and *Pine Bluff Commercial*) and the *Philadelphia Inquirer.* His comments about politics and political reporting sound as though they come from a combination scholar and street fighter.

He's right at times. He's dead wrong at times. He's always thoughtful, precise, and provocative. Here's a sample:

Question: What should be the focus of political coverage?

Answer: "The more I see of American public life, the more I'm convinced that hardly anything original or worthwhile has happened in American politics since the Jefferson-Hamilton dialogue. Andrew Jackson 'rabbelized' American politics, to coin a word, and that's caused subsequent great deterioration of quality. But insofar as anything valuable going on, . . . well, maybe in the judiciary. Some of the judicial activism is interesting. It's amusing sometimes, but it's not often really innovative."

Question: If there's nothing interesting going on in American politics, why do journalists cover it?

Answer: "There's a very practical and disillusioning reason for that. American newspapers historically have been really cheap operations. They wanted to hire people for as little money as possible, and the one thing any dimwit off the street could write about with some conviction was politics. Everybody could understand sleazy political maneuverings. It didn't require any great education or sophistication to understand the crudities of what was going on. So the papers could hire deadbeats to 'write' about it, and pay them very little money and get away with it. I suspect that's how the tradition of exaggerated newspaper attention to politics got started. And, of course, the tradition continues."

Question: Aren't the people interested in politics?

Answer: "I think the political tomfoolery we pass off as 'news' interests intelligent people in the same way zoos do. There was something vital and challenging about early American politics, but since the Bill of Rights, it's just been a sideshow for the most part. The first-rate minds have turned their attention elsewhere. To borrow an image from Cyril Connoly, journalists writing about politicians now are like jackals snarling over a dried-up well."

Question: Doesn't politics have an impact on the quality of people's lives? On their pocketbooks? Shouldn't journalists be there to report that impact?

Answer: "I think it probably does, but that influence has been greatly exaggerated because of the close attention we journalists pay to politics. We don't pay that close attention to religion, for example. Probably the good religion journalists in America you can count on one hand. And yet it seems to me that religion is a much more influential factor than politics in determining the quality of our lives. I think it was Thomas Mann who said the tragedy of the modern man is that we can't conceive of any aspect of our lives except in political terms. And we, as journalists, are partly responsible for that because of the exaggerated attention we pay to politics."

Question: Well, you're part of this, too. What's different about your columns?

Answer: "Well, all I try to do is to be honest. If something is silly, it's silly. If something is evil, to say it's evil. If somebody is a joke as a candidate for public office, to say that. That's not much, and it's considered bad form in some journalistic quarters. It's considered a violation of our standard of 'objectivity.' But it seems objective to me. If something is stupid, calling it stupid seems to me both natural and objective. The concept of the newspaper as a passive conduit of information is a relatively new one, and network television reporting shows just how ghastly an aberration it is."

Question: All right, who declared you god? You say you like Mencken. Who made him god? Or Tom Paine? Why them?

Answer: "I think the United States Constitution did. It made us all gods—not just journalists: Everybody. It made a fundamental human right out of free expression of ideas, and it was just a technological accident that newspapers grew up the way they did, and some of us were singled out to practice this right on a larger scale. But that doesn't give any more substance to my opinion that it does anybody else's. There should be a great diversity of opinion writing and of opinions. And for people to gain some perspective on this blizzard of conflicting opinion, they're going to have to look to somebody with the vision and the time and the patience to put it all together."

Question: In politics, that's the reporter?

Answer: No. We shouldn't look to journalism for that. That's why we have novelists and playwrights and essayists. Those are the great generalists. People should read them more and read newspapers less anyway. The irony sometimes get me, you know, that there may be 50,000 people reading some garbage that I write when they could be reading something Joseph Conrad wrote which would be more instructive and encouraging and pertinent. And yet they don't do it, and I don't know what to do about that. But journalists can't be everything. We are particularists, detail men and women, like the little studio assistants daubing the beards and the crockery in 'The Last Supper.' And I think that's what we ought to be. We provide specific information about specific events and situations and opinions about those events and situations."

Question: And occasionally some great person comes along who can provide that perspective?

Answer: "Yes. We can only hope so. And I can't think of any journalists who'd been able to do it. The ones who have tried have not been successful. There's a book that I reviewed not long ago about . . . some pretentious title . . . it was about Mencken, and it was a book about Mencken as a 'thinker.' Well, it's ridiculous to regard journalists as formal thinkers because what they do is catch-as-catch-can. Every day there's something new and usually something trivial that they have to occupy their minds with. The best journalists are people who know how to get compartmentalized information in an increasingly complex and compartmentalized society."

Question: Don't you think that's simply going to breed confusion?

Answer: "It depends. In the last decade or so, journalism has made some encouraging progress in some ways. There's been a trend to specialized reporting, for example. That is, the reporter who has been extensively educated in the field he or she eventually will write about."

Question: A good political reporter, then, is an intellectual—one who has studied and understands politics?

Answer: "It's not necessarily intellectual. You can have a good reporter in auto mechanics, for instance, if he knows the technology and can write adequately. The trick is to have reporters who can express themselves well, who know something about this incredibly complicated English language, who have some kind of specialized education or knowledge and who are working for an organization that recognizes the need for reporters with proficiencies in both these areas."

Question: You've been labeled an excruciating writer.

Answer: "Yeah. It's not easy for me. I do the Flaubert bit. You know, my great dream is to some day be able to write as well as E. B. White, and I know I never will. But it's something to work toward. I think it was Whitehead who said when you work you don't work for the mass audience out there. You work for a few people that you respect, that you know will care about certain things you do and certain pains you take. And if you can write it so it will satisfy—maybe even delight—those few people, then everything else that happens is just a bonus."

POLITICS IS MORE THAN JUST ELECTIONS

It may be that such blasphemy is uttered with Bob Lancaster's tongue planted firmly in his cheek. Or it may not be. But his comments are designed not to be ignored. It's difficult to be blasé about someone who deliberately steps on everyone's toes. The more journalists think about what they're doing well and why, the greater the chances that what they provide is pertinent and meaningful.

That's the beauty of a Bob Lancaster. In just a few paragraphs, he has assumed the role of being an extreme critic of political reporting and of the American government, sought to guide reporters' efforts to cover the political process, intermarried a new journalistic trend with an age-old philosophical justification, panned much of the conventional wisdom of political coverage, and outlined what he thinks are qualities of good reporting both individually and institutionally. That's a good day's work.

One doesn't have to agree with all the specifics as Lancaster lovingly flogs the institution he serves to see in his comments a number of recurring themes from the pages of media criticism. Questions such as: What is the value of political coverage? How much balance in political coverage is necessary or desirable? Are reporters politically biased? What should be the focus of political coverage?

Reporters will take differing approaches in their answers to these questions, depending, of course, on what they think their jobs are and on how they define politics. Too many reporters seem to function on definitions that are so narrow that coverage is naturally limited to the commonplace. Does politics equal an election campaign? If so, maybe Lancaster is right. Anyone off the street, without education or training, can write about speeches, rallies, and baby kissing. Maybe he's also correct in stating that nothing significant has happened in American politics for years.

One shouldn't deny the importance of campaigns. They do represent breaking news stories that end in the necessary reporting of who won and how those persons will attempt to direct government in coming years. But that can't be all that's reported. In a large sense, politics is the basis of everything from who drives what on which city streets to whether a citizen can buy the preferred food for this evening's dinner and where and in what way athletes participate in "nonpolitical" Olympic games.

The urgings of media critics are part of a chorus that includes many political writers. Their cry is similar to one heard throughout journalism. It's a cry for more understanding of the system, greater depth of reporting, and greater recognition that politics is a process of complicated dependencies. It's a call for reporting about the fabric instead of the individual threads. It's also a plea for greater emphasis on the citizen's perspective rather than mere one-way communication from the system to the people.

THE IMPACT OF POLITICAL REPORTING

The need for broader coverage does not depend upon one's theory or even proof about the type or degree of impact that political communications have on individual voters. Do the news media directly influence the specific decisions of individual voters? Probably not in most cases. That's more likely to result from interpersonal relationships and deeply held attitudes. What about the impact of information on citizen decision making? It is a factor, but basically a long-term influence and one, again, which is filtered through significant mediating factors.

But even if they do not directly influence specific decisions, don't the media set the agenda of what subject matter is under public consideration? Yes, but personal considerations again provide a filter, and this may be a chicken-egg question. It may be equally likely that the news media emphasize what already is in the public consciousness more than they place agenda items into that consciousness.

The greatest potential impact is much more subtle than what has been considered by researchers. Though it is yet to be proven, it is conceivable that the quality of political coverage helps establish public attitude and the public mood about the political system. How one covers politics in an age of anti-politics is an important question. But it may be more important to consider the forces behind anti-political attitudes. It's more than likely that the news media represent one of those forces.

The lack of systematic presentation takes several forms, only one of which is the lack of depth in reporting of real programs. Three forms, specifically, merit discussion.

One is what political scientists refer to as *now-ism,* the journalist tendency to emphasize what happens today as if it were a pattern or a trend, but with inadequate explanation of how today relates to yesterday's activity and how today's news story is part of a larger picture. Worse than the cause of journalistic incompleteness, now-ism often results in journalistic error as reporters hastily and with inadequate thought assume that today's event is a predictor of the future. Examples occur daily, but perhaps the most frequent occurrences in politics grow from reporters' early and quick assessments of leading candidates based on the results of a single primary election or, locally, from the results of a party caucus or reception at a public rally.

A second source of public confusion may be said to grow from the news media's *dramatization of apparent political conflict.* Political scientist Richard L. Rubin of Columbia University, for instance, charges that reporters treat the strategic conflict of primary contenders as if the conflict were genuinely substantive. Public cynicism may easily be fed by reports of what candidate X said about candidate Y during a primary campaign when those reports are followed by accounts of the two candidates getting together after the primary.

"It is not simply the exposure of intraparty battles that has served to further fragment already unstable conditions," he adds, "but rather the media's relentless dramatizing of the differences between the candidates and their supporters without properly identifying and affirming the substantial common ground shared by many of the candidates. Differences in style rather than substance are exploited for dramatic purposes and 'probes' by the media often serve to make minor differences of degree evolve into apparent 'confrontations' of principle between candidates— who actually share much in common."

Conflict and differences of opinion, of course, must be reported, whether they are during primary or general campaigns or whether politicians seek to perform the duties of their elected positions. They do make good copy, and they represent a significant part of the political process at all levels. But clarity of reporting requires that conflict not be highlighted for dramatic purposes when the conflict is only on the political surface or is only a small part of the circumstance.

The third form of the problem, *negativism,* may arise from the greater tendency toward investigative reporting and the subsequent increased number of negative stories about politicians that affect public attitude about the political process. Uncovering unethical or illegal behavior by public officials may rank among the greatest achievements of twentieth century journalism. From Watergate to countless similar exposés by local news organizations, journalists have methodically exercised function as watchdogs of the public. But, as in stories of political conflict, sometimes the tendency goes too far.

In situations that provide possibilities for negative, neutral, or positive stories, reporters have proven themselves more anxious to provide negative stories. For example, among the most productive materials available to the political reporter are those campaign finance records kept in state secretary of state offices and by the Federal Election Commission. Use of these public records has declined as Watergate recedes further back into memory. But of the campaign finance stories that are produced, the majority of them are negative; they tell of improper contributions, financial connections between officials and special-interest groups, or improper filing procedures. Although these are legitimate stories, one Federal Election Commission official considered it a problem that "most" of the stories were negative, "many were neutral," and "a very small number" were positive.

The problem of now-ism, conflict coverage, and negative stories is not their focus. They have valuable elements. The problem is that despite numerous examples to the contrary too many reporters place too much emphasis on them, which distorts the overall coverage. Whatever their impact, they represent a problem for political reporters especially if their goal is to provide the whole truth.

IT'S PROFESSIONAL VERSUS PROFESSIONAL

Reporters are aware of these problems. It is not just in politics that many fail to move beyond the commonplace, and their immediate response is correct, to a degree. To do the kind of job everyone would like to see them do requires more time than most reporters have available. Campaigns are hectic and complex, and just the simple act of keeping up on specific events can be massive. Covering the politics of public policy is complicated by the need for hours to interview officials and to review piles of documents. These hours are limited by the fact that many political journalists are expected to double as governmental beat reporters.

What makes the task of political reporters more difficult, however, is that the people with whom they deal may know as much about the techniques of journalism as they do. If politicians themselves are not at least "semi-pros" in communication, they make it a point to hire professionals and to carefully train others on their staffs in the art of dealing with reporters. Many political press officials are former political reporters. Often they're veterans who know how reporters think and how to use that knowledge to gain what they want.

It's true that reporters may benefit because these former journalists better understand their needs and may even retain some journalistic loyalty. But when push comes to shove, where will the loyalties lie? How long will the former journalist keep his or her job if cooperation with reporters works to the disadvantage of the politician? In most cases, these are rhetorical questions.

Who Manipulates Whom?

The struggle between the professional journalist and the professional political communicator is the basis for the adversarial approach, which is accepted as perhaps necessary but certainly inevitable. Anne Saker, a reporter for Gannett News Service in Washington, D.C., believes reporters must be aware that politicians are often out to manipulate them for their best interests. However, that also works both ways. "When you cover elections, you make the assumption that the candidate will try to manipulate the press," she said. "They believe they can influence the press to their advantage."[1]

But reporters, too, often "use" politicians as sources, whether or not the information in a story is of use to the politician.

It is up to the reporter, Saker believes, to decide what is news. "A statement about the economy on any day may or may not be news," she said. "But when the GNP (gross national product) drops, it's probably news. You have to put everything in context and know what's going on in the world."

Saker and others who cover campaigns and politics realize that constant sparring with sources is part of the job. The only deals reporters make are those that involve protection of sources. They may not identify a source, or they may not use a story if it endangers the relationship with a good source or places the source in danger. Otherwise, newsworthiness is the only reasonable criterion for any story.

Variations in degree of newsworthiness, however, do give reporters some flexibility, which permits them to write stories for the deliberate purpose of cultivating a source. The priority of political reporters is to write the page one or top-of-the-newscast story, but they daily must make decisions about whether to devote time to marginal stories that have less than blockbuster news value.

For Immediate Release

Perhaps there's no better example of this give-and-take than the specific efforts of politicians to control media content and coverage direction through production of news releases and taped actualities. Reporters know releases are prepared for one reason: to gain publicity. Releases actually assist reporters in keeping up with day-to-day requirements of their jobs. They need not feel guilty about supplementing their normal coverage with some releases. But they usually try to do some additional research and rewriting.

Some critics charge that reporters as a group don't do enough additional research and rewriting. They simply take the releases, perhaps make some perfunctory revisions, and that provides their major coverage of governmental or political activity. That is not the work of professionals. Actually, one can make their coverage-by-release look relatively authentic. The problem is that it places virtually all news judgment in the hands of the politicians. Certainly, it won't uncover a scandal, provide any negative information, or demonstrate a less than effective performance by a politician.

Veteran politicians know—and new politicians quickly learn—the value of the news release. They learn, especially in more rural areas, that if they're going to get the publicity so valuable to their campaigns, they will have to generate most of it. So reporters will continue to face the necessity of making daily decisions about whether to use the releases with only minor modifications, whether to ignore them, or whether to pick up an idea or two from them and combine them with other sources as well.

A political reporter may generate a rather good story, for example, by taking a basic release on a governor's appointment and expanding it with an interview of the appointee about office organization, program goals, procedures, and possibly how mistakes of the previous administration may be overcome. Also, in many instances, a handout from a candidate should prompt a nearly automatic call to that person's opponent.

Another way to use releases to a reporter's advantage is to compare them with what an official is saying in office or during a campaign. A reporter who saves releases has a record of what has been said in the past, of campaign promises, and of statements of opinion.

In short, news releases can represent a source of some factual information on minor stories, of the beginnings of major stories, and of a means of allowing busy reporters to expand the scope of coverage. Problems occur when reporters get too busy or lack the initiative to uncover their own stories and prefer instead to wait for the latest handout.

Gaining the Advantage

Of course, written news releases are not the only ways politicians attempt to manipulate the press. During the 1988 presidential campaign, some network television reporters came under criticism for airing "canned" events of candidates, while those candidates refused to answer questions about many of the issues of the campaign. Bill Plante, a White House correspondent for CBS during that campaign, said most network reporters realized that the candidates wanted to get publicity while trying to avoid discussing the issues. Yet, he said, many reporters and viewers want it both ways: "We want to say we're not just conduits for the candidates, but we do want access to them," he said. "We're supposed to be objective, but when we tell them, 'you're not discussing the important issues,' then we're setting the agenda."[2]

In fact, rehearsed footage of the candidates in the 1988 election came to characterize that election in the eyes of some. As one reporter wrote after the election, that year "will be remembered as one in which the candidates dispensed with substance, dispensed with being themselves and instead conducted well-scripted and well-choreographed campaigns against one another on the evening news. . . . Reporters on the campaign trail, with little access to the candidates, said they often had nothing to report beyond the candidates' 'prepackaged' message."[3]

Although reporters are manipulated, they need not sit back and accept it. It sounds like standard and stale advice, but it's true that the degree to which a reporter avoids being manipulated is the degree to which he or she is aggressive. That means more than just fighting back. Defensive journalists do little more than just hold their own. It means being on the offensive by aggressively seeking the story behind or beyond the facts or the comments provided. It means seeking, searching, pushing, testing, and asking. The reporter who can do that effectively is the one with a full knowledge of the political and governmental systems and the one with the kind of personal drive that makes reporting more than just a conduit. It's a learning experience that, says Pulitzer Prize winner Walter Mears of The Associated Press, must be constant.

"If you wake up one morning and think you didn't learn anything yesterday as a political reporter, then you probably are a lousy reporter and should go do something else," Mears says. "The effectiveness of any reporter depends on whether there's still a creative process or an educational process in what that reporter does."

Reporters stress that learning is a combination of formal education and on-the-job experience. Textbooks are helpful in establishing the structure, but only battle scars provide the wisdom to apply that knowledge. Politics functions within a structure, and reporters need both political knowledge and political instinct to give it meaningful perspective.

Walter Mears
of The Associated Press (Associated
Press photo)

Combining knowledge and good instinct into political wisdom makes possible the best use of standard journalistic techniques to diminish control by those who would otherwise use the reporter.

Principal among those techniques is the development of a wide variety of sources. The American press was developed originally on the notion that a multiplicity of voices is needed if citizens are to discover truth. Effective political reporters today function on the same notion. The best balance of voices that cry in behalf of special political interest comes from other voices, other viewpoints, and other alternatives. Therefore, numbers and varieties of sources are important. Deliberate efforts need to be made to cultivate at least four types of people from whom information may be sought.

Inside sources. Persons with the party or government organization. The most obvious is party leaders at the appropriate levels: local, county, state, or national. These may include legislative party leaders or individuals who have been selected to chair party organizations in efforts to select candidates and coordinate campaigns. But reporters also must go beyond political leadership to workers within party organizations—either professionals or volunteers—who are veterans of political conflict.

"Enemy" sources. Persons from the opposition who usually are quite willing to comment upon activities, programs, or statements by government officials or party leaders. Again, this may be the leadership of the "loyal opposition," individual legislators, former government officials, or other individuals who have specialized knowledge. The effort partly is one of gaining alternative comment, but, predictably, it also is in the hope of receiving tips that could develop into investigative or depth pieces about wrongdoing, bad decisions, or program plans of significant public impact.

Special-interest sources. Individuals who are close to the political scene but not directly involved in party or governmental activities. Some may be lobbyists, but others may function in more informal ways. They may be business executives, labor leaders, scientists, or simply individuals who are part of a cause and who advocate or oppose certain types of governmental programs.

Grapevine sources. Persons with their ears to the political ground, who perhaps are lower level governmental workers with whom reporters become familiar. Often, the reporter automatically stops in and asks what's going on that day. Government employees like to talk; and that is often the best way to get stories.

Sources beget sources. A reporter who needs information but doesn't have an automatic line should be able to make a call and say, "I need to know such-and-such. Where can I get it?" But it doesn't all happen on the telephone. Personal contact develops the kind of trust that produces information, especially confidential information, on a regular basis. The key is regularity. A reporter doesn't have to see a source daily, but the contact must be regular enough that the source is comfortable talking about sensitive issues.

Part of the contact may be in social settings. Political and governmental reporters usually try to attend as many receptions as possible, even though the practice does contain dangers. The main purpose is to get to know the political figures in a more informal setting. Occasionally, something will be heard that results in a story, but it is seldom that reporters can run immediately to their terminals as the result of a social encounter. One reporter, for example, has a personal rule that after three drinks everything is off the record until he can contact the source the following day to confirm the information.

Socializing, while necessary, also provides the potential for the relationship between the reporter and the source to become too close. It doesn't have to be in a social setting. It could result from strictly on-the-job contact. But it's axiomatic that friendships can erode the necessary professional relationship between reporter and source. It's a fine line between friendship that produces professional trust and friendship that chips away at the independence of the reporter.

CANDIDATES AND CAMPAIGNS

Covering a political campaign is frustrating hurry-up-go-get-'em-meet-a-deadline-dash-to-the-next-meeting journalism. Reporters chase candidates. Candidates chase reporters. It's confusion with a capital C. It's tiring. It's often boring. But it's gratifying and ego building. Reporters get to know the leaders of the community, state, or nation on a first-name basis. As the campaign progresses, they know that they are writing the top news of the day. They know they're being read or heard.

Maybe that's why the job of covering politics is the job most sought on any staff. It may be the most public of all reporting. Candidates and citizens alike consider political news fair game for criticism, comments, and complaints. Most of all, it means dealing with individual candidates who may understand journalistic goals but seldom agree with them. It means sorting out candidates who have varying motives, personal characteristics, and qualifications for the jobs they seek.

Distinguishing the Candidates

If citizens need to know which candidates merit their votes, then they first need to understand how one candidate differs from another. They should know (as the basis of that sorting process) the candidates, why they want the office, and what they propose to do with the position if it is obtained. Perhaps a cynic would say that voters don't use that kind of information. But there is more evidence of voter sophistication than such cynics are willing to accept. Anyway, if reporters operated under that assumption, they would be thinking themselves out of a job. Therefore, they must assume that the democratic process functions with vitality and must accept three major responsibilities in their campaign coverage.

First, they must find means of effectively determining which candidates are true contenders for the office. Second, they must place considerable focus on how candidates differ from each other. Third, they must seek authenticity instead of the imagery preferred by most candidates.

None of these tasks is easy. They're all impossible unless the reporter has a thorough understanding of politics and is willing to do the legwork necessary to overcome the manipulative efforts of politicians and their staffs.

There are those who regret that the news media have the function of determining the relative significance of any candidate in a campaign. Among them are some reporters. But it is a fact of journalistic life that reporters' impressions, when translated to copy, can make a big difference in how seriously a candidate is considered.

Political history is full of examples of candidates at all levels who have surprised reporters and done well even though they were, in effect, written off early in the campaign. Many reporters and editors, for example, didn't think that Jesse Jackson had a chance to win the 1988 presidential election when, indeed, he was one of the leading contenders. Knight-Ridder correspondent Doreen Carvajal remembered when, early in the campaign for the primaries, she was one of the few covering the Jackson campaign. "I felt the problem was the editors back in the newsrooms of America had decided he could not win their kind of victory, and they forgot there were all kinds of things to measure (in a campaign)."[4]

Part of the answer must be observation. How well is a relatively unknown citizen received in public situations? What is the reaction of citizens who come into contact with this person? Another part must be based on how well the person fits into current controversial issues. Another must grow from assessment of the strength of the candidate's financial support, political organization, and his or her primary supporters.

But politics is full of surprises, and it is most important for reporters to maintain their flexibility in order to be constantly alert for apparent shifts of political opinion. The biggest mistake a reporter can make is to develop such a strong opinion about a candidate that there is an unwillingness or inability to recognize change in public mood.

On the other hand, while it is crucial that every serious candidate gain news media attention and that no candidate be virtually ignored, reporters do have to ration their limited column inches or minutes of air time. They are especially wary of making a person a candidate he or she is not capable of being.

Another fact of political life that affects reporters is that most candidates, regardless of their political philosophy, will make every effort to avoid offending voters. The effort is based on the notion that candidates will automatically get a substantial portion of the votes from members of their party and that their major need is to gain the uncommitted votes of independents and some person in the other party. Often, this is translated into an avoid-the-negative rather than saying-the-positive approach. Often it means avoiding the specifics and concentrating on broad philosophical statements and image making.

It leads to the kind of political strategy admitted in one instance by one of former California Governor Edmund G. (Jerry) Brown's top campaign aides, and one noted by many reporters and editors who covered the 1988 presidential race.

The issue of personality and wrongdoing in the past of candidates became such a big issue in the 1988 elections that the winning candidate, at least in the Democratic primary, won by a sort of "process of elimination," said Manuel Galvan, a member of the editorial board of *The Chicago Tribune.* "Michael Dukakis was nominated because he survived," Galvan said. "Everyone else stepped on landmines."[5]

Similarly, former Governor Brown knew he had to avoid trouble at all costs when he ran for governor, an aide recalled:

"If there was a strategy in the campaign, it was to try to keep out of trouble and not get involved with issues like the death penalty or victimless crimes or marijuana. . . . We were very careful. . . . The issues we picked were obscure and boring and dull. . . . The press coverage never bothered us. It was as adequate as we wanted it to be. It was our feeling that the less coverage the better. . . . The duller the race the better. We wanted this dull, dull, campaign."[6]

Such a situation means conservative Republicans and liberal Democrats all begin sounding like moderates. Everybody is moving toward the center to get the vote, and it becomes the political reporter's job to get candidates to say something significant, better, or controversial.

In the absence of such an effort, it's little wonder many voters make their choice on the basis of perceived personalities or uninformed expectations. That's why reporters need to step back from the day-to-day campaign and assess what they're doing. Is there a need to work harder to force candidates out into the open? Should they take the campaign disclosure route? What specific questions should be asked at every opportunity—with news accounts if the candidates didn't answer the questions—until they are forced to come up with specific answers?

It's standard textbook lore to say reporters seek the truth, but there's no way to avoid it. "Everyone" knew, when Joe McGinniss wrote *The Selling of a President 1968,* that candidates were being merchandised on the basis of an image which may or may not have related to their true character or beliefs.[7] Today, that's a much discussed situation, and to reporters it's a circumstance with which they must deal daily.

Candidate Mistakes, Inconsistencies, and Naivete

Part of the truth about candidates is that they don't always say or do the right thing. They are overworked during a campaign. Political newcomers may have problems because they have not learned to handle reporter or citizen questions or because in their enthusiasm they talk about subjects on which they are inadequately informed. But even the most seasoned veteran will blunder from time to time, and reporters will be faced with how to deal with it.

Reporter reaction, of course, will depend on the nature of the occasion and the significance of the mistake in terms of the overall campaign. A slip of the tongue in a private conversation probably will be ignored unless its significance is worthy of follow-up. A public misstatement, perhaps before thousands at the scene or on television, must be dealt with. If the mistake is relatively minor, the reporter may give the candidate the opportunity to clarify it and then determine whether to ignore it or cover it with the clarification.

For major misstatements, however, the general attitude of reporters would be to use the story, giving opportunities for comment to the candidate, the candidate's party, and representatives of the other party.

One type of "mistake" for which reporters must remain alert is inconsistency of statement by candidates. Persons legitimately change their minds, especially over long periods of time. But reporters are alert to the possibility that the changes represent an effort to tailor remarks to the attitudes of particular audiences.

This practice was more prevalent in earlier years of American politics when speeches remained more local. While it's not as easy for them to get away with it today, candidates nevertheless may make the attempt.

"It's up to reporters to catch it if what a candidate says today is different from what he said yesterday and that is different from what he said two years ago," says the AP's Walter Mears. "It's important for people to know about such things. And you do it the same way you do anything else. You study, talk, and read as much as possible to find out where the candidate has been and what he has said when he was out of your hearing."

This involves careful record keeping, a file of clips and news releases, and periodic comparisons. Usually, however, it is the type of thing that only good solid homework before the campaign can uncover. In the heat of a campaign, reporters seldom have the time to review past materials unless memory lights a spark. If the inconsistency represents a legitimate change of opinion, a good story may result from a candidate's explanation of that change.

Charges of wrongdoing in a campaign also represent a challenge to reporters seeking to be fair to all parties. They're common, and they vary in degree of severity from statements that the opposition candidate is being inconsistent or vague to charges that campaign or other laws have been violated. In too many instances, such charges are little more than efforts to degrade the opposition. But they are legitimate and necessary stories, and reporters must cover them with caution.

"Usually something like this will unfold and you say, 'Okay, you make this charge. Give me your explanation.' Then you give the other guy a chance to answer, which is usually the first day's work on that," says Dotty Griffith of the *Dallas Morning News.* "Then, after that, you try to ascertain the situation or the law as much as possible by using documents or interviewing experts. But you have to be careful. It's not our job to try a case. Our job is to report the news responsibly. Some of these things are off the wall and totally unfounded, but I don't feel the obligation to go out and prove somebody right or wrong before I put in print that the charge has been made."

Griffith does, however, urge follow up. She notes that too frequently news will break that a candidate has been charged with some improper or illegal activity, and the story will end right there, especially if legal authorities do not get involved. It's unfair to the candidate and to the citizens if reporters do not follow up with the story that no action was taken on the charge. If the lack of official action results from the influence of persons in positions of importance, that is a story. If inaction is because the charge lacks validity, that is a story. Allegations of wrongdoing are too important to allow them to simply fade from the scene.

Playing Favorites?

Reporters are human. They like some people better than others. In politics, they spend a lot of time with candidates, and it is inevitable that they are going to develop preferences. Sometimes, this is just a personal decision. Other times it results from on-the-job treatment received from candidates or a combination of the two.

That raises the obvious question: To what degree does this human characteristic influence a reporter's coverage? One can find evidence for answers all the way from "a lot" to "very little." Certainly, some reporters and news organizations have taken it upon themselves deliberately to help a candidate win an election, using whatever power they have. This will be almost universally criticized. Whatever one's notions about the possibility of being truly objective, very few will condone the practice of becoming an integral part of a candidate's efforts to gain office.

Most reporters will place themselves at the other end of the continuum. "Very little," they say, not because they don't like one candidate more than another, but because they take calculated—sometimes extreme—precautions to be fair. Most, for example, make a point not to develop close personal relationships with politicians, to avoid temptation, and to avoid the appearance of a relationship that is too close.

"In Washington, reporters and sources socialize," says Anne Saker. "It's an intensely linked society." But, she adds, that usually doesn't stop reporters from writing "tough" things about Congress or the President. "A reporter who gets too friendly with sources usually doesn't last long," she said.

Reporters must trust their own judgment and journalistic instincts to provide accurate coverage. Campaign coverage thus becomes a matter of providing candidates with breaking news coverage of specific events, asking specific and detailed questions, and looking for contradictions or inconsistencies.

Providing coverage that goes beyond the individuals is another strong link in a reporter's efforts to do the job well. Rather than giving wall-to-wall coverage of individual activities, the reporter will create packages that include the candidates' views on issues. This could, for example, concentrate on one subject, such as education. Or it could be a story that provides a general lead, then segments the candidates compartmentally on several issues.

PAINTING THE WHOLE PICTURE

An artist who paints only half a picture seldom wins acclaim. But an incomplete picture is often the result of American political coverage.

Most journalists are sincere and professional, despite those who suspect their motives. Criticism that does appear mostly grows from the sheer complexity of a campaign and the lack of time to provide the kind of comprehensive coverage reporters would prefer.

It's difficult to discuss fully the relationships between individual candidates and the campaign issues when one has countless day-to-day duties. It's difficult to find time to sit back and think about or investigate the larger picture of a campaign when reporters must deal with editors' expectations of daily stories. To be on the road is a dream of young reporters, but it's tiring and mind numbing. Too many reporters do find it easier either to rely on the candidates themselves to establish the focus of the coverage, or to join the pack and follow the leads of their fellow campaign journalists.

That's not to make excuses. Less than adequate coverage does create misimpressions, does fail to inform voters, and does tarnish the reputation of political reporters in general. Quality coverage is not impossible. Many good journalists have served their readers, listeners, and viewers with distinction, and they have done so with a combination of knowledge and sheer hustle. They have provided comprehensive coverage because they have taken a comprehensive approach. That means they have accepted the difficult responsibility of covering all elements of a campaign—the candidates, the issues, the strategies, the support, the events, and all those broader social factors that play a part in any election.

No individual reporter, of course, can do it all. Even local elections require teamwork. Successful news organizations have organized their efforts to deal with some combination of at least seven types of campaign stories. None of these stories is adequate alone, and the balance among them will vary according to local circumstances, the personality of a campaign, and news media preferences. But each has something to offer that is difficult to ignore.

Breaking News Is Essential

In spite of overall requirements, breaking news remains the backbone of campaign coverage. Candidates make appearances, they speak, they answer questions, and they relate to voters in specific ways. Their activities must be given straightforward coverage. Reporters tire of hearing speeches and attending meetings, but only by being on the scene can they provide the raw material that citizens need.

This raw material consists mostly of what the candidates have to say, but there's more. It includes how the candidate is received, the level of audience enthusiasm, and how the candidate handles questions and complaints. A reporter may get an early indication of the constituency of a candidate by observing his particular part of the community, state, or county.

In spite of efforts by candidates to structure the content of their campaign and in spite of ideas about the media's agenda-setting function, human beings have their own ideas about what is important to them. The perceptive reporter on the scene can develop greater insight on campaign issues from what citizens say and ask when given the opportunity.

Breaking accounts of campaign activities also provide the foundation of more detailed and analytical coverage of a campaign. Failure to observe the candidate in specific situations creates a disadvantage when reporters want to discuss the issues, a candidate's political philosophy, or the possibilities of election success. Without such observation, reporters must depend on interviews and are subject to being manipulated.

The Issues Are the Context

One of the basic jobs of reporters is to show readers how candidates would run things if elected. That means they must go beyond covering the events and the personalities involved in a campaign. Candidates become public officials, and public officials have ideas of what is important and what should be done. Is it therefore necessary to say that the voter deserves to know about these directions while time remains to influence decisions? Many editors and reporters believe that their responsibility to the public is to describe an event in context—to describe where it fits in the present and past performance of the candidate.

The reporter should provide a broader perspective of how candidates relate to an issue, how that relationship varies during the campaign season, and how they are likely to govern with respect to it. This also involves deciding the subjects that will be placed in the journalistic spotlight.

Who decides the issues? On the surface, the answer must be the reporters. They decide what stories to write. But that answer is incomplete. Reporters look to others for cues, and increasingly, the tendency is to look less to the candidates themselves and more to the public. By giving the public more weight in the process, reporters are reinforcing the democratic process.

It is clear that issues are the main focus of editors who coordinate campaign coverage. In a survey of twenty-three newspapers in twenty-two states about coverage of the 1988 presidential campaign conducted by *presstime* magazine, "identification of issues is one of the strongest underpinnings of newspapers' campaign coverage. Every newspaper in the survey has tried to avoid slavish attention to the daily stump speeches; instead the papers are trying to move into (what one editor called) 'an in-depth exploration of the real problems of the country, and what the candidates would do about them.' "[8]

Concentration on political issues important to citizens raises three significant journalistic requirements, the first of which is political knowledge and instinct on which to base judgments. Often, the public's perception of important issues is discovered through news-media-sponsored surveys. At other times, the choice depends upon the abilities of reporters to understand and to identify individual and collective public concerns. Both methods require more than casual understanding of the political process.

The second requirement is one of time and space. It simply takes more time to analyze a political issue than it does to cover a campaign speech. It takes more digging. When the result of that effort appears, it usually requires more column inches or air time, something that will be provided only if news organizations are dedicated to fulfilling the need for greater depth of campaign coverage.

Third, unless people are emphasized, stories may be dull. The problem grows out of an attitude that emphasizes things over human beings. Inflation as an abstract concept is deadly. But inflation has direct local impact on the lives of individuals. It is an issue of local political concern. Stories that relate that point and those in which candidates are required to address themselves will capture reader and reviewer interest.

Campaigning Shows Character

Speaking about the 1980 New Hampshire presidential primary, Meg Greenfield of the *Washington Post* and *Newsweek* presented what she called a "way-out theory" of why candidates Ronald Reagan and Jimmy Carter won: "They looked better—more reasonable, competent, authentic—to their parties' voters than the other guys did."[9]

It is significant that Greenfield's thoughtful discussion of the fictions and illusions of political campaigns concludes on that personality note. Under all that candidate playacting, there are real persons who have feelings and emotions, who live real lives and have real families, who work and play like everyone else, and who have very human strengths and weaknesses. Or, as Bill Plante of CBS says, "A presidential election involves dreams, ideas, hopes, goals. Pragmatism and competence sometimes don't seem very important."[10] This could hold true for any election. What kind of public officials candidates will become depends in parts on their human qualities. That's one reason why citizens are interested and why they expect reporters to devote at least some attention to personal qualities of those people seeking office.

The election of 1988 refueled the debate about how much a candidate's personal life should be reported by the press. This came about when Gary Hart, a Democratic hopeful who, it appeared, would get the nomination, dropped out of the race after reporters followed him and learned he was in the company of a woman who was not his wife. After that, the debate raged: Was the press "correct" in its coverage of Hart?

During a seminar of top editors and columnists at the American Press Institute in Reston, Virginia, the "Hart incident" and its ramifications were a major topic of discussion. "The floodgates have absolutely opened," said *Los Angeles Times* Washington bureau chief Jack Nelson.[11]

Many of those present at the seminar agreed with Pulitzer Prize-winning *Washington Post* columnist David Broder, who believes that often personal idiosyncracies or problems of candidates are known by reporters, but never printed or aired: "I think we have a resource we tend to ignore, and that's all of these people have personal histories and they are well known to reporters."[12]

The discussions of personal characteristics may be beneficial or detrimental to candidates. But this is not the journalistic point. The task of the reporter is to provide the full picture and to allow individuals to assess candidate character traits.

Providing that information requires much more than a single interview or perhaps listening to a speech. It's not the sort of material that is likely to be the subject of a news release. The reporter has to take the time to get to know the candidate well and to seek understanding of personal as well as political motivations.

The danger that character stories may border on gossip does worry journalists. But the sensitive reporter truly interested in serving voters a slice of the candidates' personalities—for no motive other than to fill in the complete picture—can deal with the problem. First, this must involve concentrating on known facts rather than speculation. Even trained psychiatrists cannot tell with assurance what motives or thoughts lie deep within a human being. It is quite possible to learn much about a person's character by concentrating on what that person has said and done and on what others say. It's mostly a matter of taking a personal focus with traditional journalist techniques.

Second, this kind of story must involve very careful use of language and all the writing skills the reporter possesses. Meaningful character presentations are not really possible unless the writer has the skill to focus the facts more deeply on the personality rather than on taking the usual journalistic approach.

Assessing the Impact of Big Bucks

The early 1970s spawned a wave of reform throughout the United States, the aim of which was to make governmental activities more open. Not the least of the results was action making political candidates more accountable for the money they handle during the campaign. It made them especially accountable for money from big contributors.

Until then, it was almost impossible for reporters to cover campaign finances. Archaic laws applying to finances were easily circumvented. Then Congress passed the Federal Election Campaign Act of 1971, and the rules of the game changed. In many instances, so did the score, as reporters flocked to study and report on records federal candidates were required to make available.

The law has been amended several times, but it still serves the same function: It establishes contribution limits and spending limits, it regulates public financing of presidential campaigns, and, importantly for journalists, it provides for disclosure of all records filed with the Federal Election Commission.

Another type of campaign finance story that should not be ignored is examining the relationships between contributions and votes on legislation, especially bills being supported by special-interest groups.

With the increasing availability of the necessary records, reporters have only internal problems to overcome in their efforts to cover campaign finances. Often they contend that a news organization does not provide enough time to study properly the thousands of pages of available records and that they have to deal with the complexity of the records themselves.

The latter can be overcome when reporters are willing to devote time to a careful study of federal and state campaign financing laws to keep abreast of reporting requirements and available information.[13] Probably more than most other journalistic efforts, campaign finance stories come from documents.

The source of a candidate's money may or may not be information a voter needs when making a decision in the voting booth. But if the reporter offers that information, voters can draw their own conclusions.

The Strategy of Political Strategy

Individuals who discuss journalistic coverage of political campaigns love analogies. They have referred to the political race as being, among others, like a horse race, a football game, and a military operation. Each comparison, in its own way, makes a point, but perhaps it is equally significant that the analogies have two common points with political campaigns that reporters consider part of their responsibilities: the victory or defeat at the end and the fact that conducting each depends to a large degree on preconceived strategy.

The emphasis reporters place on campaign strategy, of course, depends upon individual circumstances: the closeness of the race, the relative importance of specific actions, and the significance of the strategic element in the campaign. Strategy should not be the essential point of coverage, although it should not be ignored. Citizens need assessments of why campaigns take certain directions as much as they need reports on specific actions. Understanding the kinds of strategies a politician uses helps citizens better anticipate the governing style of that individual. The conclusion may be that the candidate uses all available techniques to move toward specific accomplishments. Or it can suggest the candidate uses the system to avoid responsibility.

Taking the Pulse of the Public

Conducting political surveys is tough. Most political reporters have neither the expertise nor the desire to do it. In larger news organizations, they often find themselves working with others more capable of gaining information on the public's attitude. Perhaps the most significant contribution of "precision journalism" is that it has opened up another avenue of public communication. It has given citizens another voice and has expanded the opportunities of journalists to broaden the scope of political coverage.

News organizations use surveys for a number of reasons, including marketing and public feedback. But it's around election time that the pollsters appear most prominently on the journalistic scene. They may want to assess the relative strength of candidates in a primary or general election. They may seek information on why an election went a particular way. Or their purpose may be broader: What are the criteria citizens are using in making their voting choice? What are the issues of greatest importance? The *presstime* survey of coverage given the 1988 presidential campaign by twenty-three newspapers found that one of the trends of coverage was a stepping up of polling, used "to identify the issues, as well as to tell who's ahead. Many (newspapers) are using focus groups, too, to help identify issues."[14]

Granted, the term "precision journalism" may be somewhat off the mark. One can find too many examples in which hindsight has proven pollsters wrong. Perhaps there is truth to charges that survey results reduce the momentum of the trailing candidate by discouraging campaign workers and slowing the flow of campaign contributions. Perhaps there is a bandwagon effect in which persons leap to the support of the leader.

And worse, there are instances in which news organizations overemphasize surveys and give their coverage the flavor of a horse race. Who's ahead? Who's behind? Who's catching up?

But the criticism is no worse for news organization polling efforts than for other aspects of political coverage. The journalistic survey technique may lack maturity. It's certainly not perfect, but it adds significant elements to campaign coverage.

From the Inside Out: The Media Story

From the candidates' perspective, the road to political success is paved with publicity. There's no political point to a good idea unless reporters pick up that idea and give it widespread exposure.

Forget all the fancy definitions of news. Forget all the theories about the democratic process. Much of what candidates do depends upon whether there happens to be a reporter around to see or hear it. They're called "media events." Sure, the goal is to reach the voter. But the techniques of today are dramatically different from those of yesteryear. In politics, more than any other aspect of society, the mass media, especially television, have had a direct impact on the rules of the game. Bill Plante of CBS remembers a top Reagan aide telling him, "I don't care what you write, as long as I control the pictures."[15]

Back to the traditional definition of news. If the media have had an impact on the way campaigns are run, it would be reasonable to consider that fact as an integral part of campaign coverage. Journalists traditionally have been reluctant to write about themselves. But more news organizations have come around to the idea that their role in political campaigns is too important to ignore.

But many reporters believe that the days of the *Boys on the Bus* are over.[16] Many political reporters believe reporters must step off the campaign bus and away from the motel television set to get the facts about a candidate's past. Sources include people who have worked with him or her, news coverage from years before the bid for office, and biographies and histories.

That coverage would include discussing the staging of media events, with at least some labeling of the purpose of such activities. It would also include presenting the campaign as it unfolds in television advertising, which many candidates use as a means of ducking situations in which they must give public answers to difficult questions. It would also include discussing how citizens seem to react to campaign polls.

Much of this has been done over the years, but not enough. Candidates for president, Congress, governor, state legislature, mayor or city council are using very sophisticated media techniques. The reporting of those techniques needs to be equally sophisticated. And that, too, will be the task of those who seek to cover American politics professionally.

NOTES

1. See, for instance, Dan Nimmo and James E. Combs, *Subliminal Politics,* (Englewood Cliffs, N.J.: Prentice Hall, 1980), pp. 158–188. (This chapter provides a provocative assessment of the relationships between journalists and politicians.)

2. Bill Plante, remarks made at "Presidential Post Mortem: Has Election '88 Changed Campaign Coverage?" national conference, Society of Professional Journalists, Cincinnati, Ohio, November 19, 1988.

3. *Minneapolis-St. Paul Tribune,* "Reporters and Editors Fault Campaign Coverage," as reported in *The Plain Dealer,* November 17, 1988, p. D1.

4. Thomas B. Rosensteil, "Press Didn't Mistreat Jackson; It Treated Him Too Much Like All the Other Candidates," *Bulletin of the American Society of Newspaper Editors,* May/June 1988, p. 7.

5. Manuel Galvan, "Presidential Post Mortem: Has Election '88 Changed Campaign Coverage?"

6. Mary Ellen Leary, "California 1974: The Browning of Campaign Coverage," *Columbia Journalism Review,* July/August 1976, p. 18.

7. Joe McGinniss, *The Selling of the President 1968,* (New York: Trident Press, 1969).

8. Elwood Wardlow, "Campaign '88," *presstime,* October 1988, p. 13.

9. Meg Greenfield, "Politics and Play Acting," *Newsweek,* March 10, 1980, p. 108.

10. Bill Plante, "Presidential Post Mortem: Has Election '88 Changed Campaign Coverage?"

11. Jack Nelson, remarks made at "Covering the Candidates," American Press Institute, Reston, Virginia, September 9, 1987.

12. David Broder, "Covering the Candidates."

13. At the federal level, for example, reporters should be well acquainted with three Federal Election Publications: *Campaign Guide for Congressional Candidates and Their Committees, Federal Election Commission Annual Report,* and *Federal Election Campaign Laws.* Similar background materials are often available in some states, usually through the office of the secretary of state.

14. "Campaign '88," p. 12.

15. Plante, "Presidential Post Mortem: Has Election '88 changed Campaign Coverage?"

16. In *The Boys on the Bus,* Timothy Crouse's analysis of the activities and problems of the campaign press corps (New York: Ballantine Books, 1973).

Education Mirrors the Community

12

Whether the subject is declining government funding to public schools, the high-school drop-out rate, standardized test scores, or the quality of teaching, the public will always pay attention to education.

Even readers and viewers who would define themselves as nonpolitical or nonreligious cannot use the same label with regard to education. Despite changing political attitudes, there is little or no change in the people's perception of education's important role in their lives and in the lives of their children and grandchildren.

For that reason education has remained a focus of American journalism since colonial days. Even if public attitudes have fluctuated, reporters have consistently chronicled the role of schools as a social and personal force. In modern times, education reporting gained impetus from four happenings that propelled the nation's centers of learning to the front of the public consciousness.

The 1954 U.S. Supreme Court decision in *Brown v. Topeka Board of Education* began the long string of school desegregation events that may represent one of the top news stories of the century. When the Russians marked human entry into the space age with the launching of Sputnik I in 1957, American education went into a frenzy of scientific emphasis in an effort to overcome the apparent technological gap between the two countries. When college campuses erupted with violence and social uproar in the late 1960s and early 1970s, the nation again turned this collective eye toward educational institutions.

In 1983, the National Commission on Excellence in Education and its report, "A Nation at Risk," once again put educational institutions on the front pages and at the top of newscasts. The commission warned of a "rising tide of mediocrity" in the schools and called for extensive reforms.

It may be that journalistic coverage in all four cases has contributed to the ups and downs of public attitude. There is no question that reporters covered education in numbers. Their coverage was extensive, and it reflected and perhaps magnified feelings that stimulated and resulted from these important stories of American history.

That thirty-year period represented perhaps the high point of journalism's dependence on the education reporter. However, as time went on, many editors felt their education reporters had very few real "issues" to cover; that is, many believed that one reporter could perhaps cover twenty school districts and considered school board coverage adequate "coverage" of education.

But, as Pulitzer Prize-winning education reporter Bette S. Orsini notes, that's not education coverage: "A newspaper (and broadcast station) whose approach to covering education is surface, superficial, naive and downright behind-the-times is not only risking credibility with its readers, but is in fact denying them informed participation in one of the nation's most vital debates."

Orsini points to several examples of excellent education reporting, including an investigative series of fifty-one stories by the Jackson, Mississippi, *Clarion-Ledger,* which checked into conditions of the state's public schools and found them lacking. The newspaper won a Pulitzer Prize in 1983 for its work.

Orsini also urges education reporters and editors to read a series of fifty-four articles and editorials by *The Dallas Times Herald* that compared Dallas students' educational achievement to that of students in other parts of the United States and several other countries.[1]

Journalistic emphasis or lack of emphasis on education seems to result from confusion over the seeming contradiction between public and personal attitudes about schools and their programs. If education as a social institution is a source of distrust and therefore lack of interest in the early 1990s, the specific impact of a school on a young person remains a subject of intense concern to parents. And, as much as anything, this may reflect upon the coverage being provided by news organizations.

These are days in which all forms of social bigness are viewed with suspicion. An institutional approach to journalistic coverage of education that concentrates on national policies and governmental actions will not be enough. A personal approach that emphasizes individual circumstances of local situations, on the other hand, will not be ignored by those human beings whose lives are most directly affected.

CRITICISM OF EDUCATION REPORTING

Complaints follow journalism, and education reporters get their share. Perhaps they get more than their share because they deal with a subject matter that everyone knows something about. The validity of the criticism depends upon the situation. Much of it is valid; some is patently unfair. But its persistence must provide at least some clues to education reporters about what is expected of them by the public and by the educators with whom they work.

The manner in which reporters react to specific criticism depends upon their news judgment and upon their sense of fair play. In no way can they go as far as most educators would like and become propaganda arms of the system. But, at the same time, they must remember that they, like all reporters, bear the burden of providing complete and representative coverage, whether that coverage has positive or negative impact. Within that context, then, reaction to criticism becomes an if-the-shoe-fits proposition. But recognition of at least three general themes of criticism should help to provide the background to the total efforts of education reporters.

"Too Much Education Reporting is Dull"

In response to the suggestion that education reporting is boring, reporters say that it's because too much education is dull and because educators themselves are rarely flamboyant. That's valid sometimes, but it's doubtful that educators have a monopoly on dullness. Reporters can't pass the buck on this one. It is not the responsibility of educators to present significant journalistic material—whatever its dullness quotient—in as meaningful and interesting a way as possible.

It is the policy of many newspapers and radio and television stations to not only report about the schools, but also to report about the school board as well. To most media outlets, education coverage also includes nonpublic schools. However, while coverage of the school board is important, it is not an end in itself. Schools are teachers, young people, and programs—not just policies, resolutions, formal discussions, and debates. Maintaining that perspective provides automatic human interest to news coverage without ignoring the value of official decisions.

Likewise, such a perspective will help overcome what is a fairly routine relative sameness to education coverage across time and news media. Too much education coverage for years has involved the same subjects, used the same approaches, and often reached the same conclusions. Such a lack of imagination, which results in established patterns of coverage, is not likely to whet the citizen's appetite for education news. It's true that school programs run in cycles. Certain events occur regularly every year. The need for annual "back-to-school" coverage, to be read or seen by the same audience, places a burden upon the news media to develop fresh and meaningful ways of highlighting this important part of the school year.

But reporters also must look wider and dig deeper to discover the meaningful stories that have not been covered over the years. Very few news organizations can boast of having done a thorough job of explaining what citizens need to know about curriculum development and meaning. This may be because reporters don't understand curriculum, because they define curriculum as inevitably dull, or because they don't have time to uncover these stories. Whatever the reason, the result has been that reporters have virtually ignored the mission of education and that part of the story that has the most impact upon the people involved.

David Hawpe, now editor of *The Courier-Journal* in Louisville, Kentucky, made sure education coverage was not ignored when he took over as city editor of now-defunct *The Louisville Times*.

"I announced to the staff that the education beat was the most important on the paper—that activities covered on the education beat touched more people in a more powerful way than do any of the activities we cover. I told them I thought that the education system had more to do with the quality of life in the community than anything else I knew about."[2]

When he became managing editor of *The Courier-Journal*, he gave the same talk.

"Education Reporting Overemphasizes Controversy"

A second criticism, that education reporting dwells on conflict, sounds like a contradiction. How can education reporting be both dull and overemphasize controversy? The answer is that education reporting too often is a matter of extremes. Noncontroversial, day-by-day coverage often is routine and not given prominent play. Much of it may be very positive, and there may be a lot of it. But it's hardly conspicuous or attention grabbing.

When controversy erupts—and it's inevitable given the political nature and personal feelings involved in education—the stories move to the front. Parental complaints about textbooks, official efforts to reduce extracurricular activities for financial reasons, complaints that Johnny or Jane can't read, and concern over violence in the schools are the stories that get widespread attention. Regretably, their polemic nature make them easier to write in an arresting manner.

So, does education reporting emphasize the controversial? In some cases, no, even though it looks that way, especially to sensitive educators in the middle of those controversies. In other cases, yes, when reporters find a competitive story that gives them the opportunity to move to page one or to the top of the newscast.

But such explanations don't really provide solutions. It's big news when something goes wrong in a social situation as important as education. It's time-honored that citizens must know of disagreements, mistakes, and problems. To what degree does this very natural journalistic effort become overemphasized? There are, of course, several answers. Educators—especially those with administrative responsibilities—will be quick to draw the line. Journalists will stress flexibility within an overall context of balanced coverage.

Therein lies part of an answer: traditional journalistic technique. The news organization—satisfied that it gives citizens the bigger picture of school life and accomplishments over time—will simply say "not so" when such charges arise. The reporter whose efforts include board coverage, features, trend analysis, and the day-to-day grind of educational activity can be comfortable in the face of complaints. Coverage of negative stories is justifiable when school officials have ample opportunity to present their side.

This will not stop the flow of complaints. It shouldn't. But it will assure reporters and editors a means of knowing they have done their jobs. And that's important.

"Reporters Are Not Aggressive"

Perhaps the most damning of all is the criticism that education reporters often do not demonstrate the aggressive drive of their counterparts in other specialties. At the extreme, this raises the specter of the very antithesis of good journalism: proeducation, pliable, overly accepting, nonquestioning, and unimaginative. Few critics intend such an extreme, and most admit to countless exceptions, but the comments persist.

To a degree that charge contains truth; it is the result of three interwoven factors that say something about education reporters themselves and their news organizations.

First, in the face of many years of massive public support for education and the fact that news organizations generally want to be supportive of the needs of schools, education journalism probably has been slower to assume an adversarial stance. It is not an absolute requirement that investigative reporting be negative, but it is usually the case. In general, it has been more difficult for reporters to be critical of individuals whose function is to help children prepare for their lives. There's a big difference between public attitudes about politicians, for example, and public attitudes about educators.

Second, education is much more complex than the concept of "covering the schools" would indicate. Understanding it involves psychological theory as well as familiarity with a wide range of specific subject matter and the processes of political interaction. While many reporters have taken political science courses, for example, few will have set foot in an education class. Thus, most reporters who move into the education specialty face a rather massive task of developing the background expertise in the field. It can be learned on the job, but few ever have the time or the opportunity to do it properly.

Third, many editors, as a result of their own attitudes about education reporting, have affected the long-range value of their organization's coverage. Perhaps there are signs that these attitudes are changing, but, as David Hawpe of *The Courier-Journal* indicates, all too frequently editors have placed low priority on education coverage. And this has been reflected in their assignments.

"It's generally been viewed in most papers as a place to put beginners," said Gene Maeroff, formerly an education writer for *The New York Times* and now senior fellow at the Carnegie Foundation for the Advancement of Teaching. "It's seen by the editors and by the reporters themselves merely as a stepping stone. There hasn't been enough concern with getting very good, experienced reporters on this beat—people who have an interest in the subject, who really want to cover it, and who want to stay with it for a number of years. If that attitude could be changed, it would be a very important step toward improving education coverage generally."

It Requires Background, Experience, Desire

The requirements for providing comprehensive education coverage are the same as for any other journalistic specialty. The news organization must be committed to providing a setting in which reporters may develop and effectively use an understanding of educational dynamics. The background expertise may come, in part, from classroom training, but it's better if coordinated with general reporting experience.

Further, any person moving into education reporting must feel an obligation to read and study extensively, with particular concentration on law, political science, the budget process, and education methodology. In many ways, the requirement of keeping abreast of the field is more stringent for reporters than for the educators themselves. The reporter seldom has the luxury of concentrating on a single education specialty; rather he or she must be prepared to deal with a broad spectrum of education-related information.

**Saundra Keys and
Vince Kasper**
of the Philadelphia
Daily News (Daily
News photo)

For example, Saundra Keyes of the *Philadelphia Daily News* covered education for seven years in Kentucky and Tennessee. She believes education writers must use skills needed on nearly all other beats. "Education cuts across virtually every other beat: local government and tax policy; state legislative decisions; all kinds of social issues, religious issues, and psychology—how children learn. Few other beats offer so much possibility for creative reporting."[3]

Most education reporters list education finances as the most difficult story with which they must cope regularly. An understanding of the budgetary process, accounting principles, and financial terminology is necessary, whether it's from formal training or from on-the-job dealings with school financial officers.

Also useful is regular reading of publications that pay particular attention to educational trends. A must on the list of any reporter concerned with higher education would be the *Chronicle of Higher Education,* a weekly tabloid newspaper devoted to tracking trends on college and university campuses. *Phi Delta Kappan* is often mentioned as an excellent source of elementary and secondary school information. The *NEA Journal,* published by the National Education Association, provides general information from the perspective of the nation's largest professional organization.

Reporters should also attempt to read newspapers and magazines that regularly provide education material, particularly *The New York Times* and *The Los Angeles Times* and the national news magazines. This diet is supplemented further with local newspapers, student newspapers, and newsletters published by professional education associations.

As in all journalism, the purpose of reading education materials and talking with educators is not always to gain information for a specific story. At times, a national story may have local application. Or the reporter may gain the name of a news source. But the real point is developing a general expertise that provides substance to any reporter's overall coverage of education. Without such background, the reporter fails to learn a valuable lesson in the constant fight to maintain control of his or her coverage.

As in several other reporting specialties, education reporters can meet regularly with their peers to discuss problems through the Education Writers Association, which was formed in the 1940s. This organization now has nearly 500 members.[4]

A STRUCTURAL APPROACH TO EDUCATION SOURCES

Educators believe in delegating authority, and the organization of most school systems proves it. It is a precise hierarchy based on categorical job descriptions, which tightly constrict the functions of everyone in the system. These boundaries are carefully maintained, especially when dealing with reporters. It is not uncommon that deliberate efforts are made to box reporters into using a limited number of sources at the top of the structure. Educators seem to be more successful at that than other government officials. The most generally accessible person in any school system usually is the superintendent at the top of the heap. Accessibility often declines dramatically as one moves down the hierarchy.

Of course, educators do not consistently seek to deceive reporters, to deliberately withhold information, or to seek to cover up questionable activities. Most educators are honest, dedicated people and are probably less self-serving in what they say and do than many other categories of public officials. But, as a group, they are difficult for reporters. The jargon they use to communicate with each other is natural to them, but a curse to journalists. Their use of qualified remarks and complex philosophical explanations is not for a general audience. Their desire to see only good news spread out before the public seems to have greater intensity than that of other news sources. And they sincerely believe what they often tell reporters: "If you publicize that, you'll hurt the school and the kids."

But such generalizations may not be fair. Some educators are more gregarious and naturally more open. Some have a better understanding of journalism and thus less fear about dealing directly with journalists. Some simply believe more strongly in the value of publicity and are willing to take their chances that the good will outweigh the bad. Some have had bad experiences and thus have resolved to avoid similar situations in which they may have been burned. Some have developed a trusting and cooperative relationship with journalists.

The subject matter often makes the difference. It is not uncommon that the greater the controversy, the greater the reluctance to speak. It makes a difference whether the questioning is about programs or policy. Educators like to talk about programs, but they reserved discussions of policy matters for the very few. That's hierarchy again.

And, as in all journalism, dealing with educators means deliberate efforts to cultivate them as sources. It means spending time with them in discussions that may or may not provide immediate stories, getting to know them and demonstrating interest in their jobs and their lives, and doing homework so that questions asked will reflect both knowledge and interest. This kind of interest will reap a considerable return when the reporter must ask about problems or must call at night for a quick response on a breaking story.

Michele Norris of the *Washington Post,* advises education reporters to "cultivate" in particular a handful of teachers and principals in a district. These people can provide background information that is not necessarily for attribution. They are also people she can always come back to if she needs information, she said.[5]

The First Authority: State Government

In spite of the tradition of local control, education is a state function. The U.S. Constitution makes no direct reference to education, and most state constitutions stipulate establishing and maintaining of a system of free public schools. Even though local officials are permitted to make most specific operational decisions at home, the states establish the rules of the game. Reporters covering education locally will find it necessary to be in touch with political and/or educational leaders in the state capital.

That means, first, the governor and state legislators. The legislature passes the laws that set educational standards and, perhaps, even more importantly, it rules on the budget, which determines how much money will be available. The governor proposes that budget, is a strong political force in how much emphasis education will receive, and often appoints the state board of education that supervises and regulates local programs.

All states have a supervisory body for education, with the most frequent organization being an appointed lay group that names the state superintendent of schools (or public instruction). In some instances, the board or superintendent or both may be elected. Reporters also have to deal with a state department of education, which may have thousands of employees, as the professional complement to the superintendent and the board.

Major functions of board members are to establish (within legal and constitutional boundaries) standards of instruction and program development; provide board leadership and direction to their counterparts on the local level; regulate, when necessary; and provide educational resources through planning, research, and evaluation. For the most part, it is expected that local superintendents and boards will run their systems in compliance with state requirements without involving state or federal officials. The system, over the years, has tended to work that way.

However, in many areas of the country that process has been changing. The state and (to some degree) the federal government are assuming more authority in how local programs are run. There are several reasons for this, but it's mostly a financial matter. As school programs have grown, local financial resources for education (principally property taxes) have proven inadequate. Thus, local officials have been forced to turn to state and national governments for financial assistance. That sort of situation, over time, is bound to have impact on the decision-making process. Indeed, it has.

It is most likely that education reporters in the coming years will find that covering local school programs involves greater attention to state government. Local control is not a thing of the past, but local officials now have much more active partners in the decisions they make about neighborhood schools. It's going to be more necessary that reporters trace those strings from the local board to the state capital or Washington, D.C.

Board of Education: Lay Control

At the top of the local hierarchy is the board of education, and it is here that reporters devote a high percentage of their attention. This is done for two reasons, one good and one not so good. First, board members, legally agents of the state, are responsible for directing the local program within the state law. Reporters must carefully follow decisions because they represent directions local schools will take. Second, boards, for the most part, operate as a group and thus have very convenient meetings that usually are subject to open meeting laws and thus make it easy for reporters to get needed information.

In some states, board members are elected, usually on a nonpartisan basis. In other states, they are appointed, often by the mayor with council approval. But in either event, their function is to set up the educational policy of the school system and thus serve the fundamental American concept that schools should be locally controlled.

The resulting political activities must capture the attention of journalists. Local control means citizens should be made aware of the degree to which the board is representing their educational interests. It means citizens must have information to evaluate a board's internal management of the school system. Since schools are such an essential part of any community, educational decisions often have broad repercussions.

More and more through court decisions, the society seems to expect the schools to serve as the focal point of social change. In desegregating schools, for instance, boards of education have been forced to serve as the most visible—sometimes the only—aspect of efforts to cope with a serious social dilemma.

Thus, reporters will be on hand as boards select the system's administrative leadership, allocate its financial resources, plan school construction programs, hire teachers, establish attendance areas, determine which federally funded programs to implement, and seek to abide by court decisions. Reporters will inform citizens not only of the decisions made but also of the process and considerations involved.

Much of this information will be gained from meetings, although it always will be supplemented by interviews with board members and other school officials. This means that education reporters occasionally may have to face traditional battles against executive (closed) sessions to ensure that the process remains open to the public eye. It means they must understand what often is very complex educational and legal material.

It also means that reporters must fully comprehend the power structure of a board and school system. Legally, all board members are equal. But that's legal fiction. As is usually the case, practical realities are that some—because of the force of their personalities, their place in the community, or their longevity on the board—have greater influence than others. Board members may also form coalitions to represent educational philosophies, a desire to gain political power, or efforts to represent specific community groups.

The relationship between members and superintendents is an essential part of any analysis of school board policies. While board members hold legal authority and technically cannot delegate that authority to anyone, many serve as little more than rubber stamps for forceful administrators. In almost all cases, the superintendent recommends and the board determines. But the process is distorted when a superintendent's recommendations are accepted automatically. Such a circumstance, of course, will dictate to reporters that they spend more time in conversation with the administrator and then rather matter-of-factly report the board's official decisions.

But even a board that maintains its legal authority does not function in a social or political vacuum. Members are subject to countless pressures from individuals and groups within and without the school system. American society has become increasingly pluralistic, and this is reflected by those who desire to influence directions a school system takes.

Therefore, reporters should monitor internal efforts of such teachers' organizations as the National Education Association and the American Federation of Teachers. They also should give attention to numerous external groups, which include educational change as part of their reason for existence. Among others, this would include minority, ethnic, and women's groups; taxpayer organizations; broad-based community groups; and citizens who form special organizations for specific curricular or other educational purposes.

The Professional Administrators

When reporters are after specific information about school programs and problems, they must deal primarily with those whose day-to-day duties are to run those programs. Most school districts—even the smallest ones—have a central office that is responsible for dotting the i's and crossing the t's of school board policy. They implement. And no reporter who wants more than generalities can ignore them.

In a sense, there are two kinds of school system administrators: generalists whose responsibilities are system-wide and specialists who deal with more narrow components of the program. It is fair to say that the lower one moves on the system hierarchy, the more likely one is to deal with specialists whose major journalistic value grows from their expertise in specific types of educational activity.

Superintendents, for example, must be generalists. The larger the school system, the more general their knowledge is likely to be. They fit the pieces of the system puzzle into place. Like the school board, they provide direction and can be expected to have broad understanding, if not specific knowledge, about given programs of schools within the system. In contrast, directors of curriculum are valuable as sources only when reporters are after that kind of information. That sounds simple enough, but it is a principle too many reporters ignore by devoting the bulk of their attention to the top of the educational hierarchy.

Reporters need large numbers of administrative sources, first, because of the differing levels of expertise, and second, because of the extreme sensitivity to publicity characteristic of many educators. They need individual experts to give depth to their coverage, and they need trusted alternative sources when traditional paths to information are blocked. This means conscious cultivation of sources at three levels within the administrative organization.

Without question, the *superintendent* will be the major source of administrative information. As chief executive officer, he or she is in charge, and it's only natural that reporters maintain constant contact. If the board of education is close to a major decision, comments from the superintendent may influence that decision. If a citizens' group is complaining about education quality or about an individual program, the superintendent must be first to answer the questions. If staff specialists are working on a new program, their action comes only on the superintendent's direction, and the reasons for that direction should be made public.

But superintendents do more than maintain the internal organization and provide educational direction. Theirs is a political job as much as it is educational. Local school systems gain their financial support through public action. The success of any school system depends upon public support. This is a major responsibility to which superintendents devote large amounts of time.

How the effort is structured depends on the style of the superintendent. It may be through numerous public appearances before citizens' groups, parents, and local government bodies. It may involve remaining constantly in the public eye and developing personal trust or even charisma. Or it may be sought through quiet circulation and attempts to cultivate lay leadership. There are limitations, but a superintendent can be less conspicuous if the school system is publicly supported by respected individuals in the community.

Whatever a superintendent's style, reporters will watch the effort to maintain educational support. The public component of that effort is easy to follow, and journalists simply make day-to-day decisions about whether to report on a specific speech or panel discussion. Quiet leadership is more difficult to follow, but it is a story that requires the effort.

A superintendent's leadership, internally and externally, is extended by a central staff that may include several *assistant superintendents.* Depending on local organization, some of these assistants may have general functions and therefore do some of the superintendent's legwork, or they may have responsibilities for specific components of the operation, such as assistant superintendent for pupil personnel services, instruction, or business. Reporters, naturally, will at times work with these individuals, but because of the nature of their positions they often are reluctant to speak on the record. Reporters seeking information will be told, "You'd better see the superintendent about that" or "Here's the information, but be sure to talk with the superintendent before you publish it."

At times, the assistants or the superintendent may refer reporters to *staff specialists* who direct specific parts of the school system's program. Given varying titles—director, supervisor, or consultant—these individuals usually are trained professionals in an educational program. As such, they advise the board and the superintendent on the areas of their expertise and supervise programs in the schools.

The number of specialists available to school administrators and reporters will vary according to the school district size, but among them could be directors of elementary education; secondary education; curriculum; special education; adult education; instructional materials; audiovisual education; publications and information; planning; research; evaluation; finance; buildings and grounds; health services; cafeteria services; transportation; and others.

It's difficult, especially when dealing with a large school system, for reporters to maintain frequent contact with the number of persons who serve as staff specialists. It is not necessary to see them as frequently as board members or the superintendent. However, special efforts should be made to become acquainted with them so that, when a need arises, both the reporter and the source will be familiar and know how to deal with one another.

Another source of assistance will be the school system's office that's responsible for *public relations* or *public information.* Pick up any educational journal and browse through it. Chances are you'll find an article about effective public relations or the publicizing of positive news in the schools. Educators are interested in good public relations, and school systems typically devote considerable attention to gaining favorable publicity about their activities and programs. Someone in the system will have that responsibility even if there is no formal office devoted to the cause.

Dealing with school public relations personnel is like dealing with them in business or government. They will produce news releases and provide information, but their chief journalistic value is in suggesting story ideas and making school system personnel available to reporters. They can provide factual information and background material, but should seldom be depended on as the sole source.

The Action Is in the Schools

Sports reporters go to the ballpark. Government reporters go to city hall. Court reporters go to the courthouse. How strange it is that many education reporters spend so little time in schools. "Don't have time," they say, and that's true as long as news organizations cling to the idea that education can be covered at board meetings and from the superintendent's office. But education is schools. That's where the action is, and that's where many of the most important stories can be found. Not only during times of crisis, but also during daily activities.

It's in the schools that programs succeed and fail. It's in the schools that thousands of feature stories—not just the "cutesys," but real, meaningful human drama—literally walk the halls. It's in the schools that value is gained or lost from the millions of dollars invested annually in education. It's also in the schools that some of the very best sources of information sit unnoticed by reporters who pass through those doors infrequently. Principals, teachers, and the students themselves may know more about a school system's education program than anyone in the central office or board room. It may not always be easy to get access to them, but there certainly isn't hope until they're approached.

Most *principals* are conscientious and nice people. Many are good administrators. Some are excellent educators, but they don't have the best reputation for cooperating with reporters. This lack of sensitivity to the need for informing the public can probably be explained in several ways. First, many principals (and teachers) believe that their job is simply to stay in the building and teach. Unfortunately, this is not always the case.

Second, in too many situations, principals are not expected by those with whom they work to be up front in public situations. Principals should not rock the boat; that's what they believe.

Perhaps a third component is that principals have been ignored by reporters so universally that few have had the opportunity to develop a journalistic understanding. They fear what they don't understand, especially when it is their perception that stepping out of line could cost them their jobs.

The answer to the dilemma is easy to state and difficult to accomplish. Principals have the same relationships within the schools as superintendents have within the system. They are generalists responsible for directing and coordinating the staff toward established goals. Thus, they have potentially great journalistic value. For the reporter, that means long-term cultivation, frequent contact, and coverage of successes as well as failures. Reporters must not allow principals' reluctance to overcome their determined efforts to develop the kind of trusting relationship that leads to more complete coverage.

The same logic applies to *teachers.* That relationship may be hampered if their immediate superior is the principal who is perceived as reluctant or if the teachers have direct orders to be silent. In some instances, reporters must get the permission of the superintendent and/or the principal to interview teachers.

But the flip side of the teacher situation is the courage gained from peer support in the form of increasing openness of various teachers' organizations. Especially on certain issues, such as teachers' salaries and working conditions, teachers—most likely younger ones who have not developed overly protective attitudes about their schools or the system— are more inclined to make statements for publication. This can make good copy and can help balance what too often is top-heavy coverage.

But what about the young people, the *students* themselves? Are they too inexperienced to speak on something as serious as their education? The answer is no, not if they are given the right kind of opportunity. Reporters, of course, must be cautious with statements made by young people, especially those at the elementary level. Questions must be asked carefully, and answers must be evaluated. But, like teachers, students are very close to education, and often their perspective is a significant addition to a news story.

Michele Norris formerly of *The Chicago Tribune,* and six other reporters spent seven months in the Chicago schools, talking extensively with students, teachers, and administrators. Their two-week series was a combination of hard news, feature, and interpretive and investigative stories (see accompanying story).

Norris, for instance, learned about one teacher whose twenty-two fourth-grade students were forced to attend summer school. "She didn't teach them enough to pass," Norris said. Norris stressed that the best stories come from inside the classroom. "Amazing things go on in the classroom," she said.[6]

In addition, opportunities for feature stories about students are great for the reporter who spends time in the schools. Some of these, of course, will be of limited substance. Their chief value will grow from humor or their quality of "kids say and do the darndest things." There's a need for that kind of story. But that's not all. Young people represent a microcosm of the community at large. They have successes and failures. They struggle to overcome problems. They make tough decisions. They react in very honest ways to their environment. Both the strengths and weaknesses of society will be reflected in the school hallways, and reporters can capture those reflections.

Selection system can make the cruelest cut of all

The majority of Chicago high school students are consigned to dilapidated, mostly segregated neighborhood schools serving a course of study that prepares them neither for college nor the world of work.

They are the discards in a three-tiered system of widely inconsistent quality, a system of educational triage that results in a separate and unequal education for the city's 111,891 high school students.

Those the system chooses to save are the brightest youngsters, selected by race, income and achievement for academic and vocational magnet schools where teachers are hand-picked and supplies are plentiful.

The remaining 66,371 students are tagged with third-class status and sent to neighborhood schools where a limited curriculum and the lack of supplies stand as a daily reminder of their shortcomings.

Most of these students do not go on to college. Yet they are fed a steady diet of academic subjects designed for college-bound students.

Most do poorly. A majority drop out. Few leave school with a good grasp of even the basic reading and math skills looked for by employers or colleges.

A third of the class of 1985 were unemployed a year after graduation, a study for the mayor's education summit found. Another third were in college and a third were working.

Selective academic schools such as Whitney Young Magnet High and Lane Technical High make up the top tier and operate much like private institutions, accepting only students with solid attendance records, excellent grades and above average standardized test scores.

More than 20,000 of the system's best students are channeled into 12 selective high schools. Another 11,760 attend community academies that offer some special programs to students who live in the school's enrollment area.

Chicago's academic magnet schools were created as a result of a desegregation lawsuit. But in a system whose students are overwhelmingly black and Hispanic, the separation of the best from the rest has spawned a different kind of segregation that discriminates on the basis of achievement as well as race.

Students who cannot get into the top schools but want a decent preparation for college compete for spots in selective vocational schools that offer academic as well as technical training.

Those schools, set up to groom students with no college plans, have become second choice as havens for college-bound students who might otherwise flee the crumbling city schools.

The selective vocational schools have become the middle tier between the elite college preparatory schools and the neighborhood schools. About 11,000 students attend five selective vocational high schools. Another 1,876 attend vocational schools that do not select students on the basis of achievement.

"A high percentage of the kids here aren't interested in vocational education," said Jack Perlin, principal of Prosser Vocational High, 2148 N. Long Ave. "They come here because it's perceived as a safe place."

The 39 neighborhood schools make up the bottom tier, the place where students land when they can go nowhere else.

"The effect on students who do not go to school with high achievers is devastating," said Alvin Lubov, principal of Douglass Middle School, 543 N. Waller Ave. "It's hard to overcome feelings of rejection."

"It anoints certain youngsters," said Jack Mitchell, field superintendent for high schools. "Their whole attitude is changed. [Those who aren't selected] are leftovers." They are the children of a lesser God.

The academic magnets and vocational schools have not only the best students but also the most involved parents and the best of the teaching staff.

"There is a great deal of pressure on our teachers because 50 percent of our parents are college graduates," said Powhatan Collins, principal of Whitney Young, 211 S. Laflin St. "They know what it takes for a child to get into a top college, and if we're not doing it, we hear about it."

Meanwhile, low-achieving students who enter neighborhood high schools must take double and triple sessions of remedial classes to meet tougher city and state mandates for graduation.

As a result, few have time to take vocational or business electives that would prepare them for work, or art and music classes that might spark their interest in learning and, perhaps, keep them in school.

"Students have to pass the requisites to graduate," said Kenneth Van Spankeren, principal of Orr High, 730 N. Pulaski Rd. "Those core subjects take up most of their time."

"They're taking two periods of English or math," said Harry Tobin, director of vocational education for the system. "So it shrinks the number of opportunities for a student to take electives like vocational education."

Ironically, the vocational courses the students cannot fit into their schedule might help them learn academic subjects.

"Teaching basic math is part of our curriculum," said Theoda Smith, a plumbing teacher at Dunbar. "About 3 percent of the kids have basic math problems. But I haven't failed yet in teaching them how to use fractions. They learn when it's hands-on."

Yet, despite their advantages in reaching slow learners, vocational courses have been trimmed from general schools due to budget cuts.

The electronics shop was dropped at Orr in 1985. A school radio station died four years ago. A commercial art class was canceled this year.

The pressure to maintain the triple-tiered system is intense. Academic magnet and selective vocational schools are the only remaining hold the school system has on the middle class in Chicago.

"I stayed in Chicago because my daughter's [magnet] school is a good one," said Jody Baty, member of the Parents United to Reform Education, who testified at a joint legislative hearing in the fall. "We would not have stayed if we could go only to our local school."

But magnet schools have triggered resentment in the parents of students who are overlooked. They complain that the magnets drain the system's best teachers and scarce resources.

"We're tired of hearing everyone complain about how the layoffs might affect the precious magnet schools," said Denise Brown, a South Side parent, when it was thought that cutbacks after the fall teacher strike might affect the magnets.

"Why haven't these people complained about the way our children are treated in the neighborhood schools? It's because they don't care about the children in the neighborhood schools."

This story, from *The Chicago Tribune,* was one of more than twenty-five written by a team of seven reporters as part of a special series about the Chicago public schools. Note how the reporters do not just rely on administrators for information, but also quote teachers and parents. © Copyrighted, Chicago Tribune Company, all rights reserved, used with permission.

There is, of course, a potential access problem for reporters who want to talk with students. Superintendents, principals, and teachers naturally are wary of anything that may disrupt the flow of school activities. They also are nervous about what young people will say to a reporter. But, surely, sensitive journalists and educators can overcome such concerns.

It is possible for the determined journalist to talk with young people (and teachers) outside the school, and there are occasions when that is the best course of action. But, unless there are reasons for going outside the school, the same atmosphere of understanding and trust that applies across the journalistic spectrum should be developed with school officials. Interviews, even with cameras and microphones, can be organized in a manner that will not disrupt a school program. While school officials can in no way be granted control over the content of the interviews, their fears can be reduced by the understanding reporter whose approach to any story—positive or negative—is honest, accurate, and well balanced.

CAMPUS SOURCES TEND TO BE MORE OPEN

The problems faced by reporters in getting information in elementary and secondary schools are duplicated on college and university campuses, although they usually are not as severe. The very nature of higher education is that academic debate is encouraged or at least tolerated. This means that campus administrators and faculty are more accustomed to answering questions, presenting points of view, and when necessary, dealing with dissent.

Yet, despite the honesty, university officials tend to be sensitive when criticized, said Joe Rigert of *The Star Tribune.* "Sometimes universities think they have the corner on truth," Rigert says. "Everything they do is right." Because of this attitude, universities are the most "unwatchdogged" institutions in society, Rigert believes.[7]

It is evident that most college and university presidents are not subject to the close media scrutiny of their counterparts in primary and secondary education. Consequently, they are more likely to put themselves into positions in which they must deal with reporters. They may hold formal news conferences or informal briefing sessions. They may make more effective use of public relations offices in informing reporters of possible news stories and in providing background information. And they may more readily submit to one-on-one interviews.

But, as in government and corporate structure, the person at the top is more likely to speak candidly. Vice presidents, for example, often are less open because of their fear of jeopardizing their positions.

Another source of information is the university board of trustees, a body that, like school boards, oversees the operation of the college or university. Unlike school boards, however, nearly all boards of trustees consist of appointed rather than elected members. In most states, the boards of public universities are appointed by the governor.

Because they are appointed rather than elected, most board members may feel more open with the press—they may feel they do not have to "play" politics to get re-elected. On the other hand, because they are not elected, they may not feel a strong accountability toward the public, and consequently towards reporters, that elected officials do.

Also, because board members do not necessarily live in the same city that houses the university, they may be more difficult to get to know. The only time the reporter sees them is at monthly or even less frequent board meetings.

Like board members, college students also represent an alternative source for gaining a fresh perspective. Perhaps the best sources are individuals who are involved in student governing bodies, although many reporters will make the campus newspaper their first stop. The goal is to find students who have a campus-wide perspective and who may reasonably be assumed to be informed. Often, higher education reporters will make it a practice to read student newspapers to gain story and source ideas.

More and more state-supported universities are placing students on their boards of trustees. For that reason, students are getting more of a voice in the operation of the universities.

Of course, as universities get larger and larger, they become a more important source of stories. Some issues of interest in the 1990s are bound to be the continuing use of standardizing testing, the shrinking educational dollar, and the nontraditional student.

Critics charge that educators and reporters alike are doing a great public disservice through their use and misuse of test scores. There is considerable debate over whether IQ tests, the Scholastic Aptitude Test (the SATs), or American College Test (ACT) actually provide the kind of information they are designed to produce. There is equal debate over the indiscriminate use of such test scores by colleges.

Also, educators today claim that fewer and fewer dollars are being allocated to public universities and colleges each year. Rigert suggests doing a comparison of actual dollars allocated to higher education over a period of ten or twenty years, adjusting for inflation.

Finally, most educators will say that what was once a "traditional" college student—a student aged eighteen to twenty-one who finished college in four years—is gradually disappearing. As more adults return to

college after establishing careers, and as more students work while attending school, the average age of college students is rising. This is a
trend that will probably continue well into the 1990s and one that will
demand coverage.

Like hundreds of other subjects, these stories are difficult, and do not
offer the kind of material that can be presented on the basis of a single
interview. The kind of understanding that makes it possible for reporters
to handle such stories is required to ensure that they will know when
pertinent information is missing. It's too easy to overlook what is absent
from an impressively detailed report. This is not necessarily deliberate
deception, although it may be. Often it's a problem that grows out of the
fact that reporters don't have opportunities or the desire to follow a story
as it is being developed. And, even if they had the opportunity, it is questionable whether many reporters could afford the time to sit through
hours of planning sessions. But they must have knowledge and the perception to fulfill the responsibility of finding the whole story.

FOLLOWING THE EDUCATIONAL DOLLAR

Reporters follow the educational dollar carefully. They know that how
funds are obtained and spent is a major factor in the quality of public or
private education. It's a subject in which citizens are intensely interested, and it's especially important because those citizens provide most
of those funds and usually have a strong voice in the amount of money
made available.

Generally, funding for public schools comes from three main sources,
with the federal dollar representing an important contribution, although
a relatively small one in comparison with state and local funds. The typical federal contribution represents about 8 percent of the total budget,
usually allocated for such specific programs as special education and
school lunches. Some state funds also are earmarked for specific programs. But the biggest proportion is provided for general support,
meaning that local school boards may allocate the funds for whatever
use they deem appropriate and necessary.

On the local level, property taxes are the biggest single source of
income for public school systems, and this provides some financial problems. In many instances, property tax systems are outdated and inequitable and do not produce adequate revenues. Often taxation rates must
be submitted for a public vote, and the public mood in recent years has
not been to support increases or even to continue present rates.

Nevertheless, school systems remain dependent upon the property taxes that are calculated on the assessed value of property within the school district. The unit of taxation is called a mill, with 1 mill being equal to 0.1 cent (1/10 cent). In some states, tax millage is based on the full assessed property value, while in other states it is calculated on a percentage of assessed property value.

If taxable property in a school system, for example, is assessed at $8 million and the system needs an additional $80,000, it will ask for an increase in property taxes of 10 mills, which translates into 1 cent on every dollar of the assessed property value. The formula for calculating mill levies is:

$$\text{Mill levy} = \frac{\text{additional taxes to be collected}}{\text{total assessed property value of the district}}$$

The importance of whether a district uses the total assessed value or a percentage of that value is thus clear. Property owners with holdings valued at $80,000, paying 10 mills on the full assessed value of that property, will owe $800 in property tax. If the system is based on 50 percent of the assessed value, the amount will be $400.

Thus, while millage rates are important, reporters also must be aware of how much of the assessed property value is used in the tax calculations. The calculations can become even more complicated because of the existence of rollbacks which, for one reason or another, reduce the amount of millage authorized. For example, senior citizens may be granted a rollback that reduces the amount of their property taxes. Or a state may use a rollback to limit the total amount that may be collected, especially in times of high inflation when property values are soaring.

The need for such mill levies to produce additional operating funds is one major instance in which many school systems call for a public vote. A related form occurs when the systems want additional income for capital outlays—expansion or renovation of present facilities or the building of new facilities. These are termed "bond issues" and usually are limited to a time period that will allow production of the funds needed to accomplish the stated capital goals.

An equally important side of the budgetary picture, of course, is how the available funds are spent. By far, the largest proportion of school expenditures comes under the heading of "personnel" (generally from 65 to 85 percent of the total). Other spending categories of perhaps greater immediate interest to readers, to viewers, and to listeners would include administrative expenses, teaching supplies such as textbooks and audiovisual materials, transportation expenses, provisions for student health care, and maintenance costs.

Whatever the expenditure category, however, the point to remember is that the budgetary figures mean little by themselves. The dollars are spent for people— students, teachers, administrators, and other necessary personnel—and have meaning only when related in human terms. Specific line items in a school system budget are best translated into how they result in curriculum, other services, or, in general, the quality of instruction.

Thus, while the documents themselves may be available to reporters, interviews with school officials or visits to the individual schools are needed to put meaning into the figures. It is not enough, but possibly the earliest opportunity for reporters to make these connections stems from the fact that most states require public budget hearings. Such hearings give reporters the chance to hear discussion by board members and any residents who attend or to interview the officials themselves.

There's one other major function for the reporter following the education budget. It's probably true that school systems provide fewer instances of fraud or conflict of interest than other public bodies, but they do handle millions of dollars. Therefore, it's inevitable that cases will occur in which some officials yield to temptation. Contracts will be awarded in ways that will financially benefit board members, or officials may seek other ways to benefit personally from their professional decisions. The large number of requirements increases the chances that legal improprieties—even though they may be honest mistakes—will occur.

Reporters will watch carefully for these situations. They recognize that in spite of the relatively good record educational officials have attained that the journalistic watchdog functions are still necessary. Reporters must understand the law and the budgetary process. That's the only way to ensure that the public will know its money is being properly handled.

Done properly, education reporting is like taking on the whole society. While the focus may be the school program, the stories represent the total community. What happens in the schools reflects what is happening on the streets of the town. The attitudes of the citizens are reflected and magnified in the offices and hallways of school buildings. The community's major social problems, in fact, may surface first among the young, who are not quite so adept at hiding their feelings.

Some of the most significant educational stories of the twentieth century have not been educational stories at all. They have been social stories which, for only circumstantial reasons, occurred in educational settings. Desegregation, for example, the top education story, is the most visible part of a massive civil rights movement which has permeated every corner of society. Desegregation will continue in coming years to absorb the attention of education reporters as this society persists in its efforts to use its schools as a means of solving its problems of human inequality.

Other problems can be added to that list: problems of violence and vandalism; efforts to expand social and economic opportunities of whole classes of people—women, minority groups, the handicapped, the gifted, and the poor.

The nation's financial problems—inflation, dwindling local resources, inequitable tax formulas, fluctuating abilities of state and federal governments—all have their educational components. Boards of education have only the authority to ask taxpayers to raise their own taxes voluntarily, and that's not a popular request these days. The quality of an educational program depends from the beginning on availability of funds to meet minimum needs or to develop innovative programs. This should make the budget one of the education reporter's most dog-eared documents.

Internal money battles, especially those between teachers and boards of education, often erupt into the streets and become volatile community issues. Often the issues for which teachers are fighting involve more control over the programs or guarantees that the atmosphere in which they work will be improved.

This latter category provides news organizations with stories about discipline, attendance, and transportation, and about the physical environment in which students and teachers have to work and the resources available to them. It provides a focus on activities that create special learning opportunities. Popular community-oriented activities such as athletics or adult education merit attention, as does the impact of the energy crisis upon the nation's schools.

But perhaps in the long run the most significant story will involve classroom learning opportunities. In spite of the often mentioned public disillusionment about education, the belief rests squarely upon what is being taught and how well that teaching is accomplished. It's a paradox that, except for occasional bursts of enthusiasm when a curricular matter somehow leaps into the public's mind, curriculum perhaps represents the weakest component of education coverage. If there is a back-to-basics movement these days, and if there is a concern over why students cannot read, it's the curricular trend of previous years that has led to that situation.

Reporters themselves admit to journalistic weaknesses. Doing the curriculum story properly requires extensive use of every skill education writers are supposed to possess. Unless the reporter understands the subject matter, knows how to deal with education specialists, understands research, and has the writing skill to make educational theory come to life, the chances are good that the story about curricular innovation will be deadly dull.

But if contemporary discussions of why young people can't read or write have captured the public's interest, it makes sense that these same discussions could be even more valuable if done before the controversy arises. It is not just the reporters who must understand this. If educators dislike the negative publicity that they occasionally receive, they, too, must look ahead. Many of them must adjust their thinking in terms of dealing with reporters.

Education mirrors the community. It's certainly the most pervasive social institution and probably the object of the most natural social interest. This makes the tasks of the education reporter interesting, and this provides the greatest challenge.

NOTES

1. Bette S. Orsini, "Reporting on Education," *presstime*, September, 1985, p. 21.
2. "Reporting on Education," p. 21.
3. Saundra Keyes, as quoted in "The Beat Nobody Wants," *Columbia Journalism Review*, January/February 1985, p. 37.
4. "Reporting on Education," p. 4.
5. Michele Norris, remarks made during panel discussion, "Getting the Basics on Education," annual conference of the Investigative Reporters and Editors, Minneapolis, Minn., June 4, 1988.
6. Michele Norris, "Getting the Basics on Education."
7. Joe Rigert, "Getting the Basics on Education."

Business and the Economy

13

On October 19, 1987, the stock market plunged 508 points, sending reporters and editors scrambling for what was to become one of the biggest national stories of the year.

In March 1985, the Ohio-based Home State Savings closed its doors permanently as news photographers from across the country snapped pictures of long lines in front of other Ohio savings and loan institutions. The savings and loan crisis throughout the country eventually became one of the biggest national stories that year and for several years to follow.

Throughout the 1980s, consumers shopped in and used products made by some of the biggest companies in the United States, such as Federated department stores (which owned Bloomingdale's and Bonwit Teller stores), Goodyear Tire and Rubber Co., and RJR Nabisco. All three of those companies—and hundreds of major companies all over the world— have either been purchased or been takeover targets within the last few years. The takeover trend was clearly one of the biggest stories of the 1980s and probably will continue to be one in the 1990s.

These stories, and many more, have helped spawn what may be considered a type of revolution in business coverage in today's newspapers and on television. Ten years ago, few local television news outlets had their own business reporters, and even many major newspapers had only one or two people covering business fulltime. All that has changed dramatically.

Between 1975 and 1985, the expenditures for business reporting by newspapers with 350,000 and above circulation increased by 228 percent. Newspapers with 200,000 to 350,000 circulations increased their budgets for business news by 184 percent; and those with circulations of 100,000 to 200,000 increased spending on business news by 113 percent. Similarly, the average number of people on business staffs grew from an average of 5.7 to 18.9 in ten years.[1]

John Wicklein, a former *New York Times* reporter, notes that the "old days" of business writing are over—those days when covering business meant reprinting corporate public relations releases verbatim. "A new breed of enterprising editors and reporters is coming along—professionals who are not interested in turning out puff pieces on companies that advertise in the paper, but in reporting corporate developments, warts and all." Further, he believes, the first-rate business journalist has perhaps a more difficult job than his or her counterpart in other fields of reporting. The business reporter must know how to investigate a story and put it together in a way that will interest general readers. In addition, he or she must pick up specialized knowledge needed to cover business and economics. This specialized knowledge can be attained by learning on the job and by taking specialized courses that enable the reporter to learn how business operates. "What is needed most," Wicklein believes, "is an ability and a commitment to do hard, digging reporting."[2]

That, of course, is easier said than done. Even the most seasoned business reporters and editors can get duped at times, either through ignorance of terms and procedures, or simply because of their gullibility, as the accompanying story illustrates.

Some tips on separating the hype from the legitimate business story

"Beware of the Muhammad Ali car."

That's the battle cry of skeptical business editors at the Washington Post. According to these editors, the "Ali car" is just the kind of hyped-business story that doesn't belong in print alongside real financial news.

When Ali's p.r. representatives called Post business editors last fall to plant the story, they got no further than when they tried to plant the Ali magic shoe polish story many months before. But this time the Ali representatives found a neat trick: they approached the Metro section of the Post and sold the story on its "local angle," since the Ali car plant would be built in South Boston, Va.

Last October 31, the Metro section of the Post carried a 942-word story on plans for Ali Motors. The story said the company would make a $35,000 sports car, have annual sales of $96 million, create 410 jobs, pay $120,000 in local taxes and begin hiring in November. The story said the cars would be sold in the Middle East and come in a dazzling array of colors, including "Knock-Out Black" and "Olympic Gold."

Although the story did say that lack of financing could be a major obstacle, it should not have run at all, Post business editors say. On Dec. 24, the Post was obliged to follow up with a story that began, "Muhammad Ali's luxury car company will not build a manufacturing plant in Southside, Virginia, company officials said yesterday, adding that Wisconsin has been selected instead."

Editors and reporters in Wisconsin should learn from the Post's mistake. They should begin by asking whether there is secure financing for the Ali project. The Post's initial story on Ali Motors said, "Financing is the big question." In reality, it is the only question.

There are lots of "Ali car" stories out there and scores of hacks looking to peddle them to business editors and reporters. After all, newspapers have credibility. With enough articles in hand about plans for an exciting venture, a good promoter may be able to line up backers. At the very least, he can earn a fee for getting the boss's name in the paper.

Real estate developers, and the hype artists who represent them, are notorious for impersonating "Ali car" promoters. They phone on slow news days and offer to drop by the newsroom. They bring an artist's rendering of plans for a giant new office building. While they have no objection to letting you use the drawing in the newspaper, their warning is clear: you only have an exclusive on the story for 24 hours, before the drawing and information will be available to your chief competitors.

Before dashing off into the sunset with the latest real estate scoop, don't forget to ask some important questions.

What evidence is there of secure financing? Who are the lenders? What tenants have signed leases? Have they been given free rent up front or will they be paying the going rate? Have building permits been issued? If you get answers to these questions, be sure to call the lenders and tenants, just to make sure.

There is nothing wrong with a minor article about plans for a real estate venture, provided the venture has financing. There is nothing right about a blazing headline proclaiming a developer's plans if those plans lack financing. If a developer is looking for tenants and financial backers, the appropriate place is in the newspaper's business or real estate section. But the appropriate format is an advertisement, not an article.

Don't be fooled by signs, either. In 1982, a real estate developer put up a huge sign in Alexandria, Va., announcing an 800,000 square foot office building. Editors say the Post ran a picture and story. Meanwhile, the developer is still running around looking for his first tenant.

When a company announces that it is building a new manufacturing plant, that typically is occasion for a big story, either in the business section or on the front page. After all, everyone loves economic growth and nothing is better for a town than new industry.

Remember to challenge the numbers. When a company announces that the plant will create 500 new jobs, ask how many of those jobs are permanent and how many are temporary positions related to construction. Often, companies will lump the temporary and full-time positions together when they sell the story. Don't let them.

Be sure to ask if plans call for building the plant all at once or in phases over a period of years. Too often, announcements are followed by headlines that create the impression that the new plant will be built and operational within days. In the real world, future "phases" of plants take years to build, if they are built at all.

A good angle on these stories is to find out what concessions local officials made to attract the new plant. That is the cost of the project to the local government and to taxpayers.

Finally, in this era of business buzzwords, don't get caught using the word "restructuring" in the headline or the lead of a story. Corporations throughout the nation have been announcing major restructurings to make themselves healthier. A senior Post business editor tells me that in the old days, when newspapers still cost a dime, restructurings were known as layoffs.

David Vise is a staff writer for *The Washington Post* business section. The article appeared in *The Bulletin* of the American Society of Newspaper Editors. (Reprinted by permission.)

SATISFYING TWO PUBLICS

For a variety of reasons, the public seems more interested in business and economic news than ever before. The increase in major business stories such as the stock market plunge in 1987, takeovers, and other stories may have spawned this interest. In addition, however, Americans today have more disposable income than they did decades ago, and they are looking for ways to spend and invest it.

The desire for information on economics today exists not because economics has a greater impact than ever, but because citizens are more aware of that impact. They're learning that the stock market affects their return on investments, pension plans, and insurance policies. They are employees, producers, members of labor unions, and taxpayers. It boils down to how much they have in their pockets or whether they are able to buy what they need or want.

As long as the United States functioned with an economy of plenty, the public had limited interest in the cornucopia that spilled forth from the good life. When the flow subsided and national economic problems hit home, the interest grew. Inflation. Recession. Tariff. Federal monetary policies. Trade balance. While just words before, beginning in the 1970s, these words became subjects of heated conversation on Main Street.

Economic journalism made its move toward respectability when reporters and editors realized that they had two audiences. Reporters had for years dealt with and catered to the business specialist—executives, brokers, big investors, manufacturers—who understood the language and the process. It was a relatively closed circle. The business section of American newspapers gained the reputation of dullness, puffery, and inside information.

Now business and economic reporters have general readers—consumers—who may not go to the business section but may want information on how the economy or governmental economic decisions impact their lives. With this broader interest, business and economic news is more frequently seen on the front page and more conspicuous on the evening news. This developing public appetite has to be satisfied.

The journalistic requirements of understanding and explaining economics have thus moved to center stage. They were less necessary when the function of journalists was to transmit information from one set of experts to another. But with the growth of public interest, discontent, confusion, perplexity and anger, reporters find it much more necessary to engage in what Dan Cordtz, a syndicated financial columnist and former ABC News business reporter, refers to as "instant anthropology," that is, helping people to understand the society in which they live, with the economy ranking among the most important factors.[3]

As Cordtz points out, accomplishing this is not easy. The typical citizen doesn't have the basic facts about economics to enable him or her to judge how much to trust the prescriptions of the experts. When people are asked to guess what the average profit margin is of American companies, they are usually dramatically incorrect on the high side.

They usually don't know what the gross national product is or what the consumer price index measures or who's included or not included in the monthly unemployment figures. "We ought to be writing stories so people can come away with some idea of how the world works," Cordtz says. "Most people are interested in business because they're employees, union members, consumers, taxpayers. We shouldn't focus as much on one company, but on economics—the whole pictures."[4]

Has Journalism Been Doing Its Job?

The national business stories that broke in the mid- and late-1980s proved at least one thing to business editors and readers and listeners: that business staffs should be better prepared for the *next* crisis. Further, it is not just the major newspapers and the networks that should be prepared to cover another stock market plunge, or its equivalent; small news outlets also need to be prepared.

At the *New York Times,* all forty-six business reporters covered the October 19, 1987, stock market plunge, and as many as thirty reinforcements were brought in to work on the story. In addition, two days after the plunge, eight full pages were cleared for coverage of the event.[5]

The *Times,* apparently, had the resources to do that. But how did other, smaller papers with circulations of less than 100,000 handle the event? For the most part, not too effectively, according to one researcher who studied the issue. James K. Gentry, director of the Business Journalism Program at the University of Missouri School of Journalism, and his associates, analyzed thirty-four small and medium-sized newspapers with circulations of less than 100,000 to see how they handled the story.

Gentry reports that he came across numerous examples of editorial initiative and solid reporting, but "we discovered even more examples of ho-hum editing and pedestrian coverage. Many papers acted as if the crisis was only a local story in New York City. Many neglected the basics of good reporting: Who will be affected by the crash? Where will it hit hardest? When will the crisis abate? Why didn't anyone see it coming? How can we avoid a recurrence?"[6]

For instance, Gentry writes, only nine of the thirty-four newspapers produced a local article on the likely impact of the stock plunge on the economy of the region; and, while eight papers explained what the Dow

Jones Industrial Average is and listed its thirty component companies, only two explained weaknesses in using the system as an indicator of market performance.

Gentry had the following tips for covering a major financial story at a small paper:[7]

- Tell local stories through the eyes of those affected (brokers, affected fund managers and affected investors).

- Answer the who, what, where, when, why, and how more carefully than normal—remember, many readers and viewers have limited knowledge of how business and economics work.

- Explain the jargon of business and economics. Glossaries can be effective.

- Editors who select wire copy for the business pages need to have a better sense of what readers need to know—more what and how stories and fewer cute stories about stockbrokers.

Some of the weaknesses revealed by the stock market plunge are general weaknesses of much of the business coverage in general. Cordtz, for instance, believes that while the stock market plunge received extensive coverage in the print and broadcast media, few reporters offered an explanation for the event. "There was little explanation as to why it happened," he said. "Coverage before the crash was cursory, superficial and misleading."

Cordtz also believed many reporters stressed the "sensational" aspect of the stock story. "They seized on the most apocalyptical quotes available. Some reporters indicated the world was coming to an end."[8]

John Lawrence, former assistant managing editor of economic affairs at the *Los Angeles Times,* agrees that better coverage of the stock market was needed *before* the big story. "Part of the problem is that in carrying stories on the market day in and day out, the media allowed themselves to be lulled into handling market news as part of the daily grind," he wrote in the *Columbia Journalism Review.* Many experts predicted that the market may be headed for disaster, he believes, but those warnings were, for the most part, not heeded by the media. "What was needed over many months of the bull market was far less of the standard analysis—the market is "backing and filling" or "consolidating for future gains"—and far more digging into the workings of a market whose players and the mechanisms had changed radically over recent years."[9]

AVOIDING THE JARGON

Part of the problem of the stock market coverage—and other business coverage as well—is the refusal or inability of reporters or editors to "translate" business jargon. William Barnhart, associate financial editor of *The Chicago Tribune,* believes that understanding the terms of business and economics is vital. "Sometimes your sources prefer you be overwhelmed," he said. "That way, they can fool you, or at least think they can."[10]

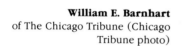

William E. Barnhart
of The Chicago Tribune (Chicago Tribune photo)

Lawrence believes that much of what he calls the "gibberish" of market analysis is quoted verbatim in stories without explanation. He uses as an example excerpts from stories in the *New York Times* reporting large declines in the stock market in September 1987, before the 508-point drop: " 'Putting the Dow's decline into perspective,' said Eugene E. Peroni, Jr., a technical analyst at Janney Montgomery Scott Inc. in Philadelphia, 'I think we're back in a climate where such retreats will be perceived as constructive backing-and-filling movement rather than perilous motions to much lower levels.' (Translation: Don't look for the market to collapse just yet. Down days like this one aren't very significant.)"

Further, he writes, The Associated Press quoted an analyst, " 'I don't believe the rally is stable or reliable at those levels . . . the breadth statistics yesterday and today have been extremely stubborn.' " (Translation: if it's possible to give one: The rally didn't include a broad enough range of stocks, so the market is going to go down.)

As Lawrence writes, "It's not the analysts who are at fault for this jargon—it's the journalists who quote them."[11] Analysts, PR people, and other sources.

Often, security analysts can provide information the reporter could not get elsewhere; but most business journalists would probably warn that analysts often have a vested interest in a story and how it is written. "Understand that their role is to serve their firms and clients," Barnhart says. "Make sure someone is not giving you a lot of superficial information just to be quoted."[12]

Paul Bernish, director of public relations for the Kroger Co., agrees that at times stock analysts can offer information; but much of what they say is opinion and not fact, he believes. "They [analysts] engage in speculation," he said. "Remember, it's only opinion, but their opinions are often inordinately influential."[13]

Clearly, developing sources is the key to quality in any reporter's work. But it is even more complicated for the economic journalist. The techniques used are the same as those used in other areas of journalistic concern, but the problems, while similar, are intensified by both the legal status and the basic attitudes of the business community.

It is obvious that those people in business who dislike or distrust reporters are less likely to cooperate. But the attitude impact goes further. Unlike politicians, who tend to be outgoing and gregarious, many business executives are uncomfortable dealing with reporters. Some feel little sense of public obligation to lead them to share the internal workings of their business. They define their business as private and often resent efforts by reporters to get beyond superficial public announcements, particularly if the information sought could have negative impact.

And, unlike the government reporter, business and economic journalists cannot call upon a Freedom of Information Act to pry open corporate file cabinets. While it is true that there are laws requiring financial disclosure, there aren't any laws that say the public has a right to know about the internal decision-making process.

At the same time, however, the ingredients for an effective mix of sources are there. The reporter has to dig them out with patience, persistence, and demonstrated professionalism. The economic community

is large; its occupants are varied in their interests; and the system functions, internally as well as externally, on competition. When that competitive spirit is joined with the natural desires of human beings to see
their names in print or their faces on the screen, the possibilities are
greater that someone will answer persistent reporters' questions.

"It's important to get to know people on a beat before a crisis," says
John Morris, former business editor of the *Cincinnati Enquirer.* "Talk
with them before a story breaks. They might be more likely to talk to us
then, when we know what we look like and who we are."[14]

IT MAY BE REFRESHING AT THE TOP

Economics journalists, like their counterparts, usually are wary of
seeking information, especially sensitive information, from persons low
in the business hierarchy. They know that too often middle- or low-level
executives either won't say anything useful or will want to provide their
conservative ideas of what the boss wants. That's why it's usually best to
start with the person at the top, if possible. As Morris indicates, reporters
often are surprised at how candid these executives can be.

Of course, they're not always candid. Chief executive officers and
company presidents vary in their willingness to cooperate. Some answer
their own telephones if the reporter gains access to their direct lines.
Some never grant interviews, preferring to delegate responsibility to
specific lower executives or public relations personnel.

Part of the problem is executive eccentricity. Reporters occasionally
find the attitude that answering questions is beneath the importance of
an executive or the belief that public relations departments exist to control the flow of information. There's also the executive who believes news
media content can be controlled through economic power, specifically
through the granting or withdrawing of advertising dollars. It is not likely
that reporters will get much cooperation from these persons.

Egocentricity, however, can work to journalistic advantage. Executives who feel the company is so dependent on them that no one else
can effectively speak for it may not be tolerant of seeing lower executives' names in the paper or on television. It certainly enhances one's
self-image to have reporters knocking at the door.

"Maybe it won't surprise you," says Dan Cordtz, "but I've been amazed
at the way successful businessmen lust after getting their faces on the
tube. They're afraid of being made to look foolish, of course, but on the
other hand, they really like having their colleagues . . . and kids and
grandchildren see them. I consider that legitimate repayment if you can
get the guy to say something of value."[15]

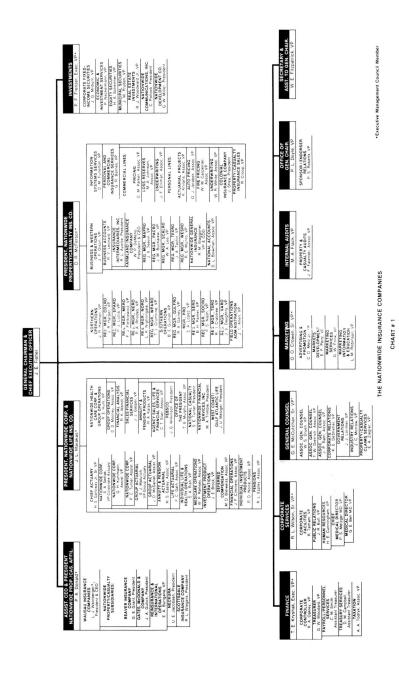

THE NATIONWIDE INSURANCE COMPANIES

CHART # 1

Office of Human Resources, Department of Compensation & Organization
September 1988

*Executive Management Council Member

251

It's not just ego stroking that gets reporters into the executive suite. Much depends on whether a journalist has demonstrated fairness, professionalism, understanding, and the ability to accurately reproduce the sometimes complex comments and information received. Executives are sensitive to reporters' knowledge. Once that has been demonstrated, many executives are hungry to talk with someone who understands what is going on.

Reporters have a similar requirement of executives to whom they pay greater attention. It's not common to expect the official to have a command of all the technical details, especially in a large corporation. Some executives demonstrate a great deal of knowledge of the intricacies of their operations, but their importance is greatest in providing the broader picture.

Lower executives are less likely to have that global view, but some are in positions from which they can be of benefit to reporters. Most companies are divided, at least, into the financial side and the operations side, with individuals in charge of each; most have a whole series of vice presidents and others with specific responsibilities for various corporate divisions. These people are potential sources of information for whatever company policy dictates to be their role with reporters.

Journalists do concentrate at the top of the business hierarchy, but they find at least three circumstances in which they may deal with lower level executives. The first, they say almost flippantly, is "when they're the only ones who can be reached at deadline time." Second, a reporter often is referred to or seeks out lower level executives whose knowledge is appropriately specific to provide detailed elaboration. And, if for no other reason, executives below the top should be cultivated as sources because these are the persons most likely to provide tips. Many executives are close enough to the top to be aware, and circumstances do arise in which they may be willing to share their inside knowledge with trustworthy reporters.

The typical corporate public relations operation does not exist. Given many titles—public relations, public affairs, public information, corporate affairs, corporate communication—the roles of the personnel in this office depend upon the philosophy of the firm's top management.

In some instances, the top public relations personnel are involved in more aspects of planning, sit in on the strategy sessions, understand philosophy and operation, and are in positions to speak officially. In other instances, they serve as expediters for those, including reporters seeking information. They know their way around the organization, understand its policy in general, and open doors to individuals who can answer reporters' questions. Some serve only as roadblocks, defining their jobs as protecting corporate executives by placing their bodies in front of targets of reporter interests. They may be little more than clerical publicists who dutifully type news releases and prepare brochures based on information provided by management and then submit their work to officials for editing.

The first job of any reporter is to determine the role or combination of roles for particular public relations personnel. Some reporters will avoid PR offices at almost any cost, and others will take advantage of some of the services they provide. The most frequent uses are for background or organizational facets, for story ideas, and for persons who know enough about corporate structure to recommend specific persons to answer specific questions.

GOVERNMENTS HAVE A SAY

Cries often are heard from business leaders, from some economists, and from politicians that government meddles too much into the affairs of business. Without arguing that point, journalists can see that the governmental role provides countless possibilities for information. That role itself must be covered. Reporters will want to talk to corporate and government officials about rules, regulations, standards, enforcement, requests, loans, and all the other economic subjects involving the government.

Virtually every aspect of business is subject to some form of regulation by local, state, and federal governments. Local government, for example, often inspects gasoline pumps and restaurant kitchens; state governments regulate telephone and electricity rates and examine dairies and the books of state-chartered banks; and the federal government regulates the activities of broadcast stations, chemical plants, and stock exchanges.

Aside from the direct connection, a byproduct of government's role in American business is its record-keeping and statistics-generating function. While not always easy to find, statistics and other background information are available to broaden almost any story, and to relate, for example, how the specifics of the local economy compare with other areas or fit into the national picture.

At the federal level, the possibilities are enormous for reporters who have the patience to sort through available paperwork. Once the proper agency has been discovered, both human and paper resources await. Among the agencies that deserve attention are the Securities and Exchange Commission, to whom public corporations report financial data; the Bureau of Labor Statistics and the Commerce Department, the Census Bureau and the Small Business Administration (which, in addition to being national, has usually an equivalent on local and state levels). The Joint Economic Committee of Congress puts out a monthly booklet called *Economic Indicators* which could serve as a general reference on national statistics. Among the most valuable resources would be *Statistical Abstracts of the United States* and its companion, *Historical Abstracts of the United States.*

BANKERS HAVE A BIG INTEREST

The nation's major financial institutions do not have offices in every town. But practically every town in the country has a reasonable substitute in the form of bankers whose job it is to understand the local economy. Such persons will not automatically share their knowledge with reporters, and they certainly will not divulge specific information about the financial condition of local individuals or corporations.

Bankers are not always correct in their assessments of the local economy, but they do have the background and usually have seriously done their homework. They're in a better position than most to make educated guesses. Some of the larger ones even have economic analyses that could be journalistically beneficial.

Reporters will not succeed with bankers if they simply burst through the door with pointed questions. It must be a continuing process of cultivation, getting to know each other, and proving that reporters understand and know how to use the information they get.

THE ACADEMIC APPROACH

Another potentially strong source of broad understanding and specific analysis that is just as close as the nearest college or university is the local business professor. Almost all colleges and universities have some type of economics program, and if a reporter is lucky, he or she may uncover a scholar of the local economy. But value may also be gained by developing sources who can explain economic trends and impact in general.

Even if these sources never appear in print or on the air—and some prefer it that way—they can help on issues with which the reporter is not familiar. Some economists have made names for themselves because of frequent appearances in the news media, but more important than their understanding is that their understanding provides scope to an economics story and contributes to its authenticity.

They tend to be cooperative, at times even excited, when asked to explain issues to reporters. It's another opportunity to teach and to talk about what probably is their favorite topic. But they seldom walk uninvited into the newsroom. They must be invited; they must be called; they must be asked.

FEDERAL REGULATORY AGENCIES

Although most federal agencies have their headquarters in Washington, many have regional offices that often can supply information to reporters on policies and actions regarding specific businesses. Each of the following agencies falls into that category.

More detailed information on all federal regulatory agencies, including names and telephone numbers of contacts, may be found in the *Federal Regulatory Directory,* published annually by Congressional Quarterly in Washington (about $25, but available at most public libraries).

Consumer Product Safety Commission. The commission establishes mandatory safety standards for the design, construction, contents, performance, and labeling of consumer products. It has the authority to ban the sale of items that do not meet established standards.

Environmental Protection Agency. The EPA has the authority to set and enforce national standards for air and water quality and for handling of hazardous solid wastes and pesticides. It supervises state and local compliance with national standards.

Federal Communications Commission. The FCC regulates radio, television, telegraph, cable, and satellite communications. Its most important function is to license and assign frequencies to individual stations.

Federal Deposit Insurance Corporation. The FDIC insures bank deposits and regulates state-chartered banks that are not members of the Federal Reserve System. It requires periodic reports on the financial condition of banks under its supervision.

Federal Energy Regulatory Commission. An independent agency within the Energy Department, the commission regulates electric utilities and the interstate transportation and pricing of natural gas and electricity.

Federal Trade Commission. The FTC acts to prevent price fixing, unfair competition, false and deceptive advertising, and monopolistic practices by businesses engaged in interstate commerce.

Food and Drug Administration. An agency within the Department of Health and Human Services, the FDA is responsible for testing and setting standards for foods, household products, drugs, and other medical items.

National Highway Traffic Safety Administration. An agency within the Transportation Department, this body sets safety and mileage standards for automobiles and trucks and has the authority to order recalls of vehicles that do not meet the standards.

National Labor Relations Board. The main functions of the NLRB are to prevent employers and unions alike from engaging in unfair labor practices and to conduct elections to determine whether employees want to be represented by a union.

Occupational Safety and Health Administration. An agency within the Labor Department, OSHA sets and enforces on-the-job safety and health standards. It requires employers to file reports on job-related injuries and illnesses and inspects work sites for safety problems.

Securities and Exchange Commission. An independent agency, the SEC regulates the trading of stocks and bonds at national exchanges and over-the-counter markets. It requires public disclosure of financial and other information by companies whose securities are traded on the national exchanges.

LABOR DOES ITS HOMEWORK

Another group of persons with an understanding of what's going on in the corporate world consists of labor union officials. They have to have good information at their fingertips. Collective bargaining negotiations must consist of more than educated guesswork. Officials need a clear picture of company finances, an assessment of its place in the industry, future possibilities, policies, and personalities of corporate executives.

To gain much of this, today's more sophisticated labor unions maintain economists and accountants on staff to review the results of various companies with which they do business. They may even issue their own reports or critiques of financial reports of those companies.

They usually are willing to talk with reporters they trust. In a sense, labor unions represent what in a political context could be called the "loyal opposition." They are interested in future development and growth of their industry, but their ideas on how to accomplish this may differ from those of corporate officials. Because they are constantly doing their collective bargaining homework, they can be very good sources of specific information about the corporation.

But union officials do have their axes to grind. Their constant goal is to achieve some desired end, and what they say often will be within that context. Thus, they are approached by reporters with the same skepticism as any other source who has something to gain.

ORGANIZATIONS FOR EVERY VIEWPOINT

This is a free country. Citizens have a right to express their opinions, and they have a right to express their opinions collectively. That particular piece of American philosophy has been used extensively in the past quarter century, and business is part of the forum. Trade associations, intraindustry organizations, and chambers of commerce see their function as one of support for business. Consumer groups see themselves not so much antibusiness as proconsumer. Sometimes, antibusiness groups oppose, almost on principle, anything that comes out of corporate headquarters.

A common ingredient among all these groups is the attention they desire and often receive from the news media. It is not easy for the reporter to pick the thoughtful comments from the din of boosterism and degradation. The temptation is to listen to the loudest cries and to follow the heaviest footprints.

Still, the activities of such local organizations as a home builders' association or car dealers' association merit attention. As with chambers of commerce, material gained from them is likely to be one-sided. That does not mean they should be ignored; it means the other sides, if they exist, should be sought. Perhaps the most significant contribution of such groups is in the form of statistics—a demonstration of business activity—and political action designed to gain or maintain special privilege or stall the latest controlling legislation.

Volumes of Written Material

Nothing adequately substitutes for general familiarity with business and economics that comes from careful, day-by-day attention. That means extensive reading. Dozens of individuals and organizations are sources for material. Governments require and issue report after report. Corporations prepare statements for shareholders and the public. Business publications analyze industries and economic trends. Special-interest groups write letters and articles and produce brochures, newsletters, and special studies.

Hospitals strive for fiscal fitness

By MARCUS GLEISSER
STAFF WRITER

Fiscal fitness is making modern medicine more of a business than many veteran medical practitioners would like to believe it is.

Doctors dedicated to professional care are being forced into a new world of strict management discipline because of the rising health care costs. As a result, mergers and sharing of expensive equipment have become commonplace among former competitors.

Experts in mergers, affiliations and preferred providers have invaded the quiet corridors of hospitals and have brought doctors and nurses new business partners in dispensing care.

Moves that were considered strange a short time ago are now a normal part of hospital planning, according to Richard J. McCann, president and chief executive officer of the Meridia Health System, the result of a merger in December 1984.

Limited payments from Medicare and insurance companies based on the Diagnostic Related Group (DRG) concept of paying a set amount of money for specific procedures—a specific amount for a gall bladder operation, so much for an appendectomy—pushed hospitals to find ways to cut costs, he said.

"The vast majority of hospitals in the country are operating on a less than 1% operating margin," said McCann. "The only other businesses running on such a tight profit margin are the supermarkets."

It used to be that a hospital would be reimbursed on a cost basis so if an administrator made a mistake, such as overstaffing or ordering unduly expensive equipment, the money to cover that would come from insurers.

All this has changed with the spread of DRGs, McCann said, adding, "What used to be a game of yards now is a matter of inches. The money supply has tightened considerably."

Charles Schetter, director of health care practice at McKinsey & Co., consultants in Los Angeles, said, "This movement to fixed fees rather than the cost-plus method, forced hospitals to respond by trying to diversify and find other sources to support their costs. Some have tried to capture efficiencies through merger.

"Mergers can be helpful in some local market settings. Those tend to be where a combination of hospitals end up having a greater share of the local market and therefore can command more power in negotiations with payers.

"Some mergers can also be helpful where they can, in fact, see real business operations improvements from having fewer support people so more efficient use of computer systems, purchasing and so on," he said.

Meridia merged such hospitals as Euclid General, Huron Road, Hillcrest and, in 1986, Suburban Community into a system with 3,888 employees and 1,100 physicians in 40 specialties. Last year they served more than 42,200 inpatients and 250,000 outpatients.

A key result is the sharing of multimillion dollar high-tech equipment that would have pushed a free-standing hospital into severe money problems if it had to go it alone.

For example, Hillcrest's $2.4 million mobile magnetic resonance imaging (MRI) equipment and $2 million gallstone lithotripter, the latter used for crushing gallstones without surgery, are shared by other Meridia hospitals.

The MRI equipment, in addition to its original cost, also carries the annual expense of a service maintenance contract up to $180,000. Computed tomography equipment can cost $1.2 million with up to $100,000 in annual service cost.

Merging of hospitals has been growing.

For example, St. Vincent Charity Hospital and Health Center has joined with St. John and St. John West Shore; Lutheran Medical Center and Fairview General have united in Health Cleveland; the MetroHealth System has the MetroHealth Medical Center and MetroHealth Hospital for Women; Mt. Sinai Medical Center and Laurelwood Hospital have an affiliation.

Henry Jacques, spokesman for Health Cleveland, said, "It has worked out well for us. Numbers are up at both hospitals. We share an MRI mobile unit and a good deal of management skills. The joining has given us a good reach into the community."

Rob Rosati, consultant for the health care advisory service of Laventhol & Horwath here, said, "The reason you see more mergers of hospitals these days are the four Ms at play— management, money, market and medical staff—each of which usually benefits from a joining."

He underscored that more mergers will come because of increasing pressure on the health care industry, which is becoming increasingly competitive.

"External forces are working against status quo," he said. "Smaller hospitals are finding that the problems of status quo are finally catching up with them."

One way of solving the problem of standing alone in the face of rising costs is the preferred provider plan, such as the Emerald Health Network Inc., where hospitals have not formally merged but simply joined to offer a joint price to business.

Under this plan, participants can go only to specified hospitals and physicians who have agreed to a joint offering of their services. This plan is available to businesses and not individuals.

The Emerald plan is a joining of six hospitals which blossomed to 23 around Northeastern Ohio. Their purpose was to offer companies insurance-rate service provided they directed patients to the member hospitals.

In a merger, hospitals join their assets and lose their individual identity.

An affiliation is a step below merger. In the Mt. Sinai-Laurelwood affiliation two years ago, for example, Mt. Sinai acquired 50% of the former Ridgecliff, which is now Laurelwood Hospital.

"We put four board members on the Laurelwood board and they kept four members, so they have a new board which, in turn, hired its chief executive officer who reports to the Mt. Sinai CEO. In effect, Mt. Sinai thus manages Laurelwood," said Glenn Levy, senior vice president, corporate development/marketing.

The benefit for Laurelwood was needed cash that paid off bonds, leaving it debt free. Money went to develop programs in mental health and chemical dependency programs.

For Mt. Sinai, Levy said, "We felt there was a real need in Cleveland for a premier mental health system and the basis of that system should be a free-standing hospital totally devoted to mental health and chemical dependency. This would further our mission in the community."

Also, mental health and chemical (alcohol) dependency is one of the key services corporations and insurance companies are looking at. The affiliation thus gives Mt. Sinai a competitive advantage "because we can provide comprehensive mental health services at a good price," Levy said.

The changing hospital scene involves a major segment of Cleveland employment. There are 26,000 people working in hospital systems and affiliations in this area, according to the Greater Cleveland Hospital Association.

But the changes to the health industry are not all clear.

Lurking in the background, for example, is the challenge from federal antitrust lawyers who view the joining as a combination that can push up the cost of health care.

One case is pending in Rockford, Ill., where two hospitals operating at a loss and competing for the same patients agreed to merge and reduce duplication of efforts. The Justice Department opposed this on antitrust grounds and a federal judge agreed. There is talk of appeal to the U.S. Supreme Court.

McCann said the Rockford problem was different from Cleveland in that it involved the only major hospitals in town and, the Federal Trade Administration claimed, the merging would eliminate major competition.

"We do not have that problem in Cleveland," he said. "We have too many competing hospitals to be charged with monopoly. That problem could arise here only if all the hospitals decided to consolidate."

Nonetheless, the potential for problems is watched very closely here. Plans to merge must be filed with the state attorney general's office where they are reviewed and the applicant is told if there is violation of antitrust laws.

Not all joint efforts are economically sound, according to Frank L. Muddle, president of the Lake Hospital System, which has two hospitals, LakeEast and LakeWest.

His two hospitals were formed originally as satellites to serve different parts of Lake County rather than the result of a merger. Muddle feels it would be more efficient to have everything in one place.

"I run into the cost of duplicating services, such as X-ray, for example, that could be combined efficiently in a single building," he said.

Soaring health care costs have been a major problem to businesses here and across the nation for many years. Major labor unions have been calling for a national health care program and some corporate leaders have joined them.

The Health Action Council (HAC) here, an association of employee benefits managers from large Cleveland companies, has been pushing for cost controls for several years. Members have proposed a law requiring hospitals to report prices for various surgical procedures so choices can be made by patients.

At Meridia, McCann said, the merger came about "primarily because board members were looking to the future and were concerned about the ability of free-standing community hospitals to survive."

He noted that Cleveland was probably four or five years behind the rest of the country in its changes.

"Our merger gives us up to $3 million a year in quantity purchasing and has helped us in our marketing efforts," McCann said. "Recently we launched an advertising program for laser surgery which resulted in a 9% increase in our surgery volume in four months. We got about 6,000 inquiries from individuals within 90 days."

This enabled the Meridia system to bring laser experts from Austria, England and parts of the United States to train physicians and nurses here and to build an infrastructure to do effective laser surgery, he said.

"The biggest advantage in mergers is that we can introduce a management discipline that you don't have as a free-standing institution," he said.

The economics of health care is a hot story—on the business pages. This story, from the *Cleveland Plain Dealer,* explains the economics of health services, and how hospital ownership has changed over the last few years. (Reprinted by permission.)

Many of these documents are sent unsolicited to journalists. Others are sought for specific purposes, at times against the will of the producer. Somebody has to read this material to extract facts of local value and to be informed about national economic trends with local impact.

The sources include newspapers considered to contain the best business news coverage, including *The Wall Street Journal,* the *New York Times,* and economics-oriented magazines such as *Business Week, Fortune,* and *Forbes.* All three news magazines devote major attention to business. The reporter may also want more specific materials: government newsletters such as housing market reports; industrial publications such as *Dollars and Cents of Shopping Centers* from the Urban Land Institute; and informational and advisory newsletters, such as the *Goodkin Report* on real estate matters, published by the Sanford R. Goodkin Research Corp.

Much more is available in the local library, says economist Richard Vedder of Ohio University: "There are a lot of data sources that reporters ought to learn to use. Two good sources published by the U.S. Bureau of the Census are *City and County Data Book* (published every five years) and *County Business Patterns,* published monthly. Another source is Sales Management Magazine's annual *Survey of Buying Power.* Most state employment services have much useful information. The Ohio Bureau of Employment Services, for instance, publishes data on a county-by-county and on a metropolitan basis. There is a lot of material that the average reporter simply does not know exists. But it's right there in the library."

Annual Report to Shareholders

Information on specific corporations likewise is available, even from firms that may be less than enthusiastic about dealing with reporters. Public corporations are required by the federal government to report routinely on their financial status. These reports take several forms. The monthly financial reports to shareholders (generally issued near the end of the following month to allow time for closing the company's books) cover activity, sales, and expenses. Every three months, companies are required to submit quarterly reports, which in fact are both monthly reports and cumulative reports of the two previous months.

At the end of the year, this information is put together in an annual report, often in a slick magazine format that may reach 100 pages. In the past, companies regarded the reports as a bother, something saddled on them by a meddlesome government. But now they are regarded as a top-priority means of corporate communication—not only with shareholders, but also with a host of other constituencies, ranging from financial analysts and customers to politicians and social activists. Now, too, companies have put major effort into interim shareholder reports, post-annual meeting reports, security analysis yearbooks, and public issue campaigns.[16]

Many top company officials consider the annual report as a marketing, recruiting, and public relations tool, in addition to simply meeting a legal obligation. Reporters, however, are not unanimous in their assessments of the journalistic value of these annual reports. They are concerned about the fluff and puffery. They recognize that a corporation has enough flexibility, even in the face of governmental requirements, to make persuasion a focus of the reports. Reporters are uncomfortable with information gained in this kind of situation. It's also true that the annual reports seldom contain new information but represent new packages for material originally published elsewhere, perhaps in monthly or quarterly reports.

Nevertheless, reporters who understand how to use the reports may benefit from them, at least in general ways. They are part of the message a company wants to present. A company having financial problems may make the report look spartan to support claims being made in the copy that everything possible is being done to control costs. The annual reports of rapidly growing companies may be designed to project the image of unlimited expansion and almost guaranteed success.

Inside the reports, among matters to which reporters pay attention, are the bottom line figures. These figures provide the news of a particular company, often expressed in the amount of profit or loss, the percentage of increase or decrease from the previous year, and the per-share impact on shareholders.

Trends may be isolated from the reports, perhaps with regard to profit patterns over time, or something more specific. For example, if a company shows a substantial improvement in its financial picture because of a specific product that may be manufactured locally, that could indicate possible expansion of local industry. The full story, of course, will not be in the annual report, but observant reporters may find the beginnings of several stories to be pursued.

Professional accountants and experienced journalists alike may moan over the growth of annual reports over the years, pointing out that the significant (and legally required) information generally is found among footnotes and/or tabular information in the back of the book. Footnotes represent exceptions, unusual occurrences that must be noted. It's in the footnotes, for example, that reporters may discover major changes in the chief executive officer's salary. Or they may get the best perspective on lawsuits and active litigation that could have major impact on a company's overall performance.

It may be that the major journalistic value of annual reports is not in the specific information. They do, however, give broad perspectives and provide opportunities to analyze formal statements from corporate executives about the past year's experiences and plans and expectations for the future. A collection of them gives a chance for comparison—either one company with other companies in an industry or one company over several years.

FORM 10-K

The most significant of all financial reports is Form 10-K, the annual report required of all publicly held corporations by the Securities and Exchange Commission. Similar to the annual report to shareholders, but much less grandiose, Form 10-K describes in rather intimate detail what businesses do, how much they make, who runs them, and the legal problems they may be having. Failure to properly report the information required by the SEC in this form could result in criminal charges against senior officers or the board of directors.

Reporters may obtain copies of a company's Form 10-K from the firm itself or from the Securities and Exchange Commission in Washington. As with the annual report to shareholders, companies are not required to share 10-K with journalists, but since the documents are made available routinely to so many persons, it's relatively easy to obtain copies. The major advantage of 10-K is that its straightforward form, one written without the gloss and puffery of the annual report to shareholders.

William Barnhart, associate financial editor of the *Chicago Tribune,* believes the 10-K is one of the most valuable sources of information for business reporters. He also believes it may be necessary at times for an analyst to read the report and go over it with reporters so they will not misinterpret the numbers. He added that some numbers must be calculated for them to make sense to the reader of the document.[17]

Despite the wealth of information it offers, Form 10-K is just the beginning of materials provided through federal government disclosure requirements. The SEC alone uses some 180 different forms to cover the broad range of business activities regulated by the agency.[18]

Proxy statement. A detailed meeting notice to shareholders, it is of special value to journalists because the SEC presumes that management includes financial information. Among the most useful information is the salaries of directors and top officers who make more than $40,000 a year. It also includes an agenda for the company's annual meeting, which may give reporters additional insight.

Prospectus. A document produced when the firm is preparing for the sale of new stock. Prepared for potential buyers, the prospectus includes detailed information about the company, its activities and properties, financial condition, subsidiaries, and plans for the future. Availability of such information opens up numerous avenues for reporters.

Form 8-K. A document that describes any shift in who controls the company, bankruptcy, and the hiring of new auditors. Such personnel changes often result from major policy changes or from mismanagement of the company. Thus, familiarity with the 8-K, which must be filled within 15 days after any significant change in operation or finances, may give a reporter a running start on major news.

10-Q. Similar to the 10-K, Form 10-Q is filed quarterly, so consequently has data that is more current than that filed in the 10-K. "You must read the fine print on these," Barnhart says. "The company may have to reveal something here to comply with the law that it would normally not reveal or issue a release on."[19]

Schedule 13D. A document that must be filed when any individual or company buys more than 5 percent of the stock in a company. Included is information on the amount of stock purchased, date of the purchase, and source of the buyer's funds.

Availability of these documents and hundreds of others is important to reporters. Companies have the legal responsibility to report any matter of significance that could affect, either positively or negatively, their financial performance. This can range from labor strife to new inventions, to the resignation of the chief executive officer, to legal battles, and to new ownership. Often, companies are not likely to call news conferences to make formal announcements.

Thus, the first obligation of reporters is to know what is available, where it can be obtained, and when it must be filed. Some reports, such as Form 10-K, are filed at prescribed times. Others, however, are sent to the SEC only when circumstances dictate, and that represents a special challenge. Keeping track of them requires that reporters know what's happening within a company well enough to anticipate such filings and/ or that they maintain regular contact with the SEC in Washington.

TRACKING PRIVATELY OWNED COMPANIES

Obtaining information about a company that does not sell stock to the public is more difficult. No Freedom of Information Act applies. No disclosure laws apply. The owners control the degree of cooperation they may extend. In the absence of such cooperation, reporters are on their own. But means of gaining information do exist.

For one thing, there are financial services that serve the total business world by making information available. While reports from companies such as Dun & Bradstreet and Standard and Poor's Corp. are not designed for media use, they nevertheless may be obtained and can provide usable information about privately owned companies and how they relate to the industry as a whole. Such reports may be obtained by a news organization's business department through a stock broker or any cooperative business executive.

One of the best sources is the union that represents the company's workers. Officials of labor organizations usually have data and an understanding of the operations of a company and its plans.

Legal documents may be available as well. A trip to the local courthouse to browse through the public records involving suits and judgments perhaps is a fishing expedition, but it could be valuable in getting reporters started on potentially good stories. (A record of a real estate transfer that indicates a company has sold its headquarters could mean, for instance, that the company may be planning to rent its headquarters because of financial difficulties.)

But, more than anything, there is a need for good, basic reporting. In lieu of documents and as a complement to documents, reporters conduct interviews. They talk to people—hundreds of people—and see what they can piece together. Officials of both public and private businesses must deal with others, and that makes it inevitable that a reporter's enterprise can turn up usable information.

A GLOSSARY OF ECONOMIC TERMS

A

absolute advantage The ability of a producer to produce a higher absolute quantity of a good with the productive resources available.

abundance A term that applies when individuals can obtain all the goods they want without the costs. If a good is abundant, it is free.

actual turnover The number of times individuals actually spend their average money holdings over a given time period. Actual turnover is determined by the proportion of income that people receive and actually retain as money balances over a given period of time.

antitrust Laws covering all sorts of business activities that are thought to involve unfair forms of competition.

appreciation A rise in the price of currency relative to other currencies.

B

bank balance sheet A bank's financial position at a given time. The bank balance sheet shows assets, liabilities, and net worth.

C

capital The existing stock of productive resources that have been produced, such as machines and buildings.

capitalist economies Economies that use market determined prices to guide people's choices about the production and distribution of goods; these economies generally have productive resources that are privately owned.

cartel A group of otherwise independent firms that band together to control their industry, usually by cutting back production to raise prices.

change in demand A shift in the entire demand curve so that at any given price people will want to buy a different amount. A change in demand is caused by some change other than a change in the good's price.

change in quantity demanded Movement up or down a given demand curve caused only by a change in the good's price.

civilian labor force All persons over the age of sixteen who are not in the armed forces or institutionalized and who are either employed or unemployed.

comparative advantage The ability of a producer to produce a good at a lower marginal cost than other producers; marginal cost in sacrifice of some other good compared to the amount of a good obtained.

competition Rivalry among individuals in order to acquire more of something that is scarce.

consumer price index (CPI) A measure of changes in the price of hundreds of consumer goods.

cost The most valuable opportunity forsaken when a choice is made.

currency Paper money issued to the government.

D

deficit spending A term that refers to the situation wherein the government spends more than it receives in taxes.

demand The maximum quantities of some good that people will choose (or buy) at different prices. An identical definition is the relative value of the marginal unit of some good when different quantities of that good are available.

demand deposits Checking accounts in commercial banks. These banks are obliged to pay out funds when depositors write checks on those numbers. Checking accounts are not cash—they are numbers recorded at banks.

depreciation A fall in the price of a currency relative to other currencies.

derived value The consumers' value of an additional unit of the productive services of a resource, such as labor. Derived value is the product of a resource's marginal productivity and the consumer's relative value of the productivity.

desired turnover The number of times individuals want to spend their average money holdings over a given period of time. Desired turnover is determined by the proportion of income that people receive and want to retain as money balances over a given period of time.

diminishing relative value The principle that if all other factors remain constant, an individual's relative value of a good will decline as more of that good is obtained. Accordingly, the relative value of a good will increase (other factors remaining constant) as an individual gives up more of that good.

diminishing returns As more and more of a productive resource is added to a given amount of other productive resources, additions to output will eventually diminish, other factors, such as technology and the degree of specialization, remaining constant.

discretionary fiscal policy Changes in a fiscal (tax or spending) program initiated by the government to change aggregate demand.

disposable income The amount of an individual's income that remains after taxes are deducted.

E

econometrics The use of mathematic and statistical techniques to solve economic problems, test theories, and predict the future.

efficiency The allocation of goods to their uses of highest relative value.

elastic demand A term used when the percentage change in quantity demanded is larger than the percentage change in price.

equation of exchange ($M \times T = P \times Q$) This equation tells us that the money supply (M) multiplied by the number of times that money supply turns over (T) will equal the price level (P) multiplied by the real output (Q).

equilibrium The amount of output supplied is equal to the amount demanded.

equity A distribution of goods that is judged fair by some ethical standard. The method of distributing those goods, as well as the final distribution, are dimensions of equity.

exchange The voluntary transfer of rights to use goods.

excess reserves That portion of a commercial banks' reserves in excess of its legal resources.

F

fascist economies Economies characterized by overwhelming government control of economy; usually that control is vested in one individual or a small group.

financial investment Those investments that do not represent purchases of final products.

fiscal drag A term that applies when the federal government's taxing and spending policies result in federal budget surpluses at full employment (which at times tend to inhibit economic growth and employment).

fiscal policy The federal government's attempts to change aggregate demand through tax and expenditure (spending) changes.

free good A good that is abundant and costless.

full employment budget The amount the federal government would spend and receive in taxes if labor resources were fully (highly) employed.

G

gains of exchange The difference between the relative values of a good to the buyer and the seller. How this difference is divided between the buyer and the seller will depend upon the price of the good. Exchange will not occur unless both the buyer and the seller expect to receive some of this gain.

good Anything that anyone wants. All options or alternatives are goods. Goods can be tangible or intangible.

GNP The sum of the prices of all the final goods and services produced in a given time period.

GNP per capita The amount of a nation's total production available to each individual.

per capita GNP $= GNP$ population

H

highest-value uses All uses of a good that have relative values that are not less than the market clearing price.

I

income statement An annual summary of income and expenses of a given business in order to determine the net income of that business.

inelastic demand A term used when the percentage change in quantity demanded is smaller than the percentage change in price.

inflation A decrease in the value of money.

interest The annual earnings that are sacrificed when wealth is invested in a given asset or business. The interest sacrificed by investing in a given business is often called the cost of capital.

inter-industry concentration The proportion of assets and sales etc. in many industries that are owned by the biggest producers.

intra-industry concentration The proportion of assets and sales etc. in a given industry that are owned by the biggest producers.

inventory A stock of goods or resources held by a buyer or seller in order to reduce the cost of exchange or production.

K

Keynesians A group of economists who emphasize an activist government role in economic affairs through planned changes in the federal government's expenditures and taxes.

L

labor supply The maximum quantities of labor services that will be offered by workers at different wages, other factors remaining constant. An identical interpretation is the workers' marginal cost of time spent working when different quantities of labor services are offered.
leisure All uses of time in which one's labor services are not exchanged for money. The uses of everyone's time can be divided between employment and leisure.
liabilities The debts of a person or business.
lowest cost uses The highest valued uses of a good.

M

marginal The additional or extra quantity of something. If one drinks six sodas a day, the marginal soda would be the sixth soda—the one on the margin. If our total points on the next (marginal) exam equal twenty, your marginal points are twenty.
marginal productivity The additional output obtained by adding an additional unit of a productive resource, such as labor. More precisely, marginal productivity is the change in total output divided by the change in the amount of the productive resource employed:

$$\text{marginal productivity} = \frac{\text{change in total output}}{\text{change in amount of productive resource}}$$

marginal propensity to consume (MPC) The percentage of new or added income that is consumed.
marginal propensity to save (MPS) The percentage of new or added income that is saved.
marginal revenue The change in total revenue obtained by selling one additional unit of a good. More precisely, marginal revenue is the change in total revenue divided by the change in quantity sold:

$$MR = \frac{\text{change in total revenue}}{\text{change in quantity}}$$

market clearing price A price that rations the supply of a good among competing consumers so that the quantity of the good demanded is equal to the quantity supplied.
minimum wage A wage below which employers may not legally pay employees for specific kinds of employment.
monetarists A group of economists who emphasize money supply changes as a central cause of price and output (income) changes in our economy.
monetary assets Assets whose money values do not change as inflation occurs.
monetary liabilities Liabilities (debts) whose money values do not change as inflation occurs.
monetary policy The federal government's attempt to change aggregate demand through money supply changes.
money Any good that is generally used as a medium of exchange and as a common denominator for prices of other goods.
money multiplier The process by which excess reserves creates new demand deposits or money; for example, with a 10 percent legal reserve requirement, $10 of excess reserves may be used to create $100 of new demand deposits of money.
monopoly A market in which there is only one seller of a given good.
monopsonist A single buyer of any commodity in any given market.
multiplier The number of times new investment spending will be respent to produce a certain amount of new income.

N

natural rate of unemployment The amount of civilian unemployment the economy tends to produce even when the supply and demand for labor are equal. The natural rate is determined by the percentage of the civilian labor force unemployed at one time or another during any given year multiplied by the average time people spend searching for jobs.

near monies Assets that are not directly exchangeable for goods and services but that may be readily converted into money. A savings account is an example.

need A specific quantity of a specific good for which an individual would pay any price. Need denies the existence of choice, for a need means that a person would not choose more of one good for less of another. Instead, a need means that a person will give up everything else rather than reduce consumption of a good by even small quantities.

net monetary creditor A person who owns more monetary assets than liabilities.

net monetary debtor A person who owns more monetary liabilities than monetary assets.

net worth The difference between the assets and liabilities of a person or business.

New Deal Programs initiated in the 1930s that were characterized by significantly increased government aid to various economic groups and equally significant increases in government involvement in the economy.

nominal wage One's wage not adjusted for inflation.

O

oligopoly A market in which most of the sales of a given good are accounted for by few firms.

open inflation An increase in the general level of money prices when market prices rise to new market clearing levels.

open market operations. The purchase and sale of government bonds by the Federal Reserve in order to change commercial banks' reserves.

option Anything that anyone wants. In economics, options (alternatives) are also called goods.

P

parity A government guarantee that the ratio of prices now received by farmers to prices now paid by farmers will equal the same ratio that existed during the years 1910–1914.

political economy Policies that emphasize the interaction between politics and economics and that have political and economics effects.

poverty level income The minimum amount of yearly money income estimated by the government for an urban family of four.

price The amount of some other good(s) that one must offer in exchange to acquire a unit of a good. Compare this definition of price to the definition of relative value. Also note that the cost of a good to the consumer can be more than its price if there are additional exchange costs, such as waiting in line, that are borne by the consumer but not transferred to the seller.

price index A tool to measure price changes. All price indexes compare the value of goods in a current year to the value of those same goods in a different (base) year.

profit The excess of income over all costs, including the interest (capital) cost of the wealth invested. The net income of a business is not an accurate measure of its profit.

progressive tax A tax that takes a higher percentage of income as income rises.

public goods Goods whose consumption by one individual does not diminish the amount available of that good for other individuals.

pure fiscal policy A fiscal policy that is effected without any change in the money supply.

R

real GNP The GNP of any year measured in the prices of a base year. Real GNP is a nominal GNP adjusted for inflation.

real investment Those investments that represent purchases of new final products.

real wage One's wage adjusted for inflation.

relative value The maximum amount of some good(s) that one will offer in exchange to obtain one more unit of some other good. An identical definition is the minimum amount of some good(s) one would accept to give up one more unit of some other good.

repressed inflation A term that applies when public officials control prices and keep them from rising to new market clearing levels. Resulting shortages cause the value of money to decline.

reserves Cash held by commercial banks in their vaults or number of deposits with the Federal Reserve Banks.

S

scarcity A term used when the quantity of a good demanded exceeds the quantity supplied at the existing price.

socialist economies Economies that are characterized by government ownership of productive resources, significant government planning, and attempts to redistribute national income more equally.

supply The maximum amounts of a good that producers will choose to produce and sell at different prices, other factors remaining constant. An identical definition is the marginal costs of producing a good when different qualities of that good are produced, other factors remaining constant.

surplus A term used when the quantity of a good supplied exceeds the quantity demanded at the existing price.

T

T account An account that summarizes changes in the assets and liabilities of a person or business.

W

waste When the relative value of a good is different from that good's marginal cost of production, waste occurs. Goods or resources are wasted when they are allocated to uses which are not the most valuable.

wealth The value of the existing stock of goods (assets); those goods may be tangible or intangible.

wholesale price index (WPI) A measure of changes in the prices of goods at the wholesale level, particularly those goods sold between businesses.

Sources: Reproduced with permission from *Choice & Change, An Introduction to Economics,* by Dickneider and Kaplan, West Publishing Co., St. Paul, Minn., 1978, and *ABZs of Economics,* by Susan Lee, Poseidon Press, New York, 1987.

NOTES

1. John Wicklein, "A Steady Stream of Well-trained Reporters Is Needed to Fuel the Boom in Business Coverage," *The Bulletin of the American Society of Newspaper Editors,* April, 1987, p. 11.

2. Wicklein, p. 12.

3. Dan Cordtz, remarks made at the Ohio Media Economics Conference, Columbus, Ohio, May 14, 1988.

4. Dan Cordtz, remarks made at the Ohio Media Economics Conference.

5. James K. Gentry, "How the Crash Hit Home," *Washington Journalism Review,* March, 1988, p. 49.

6. Gentry, p. 49.

7. Gentry.

8. Cordtz, Ohio Media Economics Conference.

9. John Lawrence, "How Street-smart is the Press?" *Columbia Journalism Review,* January/February, 1988, pp. 23–28.

10. William Barnhart, remarks made at Ohio Media Economics Conference, Columbus, Ohio, May 14, 1988.

11. Lawrence, p. 25.

12. Barnhart.

13. Paul Bernish, remarks made during panel discussion, "Covering Corporations," national convention, Society of Professional Journalists/ Sigma Delta Chi, Cincinnati, Ohio, November 18, 1988.

14. John Morris, "Covering Corporations."

15. Dan Cordtz, Ohio Media Economics Conference.

16. "The 40th Annual Report Awards," *Financial World,* October 15, 1980, p. 63.

17. Barnhart.

18. Steve Woodward, *Public Files of the SEC,* (Columbia, Mo.: Freedom of Information Center, August 1979), p. 1. This Freedom of Information Report No. 408 is a very good overview of SEC documents of value to reporters. A complete list of forms used by the SEC is available in Title 17 (Commodities and Securities Exchange) of the Code of Federal Regulations. The SEC publishes another source of general information, titled *Manual of General Record Information.*

19. Barnhart.

Economics Coverage and the Standard-of-Living Beats

14

When it comes to discussions about the economy, most people's eyes glaze over, and they may find an excuse to change the subject. While many people may be vaguely aware of and interested in concepts such as the gross national product, they are interested in how it influences the local economy. They want to know how it impacts them, their family, and their friends.

The economy is not difficult to relate in local and personal terms. The corner market is part of the economy, as well as the factory on the edge of town. Farmers, too, and plumbers.

The high-stakes wrangling that could lead to a corporate takeover may seem at first to have little effect on the average person; that is, until a favorite store or restaurant is closed or relocated, or layoffs occur.

JOURNALISM'S DIVERSIFIED APPROACH

It takes teamwork and diversification for news organizations to cover the economy. No single individual can know all there is to know, cover the territory, and write even the most necessary stories. The organizational chart may not show it clearly, but newspapers, magazines, and some broadcast facilities will have several—if not several dozen—reporters directly responsible for news and analysis of the factors having economic impact; namely, corporations and smaller businesses, financial news, real estate, transportation, labor, consumers, energy and the environment, agriculture, and government. They may be supplemented by an individual or team focusing investigative skills on economic activities.

Through such diversification, news organizations are reaching into many corners of the economic world. This has greatly improved coverage, of course, but there's room for more.

Covering Mergers and Takeovers

One major business and economic story through the 1980s was the continuing advent of takeovers of small and large companies throughout the world. The number of corporate mergers and acquisitions valued at $1 million or more increased from 3,156 in 1984 to 3,412 in 1985 to 4,218 in 1986. That means an average of about 10 a day for three years.[1]

As most business writers and editors would probably acknowledge, a takeover attempt—whether it is successful—affects scores of people. Certain areas of the country, for example, have large senior citizen populations, which might indicate a sizable number of stockholders or people whose pensions are vested in stocks. If a specific company is in trouble, it may mean a reduction in the dividends it pays. This would affect those in the community who depend upon those dividends.

For example, a fairly large number of retirees who have settled in Lakeland, Florida, are from the Detroit area. The chances are good that they carry stock portfolios and pensions that are tied to the fortunes of major automobile manufacturers. This opens an opportunity for special efforts to provide news from Detroit even though it is hundreds of miles away.

Of course, the presence of a local plant or office of a major firm also broadens community interest in news about the industry in which it is involved. The reader or viewer may work there or simply be aware of the economic importance of the firm to the community. The local news organizations should therefore cast eyes toward the financial centers for information in addition to what is gained from local sources.

So there are situations in which news organizations—however small they might be—should attempt to develop a ready list of sources who can be called when something unusual occurs or called for periodic status reports.

William Barnhart, associate financial editor of *The Chicago Tribune,* stresses that takeovers do not relate only to shareholders. "Many people have money invested in company pension plans and the like," he said. "The overall theme (of a takeover) is important to readers. Ask yourself what the stake of your readers is in this."

Barnhart advises reporters to put any takeover attempt in context of the structure of the industry. That is, in the case of an airline takeover, for instance, airline analysts can be sources. Also, he suggests that reporters look at previous takeovers in that industry to see if they could have been the impetus for future takeovers.

He also urges reporters to look not just at the "who, what, where" of a takeover attempt, but also at the "why." "You're not defending or opposing it," he said. "You're giving background. Sometimes we cover takeovers like sporting events. 'Here's what happened,' a source says. This can be fine, but there is an overall economic context. Talk to suppliers, to customers, talk to employees and employers."[2]

Also, don't forget the people and the government angle when covering takeovers. Takeovers often mean dislocating hundreds of people and their families; therefore, don't forget this human angle.

Obviously, the takeover target and the company that is taking it over must be contacted for details of the story. But if they do not offer information, a rich source could be state and local governments, particularly the offices of the mayor or governor and economic development offices. They often know what's going on and are willing to talk about it.

Don't Overlook the Human Aspect

An attempted takeover of the Goodyear Tire and Rubber Co. in 1987 is not something the city Akron, Ohio, will soon forget. It is also not something Doug Oplinger, assistant managing editor for news of *The Akron Beacon Journal,* will ever forget. His staff won the Pulitzer Prize for General News Reporting that year for its coverage of the attempted takeover by Sir James Goldsmith.

Oplinger, who was business editor at the time of the takeover attempt, knew that he had to get his readers involved in the story. "We tried to turn it into a people story," he said recalling how staff members interviewed Goldsmith himself, Goodyear workers, and members of the community who were afraid they'd lose the city's biggest corporation if the takeover attempt succeeded.

Oplinger recalled how hundreds of Goodyear workers traveled to Columbus, the state capital, to attend a legislative hearing about the subject. The workers, all wearing Goodyear caps on their heads, filled the room and stood outside in the hall. This in itself was an excellent story, Oplinger said.

The *Beacon Journal* business staff was at an advantage in some ways because most Akron residents knew someone—either directly or indirectly—who worked for Goodyear. "Goodyear was an important factor in the community," Oplinger said. "Twelve thousand people worked there at the time of the attempted takeover. People read about the company and knew the names and the faces."

Still, it was difficult to put the details of the takeover in easy, readable form. It also was a challenge to put the entire Goodyear story and not just the takeover attempt into perspective. Oplinger said that shortly before the takeover attempt, the company built a large technical center and a new plant that brought hope and jobs into the community. Two years before the takeover attempt, however, the company began running into financial problems. Part of the job of the newspaper's business staff was to weave that information into the "takeover attempt" story, Oplinger said.

Another challenge of the staff was simply to get the information. The staff knew it had to go beyond talking to public relations people, but, for legal reasons, Goodyear officials were reluctant to talk. "It was a matter of weasling our way into places, such as the floor of the New York Stock Exchange, to interview traders," Oplinger recalled.

Oplinger said the newspaper's circulation during the takeover attempt rose, indicating to staff members that "we were doing things right."

It also showed them that business and economics affects everyone. "Take the time to show that there are people behind the numbers," he advises. "Then business reporting can come to life for everyone and go on the front page. Bring business writing down to a personal level."

One tip he gives reporters is to write business stories as though they were telling the story to a friend or relative: "My goal was to write stories that would interest my mother; she was typical. When I first came to the business desk, I thought, 'Mom would never read this.' So I tried to think of ways to report things that were different."[3]

Paul Bernish, director of public relations for the Cincinnati-based Kroger Co., was on the other end of a corporate restructuring. He said there were reasons his company talked little to reporters in 1988 during a restructuring of Kroger. The restructuring was implemented to prevent a corporate takeover. "We were fighting for our very existence," he said. "Part of our plan was not to say much." The reasons? "Takeovers are high stakes," Bernish said. "There are billions of dollars on the line and often the battleground is on the pages of newspapers. It's a way for various sides of the struggle to sway the other side through trial balloons or by creating or dispelling rumors."[4]

John Morris, former business editor of *The Cincinnati Enquirer,* one of the newspapers covering the Kroger restructuring, agrees that newspapers and other media outlets are often pawns in the takeover game; that is, they are indeed used by the players. Still, be believes, the failure of companies to talk to reporters inevitably leads the reporters to talk to other sources such as analysts. Those analysts often offer information that the company does not want to get out, he said.[5]

COVERING CONSUMER AFFAIRS

Lea Thompson, an investigative/consumer reporter for WRC-TV in Washington, D.C., enjoys her job because she knows what she does helps people. Thompson reports on consumer issues, and therefore, gets a chance to change the system.

Thompson is representative of what might be considered a new breed of reporters who emphasize the needs of citizens who historically have had little journalistic attention. Consumer reporting is a twentieth century development that goes hand in hand with environmental reporting in gaining much of its impetus from ordinary citizens. This provides several approaches to the subject matter.

The most common approach could be labeled the how-to story (e.g. how to do a more effective job of purchasing, how to save money in the supermarket or buying insurance, or how to determine quality). The emphasis is on helping consumers understand the process and on giving them information they can put to use. Often seasonal, it may involve comparison shopping and informing the audience of the best price or the best buy in terms of quality and price. Or it may consist of explanations, for example, of income tax deductions or what the consumer price index means in everyday life.

A second approach is reporting on regulatory action. One of the paradoxes of modern journalism is the way that it often joins forces with government in efforts to correct practices that are detrimental to citizens. Some would say governmental efforts have been inadequate, but it is fact that in recent years, American government has taken a stronger consumerism approach through its regulatory agencies. Investigations and decisions of such groups often provide the stories that reporters follow or often represent the starting point for deeper journalistic analysis.

Providing information about citizen-consumer-neighborhood-community action groups represents the third concentration. Citizens do not sit still and calmly accept everything these days. Spurred on by leaders of the consumerism movement and even governmental agencies, they organize, protest, request funds to be set up and run self-improvement programs. Journalists fan these local blazes by providing the encouragement of publicity and by helping document the concerns for which solutions are sought.

Among the most complex of journalistic consumer-reporting efforts is the reporting of corporate power and corporate activities with direct (perhaps negative) impact on the community and its citizens. This may be as simple as reporting the economy in terms of consumer issues, for example, or whether campaign contributions influence votes in legislative bodies.

There is also the investigative approach. Reporters define the problem, ascertain the need, conduct their inquiries, and spread the word. More than anything, investigative reporting represents a willingness to take the initiative and devote the time to finding explanations for social circumstances. This may be the reporting of deliberate consumer fraud. It may involve questionable practices—perhaps inadvertent—that raise prices, lower quality, or create health and safety problems. It may be an explanation of a local situation that has affected prices, such as shop owners' increasing prices to compensate losses due to shoplifting.

Few journalists fit exclusively into a single mode of consumer reporting, nor should they. A news organization will establish policies about emphasis, of course, but the best coverage involves all these levels. An exposé may be more exciting journalistically than discussing how to select a good cut of meat at the best price, but overall, the value of consumer journalists will depend on how well they cover the spectrum.

The quality of their performance is a subject of some disagreement, and it has been for several years, especially among those people such as consumer advocate Ralph Nader, who says the journalistic effort has improved but remains inadequate: "First of all, media are now willing to name brand names in the context of critical stories. Second, the media are willing to report citizen research and commentary more than before when it was primarily official-source journalism. Third, more newspapers and television stations are devoting resources to having full-time consumer reporters.

"Having said that, however, one must keep in mind that there's a long way to go, that the local department stores and local drug chains and local factories carry a lot of implicit opportunity for self-censorship by newspapers, and the coverage of Main Street USA is not very good," Nader believes. "Many reporters will report a dangerous drug finding by a national drug company, but they won't report a local chemical waste dump hazard by a local company that is an economic force in the community."

Nader is particularly critical of journalism's efforts to report the impact of the political system on the consumer. This, he says, is the broadest and most important type of journalism, but it's the most poorly done because the more consumer news focuses on point of sale, the less opportunity it has to provide public information directed toward prevention of the problem in the first place.

"For example, 'Well, here's how you choose different cuts of meat,' but there's very little reporting on the meat plant, on sanitary standards, on U.S. Department of Agriculture regulations. Under those circumstances, the light of public information which might lead to change at the source of the problem far removed from the point of sale in the store is minimized."

Others, without denying the importance of larger perspective advocated by Nader, take a different approach, criticizing reporters for over emphasis on stories about business versus the consumer. They say too much consumer news is after-the-fact reporting, and greater attention should be placed on helping the consumer in the marketplace.

Bringing It Home

Whatever the approach, the essential ingredient of consumer reporting is its emphasis on people. The term itself is the clue. It's a broad concept, made up of anything that affects people, the way they spend their money, who has the money, where it comes from, what products and services are available, and any possible health or safety hazards involved.

To many consumer reporters, ideas can come from everywhere. This is one advantage the consumer reporter has over other journalists. The political reporter is not a politician. The education reporter is not an educator. But the consumer reporter *is* a consumer and can uncover stories just by being observant during normal day-to-day living.

The best consumer reporters also stress that the human approach involves more than just writing about consumers and to consumers. It means using consumers as sources in the story. It has been stated, probably correctly, that average citizens were aware of this nation's economic problems in the late 1970s before the professional economists. They knew it because they experienced it, and they tend to be willing to talk about it. Consumers intuitively know that their problems will not be solved unless public discussion is stimulated. They know public discussion results from publicity. Maybe that's why they're so willing to open up and talk about private financial problems.

For all its value, using consumers as sources also adds a burden to reporters—a burden which necessitates going to economic and/or government experts. Individuals who are having problems, as well as consumer groups organized to fight such problems, often are emotional and have a right to be. They're dealing with an emotional subject. Reporters usually find it necessary to consult others who have broader and deeper knowledge who have access to specific facts, and who can be objective.

That's why the advocacy role of consumer reporting may pose problems. It is true that the consumer reporter is an advocate in the sense that he or she may represent the consumer. But that is not an excuse for one-sided coverage. The consumer needs a full report; the country needs a full report.

Of course, newspapers and broadcast outlets may suffer economically because of top-notch consumer coverage. Lea Thompson of WRC-TV in Washington, D.C. acknowledges that her station has undoubtedly lost

Lea Thompson
of WRC-TV, Washington, D.C.
(WRC-TV photo)

advertising dollars after advertisers were the subject of some of her stories. Fortunately, she said, officials at her station have not let that keep them from allowing consumer stories to air. But other reporters may not be so lucky, she believes. (Interestingly, Herb Weisbaum, a consumer reporter of KIRO of Seattle, said he worked on a television station once that took him off the consumer beat after a subject of one of his stories sued the station. The station won the suit, he said, but he thought it wise to find work at another station that would allow him to continue his consumer work despite the attitude of some advertisers).[6]

Weisbaum and Thompson agree that the consumer writer must be a voracious reader to find out what's going on in the world. Thompson suggests that consumer writers read religiously such publications as *Business Week, Money,* and *Consumer Reports.*

Thompson stresses that most of the stories she does affect almost all consumers; that is, she has tested the amounts of fat and sodium in school cafeteria food and found that it is higher in those substances than the food in most fast-food restaurants; she has tested the quality of the water in city-run swimming pools and found that most pools are not up to health-department standards. She has also analyzed grocery-store beef and learned that some of it is not properly labeled.

Other ideas she recommends are investigating baby formula and, over-the-counter drugs to see how many are outdated, and testing sulphites in salad bars. Although such sulphites are not banned, they still are dangerous and exist in salad bars, she says.

But she and Weisbaum stress that such testing cannot be done in a haphazard manner. For instance, she tested the swimming pool water by using the same kits used by pool management and by using the same testing techniques. Thompson also recommends that reporters find "authorities" or government officials to help test such items as meat or other foods. That way, the results of the tests are legitimate when presented to the businesses and consumers.[7]

There are, however, some tests that reporters can do themselves. Weisbaum once did a story that tested the efficiency of mail services by sending several wrapped, breakable items to friends. He then noted how quickly the packages were delivered and whether the products were damaged. In addition to letting viewers know the best way to send items, he included a small segment on the best way to package items so they do not break.

Of course, many consumer writers have the latitude to do longer, more involved stories. Weisbaum and Thompson said that they both have done stories on questionable practices of some children's beauty pageants, which might be run by shoddy organizations out for high entrance fees.

Investment scams, such as investments in fake diamonds or rare coins, often catch innocent victims, Weisbaum believes. Customers, who are usually reached by telephone, are told that such investments are risk-free.[8]

COVERING LABOR AND WORK

It's difficult to avoid the conclusion that American journalism has taken an elephant's tail approach to coverage of labor. The attention reporters give to unions in the name of labor reporting simply ignores the size of the animal with whom they're dealing. More than 100 million persons are employed in this country, with less than one-quarter of them involved with labor unions. Yet, by far, coverage has focused on mainly organized labor.

Even the news devoted to unions has been narrow. In many instances, it has represented only the coverage of unions on strike. A "work stoppage," as it is now being called, is only part of the process of collective bargaining. Union and management representatives negotiate, the union makes a proposal, the company responds with a counteroffer, they go back and forth (perhaps there is a strike, perhaps not), an agreement is reached, ratified, and put into effect, and it has a specific impact on workers and the company, or it has a broader impact on the community at large. Each stage represents a component of the total process. Each merits journalistic attention.

Other aspects of organized labor have been covered but deserve more coverage. Unions don't come into being at the time of a strike. They exist, elect officers, develop philosophies, and implement programs. Coverage of these operations might help eliminate some of the surprise and anger when conflict does arise. Union leaders have considerable authority and often handle millions of dollars of union funds. Occasionally, they get into trouble with legal authorities. Reporters have paid only periodic attention to these matters.

Union leaders—themselves politicians who depend on votes to maintain their positions—more often take stands on political issues, particularly those which have to do with social welfare. News organizations have noted that the leaders of the nation's largest labor unions have endorsed a political candidate or have spoken for or against specific legislation.

But such coverage has not been prevalent on the local level in spite of the fact that almost all labor unions from time to time act as lobby organizations, support candidates, and contribute campaign funds. Political activities may be concentrated in state capitals or in Washington, D.C., and thus may be covered by the statehouse or federal reporters. But they must be an essential part of a news organization's coverage of labor.

It is much easier to cover the organized portion of the nation's work force than the amorphous and far-flung portion that consists of millions of individual workers without a centralized philosophy or method of communication. But labor reporting must be bigger. It must be categorized as union and nonunion. Frank Swoboda, a national correspondent for *The Washington Post,* believes the labor beat includes any trend or happening in the workplace, including coverage of the role of women, minorities and teenagers.[9]

It's the nonunion coverage, other than periodic presentation of employment statistics, that is most likely to be ignored. Most people who work don't belong to any type of union. But they provide good—although admittedly difficult—opportunities for reporters who want to feel the pulse of the nation and its economy.

On and Beyond the Picket Line

Swoboda believes changes that took place in the work force since the late 1970s have been "stunning;" that is, the dramatic growth of the number of women and minorities in the work force has changed its makeup entirely and "brought different demands and qualifications."

Another major change that will forever impact the work force is a switch from a manufacturing to a service economy, which changed the necessary job requirements of applicants. This switch has a particularly damaging effect on young people without college educations, most of whom could have, in previous decades, found high-paying nonskilled or semiskilled jobs.

In addition, the concept of the "company person"—one who stays at one company his or her entire life—is rapidly disappearing. Swoboda said the average person changes jobs six times during his or her lifetime and changes occupations three times.

Finally, the rise in the numbers of temporary, part-time and what Swoboda refers to as "contingent" workers also merits extensive coverage. "There are people who are no longer a part of the core workforce," he said.[10]

However, it is not just the type of employee and the type of job that have forced changes in labor reporting. Dennis McCabe, director of corporate information for Indiana Bell, believes public sentiment regarding labor and management has also changed over the years, as has the positions of labor and management during strikes.

In the late 1960s, for instance, "there was the tendency to assume that during a dispute, the union was probably right because it represented the working people," McCabe said. "Now, it's more even. People believe there's good and bad on both sides."

In addition, McCabe believes management and labor have more common interests than ever before and during labor disputes, "the two sides are not at extremes as they used to be. . . . They work together for the common good."

The changes in the demographic makeup of the work force and the move away from a manufacturing economy also affect labor-management relations, McCabe believes. For instance, an older work force is not as likely to strike as younger workers. And fewer manufacturing jobs translate into a decline in numbers of union members, McCabe believes.

Furthermore, strikes today do not have the impact on customers that they did decades ago because of foreign competition. For instance, if production of a particular American automobile declines because of a strike, consumers now can easily buy a car made overseas, McCabe said.

Because of the changing environment in the work force, union officials have during the last decade or so turned less to collective bargaining and more to local and state legislatures to meet the demands of their workers, McCabe believes. That is, they are now more than ever attempting to get laws passed they believe would be of advantage to workers.[11]

Problems of Labor Coverage

Labor clearly has its own views of how it thinks it is being treated in the media. Those views are not always favorable, even though reporters are getting more sophisticated about defining "labor coverage."

Charles Deppert, secretary-treasurer of the Indiana AFL/CIO, believes that many reporters are too reliant on "buzz words" that are either outdated or simply inaccurate. "We hear phrases like 'strikes,' 'big labor,' 'union bosses.' We feel these phrases cast labor in a bad light." For instance, he said, persons other than union members can go on strike, but when nonunion members strike, the connotation of the word is not severe. When unions strike, "it conjures up bad things like violence." The use of the word "picket" is used only in conjunction with union members, he believes. "Everyone else demonstrates; unions 'picket.' "

Deppert also thinks that terms like "demands" and "big labor" are erroneous. "Proposals become 'demands,' " he said. "And 'big labor.' What is that?" He finds the term "union bosses" outdated. "Labor representatives are elected," he said.

Unfortunately, Deppert said, most labor disputes get media attention only if there are incidents or strikes, when, in fact, the vast majority of labor-management disputes are settled without strikes or incidents, he said.

Deppert also believes the media convey the idea that all labor unions are alike and all are sympathetic and supportive of each other at all times. In truth, most unions are run in different ways, have different goals and are dissimilar to each other in many ways, he said.[12]

Many reporters would disagree with Deppert, perhaps justifiably in countless incidences, but his complaints are not uncommon. They stand as constant reminders of the need for providing readers, viewers, and listeners with broader perspective on the exiting events of the day.

COVERING AGRICULTURE

Agriculture is a paradox in this country. It is somewhat akin to Charles Dickens's opening line in *A Tale of Two Cities:* "It was the best of times, it was the worst of times. . . ." It's confusing. The American people are aware of the importance of food production, but they also must know that 2 percent of the population feeds the rest, and the number of producers has declined rapidly as farmers migrate from rural areas in search of better opportunities.

Americans believe that farmers take pride in their independence and show disdain for welfare and other types of public support. But, at the same time, society provides special assistance so that farmers can survive on the farm. We say agriculture is basic to the American economy. It provides the force that has made this country great and holds the key to developing other countries. Yet, the impression that farmers are not sharing in economic gains is strong.

The problem is that farmers do not speak with one voice. The message changes with time and geography. Urban America believes there is a category of concern called "agriculture," but that may mean anything from the farmer through the retail grocer.

This confusing picture has been reflected by American journalism. The confusion has been fed historically by news organizations concentrating on breaking news, events, and stories that report what another agricultural expert had to say on a topic. This policy reflects the many messages regarding agriculture without providing the context that urban America needs to understand those messages.

It is not possible or desirable for news organizations to adopt a uniform coverage philosophy. They serve different audiences with different needs. Journalists in metropolitan areas have correctly assumed that their audiences have little need for or interest in the kind of agriculture news that emphasizes the how-to aspect of farming, the technological developments, or the discussions of the latest pesticides. They leave that kind of coverage to their colleagues in smaller towns or rural areas which serve audiences that do need it.

Even in small towns, the focus of coverage depends on local agricultural activity and on what types of products are grown. An Iowa newspaper would provide little news about cotton production. Audiences in Maine would have little need for information on the latest techniques for citrus crops.

Agriculture as a business and as a major force in the nation's economy, however, is a subject of interest in both Iowa and Maine, as well as to metropolitan centers across the country. When bad weather damages the citrus crop, that means the price of oranges will be higher. When corn blight hits the nation's midsection, market prices will be affected. When beef producers cut back on the size of their herds because of the high cost of feed, urban residents will feel the pinch.

Those kinds of stories exemplify the broader treatment that journalism is giving agricultural issues. News organizations continue to provide announcements and to break news pertinent to the area, but they are more unlikely to see themselves serving a general audience of consumers, which includes farmers.

The broad effect of farm news on farmers, consumers, and other businesses was studied by Michael Hoyt, who visited a small-town Iowa paper in 1987 to examine the coverage of the farm crisis that drove many farmers out of business during the 1980s. During that time, many farmers borrowed money to expand and were caught by declining prices of crops. Subsequently, they failed to repay their loans.

Hoyt examined the coverage by several major newspapers and by the weekly *Adair County Free Press* in Iowa. He learned that major dailies like *The Los Angeles Times, The Philadelphia Inquirer,* and *The Kansas City Times* wrote stories about such subjects as the changes that led to the world's food glut; the grass-roots efforts to shape federal farm policy; and the effect of manufacturing, mining, and even the fishing industry on the farm crisis.[13]

Smaller newspapers in farm communities, however, were faced with a bigger challenge, Hoyt wrote. First, they had to learn how to continually cover the "bad news" of the farm crisis while still emphasizing the positive side of life. Hoyt writes about *Free Press* Editor Ed Sidey:

> "There's an attitude," he says. "Nobody is in a more powerful position to do something about that than the newspaper people. For a community to turn around, you've got to have hope. If you keep talking too long about the problems, everybody gets more depressed. On the other hand, if you are too upbeat, people think you don't understand and you lose your credibility. It's a fine, fine, line. . . ."
>
> "In the beginning, Sidey's farm-crisis coverage included plenty of meetings of angry and dispirited farmers—organizing efforts, seminars, and the like—but those have tapered off now. Farmers have emotionally adjusted to the crisis, Sidey says—'the folks have finally realized it's not something they did wrong'—and his agricultural coverage is fairly routine again. He never was one for covering the human drama anyway—the family is losing its farm, the tears and the rage. "I know these people," he says. "That would be like breaking into the house of a friend to take a picture of his grief at a death. I don't do that."[14]

Sidey's job also includes intense coverage not just the farmers and the prices of food, but also of nonfarm businesses in his community that suffer because of the community's declining economy.

Getting to the Issues

The general consumer approach to the coverage of agriculture requires the integration of the subject matter and sources. It means the agriculture reporter must be more than someone who was reared on a farm. It dictates detailed knowledge and an understanding of economic and political activity. It requires a reporter who reads broadly and who at the same time understands the thinking and the problems of the agricultural community.

Without such a combination of a broad and specific perspective, the reporter will be forced into continued passing along of superficial and often contradictory points of view from various representatives of agriculture. To succeed at an issue approach without such background would not be possible.

The journalist's goal is to explain the place of agriculture in important social issues. What has public impact? Why? What are alternative courses of action? What can influence decisions?

Once the commitment has been made to issue analysis, there must be decisions about what those issues are. Issues will vary as social circumstances change. But for the 1990s, it is likely the issues will remain relatively constant. These issues include the following:

Health and Safety. Americans in recent years have become increasingly interested in the quality and healthfulness of their food. Many are skeptical about freshness, nutritional value, purity, and flavor. They seek alternatives. Likewise, there has been an increase in questions about the effects of herbicides and pesticides used in agriculture on people.

Government's Role. The role of government in agriculture merits constant journalistic attention. The impact is large and not publicly understood. Farm subsidies as a means of controlling production remain controversial. Buying and selling by governmental agencies is puzzling. What role does government regulation play in health and safety? To what degree are regulatory activity and farm subsidies political footballs? Is government adequately dedicated to agricultural research as a means to solve recurring concerns?

Land Use Planning. As urban sprawl continues and more land is consumed for residential and industrial purposes, the question remains whether land needed for agriculture will be available. Legislation on this question is considered and passed from time to time at all levels, but the public has demonstrated little concern. This is a subject, therefore, that opens up an avenue for journalistic leadership.

Financial Concerns. The public is aware that huge investments are required by those people who farm on a large scale, and the public has been told that the profit margin is slight. Therefore, as in every area of journalistic concern, finances must remain a major consideration. What are the problems of small farming units? Can they survive? Should they survive? What are the long-range implications of a situation in which only the very large can operate effectively? What impact are financial problems having on the farm family and on such social necessities as education in predominantly rural areas?

Local Parallels. If these issues are national in scope, they also have local parallels. News organizations seeking to serve hometown audiences will not ignore such important issues as zoning decisions when a public usage of land (e.g., airports) would remove farmland from production and when public decisions are involved in renovation and restoring strip-mined land. They also will not ignore such issues as hunting rights, predator control, and debates over such matters as the sheep producer's need to control losses versus the conservationist's concern about coyotes.

This listing is not comprehensive. The agenda will include other issues, other unanswered questions, and other needs for public understanding. What about food import-export policies that touch on the question of using food as a political weapon? What about alternative energy sources, such as gasohol, which use farm products as a substitute for imported petroleum? If solutions are found, one of the requirements will be continued comprehensive journalistic attention.

Jane Dwyre Garton, a former agriculture reporter for the *Appleton* (Wisconsin) *Post-Crescent,* believes agriculture reporters in the 1990s will have to deal with several issues that require skills in such areas as business and medical writing. "Biotechnology," for instance, the entrance of high technology into the farm, must be dealt with. In addition, stories are waiting to be written on the health hazards of farming. These occupational hazards include diseases that are spread from animals to humans or from humans to animals; respiratory illnesses that are often caused by inhaling large amounts of dust; and stress-related illnesses.[15]

The Commodity Markets

One point at which breaking news coverage and issue coverage coincide is the point of sale. Today's prices are breaking news, and today's prices are part of long-term financial trends. Perhaps the most conspicuous point of sale for agricultural products is in the commodity markets scattered across the country. Buyers and sellers come together and action is concentrated, which gives experts and journalists ready opportunities for analysis.

Commodities are not exclusively agricultural. However, the oldest and most extensively covered markets are those involved with grain and livestock trading, and the number of products getting attention is increasing. A typical list over the wire service could include coffee, orange juice, cotton, copper, silver, gold, lumber, eggs, potatoes, money futures, U.S. Treasury bills, and U.S. Treasury bonds.

The major coverage attention on the commodities market usually is on products of most local interest and, at times, on general summaries of price trends. This involves both what is called the sport market (real goods for immediate delivery) and the futures market (providing for delivery at a future date).

But reporting simply the prices may not be enough. Readers and viewers need to be shown the bigger picture of what's going on in the market, and how that affects the local picture.

Like other specialists, agricultural reporters must be avid readers. They must read the agricultural trade journals, as well as general-interest and business publications such as the *Wall Street Journal, New York Times,* and news magazines.

NOTES

1. Dan Rottenberg, "Missing the Message on Mergers," *Washington Journalism Review,* June, 1987, p. 18.

2. William Barnhart, remarks made at Ohio Media Economics Conference, Columbus, Ohio, May 13, 1988.

3. Doug Oplinger, remarks made at Ohio Media Economics Conference, May 13, 1988.

4. Paul Bernish, remarks made at "Covering Corporations," annual conference of Society of Professional Journalists, Cincinnati, Ohio, November 18, 1988.

5. John Morris, "Covering Corporations."

6. Lea Thompson and Herb Weisbaum, remarks made at "A New Look at Consumer Reporting," annual conference of Investigative Reporters and Editors, Inc., Minneapolis, Minnesota, June 3, 1988.

7. Thompson, "A New Look at Consumer Reporting."

8. Weisbaum, "A New Look at Consumer Reporting."

9. Frank Swoboda, remarks made at "Covering Labor/Management Issues," annual conference of Society of Professional Journalists, Cincinnati, Ohio, November 17, 1988.

10. Swoboda, "Covering Labor/Management Issues."

11. Dennis McCabe, "Covering Labor/Management Issues."

12. Charles Deppert, "Covering Labor/Management Issues."

13. Michael Hoyt, "A Small-Town Paper Confronts the Farm Crisis," *Columbia Journalism Review,* September/October, 1987, p. 36.

14. Hoyt, p. 37.

15. Jane Dwyre Garton, "The Road to Better Ag Stories," *The Quill,* November 1986, pp. 30–32.

Tracking the Ups and Downs of Medicine and Science

15

A few decades ago, it was only in the context of science fiction that we could think of something as unbelievable as a heart transplant. Or hospital stays of two or three days after major surgery.

Only in movies could we have traveled to the moon and found cures to previously incurable diseases.

But science and medicine attacked many problems. The results provided new drugs, new methods of treatment, new forms of transportation, satellites, and television. Without question, the twentieth century has been history's greatest era of scientific and medical discovery.

On the other hand, advancements in science and medicine have brought with them problems. Adverse reactions by some to the Swine flu vaccines of the late 1970s caused paralysis in some, and the most advanced space technology could not prevent the tragedy of the explosion of the space shuttle Challenger in 1986.

Billions of dollars have been pumped into an unwon "war on cancer." Technology has not been able to develop economically feasible alternative sources of energy to replace our finite supply of fossil fuels.

To a great degree, the general public knows about such achievements—and tragedies—because journalists are there to witness and record them.

Rita Rubin, medical writer for *The Dallas Morning News,* enjoys her job because she considers her beat one that solves problems for readers. "The medical beat is the most personal beat," she said. "It hits closest to home for the readers. Everyone is concerned about their health." She gets great satisfaction, she said, out of telephone calls she gets from grateful readers who read her stories. "It can be extremely satisfying. People have thanked me for helping them."

The wins, the losses, the gains, the discoveries, the applications, the relationships to society, and the long- and short-term impacts of medicine and science on individual human beings are the domain of medical science reporters. Those beats, however, are so big that the task of covering them is often subdivided even further. Part of science writing, for instance, has been delegated to "environmental" reporters, "energy" reporters, and even "new technology" reporters. The medical beat can be divided into those people who cover personal health issues, those people who cover health agencies, and most recently, those people who cover specific diseases, such as Acquired Immune Deficiency Syndrome, or AIDS.

AIDS AND PUBLIC PANIC

To Rubin of *The Dallas Morning News,* the biggest medical story of the 1980s unquestionably was AIDS. In covering that disease more than any other, she believes, editors and reporters have had to rethink the way that they treat the medical beat. "AIDS has brought all the problems of our health care system to a head," she said. "We (medical reporters) have had to rethink the way we do lots of things."

It's true in all reporting, but medical reporters particularly face the rather frightening prospect that what they write about has direct impact on the every life or death of readers, listeners, and viewers. On one hand, those who suffer are apt to see any discovery as a miracle cure. Or some may suffer unnecessarily from, say, polio or tuberculosis because they are lulled by reports that modern science had conquered those diseases. Or, thousands may experience needless trauma because of exaggerations of a possible serious epidemic. In medical writing, as some reporters believe, there's new hope and no hope.

The advent of AIDS and the coverage of the disease have brought to light all the problems associated with medical reporting, as well as the responsibilities of medical writers to their audiences. Thousands of AIDS victims are affected, of course, by reports of cures, treatments, or any hope of conquering AIDS. Conversely, news of stumbling blocks to those cures and treatments could cause victims to suffer even more.

Ironically, when AIDS was first reported in large numbers in the early 1980s, some reporters had trouble getting stories in print and on the air. In 1987, major metropolitan newspapers ran more than 10,000-AIDS related articles. Some editors and health practitioners believe that the stories were "reactive" rather than "reflective," and unwittingly added to the confusion about the disease.[1]

In the mid-1980s, many large newspapers and broadcast outlets found it useful to simply assign a reporter to the AIDS beat. At *The Dallas*

Morning News, for instance, the AIDS reporter covers the social rather than the medical aspects of the beat, including the availability of patient care, the special programs for AIDS patients, and the ethics and other nonmedical issues. The AIDS beat reporter may also cover public policy and religion, and their relationship to the disease and its victims.

During the first few years of coverage of the AIDS epidemic, newsrooms had to piece together coverage guidelines, says Carol Riordan, an associate director of the American Press Institute in Reston, Virginia. For instance, how graphic should stories be to detail how AIDS is transmitted? Should newspapers list AIDS as a cause of death in obituaries?

To deal with the problem of AIDS coverage, some news outlets brought in local officials from state and local health departments to talk to reporters and editors. Others used such officials as "resident experts" when reporters had questions.

Other news outlets have compiled written guidelines that outline AIDS coverage. One such policy, in *The Milwaukee Journal,* outlines the use of names in AIDS stories and spells out when to list AIDS as a cause of death in obituaries. It also spells out how to counteract hysteria when reporting on an incident "that could feed panic or distort understanding."[2]

The San Jose Mercury News stylebook stipulates that the overall policy of the newspaper regarding the coverage of AIDS is "to treat AIDS stories in the same manner as stories on any other disease. To do otherwise simply perpetuates the social stigma that has been attached to it." For that reason, the newspaper attempts to list the cause of death in all its obituaries.[3]

Edward M. Brecher, a Fellow of the Society for the Scientific Study of Sex and the author of several books on sex and health, believes the media have routinely exaggerated the spread of AIDS in the heterosexual community. And once reporters learned the numbers of heterosexual AIDS cases were relatively small, "data demonstrating the rarity of heterosexual AIDS-virus transmission sank from sight under the barrage of ominous predictions and warnings."[4]

Brecher does not believe the media purposely misled readers and viewers about the effect of AIDS on the heterosexual community. Instead, he believes, such misleading reporting, in some ways, gives people what they want: "Americans these days take delight in being scared out of their wits—by horror movies, bloodcurdling TV . . . and Stephen King's novels for instance," he believes. "The news media know that scare stories, including stories about heterosexual AIDS, sell papers and attract massive audiences. . . ."[5]

THE RUSH TO REPORT THE BREAKTHROUGH

One thing most investigative reporters learn early in their careers is to listen to and talk to top officials, but also to go beyond taking the word of top authorities. Many times, the best stories cannot be found simply by talking to the person at the top. Walt Bogdanich, an investigative reporter for *The Wall Street Journal,* won a Pulitzer Prize in 1988 based on information he thinks he never could have learned had he been content to base a series he did on the comments of top doctors. Bogdanich won the award for a series he wrote on faulty medical laboratory tests around the country—a story no other reporter had done.

Walt Bogdanich
of the Wall Street Journal (Wall Street

"Look beyond the predictable stories. Be innovative," Bogdanich urges medical and science reporters. One "fault" of science and health reporters is that they spend too much time seeking what he calls the "miracle-cure stories . . . these are the gee-whiz stories, the wonderful stories." Legitimate "miracle cure" stories are rare and are sought after by most reporters, he said. Or sometimes reporters have a good idea but they simply do not go far enough with it. When he started his series on medical laboratories, for instance, many other reporters were writing stories on inaccurate results of drug testing; they did not go one step further, as he did.

Bogdanich began his investigation into faulty laboratory testing procedures after he received a wrong finding on his own cholesterol-level test. In addition, he had, over the years "collected" stories from friends and relatives about laboratory test results that they believed were in error.

He suggests that reporters can get their best information from talking to "front-line" people—consumers, attending physicians, and nurses. "You don't need the experts to tell you what a good story is," he believes.[6]

Still, medical breakthroughs are becoming more and more common, so it is natural more media outlets are carrying reports of those breakthroughs. But to one correspondent for *The Lancet,* a leading British medical journal, too many reporters are suckers for the miracle cure story.

Jim Sibbison remembers how many of the national media—including *Newsweek, The New York Times* and ABC World News Tonight—reported as fact a finding that aspirin can reduce the risk of heart attack by 50 percent if taken every other day. Most of the news outlets based their stories on a study published in the *New England Journal of Medicine,* which called the finding a "breakthrough."

Two days after publication of the *New England Journal* article, the *British Medical Journal* reported that aspirin could not, in fact, prevent initial heart attacks; other studies showed that aspirin might, indeed, increase the chances of a stroke in some cases. As Sibbison points out, some media outlets refused to retract or change their stories; meanwhile, the Food and Drug Administration and the Federal Trade Commission asked aspirin manufacturers to refrain from advertising their product as a preventive for an initial heart attack.

Are reporters too quick to report on sometimes unsubstantiated breakthroughs? Sibbison points to a 1985 survey of medical scientists by Jay A. Winsten of the Harvard School of Public Health. That survey indicated that the chief fault of science writers, according to the scientists, is their habit of reporting "breakthroughs" on the strength of tentative findings that later can be contradicted.[7]

Statistics, too, can be misused and provide an inaccurate picture to the reader. In 1977, T. Gerald Delaney, director of public affairs for Memorial Sloan-Kettering Cancer Center, asked journalists to use restraint in their use of statistics, especially long-term survival figures.

He uses the illness of the late Senator Hubert Humphrey of Minnesota as an example, saying news reports that the senator had a 20 percent chance of survival from his cancer provide an example of the statistical fallacy of predicting the fate of an individual on the basis of a group.

In addition, Humphrey read these stories and, according to his doctors, was visibly shaken by them, Delaney said. There is also a strong possibility that these same news stories may adversely affect the attitudes of those people linked to the patient as well as others who may improperly relate the published information to their own cases.[8]

ASSESSING SECOND-GENERATION IMPACT

Controversies have become so publicly pervasive that reporters find themselves more frequently covering the broader implications of science, health, and technology, while paying attention to the long-term public impact of technological advancements. What happens later? What, for instance, is the long-term effect of radiation from a nuclear power plant? Or artificial sweeteners?

These kinds of questions represent the potential second-generation problems of technological application of scientific findings. Americans did not anticipate the problems of air pollution from automobiles, and it's going to take more knowledge to find the solution. The painful awareness that dangers lurk in the midst of great achievements has developed slowly. The potential problems were not analyzed. Most Americans, including reporters, had little understanding of the risks of technology and, significantly, this failure seems to have become an inherent part of the American character.

Jonathan Beckwith, a geneticist with Harvard University, warns reporters to be particularly careful with genetic research that indicates that one gender may be more talented than another at certain intellectual pursuits; for instance, that boys are better at mathematics than girls. Often, researchers and reporters fail to look at sociological factors that may account for those differences. He also warns reporters to be aware of social biases on the part of the researcher. "The social biases of researchers always come into play," he says. "It's often extremely difficult to separate socialization and environmental factors." Beckwith added he has often seen stories, particularly about genetic research, "overblown" in the media.[9]

James Detjen, a science writer for *The Philadelphia Inquirer,* warns against any seemingly perfect scientific breakthrough. "Remain skeptical of official sources," he says. "Nothing is foolproof. Nothing is perfectly safe. History has shown everything fails from time to time."[10]

It's not simply a negative matter. Future impact of a discovery may be positive; in the long run, there may be hope for solving another human problem. The point is that even though many researchers are reluctant to look beyond the moment of a research project, it's the reporter's task to pry some of the information loose. Scientists and physicians do not work in vacuums. They don't do research without some sort of an idea of where it fits or what it might mean.

Jim Detjen
of The Philadelphia Inquirer
(Philadelphia Inquirer photo)

SCIENCE AND MEDICINE ARE POLITICAL ISSUES

Assessing the future implications of scientific developments involves more than scientific understanding, for the role of science, medicine and technology as a national priority is as political as it is technical. This places additional responsibilities on journalists, who must be acutely aware of how science and medicine fit into the whole fabric of society and how the distribution of power influences that fit.

Expert coverage of the politics of science and health involves the familiarity with the court system; with agency procedures for establishing regulations for food and drugs; with organization of health delivery agencies; and with legislative bodies at the local, state, and national levels.

Margaret Engel, a science reporter for *The Washington Post,* suggests science and health reporters make a habit of checking local courthouses routinely for information regarding lawsuits filed by and against hospitals and doctors. In addition, she says, state health insurance regulators and state attorneys general are usually good sources of medical fraud stories.[11]

The list of possible sources of information also includes local health planning agencies, for instance, that have on file information about hospital operation and ownership and the Nuclear Regulatory Commission that has bureaus that inspect X-ray equipment and outline charges against hospitals regarding use of that equipment.

Detjen of *The Philadelphia Enquirer* agrees that public documents can be indispensible when covering science, particularly the energy beat. The NRC, for instance, gives each nuclear power plant a specific docket number. All of the documents regarding each plant are filed in the NRC's Public Document Room. A reporter need simply locate the file for a plant by using its number.

The NRC also is a rich source of information regarding inspection reports at each plant; notification by the plants of "unusual occurrences," which could mean safety problems; and inspection reports.

Other public agencies that keep files about nuclear plants include the Securities and Exchange Commission, which details regulatory and legal problems faced by utilities in 10-K reports; and the U.S. Labor Department, which keeps files on whistleblowers' complaints; and state public utility agencies.[12]

Bogdanich of *The Wall Street Journal* used court records as part of his research to learn who was harmed by incorrect laboratory test results. As he and others learn quickly, lawsuits are rich with a variety of information.[13]

It is possible to argue that these kinds of stories fall into the domain of the political reporter or the economic reporter or the consumer reporter. But many will argue for the science or medical reporter, stressing the background in dealing with medical sources. A science writer understands how to talk to scientists and how scientists think.

Still, that doesn't keep some science and medical reporters from getting caught in a game of politics, particularly regarding health care.

The politics of medicine is particularly well illustrated by the AIDS crisis. Brecher, who believes the spread of the disease into the heterosexual community was exaggerated in the media, blames this in part on an attempt by researchers to get money for AIDS research. Some physicians may believe, for instance, that if AIDS is not viewed by the public as a heterosexual problem, money will not be awarded for research.[14]

Tom Lee, former reporter turned physician, says the media's coverage of cancer has had a double-barreled negative impact.

"A suspicion is growing that the influence of the press on the cancer program is complex and dubious—that sensationalized, intensely personal stories about the disease and its victims have resulted in an exaggeration of cancer's importance in the country's overall biomedical research, and thrown the emphasis on possibly futile attempts to cure it rather than trying to understand and reduce its environmental causes," he says.

Lee points out that one byproduct of popular interest and public money is an extraordinary pressure on researchers to come up with the kind of findings that will make headlines, please politicians, placate voters, and bring in more funds.

"The nuts and bolts of science appear in the professional journals," he says, "but a researcher who can get his work and his institution covered by *The New York Times* is nevertheless a valuable commodity. Having 'star quality' depends on more than IQ, and researchers know that their work must have obvious clinical implications to draw attention and support. Winning grants often seems a more consuming goal than whipping cancer."[15]

Similar politics enter into the tragic explosion of the space shuttle Challenger. William Boot, a contributing editor of *Columbia Journalism Review,* believes that many reporters were "dazzled" by the "glamour" of the space program and the National Aeronautics and Space Administration and ignored hints that Challenger could be headed for disaster. Boot claims reporters were reluctant to question NASA on anything it did because of its success in the late '70s and early '80s when the shuttle moved from the drawing board to experimental flight. They were also overwhelmed by the mystique of the program, and too eager to dismiss the dangers of space flight.

In addition, Boot maintains that some reporters felt the NASA scientists, of course, knew more than the reporters about the technology, so they felt intimidated when questioning the agency. "Beyond space reporters' technical insecurity and preference for glamour lay another impediment to criticism of NASA: the agency's powerfully positive image. It had been polished by the triumphs of Project Mercury and the moon landings and by the accolades of reporters themselves."[16]

DAY-TO-DAY CHALLENGES

Covering individuals and institutions that are among the nation's elite, dealing with material which literally represents life or death to some in the audience, and coping with some of the most complex information available places continuous demands upon science and medical reporters. Their successes at meeting the demands, of course, will vary. But all will face daily challenges that must be overcome.

Dealing With Scientists and Doctors as Sources

Unlike the political reporter, who is courted, invited, visited, and assisted by politicians who know they need the media, science and medical reporters often have to deal with individuals who neither know how nor care to deal with them. It's true that more and more scientists are learning the value of the news media, but it's also true that at times reporters face lack of cooperation or outright censorship, sometimes prompted by local medical society codes.

Many scientists simply do not know how to cope with an individual who insists on simple nonscientific explanations of complex scientific subjects, who writes in what many regard as a frenzied and incomplete matter, and who pays little regard to the subtleties of science and medicine. Others have a basic distrust of reporters because they have been burned by journalistic misinterpretation or exaggeration. Very few reporters have good technical backgrounds from which to write, and this creates an awkward situation when one is dealing with highly trained scientists.

To Rita Rubin, however, the best doctors and researchers can also explain their field to a layman. "The top researchers are those who can explain their work on different levels," she said. "Some Nobel winners can explain their work to junior high students."

She admits, however, that at times physicians are difficult to contact. "I've had to call China," she said.

Sources of information are everywhere, and science and medical reporters must be careful not to rely too much on "expert" sources. In addition to contacting consumers, including his own relatives, Bogdanich of *The Wall Street Journal* talked to lab technicians and other "front line" people. "Forget the head of the AMA (American Medical Association) and all those glorious figures," he advises. Further, to get an idea of the accuracy of various laboratories, Bogdanich sent in five of his own blood samples to five different laboratories to see if the results of the tests were the same; they weren't.[17]

Engel of *The Washington Post* also believes that sources for science stories surround most reporters. She gets to know medical attorneys and medical suppliers. In addition, members of nurses' and other medical unions help provide information and sources for her.[18]

When covering the energy beat, state and local regulatory inspectors have been Detjen's single best source of stories and information.

Sources of information are everywhere, from the smallest town to the largest city. And science and medical reporters must avoid the twin problems of ignoring good local sources or of not reaching far enough. Locally, every rural area has county agricultural agents and high school science teachers; most have nearby university science staffs and industrial scientists. Reading scientific literature and even the popular media will provide long lists of names for the enterprising reporter. Also, specific trade or professional publications aimed at a certain group of people also can provide story ideas.

One question reporters must also answer for themselves based on specific circumstances is how willing they are to use material from public relations sources.

Dependence on a PR person relates directly to the role that person plays in the overall organization. Rubin says she is usually reluctant to rely on most public relations people, simply because most of them do not know the kind of stories she does and the type of material she needs. "I just get inundated with news releases," she says. "Judging on most of the information I get, it's obvious these people don't read the paper."

America struggles to kick the habit

By Paul Hayes

Michael Loewe, a 42-year-old financial consultant in Milwaukee, has cut his 30-year-old cigaret smoking habit in half. After hypnotism, bets with friends, group therapy and unending pressure from his wife and children, he's down to a pack and a half a day.

"I've wanted to quit smoking for a long time," he said. "I even went to a hypnotist in St. Louis in 1976. He had a heavy German accent and he pronounced my name Lou-vee. I found it humorous rather than serious. I paid him $87 and lit up on the way out of the hospital."

The nation has millions of Michael Loewes. They represent a tobacco tradition centuries old and global in scope. They also represent the 20th century tobacco tragedy, the conflict between an engrained cigaret habit and health.

In 1985, Loewe attended meetings once or twice a week for six weeks with a group of smokers who were trying to quit. It was as close as he came to quitting, he said, far closer than when he and three friends each put up $200 to encourage each other to stop smoking.

"No one collected," he said. "After a while we were all so uncomfortable that we agreed to take back the money, take each other off the hook and go back to smoking."

It is the cigaret he unconsciously lights while talking by phone to a client, for instance, that is his downfall. Sometimes he's had three cigarets burning simultaneously in his desk ashtray, he said.

He recalls with embarrassment that, not too long ago, he would leave the house frequently in the middle of the night to find a pack of cigarets. His son Christopher, then only 4, drew a cartoon mocking his behavior.

As psychological and physical compensation for his smoking, he rides a stationary bicycle 10 miles a day. He had no problems with his last physical. His heart and lungs seemed sound. He believes he still has his health.

"But I won't lie to myself," he said. "When I think about it, I'd rather live to be 80 than 65, and without emphysema and the rest of it. There are one of three ways I'm going to quit; I'll quit, I'll die, or when they pull the first lung out."

He added one other note of interest:

"I'm noticing more and more that I'm one of a few in any group that smoke. Today, out of a random group of people there might be two smokers where there used to be six or seven."

HIS OBSERVATION is accurate. Loewe is a member of a dwindling minority of cigaret smokers. There is every good reason to think that the era of the cigaret has peaked and is in decline.

According to the Tobacco Institute, cigarets consumed for each American man and woman older than 18 averaged 4,345 in the peak year in 1963. That dropped to 3,378 in 1985.

For years, population growth—the coming of age of the baby boom generation—kept gross cigaret sales rising, but that has ended as well. The institute said that the industry sold 594 billion cigarets in the US in 1985, down from its peak of 631.5 billion in 1980.

One measure of the decline came in December, when the National Cancer Institute reported a 4% decrease in lung cancer among US males from 1982 to 1983. This ended a trend that had seen annual increases of as much as 10% a year until it began leveling off in the mid-1970s.

Epidemiologist Richard Doll and Richard Peto anticipated this downturn in 1981 as a result not only of fewer cigarets consumed per smoker, but of the introduction in the 1950s of filtered cigarets with lower levels of tar and nicotine.

But the National Cancer Institute said that while there probably were 7,000 fewer cases of lung cancer in men in 1983 alone, lung cancer cases and deaths among women continued to climb.

There were an estimated 41,000 new cases and 35,000 deaths by lung cancer among American women in 1983. Epidemiologist attributed this to the increase in women smoking cigarets in the mid-1970s, while many men were quitting.

This year, lung cancer is expected to overtake breast cancer as the leading cancer-caused death among American women. This results from smoking habits begun by women in the 1940s, when thousands went to work during World War II.

Today many women have joined men in trying to quit, and enough are succeeding that the overall number of smokers continues to decline.

LOSS OF NUMBERS means a loss of political power, and this helps explain the increase in anti-smoking legislation.

The past few years have brought two congressional acts upgrading warnings on cigarets and smokeless tobacco, and restrictive smoking laws or ordinances in 37 states, including

Wisconsin, and hundreds of municipalities, including Milwaukee.

There are higher excise taxes on tobacco, a wave of new liability suits filed against the companies, a call for a ban on all cigaret advertising, and pressures to ban smoking in work places and commercial airliners.

The six big American cigaret manufacturers know that the US market will continue to decline. In fact, said one insider, the industry expects that cigaret smoking will decline by at least 1% a year for the rest of the century.

But don't mourn for the big companies. They have been and remain enormously profitable. By raising prices and cutting costs, tobacco companies have increased profits an average of 15% a year for a decade.

John Mullahy, analyst for Resources for the Future, a study group in Washington, D.C., cites studies that show that each 10% increase in cigaret prices causes a 3% to 7% decrease in sales.

Obviously, there is a point where higher prices no longer will mean higher profits, but it hasn't been reached yet.

Cash-rich from profits, the cigaret companies are putting much of their resources into diversification rather than an overall increase in cigaret making capacity.

What could quickly change this overall picture? What could accelerate the gradual decline in cigaret smoking?

A tobacco prohibition act obviously would, but few people seriously believe prohibition to be politically possible or any more workable than the prohibition of alcoholic beverages was in the 1920s.

An increased use of excise taxes imposed on cigarets would change the picture, by diverting to state and federal coffers an increasing share of tobacco revenue that otherwise would have gone to the companies.

A COURT JUDGMENT holding the manufacturer of a tobacco product liable for a death would shake up the industry, but perhaps not as much as many anti-smoking activists believe or hope. The industry is confident that this won't happen, insiders say.

The industry closely watched a case this year in which a woman in Oklahoma blamed the mouth cancer death of her son on smokeless tobacco, or snuff. The snuff was sold without a warning on the container. Even so, the tobacco company won.

The tobacco industry has yet to pay a dime to a plaintiff for the health consequences of smoking, either as a court judgment or as an out-of-court settlement.

If the tobacco company could win in this case in Oklahoma, it's hard to see how the industry could lose in cases involving products that carry warnings. Thus, an insider said, that industry's confidence that it can withstand whatever court challenges are ahead is growing, not shrinking.

DOES THE industry fear anything? Yes. Its greatest fear is that cigaret smoking will become socially unacceptable, that peer pressure will move smokers to quit and keep prospective smokers from starting.

The US has 53 million active cigarette smokers, and 90% or more of them already know that the habit is dangerous. But segments of society respond differently to the knowledge. Smoking clearly has become more of a blue-collar habit.

"Once glamorous, smoking is now simply gauche," said a headline in the August issue of Vogue, the fashion magazine, an issue that carried five advertisements for cigarets.

This emerging attitude, more than anything, has provided the political power to restrict the spaces in which smoking can occur. Today, a push is on to persuade corporations to banish smoking in the work place.

Meanwhile, all of these issues are irrelevant to smokers such as Michael Loewe, who say they want to quit, but haven't.

What is important to Loewe is that he's smoked heavily for 30 years, he's convinced it's dangerous, and he's tried to quit many times but failed in each. He'll keep trying.

Loewe symbolizes the essence of the cigaret problem. Regardless of public policy, smoking is an intensely private problem, a personal battle that only smokers can fight with themselves—win or lose.

This story localizes a national health issue—the health hazards of cigarette smoking. Note how the reporter mixes the local and the national for an informative, easy-to-read story. It appeared in the *Milwaukee Journal,* and is reprinted with permission.

She does, however maintain a good relationship with many university public relations people, most of whom genuinely want to help her with stories. Most college and university public relations people are happy to make sure reporters get in touch with the "right" person for a story, she said, and are not concerned with pushing a product or service.

Detjen, too, believes public relations sources can be helpful, to a certain extent. But it is not always wise to rely on them, he believes, because sometimes they simply are not told all the facts and inadvertently give wrong information or fail to tell the whole story.[19]

Parlez-Vous Science?

Reporters usually are not scientists or doctors themselves. They don't have advanced degrees. Yet they find themselves daily serving as the link between scientists who speak a virtual foreign language and a public that needs translation and critiques, not parroting. There is, of course, no journalistic secret. The point is not to know all about nuclear physics, astronomy, or psychology, although any background knowledge is helpful. The real talent is to ask intelligent questions and to feel no embarrassment over saying: "Let's try that one again. I don't understand."

Rubin says she keeps pressing physicians and researchers into speaking about their jobs in layman's terms. "I'll keep on them to give analogies," she said. She, in turn, tries to compare often intricate surgical procedures in ways readers can understand.

Although she keeps a medical dictionary on hand, "I can't expect to keep thumbing through it during the interview," she said. If she is reviewing her notes after an interview and finds she did not understand something as well as she thought, she always calls the researcher to get a better explanation that she can pass on to her readers.

Detjen of *The Philadelphia Inquirer* agrees that analogies help the reader. If, for instance he is talking about the acid content of acid rain, he is not content to simply say it has a "PH" of 3. "It helps if you can say, 'that's as acidic as vinegar, or as acidic as tomato juice,' " he said.

Detjen also believes narratives or case studies about people can help people understand the personal side of research and understand technical material. If a reporter is describing, for instance, the appearance of technical equipment, he or she should try to compare it to an item familiar with the reader.

The concepts of nuclear power—which were new to most reporters—suddenly became extremely important for the reporters who covered the nuclear accident at Three Mile Island in Pennsylvania. The Three Mile Island incident was so widely reported that by 1989—more than a decade after the accident—the public still mentioned safety as its top concern of nuclear power, says Andrew Morrison, who conducts public opinion research into energy and environmental issues. This concern with safety was second even to energy efficiency and monetary savings.[20]

But Three Mile Island was not the only incident that made people aware of energy in the late 1970s and early 1980s. The energy crisis during those years drove home to many citizens the problems of limited resources. But once the "crisis" died down, so did concern for energy issues, says Ann Bisconti, vice president for research and program evaluation for the U.S. Committee on Energy Awareness. In 1979, at the height of the energy crisis, 69 percent of Americans polled mentioned energy as one of the two biggest problems in the United States. By 1989, Bisconti says, only 1 percent of those polled listed energy as a serious problem.[21]

MOVING TOWARD MATURITY

Science and medical writing have always been part of American journalism. But it was not until World War I and World War II in the twentieth century that the media came to recognize the essential value of covering scientific developments in detail. It also was not until the Russian launched Sputnik 1 in 1958 that science reporting became a genuine specialty. Hundreds of journalistic "science experts" covered the subsequent space race.

As the twentieth century progresses, perhaps science and medical journalism are reaching maturity. Reporters seem to be much less anxious for miracle-cure stories and more determined to chronicle scientific, medical, and technological developments from the perspective of their role in social development, whether that role is positive or negative.

That maturity could be reflected in the development of three trends that demonstrate changes in science and medical writing and portend future developments.

Less Breaking News, More Interpretation

Meetings of scientific and medical organizations, news conferences by leading researchers, specific technological and medical developments, and technological accidents will always receive journalistic attention. They deserve it. But these reports don't always give a sophisticated audience what it wants or needs. Reporters are paying and must continue to pay greater attention to the background, broader implications, and meaning of scientific developments.

Reporters are more likely to be evaluative, at times more critical, of scientists and technologists, of their work, and of the social implications of their efforts. To accomplish this, reporters themselves are becoming more knowledgeable and using more alternative sources in their stories. This includes not only scientists, but also government officials and other citizens. They are beginning to keep their own personal libraries of books and information that they know will help them in the future.

For instance, Detjen of *The Philadelphia Inquirer* predicts that the use of laboratory animals in medical research will continue to become a hot issue for science reporters into the twenty-first century. He predicts that other areas of interest in science reporting in the next few decades will be genetic engineering and its effects, both biological and political; global climate changes and the decay of the earth's ozone layer; and occupational health, including such topics as radiation exposure. He also sees the emergence of more stories about earthquakes and the factors that lead up to them, and, interestingly, astrology and the occult. Although that last topic hardly seems scientific, "the fact remains, there is a thriving industry (in the occult) exploiting the elderly, the poor, the uneducated."[22]

David Lore
of The Columbus Dispatch (Columbus Dispatch photo)

David Lore, science writer for *The Columbus Dispatch,* sees a reemergence of the importance of energy reporting. Lore, who covered the energy crisis of the 1970s, remembers when Christmas trees were dark and gasoline was rationed. "Energy will be a hot beat again in the 1990s," he says. And it will be a beat that will affect everyone's lives: "We're talking about people's power supplies, people's pocketbooks, people's very lives."

Issues emerging in the 1990s are acid rain, the Greenhouse effect on climate and temperatures, changing weather patterns and more on nuclear power. "Will nuclear power be resurrected?" he asks.[23]

Focus on Audience Perspective

Science and health journalism, in spite of notable exceptions, has tended in the past to echo the journalistic practice of presenting news from the official source to the general audience. It has passed along "the word" from the experts. But many readers, viewers, and listeners are becoming too sophisticated to simply believe what they are told. Some are becoming more vocal about what they want from science and medicine and what they want from journalism.

Science and medical reporters are aware of this need, and they are responding. In medicine, they are writing more from the perspective of the patient; in all of science, they are placing greater emphasis on the social consequences of science and technology. A greater tendency toward consumer orientation to science coverage is apparent, and the traditional flow of news has been made a two-way street. Journalism is seeking to inform government, corporate scientists, and officials of public attitudes about what they are doing.

It Doesn't Have to Be Dull

Most high school students, perhaps for good reason, have the attitude that science is dull. Too many reporters—even some of those who write about science—have carried that attitude in their professional lives. But while science may be complex, many reporters and scientists stress that it is among the most naturally dramatic fields of inquiry. Many reporters simply have not been taking advantage of this.

A change is reflected in efforts to use writing styles that highlight this natural drama and that attempt to humanize the potentially cold facts of scientific and medical developments. This is not simply translating scientific terminology, although that is important. It's writing as though science has a direct impact upon the person reading the magazine or newspaper, watching television, or listening to the radio. It does. This must be reflected in a professional style that avoids sensationalism for its own sake and stresses the human, the personal, and sometimes even the lighter side of science and medical news.

The Spotlight is on Health

The American public probably is more interested these days in the state of its general health than it has ever been in history. People of all ages jog along highways, country roads, and formal running paths. Local recreation programs are booming as more individuals seek physical activity. But more than exercise is involved. People are interested in their health and in the health of others. When people are interested, it's reasonable to assume that authors and journalists will provide them with ways to feed that interest.

The journalistic spotlight will focus on more news accounts of efforts to find cures for cancer and AIDS, on research into the causes of birth defects, on the cost of medical care, and on other economic health issues.

These topics have always been important. But medical writers have also rediscovered the how-to format, and they are providing more and more information of practical usefulness to those in the audience.

Human beings, however, don't always live according to the health advice they receive. But their interest is enough of a spark for journalists to continue to emphasize health.

That could save lives, and that's reward enough.

NOTES

1. Staci D. Kramer, "The Media and Aids," *Editor & Publisher,* March 12, 1988, pp. 10–11, 43.

2. Carol Ann Riordan, "Covering AIDS," *Presstime,* May 1988, p. 28.

3. Stylebook, *San Jose Mercury News,* as quoted in "Covering AIDS," *Presstime,* May 1988, p. 28.

4. Edward M. Brecher, "Straight Sex, AIDS, and the Mixed-Up Press," *Columbia Journalism Review,* March/April 1988, p. 46.

5. "Straight Sex, AIDS and the Mixed-Up Press," p. *50.*

6. Walt Bogdanich, remarks made during, "Health and Science: On the Record," annual conference of Investigative Reporters and Editors, Minneapolis, Minn., June 4, 1988.

7. Jim Sibbison, "Covering Medical 'Breakthroughs,' " *Columbia Journalism Review,* July/August 1988, pp. 36–39.

8. Gerald T. Delaney, "The Human Impact of Cancer News Stories," *Columbia Journalism Review,* March/April 1977, pp. 30–32.

9. Jon Beckwith, remarks made during "Covering Science: Problems and Perspectives," annual conference, Society of Professional Journalists, Cincinnati, Ohio, November 19, 1988.

10. James Detjen, "Health and Science: On the Record."

11. Margaret Engel, "Health and Science: On the Record."

12. James Detjen, remarks made during Ohio Journalism and Energy Conference, Columbus, Ohio, October 21, 1988.

13. Bogdanich, "Health and Science: On the Record."

14. "Straight Sex, AIDS, and the Mixed-Up Press."

15. Tom Lee, "Cancer's Front-Page Treatment," *The Nation,* September 18, 1976, pp. 237–238.

16. William Boot, "NASA and the Spellbound Press," *Columbia Journalism Review,* July/August 1986, p. 24.

17. Bogdanich, "Health and Science: On the Record."

18. Engel, "Health and Science: On the Record."

19. Detjen, Ohio Journalism and Energy Conference.

20. Andrew Morrison, remarks made during "Public Opinion and Public Acceptance of Energy Decisions," Ohio Journalism and Energy Conference, Kent State University, November 3, 1989.

21. Ann Bisconti, "Public Opinion and Public Acceptance of Energy Decisions."

22. Detjen, "Health and Science: On the Record."

23. David Lore, remarks made during panel discussion, "Energy Needs in the '90s," during Ohio Journalism and Energy Conference, Columbus, Ohio, October 21, 1988.

In Search of Cultural Diversity

16

Cultural diversity (inclusiveness) in the newsroom remains a goal of the 1990s as American journalism continues its response to the need for attention to the total community. The term means several things. First, it describes the need for increased hiring of nonwhite journalists so that news organizations themselves are representative of the public they serve. If this is accomplished, it is more likely the content of the pages and airwaves will better reflect the cultural diversity of the communities in which they function.

Likewise, since social and ethnic groups are a part of the total community, a goal of news organizations must be an understanding by all their employees that coverage is of issues. Social and ethnic groups should not be isolated and used as examples of problems that involve everyone.

In spite of efforts by many news organizations, achieving these goals remains illusive. Charges of lack of progress are equally valid today as when they were made originally by the National Advisory Commission on Civil Disorders. That group, popularly known as the Kerner Commission, was appointed by President Lyndon B. Johnson to study the violence that occurred in the summer of 1967 on the streets of twenty-three of the nation's cities.

Blacks—the majority of the residents of metropolitan ghettoes—sought to overcome their frustrations and vent their rage by striking back at the system they felt had betrayed them. This predominantly white society was not ready for such rage. Then a year later came another shock: The blame was placed on white society.

"White racism," the commission said, "is essentially responsible for the explosive mixture which has been accumulating in our cities since the end of World War II."[1]

About halfway through its report, the commission provided another surprise, this time for those involved with the nation's news organizations. The news media, it said, shared the responsibility for creating the circumstances that ultimately led to the eruption.

"The news media have failed to analyze and report adequately on racial problems in the United States," the commission said, "and, as a related matter, to meet the Negro's legitimate expectations in journalism. By and large, news organizations have failed to communicate to both their black and white audiences a sense of the problems America faces and the sources of potential solutions.

"The media report and write from the standpoint of a white man's world. The ills of the ghetto, the difficulties of life there, the Negro's burning sense of grievance, are seldom conveyed. Slights and indignities are part of the Negro's daily life, and many of them come from what he now calls 'the white press'—a press that repeatedly, if unconsciously, reflects the biases, the paternalism, the indifference of white America. This may be understandable, but it is not excusable in an institution that has the mission to inform and educate the whole of our society."[2]

It's been a quarter of a century since the Kerner Commission issued its indictments. But few since have stated the need more precisely or with greater authority. Few have been so extensively quoted. The specific recommendations of the commission have provided the benchmarks for evaluating the news media coverage of race and race relations. Among those recommendations were:

- Recruit more blacks into journalism and broadcasting and promote those who are qualified to positions of significant responsibility.

- Expand coverage of the black community and of race problems through permanent assignment of reporters familiar with urban and racial affairs and through establishment of more and better links with the black community.

- Integrate blacks and black activities into all aspects of coverage and content, including newspaper articles and television programming. The news media must publish newspapers and produce programs that recognize the existence and activities of blacks as a group within the community and as a part of the larger community.

- Accelerate efforts to ensure accurate and responsible reporting of racial news through adoption by all news-gathering organizations of stringent internal staff guidelines.[3]

DIVERSITY IN THE NEWSROOMS

It is unlikely that the final three of these goals will be achieved until news organizations take care of their own need to attain cultural diversity within their own staffs. Loren F. Ghiglione, editor of The News in Southbridge, Massachusetts, and 1989 president of the American Society of Newspaper Editors, expresses considerable concern over lack of progress in this regard. The need, he said, is clear:

Loren F. Ghiglione
of The News, Southbridge, MA (The
News photo)

"To serve a diverse readership and marketplace, the newspaper industry has to become more than a 92.5-percent white symbol of the status quo." Ghiglione's comments came in the aftermath of a 1978 ASNE resolution to hire minorities by the year 2000 in percentages equal to their representation in the society. In spite of that, he noted what appears to be a diminishing of that dedication.

"ASNE's Minorities Committee, once this Society's largest, now has about half the editors it had only a few years ago," he said. "Employment freezes, layoffs, and last-hired, first-fired policies threaten to undermine years of minority recruiting. Talk of racial diversity has given way to talk of marketing, competition, and circulation. Editors who have established intern programs for minority students ask whether, given the tone of recent U.S. Supreme Court decisions, they face reverse discrimination suits."[4]

The statistics are not encouraging. As of 1989, Ghiglione notes that 54 percent of the country's daily newspapers were without minority staffers, and an ASNE census reported that only 7.54 percent of newspaper newsroom employees were black, Hispanic, Asian-American, or Native American. Compounding the situation, a survey by the American Newspaper Publishers Association showed that 7 percent of the industry's executives are minorities. In broadcast newsrooms the percentages of minorities has been declining from 15 percent in 1978 to 14 percent in 1984 to 13 percent in 1986.[5]

What makes the need for larger numbers even more compelling, however, is the fact that minority populations are growing rapidly. Demographers suggest that sometime during the twenty-first century, they will become the new American majority. David Lawrence, publisher and president of the Miami Herald and chair of the Task Force on Minorities in the Newspaper Business, noted the significance of this fact in the preface of a task force report on the future of minorities in the business.

"You and I both know that over the years, much of the energy behind minority hiring and advancement in our business has been the moral obligation to do what is right and fair," he said. "Rightly so. But the results—or the lack of results—tell us that this approach has not been enough. So we are here to make the case that what is right and fair is also smart business."[6]

Lawrence's emphasis on the good business angle should not be construed, however, as diminishing the value of the earlier goal—the journalistic need for minority staffers because it is the "right and fair" thing to do. It is, in fact, good journalism if one accepts the fact that news organizations exist to provide information about and to the community at large. Cultural diversity means more than just minority staffers. It means a broader perspective about what news is; it means sensitivity to the needs, contributions, role, and wishes of all elements of society; it means understanding the important backgrounds of all elements of society; and it means reflection on community issues as they relate to citizens in general.

IT'S MORE THAN BLACK AND WHITE

It is significant that the Kerner Commission of the 1960s and the Task Force on Minorities in the Newspaper Business of the 1980s demonstrated differences in what they accepted as the focus of their discussions. The Kerner Commission described frustrations of one social group—African Americans. The Task Force, however, recognized that the commission's themes applied more broadly. Thus, as the twenty-first century approaches, the emphasis is on blacks, Hispanics, Asian Americans, and Native Americans.

History has demonstrated the need for this expansion of perspective. The civil rights struggle emerged first among blacks and then spread to other groups, who also complained about social injustice and about media coverage. Other ethnic groups—particularly Hispanics and American Indians—echoed the outrage. Women, too, charged that journalism either ignored them or took a paternalistic approach.

But the awakening went beyond that. Persons with disabilities began to demand full physical and social access to the means of livelihood. They pointed to a lack of general awareness of the problems they face in coping with a society structured for those without disabilities. They blamed the media, in part, for this lack of awareness and strongly suggested that their needs deserved attention.

"You should realize that handicapped people are involved in a civil rights movement," Siggy Shapiro, then of WWDB-FM in Philadelphia, told a convention of the Society of Professional Journalists. "And I think that it's important that you realize that there's a great need for information about the rights of people with disabilities. The media, as you know, can do an enormous amount to change attitudes."[7]

The elderly, likewise, expressed dissatisfaction over their insignificant status in society and in the media. Some organized, called themselves the Gray Panthers, and began a struggle to move from the confinement of rest homes. That struggle against discrimination today is being led by the American Association of Retired Persons. At the other end of the age spectrum, some persons began to speak of the rights of children to media attention other than in crisis circumstances.

The situations about which all these groups and individuals complain, while perhaps not identical, are similar, and their suggestions to the news media run parallel to those of the Kerner Commission.

They question traditional news judgment when much legitimate news about them, their activities, and their needs is ignored, treated in stereotypical fashion, relegated to insignificance through placement, or given once-over-lightly, often "cutesy," treatment. They question journalism's collective intent when the tone of news inevitably appears negative. They doubt journalism's role as protector of citizens when they seldom hear the investigative whistle blow on what they perceive as serious social injustices. And they see little evidence that news media are attempting seriously to solve these problems by making their staffs more representative of the total populations.

Perhaps the charges are exaggerated and overly emotional. A general social consciousness truly has swept through American newsrooms. There is more attention to a larger variety of social groups. Statistics and examples also would show that news media recruiters are actively seeking individuals who will help broaden journalism's overall perspective. But is it enough? The answer, even from most journalists, is a resounding "no."

RACISM, SEXISM, AGEISM

Especially during the early years of the civil rights movement, it was common to hear the charge of "racism" leveled at government leaders, law-enforcement officials, members of the clergy, or journalists. The automatic response to such charges—then and now—is defensiveness. The charges were made by individuals with good intentions and sometimes leveled at individuals with good intentions. Often they did not understand each other or place the same meanings to the term.

Prominent civil rights leader the late Rev. Ralph Abernathy was asked if he felt the media had improved their coverage of black life. Abernathy's response was direct:

"I certainly do not. I don't think there has been a marked improvement at all. I think that's simply because of racism on the part of those who make up the press. The roots of racism are so terribly deep that it is impossible to separate one from his background in the white community—whether he lives in Georgia or Alabama or New York or California or Michigan. That is, in any particular walk of life, if a person comes out of a racist background, he takes that racist feeling and attitude into that chosen field. And, unfortunately, those who control the news media in our country are from the white community."

Stated another way, it is extremely difficult for any person to overcome those factors that provide the basic perspectives of life. Decisions are made on the basis of what we believe. They are not necessarily intentionally detrimental, but a white journalist may exercise news judgment that is counter to what a person from a different background might do. And the attitudes are not always racial. They may concern gender, for those who control the news media also tend to be men. They tend to be less than elderly or to have gained their positions and wealth in their younger years. They seldom are physically handicapped. What they are will be reflected naturally in the decisions they make.

It is not that journalists, as individuals, make their decisions on the basis of race, sex, or age. Perhaps some do, but the majority fall into the trap on the far end of a continuum that is comprised of what scholars consider three types of attitudes.

Expressed in racial terms, the lowest rung of the ladder is individual racism (sexism or ageism). This represents action based on the belief that one's own race is superior. When individuals transfer that attitude to social institutions and consciously manipulate those institutions to achieve superiority, the label is institutional racism. To the degree that persons do make such conscious use of their news positions, they are a disgrace to journalism. But they are small in number and usually are taken care of by the system. The most far-reaching and evasive problem, however, is that which grows from cultural contributions of an entire group or race are overlooked, says author Andrea L. Rich.[8] That sounds very much like the statements of the Kerner Commission, women, the handicapped, and the elderly.

If it were simply a matter of attitudes that create coverage voids, the problem, though continuously difficult, would be easier to handle. Journalists could resolve to do better and then institute a program of pointed coverage. But the problem is more complex. Even when attention is paid to a group, there is the danger that it may be equally negative. The attention may take the form of *colonialism,* which is degrading because it implies authority and the need to help those who cannot help themselves. Yet another form, equally degrading, is *paternalism,* in which the subjects are looked down upon and overly patronized.

The historic journalistic result of such cultural racism, sexism, or ageism is that most news has been about, by, and for white males who are part of the central order. In most cases, this has not resulted from deliberate decision to degrade or ignore any section of the population. Journalists are aware of their responsibilities to the total community. But they must make judgments about what news is important and what is significant to society. And these judgments are based on the perspectives of the decision makers.

Much of the blame for the skewed coverage may have to go to unconscious neglect.

"First of all, there's the news selection and the perception of what's important," says Mary Gardner of Michigan State University, former national president of the Association for Education in Journalism and Mass Communication. "We have to be very honest that one of the reasons there's so much news about male activities is that males do control the budget and have attained higher positions and therefore are more newsworthy in general. But I get impatient, particularly in this day and age, because men who make journalistic decisions should be making more effort. They have been socialized, though, and it doesn't occur to them that anything a woman says could be important. They tend not to think about it."

But journalists must think about it, in two ways. First, as Abernathy says, "They have to overcome themselves, and they have to be aware of the fact that they have been molded by a certain type of society." But that would not be sufficient. Witness the number of reporters whose interest in providing solid coverage of the total community has been stifled by institutional traditions or unyielding editors. Journalism is moving into a new era, one in which the traditional patterns of news must be modified institutionally.

"Empathy is perhaps the key to overcoming the shackles of our own belief and value systems," Rich advises. "We must try in interracial settings to step outside ourselves in order to gain an understanding of the reality of others."[9]

GETTING TO THE ROOTS OF UNDERSTANDING

Peter MacDonald, then Navajo tribal chairman, concluded his portion of a panel discussion at an Associated Press Managing Editors convention with a plea:

"So there's a great deal of understanding that needs to occur between you and us (Native Americans). I feel that you, the people of the press, can do a great deal in this area. Ultimately our fate rests upon the conscience of the American people, and the media, more than any other institution, will determine whether their conscience is asleep or awake when the fate of our people is decided."

MacDonald had said earlier in the discussion: "In the Indian world we always say that before you judge a man you must walk several moons in his moccasins. Well, you need reporters who can understand the thinking about the concept of a dependent nation but also a sovereign nation. That's a very strange concept for America, but it does exist. And you need reporters who understand our attachment to our land base, our nonindustrial way of life, our values, and our needs."[10]

Gaining an understanding of the "reality of others" is one of the challenges for reporters who find themselves covering ethnic and other social groups. Journalists long ago accepted the fact that the successful science writer is one who understands science. That means knowing how science developed as well as knowing how in contemporary society it works. The greatest political reporting comes from individuals who know the political system and who have developed political instinct based on study and observation.

The same requirements must be applied to those who cover the lives and activities of this nation's cultural groupings. Without such knowledge and understanding, reporters are doomed to continue their superficial coverage.

Cultural values are learned best through personal contact. Reading textbooks, doing scholarly analyses, and talking with experts are activities the conscientious reporter must find time to accomplish. They provide the background and help establish the proper questions to ask. But another necessary requirement is to be on the streets, to visit the reservations, and to visit the black or Hispanic or Asian neighborhoods. Too much journalistic information comes from the power structure. It comes from government or law enforcement officials. This is information from an outsider's perspective. It is, at best, marginally helpful, and sometimes it is just plain wrong.

Without an understanding, for example, of the nonindustrial lifestyles of native Americans, it would be too easy for a reporter to be appalled at life on the reservation and to miss important stories. Associated Press veteran Howard Graves, who has covered Indians in the Southwest, believes strongly that reporters have to spend time on a reservation to fully appreciate their lifestyle preferences.

Howard Graves
of The Associated Press (Associated Press photo)

"They have been exploited by the white man for so many years that they don't care to be exploited again," says Graves, former national president of the Society of Professional Journalists. "They've had anthropologists and sociologists come on the reservation to get them into some kind of a program, and they're turned off by that. They don't like tourists driving through their holy grounds or their living areas and seeing all the debris that is around—old furniture, old car bodies, trash.

"That's the way they want to live, and they don't care how the white person feels about it. They don't want their lifestyle disturbed. If they wanted to live in the white man's world, they would move into the white man's town. A lot of them have never had any dealings with the media unless they are Indian government officials who have been off the reservation or have been involved with the police. The reporter has to know these things to deal with Indians effectively and to do the kind of job that needs to be done."

Separation of blacks and Hispanics from white society is not quite as total as that of Native Americans who live on reservations, but separation often does result from residential patterns. When this occurs, cultural backgrounds and residential socialization result in perspectives that differ from those who have not shared that experience. These differences, of course, should not be surprising. In many instances, such ethnic differences are encouraged and, in fact, make up the substance of much of this country's tourism business.

Therefore, it should be no surprise that what is important to members of a group is predicated, at least in part, on their cultural perceptions of what they are and how that fits into the majority culture. The understanding of such influences can help a reporter avoid errors.

Frank del Olmo of the *Los Angeles Times* urges reporters to be sensitive to the backgrounds, history, and demographics of social groups. He notes one instance in which a common perception—that all Mexican-Americans are farm workers—is patently incorrect. Knowing that 85 percent of the Spanish of this country, including Puerto Ricans and Mexican-Americans, are urban dwellers, he says, will make reporters a bit more sensitive and will help them to avoid incorrect preconceived notions about how a community will react to a given issue.

The women's movement provides similar examples. Even though women have battled since the nineteenth century against the idea that they should occupy a separate sphere, reporters who sought to cover the modern movement as it emerged in the 1960s found that their biggest problem was a general lack of understanding. Some editors did not recognize the potential of the story. Many chose to ignore it, to treat it lightly, or to heap scorn upon it. Even today, questions remain about whether those in journalism fully understand. Peggy A. Simpson of The Associated Press, for example, asks:

Can the movement continue to make its case with the news media, let alone the general public? Can it educate reporters and via the newspapers tell the nation about the inequities that still remain and, in some cases, are worsening? Are the enormous changes throughout society affecting men as strongly as women, or seen as significant enough for editors to assign reporters to monitor them? Are news writers developing the expertise to go beyond personality conflicts between the White House and activists to report on conditions facing women in factories and typing pools, about the resentments of men facing serious challenges for jobs from women, about the anger of millions of women isolated in low-paid, dead-end work ghettos? Are reporters aware of the new frontier facing many women in professional jobs, or concerned about the conflicts between careers and personal relationships?[11]

It's axiomatic in journalism that no reporter can effectively explain what he or she does not understand. It's also accepted that journalism exists to provide information about the community to the community. Yet, millions of people are seeing neither understanding nor adequate information about their lifestyles, their problems, and their role as American citizens.

"If we accept a cliche that I think has a lot of validity, that newspapers are in a sense writing a first rough draft of history," says Dorothy Gilliam of the *Washington Post,* "then the importance of getting the black (Hispanic, Indian, female) perspective is of significance not only to blacks (or other groups), but to the wider audience. And it seems to me that one of the perceptions that is most difficult for whites to understand is what a great stake they have in racial harmony in this country. So it is not enough to simply say that we have done this, or we have done that in terms of pacifying blacks. The real issue has to be that both interests are served, when this job is done and done well."[12]

SEEKING COMPREHENSIVE COVERAGE

Recruitment programs and seminars on cultural understanding, however important they may be, are no more than a means to an end. If those efforts are not reflected on the pages and in the airwaves, little has been gained. "The news media must publish newspapers and produce programs that recognize the existence and activities of blacks as a group within the community and as a part of the larger community," the Kerner Commission said in its 1968 report.[13] Has more than twenty years of effort produced the kind of journalism the commission was recommending? The answer from almost all quarters is resoundingly negative.

Nationally syndicated columnist William J. Raspberry of the Washington Post Writers Group sees little reason for pride in how journalism has responded to the challenge of covering its ethnic communities. Part of the reason, he says, is that the story these days is much more complicated.

"Journalists who only had to be there when the story was Jim Crow now have to find and develop the story of racial progress, or its absence," he said. "It takes more insight than most of us possess to uncover the impediments to black progress in the absence of such obvious villains as Bull Connor, Orval Faubus, and Lester Maddox.

"We're not even sure as journalists whether our role should be as active advocates for justice or merely mirrors of the obvious. Our forays, when we make them, into the depressed black communities are likely these days to be seen by the residents there not as attempts to correct injustice but a cold-hearted attempt to humiliate an already battered community."

And Raspberry lists one more important problem.

"Here's another reason," he says. "Journalism, to a dismaying degree, has lost interest in the story. We are far more interested in nailing individual miscreants, black or white—although we seem to feel there is too much focus on the black—than in pursuing the story of racial progress, or in being part of the story of racial progress."[14]

Yvonne Shinhoster Lamb, an assistant city editor at the Washington Post, discusses a report presented at a 1984 conference on blacks in the media at the Aspen Institute, which identified three dominant views among editors about coverage of the black community:

Yvonne Shinhoster Lamb
of the Washington Post (Washington
Post photo by Kim Arrington)

"Many, maybe even most, see no imperative whatever for the employment or coverage of minorities by their newspaper. Not surprisingly, these tend to be editors of newspapers that employ no minority journalists. Many serve communities with few, if any, minorities.

"A second group seems to view the minority question as important but important primarily as a matter of fairness or morality or good PR.

"The final group sees minority employment and coverage as necessary components of good newspapers and good journalism. They attach a very high priority to developing or maintaining integrated news staffs."[15]

Similar criticism is coming from college campuses, where research is showing little progress on coverage of minorities. One study of a midwestern daily, for example, found no change in the amount of coverage devoted to the minority community between 1965 and 1989.[16] Another national study of the attitudes of elected black officials demonstrated major dissatisfaction with treatment received from the predominantly white reporters. Most elected black officials in the study perceived discrimination, if not neglect, in press coverage of blacks across an array of areas, including public office, crime, business and industry, education, and the professions.[17]

If the major problem is news organizations' failure to develop the story, observers within and outside of journalism voice legitimate specific complaints about coverage of minorities in their communities. They say too much coverage is negative, especially in the sense that it focuses on minority examples of problems that are community-wide. They note too much emphasis on race, with selective use of pictures and provision of racial identification in stories that have nothing to do with race, especially crime stories. They charge that the result of this type of coverage is perpetuating stereotypes and failing to recognize that the lives of minority citizens reflect the same kinds of ups and downs as those of non-minorities.

Acel Moore, associate editor of the Philadelphia *Inquirer,* once conducted a six-month study of his paper's coverage of blacks. He found a pattern of coverage: Blacks were depicted in the paper primarily in the context of social problems, as politicians who could not be avoided, or in sports or entertainment stories.

Moore said his research uncovered several examples in which pictures of minorities were used to illustrate stories about specific social problems. One three-part series on young people and drugs, he said, was a case in point, and one that raised concerns among black staff members. The series portrayed black, Hispanic, and white youths. Photographs of the black and Hispanic youths were used on the front page, but the white youth's photo was not.[18]

Some news organizations—including the Seattle *Times* and Philadelphia *Inquirer*—have sponsored seminars on inclusive and balanced coverage in efforts to overcome these problems. The goal is to help reporters and editors to become more aware of how their coverage affects all readers. As Lamb says:

"Coverage of the black community, in particular, has long been a topic of discussion and probably will remain so until newspapers begin to deal squarely with the fact that we live in a pluralistic society. We must begin to treat ethnic groups as integral parts of that society, not as anomalies. Coverage of black or other ethnic communities will not change substantially until all reporters and editors are sensitized to the need to make coverage of the communities in which we live inclusive and balanced."[19]

Gaining such balance is a function of taking more seriously the journalistic charge to cover the total community—to reflect the current situation, to provide a forum for discussion of alternatives, and to help lead toward solutions. These goals are not matters of race, age, or sex. They are matters of thoughtful and serious thought about the human condition. Raspberry provides this advice for journalists who are searching for what to do about the plight of minorities today:

" . . . We should do what we do with any other complex story, whether it is the budgetary shell game of the White House and the Congress, the Alaska oil spill, or the controversy over fusion versus fission. First, try to understand it, in all its complexity. Then, undertake to explain it to our audience."[20]

Pulitzer Prize-winning syndicated columnist Clarence Page of *The Chicago Tribune,* likewise, advocates an inclusive approach to coverage of minorities. In fact, he says, a well-researched story should lead, almost automatically, to a look at the context in which minorities live.

"It's happened to me numerous times," he says. "I set out to write what I thought was a black story or an ethnic story, and it turned out to be an education or an economics story by the time I finished. It had little to do with race. This kind of class consciousness is something that we've gotten to be aware of nowadays. But economics, inflation, energy are the news. That's where the action is whether it's the black community or anywhere else. It's that poor people, once again, get hit the hardest. They always do."

Clarence Page
of The Chicago Tribune (Chicago
Tribune photo)

This message struck home with Page some years back when he was part of a *Tribune* team that studied the history of blacks in that city. The team found that three traditional issues had been dominant in the minds and lives of blacks: jobs, housing, and schools. It is Page's opinion that these are still the issues.

"I think more and more people are realizing that race is declining in its significance in America," Page says. "Civil rights leaders are shifting their thrust from race to economics. The thing is, there is a widening gap between blacks who are making it economically and the blacks who are not making it. This is the modern tragedy now."

Examples abound of similar economic focus among other groups as, in effect, they seek their civil rights through efforts to gain economic self-sufficiency. Much of the struggle of Native Americans, for example, concerns control of natural resources (e.g., water, coal, oil, and uranium) found on the reservations. A major thrust of women and the handicapped is for employment and for equal pay.

But it is not all economic. The insistence on programs to help battered women and to counter growing problems of rape and/or sexual harassment—pushed predominantly by feminist groups on behalf of women—are law enforcement stories that cut across male-female lines. One of the major stories of the early 1990s was this country's efforts to come to grips with serious disagreements about abortion. The abortion debate started as a women's issue. But the story expanded quickly and soon focused on a myriad of topics, including religion, family, politics, and law enforcement. It was not a woman's story; it was, and is, a social story.

Lois Wille
of The Chicago Tribune (Chicago
Tribune photo)

These facts prompted Lois Wille, *Chicago Tribune* editorial page editor, to suggest that journalists seeking to cover minorities in their communities should:

- Examine the amount of money spent per pupil in city public schools and compare that to the amount spent per pupil in adjacent suburban areas.

- Look at the conditions under which children whose families can only afford to live in public housing projects spend their days.

- Examine public transportation, and whether it serves the needs of poor city residents who may need to get to the suburbs to find jobs.

- Study fraud in minority set-aside programs, which too often become tools for majority-owned contractors to "take advantage of minority contractors, without getting jobs down to the people who need them."

- Report on successful projects and experiments that help eliminate inequality.[21]

Because of the need for such broader coverage, the attitude that news organizations can meet their needs by labeling a reporter as "minority writer" or some such title is placing too great a burden on that person. The ideal is that such coverage should be provided by the news organization's total staff as its members go about their business of covering issues of social concern.

Another part of that ideal would be eliminating the notion that one must be a member of a group to cover that group adequately. There may be certain short-term communication, attitudinal, and reporter interest advantages by having a black reporter covering blacks. But, in the long run, special consideration must be given to the fact that this attitude runs counter to journalistic norms.

For a number of reasons, news organizations ordinarily do not want a member of any group covering that group. One reason is the potential for actual conflict of interest or the appearance of a conflict. Another reason is the added burden on that reporter, who must deal with the expectations of his or her colleagues.

The ideal must be functional integration of a news organization's staff, with reporters assigned to coverage areas in which they have expertise and interest. Sensitivity would be facilitated by that expertise as it is demonstrated in understanding and knowledge of specific social groups. In addition, perspective would be broadened by greater individual representation in newsrooms of the social groups themselves.

NEWSWORTHINESS AND STREET THEATER

Of course, all stories do not develop in situations that provide reporters with ample time to conduct many interviews, review documents, or analyze statistical data. Frequently, the story occurs when a group stages an event.

Sometimes, these are carefully orchestrated theater in which all participants know the rules and the timing. At other times, however, they are spontaneous reactions and expressions of rage. The point in both instances, however, is attracting attention, making people notice, and making others want to listen. Social groups have, in fact, become very sophisticated in developing strategies that force others to pay attention. The specific actions take several forms:

- Pro-choice or pro-life forces gathering in Washington, D.C., in efforts to convince, by the force of their large numbers, the U.S. Supreme Court of their point of view.

- Farmers from across the country disrupting traffic in Washington, D.C., by driving their tractors slowly down the city's main streets.

- Blacks staging sit-ins at restaurants, movies, and other public establishments in efforts to desegregate them.

- Hispanic homemakers, workers, and retirees packing San Antonio, Texas, city council meetings to demand that something be done to improve public services in their neighborhoods.

LaDonna Harris, a Comanche and founder of Americans for Indian Opportunity, is one who has given considerable thought to the various strategies of attracting attention. She notes that when people see disruptive Indian actions at Alcatraz, Wounded Knee (South Dakota), and Washington, D.C., they consider such actions irrational.

"We came to the conclusion that Indian people were acting rationally in an irrational situation," she says. "When there is no one paying any attention to you, you have to go crazy. And so all that the Indian people were saying is 'We're here. We want you to pay attention to us. We're here. We have a right to exist, and we have a right to exist in the style that we believe in.' "[22]

The audience for such actions is fourfold. In the first place, groups may be seeking to persuade others to join the movement. Second, they have a message for those in power, whether the state or federal government, corporate executives, or local business operators. Third, they want the attention of citizens in the hopes of gaining sympathy or support for their cause.

The fourth audience is comprised of news organizations that have the means of spreading the message. Often, the activities depend upon what the news media, particularly television, are most likely to cover. Journalists are aware of their role in such events. They have mixed emotions about them. On the one hand, they dislike being manipulated, being forced to cover the complaints of a group through stagings they cannot ignore. "Media events," they call them. Sponsors say such events would not be necessary if reporters did a better job of discussing their complaints and their frustrations. Sometimes there is truth to that statement, but reporters respond that too often the issues have been discussed thoroughly and the sponsors cannot be satisfied in their desire for constant attention and repetition.

The debate is unnecessary, however, because when an act—especially one which is illegal or disruptive—is committed in a public place, often in the presence of thousands of people, it must be covered. Of course, reporters have the option of deciding that the event is only theater and of little substance and thus giving it minimal play. But they must be on the scene.

Given the public nature and obvious newsworthiness of most of those events, reporters such as William Greider of the *Washington Post* don't worry much about manipulation. They point out that there's little distinction between such activities and a presidential press conference. So the major decisions concern how, not whether, to provide coverage and how to cope with some special journalistic problems they offer.

"I think probably the major frustration of speakers at a major rally—this used to be particularly true in the antiwar period—is that they cannot get the rhetoric into the newspaper because of the theater," Greider says. "You go to a monster rally, and the stories concentrate on 'God, look at this crowd' and 'There will always be some, maybe a lot of, violence.' Clashes between police and demonstrators, lots of colorful people smoking pot. The newspapers would be filled up with that. There may be very little of what speakers are saying.

The activities, the disruption, the violence, the unusual nature of any rally or demonstration must be covered. The task may require a team of reporters. At the same time, however, "you have to give every group at least a clear shot at getting its rhetoric taken seriously," Greider says. Someone has to ignore the throngs and pay attention to the speakers, interview the sponsors, and attempt to get meaningful comments from the crowd.

In addition, every situation of this type has another side. Someone opposes. Someone disagrees. A government official may feel that the complaints are unfounded. What is being requested may be impossible in the eyes of those responsible for taking official action. Perhaps officials believe they have done as much as they can. Or they may agree with the complaints, promise action, or pass the buck. Perhaps reporters will be unable to do all of the follow-up concurrent with the rally or demonstration. It may be the next day or several days later. But the response is part of the story.

How circular the follow-up process gets depends upon the reporter's judgment. Sponsors of the rally may want to respond to the response. That may be valid. It may not. The decision is journalistic and is dependent upon individual circumstances. However, in some instances a need does exist for long-range follow-up. Issues, promises, plans of action all should be evaluated later. It's unfair and unwise to report the big splash and ignore how the water settles.

WOMEN: THE MAJORITY MINORITY

Among the most noticeable trends in American journalism is the rapid growth in the number of women now involved in what once was an exclusive male domain. American Society of Newspaper Editors' statistics indicate that women now make up 35 percent of the newsroom work force and 46 percent of the youngest newsroom group.[23] Increasingly, women are moving into positions of prominence, and a growing number of women already have or will be moved into managerial positions.

Among the evidence that these are long-term trends is the fact that an increasing number of the nation's college journalism programs are populated by a majority of female students—up to 70 percent in some cases. Even though the ASNE survey indicated that newspapers continue to hire slightly more men than women, it is clear that the nation's news organizations in time will see their male-female staff ratios much closer to community ratios.

This fact is bound to have an influence on community coverage for precisely the same reasons journalism is seeking cultural diversity: a sense of representation, a greater sensitivity to the female perspective on social issues, and a conscience that will help news organizations avoid serious mistakes based on misunderstanding.

This does not mean that female journalists have a different approach to journalism from their male counterparts. Indeed, the ASNE survey found that "women rarely differed significantly from other groups in the survey in terms of their attitudes toward work, ethics, and news judgment."[24]

Women, therefore, represent what ultimately will be a major success story for American journalism. They have come a long way. The Census Bureau tells us that women outnumber men, and demographers say they control much of the nation's wealth, but their struggle has been essentially the same as any minority group.

"Just a few years ago," says Sara Fritz of *U. S. News and World Report,* "any American newspaper might have carried a story saying: 'Margaret Thatcher doesn't look the part, but this glamorous mother of twins has shed her apron for a fling in British politics.' Stories belittling the ambitions of women have since disappeared from the pages of most newspapers—the result of a hard-fought feminist campaign begun in the early 1970s. . . . Yet some major issues involving the portrayal of women in newspapers remain unresolved."[25]

Part of that success came in 1977 when United Press International and The Associated Press issued new stylebooks in which they accepted some relatively new thinking about the coverage of women. The importance of the major news agencies cannot be underestimated, since most of the nation's newspapers and broadcast outlets tend to accept UPI or AP style as their own with only few modifications.

Perhaps the most significant contribution of the stylebooks was not in the recommendations about how to handle specific situations. Indeed, debates continue over some of the specific rules. But the news agencies did specify, "Women should receive the same treatment as men in all areas of coverage. Physical descriptions, sexist references, demeaning stereotypes, and condescending phrases should not be used."

Among specific examples, the stylebooks say that copy should not assume maleness when both sexes are involved (e.g., use of the term "newsman" instead of "reporter"), that copy should not express surprise that an attractive woman can be professionally accomplished, that copy should not gratuitously mention family relationships when there is no relevance to the subject, and that the same standards should be used for men and women in decisions of whether to include specific mention of personal appearance or marital and family situation.[26]

Whether news organizations are living up to these rules remains a subject of debate. One inconsistency often pointed out is the fact that many of the news media—including UPI and AP—continue to use courtesy titles for women and not for men. Such usage represents automatic reference to family relationships, they say, and is a waste of reporter time as well as offensive to some women. Few news organizations—with the *New York Times* representing a major exception—use courtesy titles for both men and women.

It appears inevitable that consistency of treatment will rule, and American journalism will eliminate use of "Miss" and "Mrs." Some major news organizations already have, including both *Time* and *Newsweek,* the *Los Angeles Times* (with some exceptions), and three major news groups—Gannett, Knight-Ridder, and the Copley news services. AP and UPI, curiously, do not use courtesy titles on their sports wires.

Another source of contention lies in the structure of the English language, which is represented by male-oriented terminology such as "chairman," "congressman," "mankind," "manmade," "fireman," and "man" as a collective ("the rights of man"). Here's where resistance has been greatest on the grounds that elimination of such references represents a major overhaul of the language. It may be relatively easy to use such substitute terms as "humanity" and "fire fighter" in some instances, and this is happening. But some believe "chairperson" or "chair," as nonsexist equivalents of "chairman," are defined as awkward. The news agencies have adopted a middle-ground policy and use "chairman" or "chairwoman."

It may be that the importance of the debate over coverage of women and what is defined as sexist language is the debate itself. Whatever the specific conclusions, the news media are thinking about the implications of what they do. Whether this would have happened without pressure from women's groups makes little difference. It is an era of concern, and a growing number of individual reporters and news executives have gained a new awareness.

MATTERS OF LANGUAGE AND STYLE

The importance of language to journalists of all types—print or broadcast—cannot be underestimated. How they speak, how they write, and how they communicate with their sources send messages beyond the dictionary meanings. The messages sent by reporters and editors may contribute to understanding, and they may open doors to information otherwise not available.

It is not an accident, for example, that American society has witnessed a transition from "colored" to "Negro" to "black" and, most recently, to "African American." The concern about a language that emphasized "firemen," "chairmen," and "businessmen" has resulted in restructuring.

William Raspberry, syndicated columnist with The Washington Post Writers Group, stressed the importance of language as he sought reasons for the current move from "black" to "African American."

"The best answer," he said, "may have been supplied . . . by Evan Kemp of the Washington-based Disability Rights Center. I had asked Kemp to explain the shift from "crippled" to "handicapped" to "disabled . . ." which seems to call attention to what they cannot do. His answer:

"As long as a group is ostracized or otherwise demeaned, whatever name is used to designate that group will eventually take on a demeaning flavor and have to be replaced. The designation will keep changing every generation or so until the group is integrated into society. Whatever name is in vogue at the point of social acceptance will be the lasting one."

"If Kemp is right, and I don't doubt it, the campaign to install 'African American' as the preferred term for descendants of slaves—no matter how compelling the argument for it—may be a reflection less of logic than of despair."[27]

Thus, language represents a three-pronged obligation for reporters. First, it is the means whereby they get the information presented on the printed page or over the air. Second, it is the tool used to present that information, and the success of communication efforts to a diversified audience depends upon its proper usage. Third, how it is used can suggest meaning that goes beyond the precise message of the moment.

These obligations become particularly crucial when the reporter is dealing with and about individuals who feel they have been objects of discrimination. They have a sensitivity to the language, which they know often goes beyond the dictionary. Sometimes it is language that provides part of the basis for social separation. Often the loudest complaints are about the specific words used. This means that news organizations must share that sensitivity. It does not mean, however, that reporters must always accept suggestions in the language. They should be willing to consider them and to make modifications when valid points have been made.

Speaking the Language

As a young reporter, Frank del Olmo of the *Los Angeles Times* was realistic about the reasons that he received some outstanding assignments. He was a member of that paper's Watergate team after only two years of professional experience. He received foreign assignments and occasionally traveled across the country in pursuit of specific stories.

"I've gotten many other kinds of fairly big assignments that normally might not have gone to a reporter of my youth and inexperience," he says. "But they needed somebody who spoke Spanish. I'm the guy who knows the language and can go there immediately and do the job. If anything, I would define my job as not so much a Chicano specialist but as a Spanish-speaking specialist because, incredibly, the paper doesn't have that many reporters who speak Spanish."

Perhaps that's part of the reason why journalism is criticized for not understanding significant portions of the U.S. population. Of course, not every newspaper or broadcast station could afford or would even want to have a full complement of reporters who could speak the many languages that contribute to U.S. cultural diversity. But when geography dictates that frequent contact will be made with Spanish- or German-speaking people, it makes sense that news organizations would have reporters on hand who could speak the language and do the story.

Sticks, Stones and Words

The old adage about sticks and stones doing damage but words never hurting is nonsense. Words do hurt. They can hurt deeply. They can demoralize. This is especially true when they are used over and over again for long periods of time. That's why many of the complaints that social and ethnic groups have about news media coverage find their most emotional expression in debates over specific word choice.

It matters only in degree whether the complaint concerns a truly derogatory word, represents oversensitivity, or is an expression of preference. Psychologically, if a group considers a word to be offensive, it is offensive. Being outside the dominant culture makes one more likely to grasp shades of meaning and intent and to want to break away from what is perceived as symbols of negative attitudes.

The problem is that certain terms, however legitimate their dictionary meaning, have become stereotypes and may be used to classify groups in a way that denies each member their individuality. The situation is worse when the stereotype is derogatory or has been given negative connotations. That, as Raspberry says, is what happened to "colored," "Negro" and "black."

Some people criticize the use of the term "illegal alien," saying it reinforces the image of what they call the "undocumented worker" as a law enforcement or public problem.[28] Likewise, some object to "senior citizen" because they feel it stereotypes older Americans as infirm, doddering, senile, and nonproductive. Indians don't have discussions; they have "pow-wows." Indians do not take issue with authorities; they "go on the warpath." "Lepers," without question, is derogatory. Siggy Shapiro, formerly of WWDB-FM in Philadelphia, provides yet another example.

" 'Cripple,' folks, is a no-no. By most standards among the handicapped community, 'cripple' is a totally negative term. It is ugly. It is nasty. And most handicapped people cannot abide by it. Also, 'wheelchair-bound' or 'confined to a wheelchair.' There are no chains around my chair. There are no ropes. I don't sleep in it. I don't make love in it, though some have tried. I don't spend my entire life in a wheelchair, and it is not a trap or a cage."[29]

How news organizations react to such attitudes depends, of course, upon their evaluation of the legitimacy of the complaint. It may depend upon the complexity of making the change. It may depend upon whether acceptable alternatives are available.

The fact that groups or individuals are honestly sensitive about a certain label should be given consideration. But that does not mean automatic acceptance. Reporters cannot please everyone. The language cannot be restructured every time someone gets a new idea. But neither is there a reason for stubbornness just because that's the way it's always been done.

Descriptive Identification

Journalists are trained to identify people in the news. Name, age, address, and title. But is it really necessary to describe a person in terms of race, sex, or physical status? Obviously, in many instances, this is an almost rhetorical question. Chances are good that Sarah Jones is a woman, that the executive secretary of the NAACP is black, and that the leader of Disabled in Action of Pennsylvania is a person with a disability.

But reporters often have options, and most say they would provide racial identification only when it is pertinent to the story. But when is it pertinent? Some say that in the past news organizations have been too quick to attach a racial label, for example, to crime stories, and that then becomes part of a broader complaint.

"Blacks and Hispanics commit crimes; their role as victims is slight. The victims are white. And the closer they are to the middle-class status of the paper's white editors, the bigger the story," says Clinton Cox of the *New York Daily News.* With only the rarest exceptions, that is the picture of the New York City homicide world that emerges from the New York media, he adds.[30]

While some research disputes this contention, it does agree with the intuition of many.[31] Without doubt, at some time it is an accusation that has been made against most news organizations.

LaTanya Hall, who was chosen Miss Colorado in 1987 and named third runner-up in the Miss America pageant, complained about the coverage she received in the Denver *Post* when she first won the Miss Boulder

County contest. The story read: "Hall, who is black, sang the song 'I am Changing' from the black musical Dream Girls about an up-and-coming black singing trio in the 1960s."

Hall asked: "How necessary was it to mention 'black' three times? Is it germane to the story?"[32]

UPI and AP try to be very specific in their instructions, listing four instances in which identification by race is acceptable: in biographical and announcement stories; when it provides the reader, viewer, or listener with a substantial insight into conflicting emotions known or like to be involved in a demonstration or similar event; when it describes a person sought in a search; and when it involves conflict that cuts across racial lines.[33]

The broader goal, however, must be to avoid such identification. Calling specific attention should be the exception. Most news stories involve human beings caught in the act of being citizens. Sometimes those stories are negative; sometimes they are positive. But usually their category has little to do with anything more specific than human nature.

Again, advice from Siggy Shapiro:

"If I could urge you to do one thing, it would be to follow what I call the 'crip-in-a-crowd' approach. I would really like to see news coverage with background shots of a person in a wheelchair in a crowd. I'd like to see crips-in-a-crowd stories in the written and electronic media.

"One of my favorite photos was of a female psychiatrist in a recent five-part series in the *Philadelphia Inquirer* on how dismally mental patients are being treated in the communities since they've been released from hospitals. The woman was depicted in a picture counseling one of her clients. She was in a wheelchair in the picture, and not one mention was made of that fact. She was just there as a human being doing her job. That's what I'd like to see more of."[34]

Write With Dignity

Reporting on People with Disabilities

The following is a booklet written by Bill Rush, who received a bachelor's degree in journalism from the University of Nebraska in 1983. Rush experiences quadriplegia.

This booklet was originally printed by the Gilbert M. and Martha H. Hitchcock Center for Graduate Study and Professional Development at the University of Nebraska-Lincoln School of Journalism. It is reprinted here with permission.

PART I

MAIN STYLEBOOK

(in alphabetical order)

Attitudinal barriers   See **Handicap** meaning No. 1.

Afflicted/Affliction   Connotes pain and suffering. Most individuals
with disabilities are not in pain, nor do they suffer because of their
disability.

Architectural barriers   See **Handicap** meaning No. 1.

Confined   People with disabilities are no more "confined to a
wheelchair" than people with poor vision are "confined to their
eyeglasses." Try "uses a wheelchair for mobility," or "has a
wheelchair," or "gets around by wheelchair."

Crippled   Avoid this word unless talking about an object.

Deaf and dumb or Deaf mute   People who are deaf have healthy
vocal cords. If they do not speak, that is because they do not hear the
correct way to pronounce words. (See **Deafness** in **Part III**). Try
"person who is deaf" or "person with a hearing impairment."

Disabled   Adjective. Do not use as a noun. Bad usage: "The disabled
are increasing." Better usage: "The disabled population is
increasing." Best: "The number of people who have disabilities is
increasing."

Disabled person   Try "person with a disability," thus putting the
person before the disability.

Disability   A medically defined condition resulting from a brain
injury, accident, virus, a combination of genetic factors, or trauma.
(Examples of disabilities are cerebral palsy, blindness, epilepsy,
multiple sclerosis, and muscular dystrophy.) Say "people with
disabilities" or "persons with a disability," not "disabled people."

Disease   Most people with disabilities are as healthy as anyone. Use
"condition."

Drain and burden   Try "added responsibility."

Gimp   Slang used by people with disabilities to mock society's attitudes towards them. However, can have negative connotations if used by a person who is able-bodied.

Handicap   Do not use to describe a person's physical condition. Persons with disabilities are not necessarily handicapped. The term *handicap* refers to environmental barriers preventing or making it difficult for full participation or integration.

1.   Attitudes and objects in the environment that hinder one's functioning. (Examples are steps, steep ramps, narrow doorways, curbs, and unaccepting or condescending people.)

2.   An athletic event in which difficulties are imposed on the superior, or advantages are given to the inferior, to make their chances of winning equal. Some individuals with disabilities may call themselves "handicappers" to show that they are capable of setting their own odds and that they are in control of their own lives, as the race track handicappers have control over betting odds. However, this term is not widely accepted.

Handicapped person   A better description is a "person with a disability."

Inconvenience   Preferred term. This word does not have any bad connotations. It also puts the disability in perspective.

Invalid   This word means literally "not valid." Everybody is valid.

Patient   Use this term *ONLY* when referring to someone who is in a hospital or under a doctor's immediate care.

Poor   Avoid this word unless you are talking about a person of low financial status. A person's financial status need not be related to his/her disability.

Unfortunate   Adjective that describes someone with bad luck, not a person with a disability.

Victim   A person with a disability was not sabotaged, nor was the individual necessarily in a car, plane, or train accident. Having a disability need not make a person a victim.

PART II

Suggestions for Interviewing People With Disabilities

1. Remember that a person with a disability is a person like anyone else. Never mind if the person can't extend a hand for a handshake. Personal contact is still important. It forms a bond.

2. Relax. If you don't know what to say or do, let the person who has the disability help put you at ease.

3. Explore the story in a natural manner. The person likely has many other aspects besides the disability.

4. Decide how important the disability is to the whole story. If it is not important, do not accent the disability.

5. Appreciate and emphasize what the person can do.

6. Be considerate of the extra time it may take a person with a disability to say or do things. Let the person set the pace for talking or walking.

7. Speak directly to a person with a disability. Don't assume a companion or assistant to be a conversational go-between.

8. If you are talking to a person who is deaf through a sign language interpreter, speak directly to the person you're interviewing, not the interpreter. Do not say: "Ask him/her what his/her name is." Say: "What is your name?"

9. If you are interviewing someone who is blind, don't grab the person—but let the person know where your arm is so he/she can hold it if he/she wishes. If you are walking with him/her, ask him/her if he/she would like to know where a curb is. (Some people are so adept with a cane or dog that this isn't necessary.) If you have the interview at a restaurant, read the menu aloud, let the person know where the water glass is, the bread plate and so forth.

10. If you are interviewing a person who is in a wheelchair and you go somewhere, see if it is accessible to people in wheelchairs before you go. This will save a lot of time and energy. NOTE: Only if the story has to do with disability.

11. Go some place with the interviewee, regardless of the disability, to see what type of barriers he/she must confront on a daily basis. NOTE: Only if the story has to do with disability.

12. Divide the interview into two parts and ask questions about (I) the disability, and (II) other subjects. Before the interview, decide what part is more important. For example, if interviewing a political leader with a disability about his/her views on foreign affairs, his/her disability is irrelevant. But, if you're interviewing the same politician about his/her views on national health insurance, the disability may be important.

PART III

List of Disabilities

(in alphabetical order)

Amyotrophic Lateral Sclerosis A rapidly progressive neuromuscular disorder of adults resulting from degeneration of the motor nerves in the spinal cord and brain stem leading to atrophy of the muscles controlled by these nerves in the hands, arms, feet, legs, tongue. Formerly known as "Lou Gehrig's Disease."

Arthritis Inflammation of one or more joints. Of the two forms of arthritis, osteoarthritis and rheumatoid arthritis, the latter is more likely to be disabling. Rheumatoid arthritis is a chronic, progressive, systemic disorder. Joint destruction, pain, and lack of mobility lead to severe disability. Rheumatoid arthritis tends to be characterized by periods of remission followed by periods of extreme exacerbation known as flare-ups. The disorder is often accompanied by anemia and is also characterized by symmetrical involvement of many joints.

Cerebral Palsy (C.P.) Refers to a group of disabilities resulting from damage to the developing brain which occurs before, during, or after birth up to the age of six. Symptoms range from mild to severe and may include awkward or involuntary movements (with or without) lack of balance, irregular gait, gutteral speech, facial grimacing, and/or drooling. All manifestations of CP stem from lack of muscle control. Muscles are dysfunctional not because they are defective but because they are not getting proper signals from the brain. Intelligence may or may not be affected, depending on the part of the brain injured. Difficulties in communication and inability to control voluntary muscles do not indicate lack of comprehension or impaired mental ability.

Cerebral Vascular Accident (Stroke) Cerebral Vascular Accident (CVA) occurs when normal circulation of blood through the brain is interrupted by an obstruction of a blood vessel by a clot or abnormal mass, or by hemorrhage. Deprived of oxygen-filled blood, brain cells are destroyed and cease to control body activities normally under their direction. CVA may result in hemiplegia (numbness and paralysis on one side), urinary incontinence, emotional instability, speech and language problems, and visual disturbances.

Deafness (preferred terminology—hearing impaired) Total or partial loss of hearing. The terms *deaf-mute* and *deaf and dumb* are inaccurate descriptions. Most people who are hearing impaired have nothing wrong with their vocal cords. They cannot speak or cannot speak clearly because their hearing is impaired.

Dwarfism (preferred terminology: "people of short stature.") There are more than eighty distinct types of short stature. Most types are hereditary. Each type, in addition to the inconvenience of short stature, has its own set of physical complications which may include arms and legs disproportionately short in relation to the torso, arthritis, fingers and toes without joints, and more.

Multiple Sclerosis (MS)   A progressive, unstable condition of the brain and spinal cord which has its onset in young adulthood. MS is caused by an unknown agent which attacks the myelin (covering sheath) of nerve fiber. The hard, sclerotic (scar tissue) patches which develop interrupt the nerve pathways of vision, sensation, and voluntary movement. MS can be characterized by periods of remission and persistently recurring exacerbations. Common manifestations can include failure of muscular coordination, oscillating movements of the eyes, slow enunciation of words and syllables, muscular weakness, intention tremor (shaky irregular motions which occur when purposeful movement is attempted), numbness and paralysis of one or more extremities, and urinary incontinence.

Muscular Dystrophy (MD)   A group of chronic, usually hereditary conditions with the common characteristics of progressive weakening and degeneration of the muscles. Sensation is unimpaired. Various types of muscular dystrophy differ in severity and in time of onset.

Paraplegia   Total or partial paralysis of both lower limbs. Paraplegia is caused by spinal cord injury or disease. Below the level of the lesion or damage, there is locomotor paralysis and sensory loss. About half of the people whose paraplegia is the result of an accident have a complete lesion, meaning that paralysis is symmetrical and complete below the level of the injury. The other half have an incomplete lesion and paralysis is uneven so that, for example, one leg may be more severely affected than the other.

Poliomyelitis (Polio)   An acute infectious viral disease resulting in flaccid (without tone or reflexes) paralysis because of damage to the motor nerve cells of the spinal cord. Sensations of pain, touch, temperature, and position are normal. The extent of paralysis may range from mild to severe affecting the arms, legs, trunk, respiratory muscles, or some combination of these. Paralysis caused by polio is stable and not progressive once the viral infection has run its course.

Quadriplegia   Paralysis of all four limbs caused by traumatic injury to or disease of the spinal cord in the neck. Extent of the paralysis often depends on the location of the injury on the spinal cord. Some limited use of upper limbs may be maintained.

Spina Bifida   A congenital condition in which the vertebrae of an unborn child fails to close completely. A sac containing part of the contents of the spinal cord protrudes through the opening, commonly at the lower end of the spinal cord. Muscles and nerves in the legs and lower trunk are often affected. Symptoms are most often present at birth although they may develop during the rapid growth period of adolescence. These symptoms include muscle weakness or paralysis, partial or total loss of bladder and bowel control, and, in some cases, deformities resulting from weak muscles.

NOTES

1. *Report of the National Advisory Commission on Civil Disorders,* New York Times Edition (New York: E. P. Dutton and Co., 1968), p. 10.

2. *National Advisory Commission on Civil Disorders,* p. 366.

3. *National Advisory Commission on Civil Disorders,* p. 21.

4. Loren F. Ghiglione, "Newspaper recruiting efforts are flagging as the minority share of the population grows," *The Bulletin of the American Society of Newspaper Editors,* July / August 1989, p. 2.

5. Diane Hall, Barbara Hines and Robert M. Ruggles, "Recruiting and Retaining Black Students For Journalism and Mass Communication Education," *ASJMC Insights,* July, 1989, p. 3.

6. David Lawrence Jr., "Preface," *Cornerstone for Growth: How Minorities Are Vital to the Future of Newspapers,* Task Force on Minorities in the Newspaper Business, 1989, p. 4.

7. Comments made during a panel discussion, national convention of the Society of Professional Journalists, Birmingham, Ala., November 16, 1978.

8. Andrea L. Rich, *Interracial Communication* (New York: Harper and Row, 1974), p. 117.

9. *Interracial Communication,* p. 120.

10. Panel discussion, "The American Indian," Associated Press Managing Editors convention, Portland, Ore., September 28, 1978.

11. Peggy A. Simpson, "Covering the Women's Movement," *Nieman Reports,* Summer 1979, p. 22.

12. Marion Marzolf and Melba Tolliver, *Kerner plus 10* (Howard R. Marsh Center for the Study of Journalistic Performance, University of Michigan, 1977), p. 19.

13. *National Advisory Commission on Civil Disorders,* p. 21.

14. William J. Raspberry, "Today's press ignores the real problems today's minorities face," *ASNE Bulletin,* July / August 1989, p. 18.

15. Yvonne Shinhoster Lamb, "Critics say newspapers foster 'stereotypes and ill feelings' about minorities," *ASNE Bulletin,* July / August 1989, p. 17.

16. Ted Pease, "One daily shows virtually no change in coverage of minorities since 1965," *ASNE Bulletin,* July / August 1989, p. 14.

17. Daniel Riffe, Don Sneed and Roger L. Van Ommeren, *The Press and Black Elected Officials at Three Levels of Public Office,* paper presented to the convention of the Association for Education in Journalism and Mass Communication, Washington, D.C., August 9–13, 1989, pp. 6–7.

18. "Critics say newspapers foster 'stereotypes and ill feelings' about minorities," pp. 15–16.

19. "Critics say newspapers foster 'stereotypes and ill feelings' about minorities," pp. 12, 14.

20. "Today's press ignores the real problems today's minorities face," p. 19.

21. "Five critics offer advice on covering minority issues," *ASNE Bulletin,* July/August 1989, p. 20.

22. "The American Indian" panel discussion.

23. Sandra D. Petykiewicz, "Profile: Women in our newsrooms," *ASNE Bulletin,* July/August 1989, p. 8.

24. "Profile: Women in our newsrooms," p. 8.

25. Sara Fritz, "A Change in Style," *Nieman Reports,* summer 1979, p. 24.

26. Howard Angione, Editor, *The Associated Press Stylebook and Libel Manual* (New York: The Associated Press, 1977), p. 240.

27. William Raspberry, "When 'Black' becomes 'African American'," *Minorities in the Newspaper Business,* American Newspaper Publishers Association Foundation, Spring 1989, pp. 1,6.

28. Felix Gutierrez, "Through Anglo Eyes: Chicanos as Portrayed in the News Media," paper presented to the History Division, Association for Education in Journalism and Mass Communication convention, Seattle, Wash., August 1978, p. 15.

29. Society of Professional Journalists panel.

30. Clinton Cox, "Meanwhile In Bedford-Stuyvesant . . .," *Civil Rights Digest,* Winter 1977, p. 39.

31. See, for example, Fred Fedler, "Newspapers, Blacks and Crime: Emphasis on People, Not Property, Affects Balance," paper presented to Mass Communication and Society Division, Association for Education in Journalism and Mass Communication convention, August 1980.

32. "Critics say newspapers foster 'stereotypes and ill feelings' about minorities," p. 16.

33. *AP Stylebook,* p. 185.

34. Society of Professional Journalists panel.

The Revival of Religion as News

17

There's little question that one of the journalistic hallmarks of the second half of the twentieth century has been the increasing journalistic attention given to religion. It is not just attention given to announcements of church and synagogue activities, and not just attention given to evangelical messages and summaries of sermons; it is attention given to religion as news and religion as a cultural force. It is journalistic attention given to members of the clergy as individuals who handle large sums of money and who are influential leaders of social movements and to religious beliefs as factors that contribute to government and social decisions.

Of course, in the late 1980s, breaking religion stories propelled religion news onto the front page and into national news broadcasts. The revelations of scandals in the PTL ministry in 1987 made the pages of probably every newspaper in the country. The visit of Pope John Paul II to the United States that year also drew attention to religion coverage. Added to these events as the society moved into the early 1990s is the subject of prayer in school, and even the debate about legalized abortion.

Admittedly, the emphasis on religion as news is late in coming. But the signs are there that it is arriving. The arguments as a result of the coverage have started. Religious groups are complaining (sometimes even threatening) about the scrutiny. They're organizing and learning how to deal with this new attention.

Within journalism, self-analysis is more frequent. Internal discussion and criticism are finding their way to the agendas of journalistic organizations. Professional reports often are more critical of public complaints. As early as 1979, Ronald I. Goble of the *Visalia* (California) *Times-Delta* told the Associated Press Managing Editors that church pages must be resurrected—they should focus on people, dig into theological issues and be committed to news.[1]

Times have changed since Goble's comments; but most religion reporters and editors still do not believe that enough space, time, and
energy is devoted to covering religion. Public interest in religion appears to wax and wane with time, but the concern is always there. Psy-
chologists, anthropologists, and philosophers will attest that religion is
a permanent and inevitable characteristic of being human.

"Every newspaper survey that has ever been taken in the last quarter
century finds religion high on the list of reader interest," says George
Cornell of The Associated Press, perhaps the dean of the nation's religion writers. "But newspapers continue to second-rate it as if it were a
peripheral or secondary concern. That aversion stems, I think, not from
attention to readership, but from habit—an old 'front page' notion that
newspaper desks must be staffed by hard-bitten cynics, that religion is
too controversial (which ordinarily is a measure of news interest), that
religion is 'soft' and not 'hard' news. All of these are wrongheaded."

Cornell and some of his colleagues are adamant that religion is news
and must be covered as news, not as the view of any particular group.
Religious organizations represent people speaking out of their deepest
convictions, and what they say is an expression of social thought.

Religion news is also part of the mix that goes into determining national and international directions. For example, the World Council of
Churches in 1957 called for a ban on above-ground testing of atomic
weapons. The council's position was denounced as pro-Communist at
the time, but four years later, the ban was signed into policy by the major
powers.

Consider civil rights, a movement dominated by churches and church
leaders. It's not surprising that the name most strongly associated with
the movement, Martin Luther King Jr., is that of a minister. Perhaps the
leading civil rights spokesman today, Jesse Jackson, is a member of the
clergy.

But of equal significance to the local reporter is the fact that churches
and synagogues often are at the front of tackling serious community
problems. Recreation programs designed to give young people alternatives to roaming the streets are supported, sponsored, or even operated by religious organizations. Efforts to clean up crime-ridden portions
of town may be spearheaded by members of the clergy. Support for the
poor, shelter for battered spouses, and even efforts to attract industry are
seldom accomplished without the involvement of religious leaders.

The best religion reporters know this. Perceptive religious leaders know it. Not only are more reporters being urged to do more about it, but also journalism schools, editors, and news directors are at least beginning to stress that the religion beat is as important—or more important—than beats such as city hall, schools, and law enforcement.

RELIGION'S GHETTO: THE CHURCH PAGE

The standard coverage by American newspapers of religion has been to devote a page or two or three to it once a week, usually Saturday, and then to fill most of the space with advertisements for merchants who believe, as one newspaper announced, "the church represents the greatest force for good." Beyond that, one finds church notices, wire stories, perhaps a column by a local minister, and occasionally a feature story about some church activity. Standard coverage by broadcasters, for the most part, has been to ignore the subject unless something controversial or exciting happens.

Historically, the typical church page was the result of news organizations placing little stock in the news value of religion and not wanting to run the risk of offending church leaders and members. They simply did not have the guts to give religion the same scrutiny commonly devoted to politics or law enforcement. It's safe to stick to a bland diet of activities, pastoral changes, or comments under some minister's byline.

The church page often was produced (and still is, in many cases) by part-time personnel who devoted the end of the week to collecting miscellaneous trivia. Over time, these efforts were helped by an increasing interest of advertisers, a growing flow of publicity handouts from religious organizations, and development of syndicated inspirational columns. This resulted in a bland and highly standardized image of church life on the religion pages.

There can be greater value to church or religion pages if a newspaper goes beyond the obvious announcements and tries to provide coverage of religious issues and personalities. That value depends on what reporters and editors decide to do.

Religion news must have the opportunity to compete with other news for locations in the paper, including page one. Given that circumstance, the church pages may be used for stories that are not of general interest

Bruce Buursma
of The Chicago Tribune (Chicago
Tribune photo)

but are important to the dedicated reader who turns to that section, just as sports fans turn to the sports pages or those interested in finance turn to the financial section. The pages may be used informationally to provide facts on upcoming major community religious events, much as the political reporter would write that the governor is going to speak.

But too often that is not the case, because many editors do not view religion in the same light as other types of news, says Bruce Buursma of the *Chicago Tribune.* Buursma has covered religion for the *Tribune* and for the Louisville *Courier-Journal.*

"It's very easy for an editor, if you're going to go out on a Monday night to cover some local religious controversy, to say, 'Well, we're a little short on space for tomorrow's paper. Why don't you hold that thing until Saturday and put it on your church page?' And that destroys the immediacy of the thing, and it gives the impression to religion writers, and I think the public too, that religion is an inferior subject to cover, and it doesn't carry as much interest as politics or crime or lust or whatever. Surveys show that's simply not true."

It's not true for two reasons. First, even in highly secular historic periods, religion remains a powerful, though subsurface, force in the lives of many people. Second, it tends to rise in its social importance to peaks of public concern and activity. Two such peaks helped transform religion reporting. One came immediately after World War II.

Church attendance became a way of life in the early postwar era, and the World Council of Churches and the National Council of Churches came into being. In part as a result of this, those covering religion in the secular press formed in 1949 the Religion Newswriters Association, a group whose goal it was to improve religion coverage. The RNA now has more than 200 members.

During the time the RNA was formed, religion began its move from the news ghetto. In some instances, church pages were abolished, and religion began to compete for space. William Simbro of the *Des Moines Register* credits magazines, particularly *Time,* with paving the way. The magazine put religion on the cover, and some larger newspapers began to follow suit.

Then came a time of seeming religious drought—the infamous 1960s—in which the mood, especially among younger people, was at least nonreligious if not antireligious. But even then, says former *New York Times* religion editor Ken Briggs, forces were beginning to collect which would result once again in religious emphasis.

"There were quieter movements going on," he says. "The whole evangelical burgeoning was in a kind of germinating stage at that point. As secularism made its inroads and more people became detached from the basic teachings of religious faiths, the ignorance level rose to such a point that it was time for people to rediscover. There was a whole repository of wisdom, belief, ways of looking at the world that they had simply not been exposed to. And what we're dealing with in the late 1970s and 1980s, to a great extent, are young people whose emerging religious awareness became very apparent, very striking."

As was the case in the late 1980s, specific news stories heightened interest in religion in the late 1970s and early 1980s. One of those stories was in the Catholic Church, with the 1978 papal deaths and elections and the growing debate over Catholic doctrine. The second was the controversial activities of the Moral Majority in and following the 1980 presidential elections.

"I don't think there has been a single field of journalism that's undergone a more stunning transition than religion," Briggs says. "The emphasis has moved away from a kind of special treatment, deference, kid-gloves approach, and bulletin-board style to covering religion as a legitimate area of newsworthy activity which can subject the institutions and the movements to criticism as well as give an opportunity to really inform the people what they're about."

Journalism's response has been inconsistent. Some news organizations, as Goble's comments verify, stayed where they were. The bland church pages continued. Others have abolished the ghetto and put religion news on the same basis as other areas of coverage. And some, like the *St. Petersburg Times,* have maintained the special-section concept by establishing separate tabloids or pullouts devoted extensively to religion. However, these publications are more than bulletin boards. They contain real news as well as announcements. And they are not restrictive. Reporters know that if they have a breaking story of importance, it may find its way to page one.

PATTERNS OF RELIGION COVERAGE

If it is a new wave of journalism to treat religion as bona fide news, it is logical to ask just what that means. It would be true, but overly simplistic, to say it means attempting to provide the full story. Equally true, but also simplistic, would be to say it means applying all the traditional textbook lists of qualities of newsworthiness. Perhaps the best question, really, is how the new religion coverage differs from its treatment in the past.

For one thing, the best religion reporters are seeking to cover their subject much more broadly. This nation has been predominantly Christian with a rather substantial Jewish minority since its inception. News organizations have attempted to reflect that. Attention has focused on the "big three"—Protestant, Catholic, and Jewish—and the result has been a widespread ignorance about other forms of organized religion, most of which are at least represented in this country. The smaller, often less organized, denominations were ignored, with the possible occasional exception of coverage in the locale in which they function. That's changing.

Despite its dusty image, religion can be an illuminating beat

By Elwood M. Wardlow

There is a growing body of thought that religion is one of the best beats a reporter could have.

That's still a minority view; the average reporter would still throw a fit if assigned to "the church page." But there are definite signs of change.

There are several reasons religion reporting fell into its long torpor:

• A secularizing process has been under way through most of this century. The church has lost some of its primal role in peoples' lives.

• Where once the church was the foremost shepherd and comfort, the state, the schools and other institutions shouldered their way in also.

• The churches forgot to take their arteriosclerosis pills. They let themselves become centers of ritual, rather than centers of learning.

• Spiritual questings came to be individual and inner-directed, rather than outer-imposed. A fluid world clashed harshly with rigid belief.

• The clergy, by and large, squandered a fine postwar opportunity for revival by emphasizing justice (a secular attribute) rather than values.

• Religion used to be a touchy subject. People tested the water before they talked about it. Newspapers finessed the sensitivities in a dull, institutionalized way—all very safe.

All that sounds pretty dismal, so we need to turn the coin over and see the shiny other side:

• Religion in its broader sense—beyond the incense, the turned collars, the white steeples—survived robustly. Even when all seemed bleakest (God dying, churches closing, clergy straying), there was the counterpoint of Jesus freaks and flower children. "Religion" took root in the streets as it wilted in the cathedrals.

• The thirst for a strong and central value system never ebbed. There were interminable arguments over *what* value system, but those arguments will go on until the last tribe disappears.

• The growth of offbeat and fundamentalist groups has put the old mainline churches to the test. There are encouraging signs that some are freshening their approaches to meet the competition.

• Some of the clergy are making it back to high ground. They got strung out for a time in the briar patches of social strife, but seem to be refocusing on their own special role: preacher/teacher.

• Newspapers, and the media at large have lifted their sights in every other area of reporting—and are finally getting around to the hoary old religion beat. Just as the police beat is more than cops and robbers, the religion beat is more than hiring new ministers, burning mortgages and announcing Lenten prayer schedules. The best of humankind's thoughts, the most lustrous of its visions, the most cherished of its values are within the legitimate jurisdiction of the religion writer.

We need to continue that movement beyond the dusty approaches of the past. The present mind-set of our society will tolerate that; indeed, cries out for it. And the mind-set of our *profession* cries out for nothing less.

That could be, and should be, a heady prospect for a reporter. Let us pray.

Woody Wardlow, former reporter, editor and journalism educator, is associate director of the American Press Institute, Reston, Va. The story appeared in the *American Society* of *Newspaper Editors Bulletin,* July/August, 1985. (Reprinted with permission.)

"We have a lot of space for religion," says Virginia Culver of the *Denver Post.* "And we run everything we know that would make a good story. It makes no difference whether it's hard news or features or pictures. We don't make judgments that we will cover Christianity of the big three or whatever. We cover anything. We cover all kinds of cults. If people think that's their religion, that's their religion as far as we're concerned. We're not in the business of promoting religions or trying to stamp them out. All we do is report."

Inexorably related to this breadth is an increasing effort to apply standard journalistic fairness to religion coverage. Covering religious "sects"—or those religions out of the mainstream in the United States—often poses a challenge to reporters. What is one person's true salvation is another person's bizarre cult.

Most reporters say that what matters most in covering sects is not the "strangeness" of a sect's activities, but the legality of those activities and their effects on children, few of whom are members by choice.[2] Reporters say many religious sects put up a wall of silence, making it difficult to get information from these groups. Michael D'Antonio, a religion writer for *Newsday* on Long Island says "defectors" or those disenchanted with a sect often leak information about it. But he also warns that reporters should sometimes be wary of such sources—they often have an ax to grind.[3]

Resources about religious sects or "cults" are available to reporters. The Chicago-based National Cult Awareness Network has affiliates in thirty-eight cities in the United States and has on file information about religious groups that are not mainstream. Has legal action been taken against any of these groups, for instance? Is there any financial information about them?

Sondra Chesky, president of the Houston office of the Cult Awareness Network, acknowledges that no "definition" of cult exists. But many researchers into the phenomenon say cults often involve charismatic but deceitful leaders who seek power or wealth, and they usually draw followers through brainwashing or mind control.

Chesky points out that the existence of religious cults has ramifications for all of American society—not just for those involved in the cults. These groups usually get tax-exempt status on property owned, and they often own millions of dollars of land and other property. In addition, because some cults prohibit members from visiting family members, these groups have a widespread effect on the family.[4] It is estimated by the Cult Awareness Network that more than 1.5 million people worldwide—and possible as many as 3 million—are involved in what can be termed "cults" or sects.

Karen Thorsen of Dallas, Texas, who says she was formerly a member of a motivational cult, urges reporters to do their homework before investigating or writing about any religious, political, or self-help organization that appears to be out of mainstream society. She also warns that reporters seeking to infiltrate these groups by joining them should be careful. After every meeting, reporters should talk to a counselor and discuss their feelings about activities of the group daily. Leaders are so subtle yet powerful than even someone investigating them can begin believing their claims, she says.[5]

Religion and Culture

No social institution, including organized religion, can function effectively for long in a way that is contrary to culture. It may hold true to old patterns for a while, perhaps even years, but change is inevitable. The reporter should be there to record that change and to relate it to the culture in which it occurred. If analysis of culture provides a yardstick with which to measure the role of religion, the coin has another side. Religion provides a means through which reporters may analyze culture.

"Religion always mirrors what's going on in the culture," Briggs says. "Particularly religious institutions because they're conservative. They don't always react as quickly, and that's sometimes why they make news. Things work through the system more slowly, but then suddenly those cultural happenings begin to filter through and the church mixes them with its own peculiar and particular way of looking at the world. There is a transcendent element there that also brings something to the culture and look at itself in ways it wouldn't otherwise."

That's why, he adds, he tries to take a thematic approach to his religion coverage. Balancing local coverage, event coverage, and national coverage is difficult, and the bigger picture is lost if the reporter fails to find and to concentrate upon inherent cultural characteristics or actions.

Discovery of the bigger picture involves a broader understanding. Religion impinges on just about every public concern and issue, from war to sex. Whether the issue is crime, foreign aid, the law, nuclear power, economics, labor dispute, consumer fraud, or the quality of television shows, religious presuppositions are involved. The basic question always is: What's the right, the just, and the good solution? That's a moral question bound with religious premises about human obligations. The role that religious premise or organized religion plays in any public concern will both influence and be influenced by the culture.

Moral Influences in the Real World

Religion is not something individuals can separate from what they do, and this applies to public officials. Closely related to the cultural approach—but on a more intimate, personal level—is the matter of how individual beliefs influence, or even predict, the position of a public official on a specific issue. This consideration, in the opinion of many, is an aspect of coverage that must rank among journalism's failures.

Wesley G. Pippert, formerly a religion writer at United Press International, says that "we in the press frequently have been uneasy, unable, and perhaps even a little unwilling, in dealing competently with the moral dimension of public issues." Author of *The Spiritual Journey of Jimmy Carter*, Pippert notes that few reporters ever understood the impact of the former president's religious beliefs because they often ignored the evidence placed before them. They seldom covered Carter's Sunday School teaching, for example.

"The thought of one of the most powerful persons in the world standing in front of a small group, speaking without benefit of researcher or speechwriter, reflecting on his values, is astounding," Pippert says. "It is some of the purest Carter that we have, inasmuch as most other remarks are crafted by his stable of speechwriters."

Pippert says that, by analyzing Carter's religious background and beliefs, reporters could have discovered much more about the man, his approach to power, his views on the presidency, his insistence on human rights, and his personal drive. Indeed, much was written about Carter being born again, but much of that coverage reflected a lack of knowledge and a lack of understanding.

Ironically, religion and its links to politics became more evident after Carter left the White House. Debra Mason, religion writer for *The Columbus Dispatch* in Ohio, says religion writers in the early 1980s frequently wrote about the political power wielded by the Moral Majority and its leader, Jerry Falwell. By 1988, two ordained ministers—the Rev. Pat Robertson and the Rev. Jesse Jackson—were candidates in the primary election that year.

Mason noted that during the Reagan presidency, photographs of the President often showed him praying. Coverage was also given to his yearly addresses to the National Religious Broadcasters, and Reagan's views on such issues as prayer in school were at the forefront of the news.

Debra Mason
of the Columbus Dispatch (Columbu
Dispatch photo

Holidays can trouble two-faith families

By Debra Mason
Dispatch Religion Reporter

Wendy Fox hasn't forgotten the time a couple of years ago when her rabbi came over to deliver a Hanukkah menorah for her to light during that Jewish holiday.

"I grabbed the menorah out of his hand and quickly shut the door," she recalled, hoping he hadn't noticed the Christmas tree not-so-subtly located near a front living-room window of her East Side home.

FOX, 28, and her husband Douglas, 30, are among the growing number of Jewish-Christian couples in the United States.

Although December can be a dilemma for some interfaith couples, the Foxes have found a way to live with Mrs. Fox's Reform Movement Judaism and Mr. Fox's Roman Catholicism.

December is shared by the Christian holiday of Christmas and the eight-day Jewish festival of Hanukkah, which this year ends at sundown Sunday.

About 750,000 Americans are in Jewish-Christian marriages, with at least that many children, Jewish organizations estimate. The couples are so common that at least two books on the subject were published last year: *Raising Your Jewish-Christian Child* by Lee F. Gruzen and *Mixed Blessings,* by Paul and Rachel Cowan.

Rabbi Howard Apothaker of Temple Beth Shalom, 3100 E. Broad St., recently taught a class for interfaith couples. He will repeat it in January.

RABBIS OF the three major Jewish groups—Reform, Conservative and Orthodox—all discourage interfaith marriages. However, if a couple is already married, the attitude is to try to accept them into Reform Movement synagogue life, Apothaker said.

He said he has found that "Christmas is so available to other people that Jewish people know so much about it, and it may be easier for a family to adopt symbols of Christmas than symbols of Hanukkah."

Although the Foxes' 3-year-old son, Jonathan, attends preschool at the Jewish Center, he and his sister, Kaitlyn, 1, are learning the religious traditions of both faiths. Jonathan has been baptized, but his sister has not. At this home, Santa Claus does come to town.

But "absolutely, they will not be confirmed until either one of them is old enough to choose" a faith, Mrs. Fox said.

THERE IS a little more disagreement when it comes to where the children will attend college. Mr. Fox said Notre Dame is where Jonathan will go; Mrs. Fox says Harvard.

While some interfaith couples think children are confused by the two religious viewpoints, the Foxes do not. When they do attend either Mass or synagogue services the whole family goes.

Mr. Fox said his first temple service was more a learning experience than an awkward episode. "I never felt uncomfortable," he said.

Mrs. Fox grew up with an annual Christmas tree, although in her Jewish family it didn't carry the religious significance it does for Christians. It symbolized family happiness and giving to others, she said.

ONCE MARRIED, "the biggest dilemma was the first year, setting up the pattern" of whose family is visited when, Mrs. Fox said.

Their situation does sometimes mean special planning for their friends, who include Jewish and Christian couples.

For example, the couple sends two sets of holiday cards—one set for Christmas and the other more general, for their Jewish friends and families.

Dennis Aig, who is Jewish, and his wife, Ann Bertagnolli, who is Catholic, also jointly celebrate the holidays. Both are 38.

"We light the menorah and plug in the tree," Aig said.

AIG SAID the key to harmonious coexistence during the holidays was the couple's decision before they were married five years ago that each would be allowed to practice his or her faith. They attend both temple services and Mass on a "semi-regular" basis, Aig said.

December is not the only time when holidays from different faiths come at similar times, Aig said. The Easter season, which includes the Jewish holiday of Passover, can also be tough.

Aig is lucky because his wife's Catholic family is sensitive about his Judaism. His late father-in-law even used to complain to the merchants in the small Montana town where he lived that they didn't carry Hanukkah cards.

Even for couples where one spouse converts, December can be a tricky time.

"When Christian partners do convert, that doesn't end the problem, because there's still the family, so it's ongoing," said Rabbi Leonard Gordon, the interim rabbi of Tifereth Israel, 1354 E. Broad St.

This story, from the *Columbus Dispatch,* December 10, 1988, humanizes an issue that is affecting more and more families today—interfaith marriage. Note how national statistics are woven into this local story. (Reprinted, with permission, from the *Columbus Dispatch.*)

Religion as Controversy

Get a group together, involve participants in something as personal and emotional as religion, and controversy is inevitable. The diverse beliefs of this nation's hundreds of religious groups and predictable variations within a given group make disagreement natural. Some news organizations in the past have ignored such controversy because they felt that it was an internal matter or because they wanted to avoid alienating members of the community's churches or synagogues.

That is changing. Reporters know that a broad approach to coverage of such an important social institution must include the failures of that system as well as the successes. They know everyone is not going to like every story they write, but they can only hope their impartiality, completeness, and fairness will be respected.

Religious controversy comes in standard packages: philosophical disagreements over the purpose and appropriate activities of an organization; power struggles; corruption; and conflicts with outside groups or government or individuals. A reporter's approach must be traditional journalism involving multiple points of view. Often there can be no solution; at times there may be compromise.

Mason lists, for example, constant tension between the views of U.S. Catholics and the mandates of the Vatican. Examples of this include the Vatican's prohibition of birth control and opposition to divorce. Many Catholics in the United States take a liberal view toward these measures. When writing stories about these topics, Mason has had to acknowledge both points of view from those she interviewed.

Religious Doctrine is the Core

Explaining journalistically what people believe and why they believe it may be the biggest challenge of the religion reporter. The term is "faith," and faith, by definition, is not explainable. For many, belief does not result from rational calculation. A particular doctrine is accepted. It is not a result of thought; it's the beginning of thought.

Add to this the fact that many believe church doctrine to be a personal or internal matter that should not be discussed publicly, especially by a person who is not within the fold. The mere mention of some subjects is a source of controversy that's heightened when the information does not agree specifically with an individual's personal interpretation. Many people are sensitive about their religious beliefs, and it's easier for them when those beliefs are not discussed.

The problem is compounded when religion reporters do not have backgrounds to tackle these sensitive and complex matters. One can argue forever about whether they should be formally trained in theology—and more are these days—but the fact is that without formal training or very careful personal study, reporters are likely to heap scorn upon or shy away from stories that get into doctrinal matters.

This is unfortunate, and, says the AP's George Cornell, is a problem news organizations just continue to address.

"Newspapers and news services need specialists in religion coverage as much or more than they need specialists in sports, financial, scientific, or political coverage," he says. "It is true that religion is a universal subject, but it is far more complex than any of the others mentioned. It also is one in which there has been more misunderstanding and tribal—read denominational—misconceptions than in just about any other field.

"Those mutual misconceptions, fed by offhand scuttle-butt, backyard gossip, and ignorance, have been at the root of some of our sorriest social sores and prejudices. Religious illiteracy is rampant, particularly in our age, even in terms of many people's own religion."

Thus, if Cornell is right (and he is), the need for explanation of religious doctrine is as great for many of the traditional patterns of thought as it is for new ideas that work their way into public consideration. Some reporters do not want to tackle the old issues, the standard arguments, and the historic debates. The normal excuse for this is that it has been done, that all of the arguments have been presented, and that no conclusion can be reached. The latter point may be true, but it's wrong to say that all arguments have been presented. Genuine biblical scholars continue their study, and they tend to be ready sources for careful consideration of traditional doctrine.

Consideration of traditional doctrine, in light of new knowledge and new theories, represents a potentially exciting phase of a religion reporter's job. Biblical scholars are as close as the telephone or perhaps the nearest university campus; the results of their studies are published in journals and books; local members of the clergy have ideas to contribute. It does take time, it does take effort, and it does take conscious study. It requires dedication, both by the individual reporter and by the news organization.

Covering the Institution

In the drive to broaden the scope of religion coverage, religion re-porters—like their counterparts in other specialties—cannot forsake the obvious need for attention to activities within local churches and syn-agogues and the church as an institution. Twenty-five million Americans profess "a high degree of spiritual commitment," due, in part, to what they say is a "disenchantment with modern lifestyles," a "pervasive feeling of emptiness," and a "growing awareness of the nuclear threat."[6]

To ignore what churches, synagogues, and other places of worship do as part of the organization would be a serious error for any community-oriented news body. The raffles, bingo, groundbreakings, pastoral changes, programs, pageants, classes, meetings, and publications are what the churches are about. Call it trivia, call it mundane, or call it less than exciting. But call it necessary coverage. That's the key, if for no other reason than that any reporter must keep in touch with specific events and specific people to retain the broader perspective of religious trends and issues.

But institutional coverage is not necessarily just announcements. Every program has content, and that content represents a potential link to the broader picture. It is not necessary, of course, that every story become a thoughtful discussion of a serious religious issue. But the reporter who understands religion will find many opportunities to make a contribu-tion to public understanding.

The solution lies in the perspective and understanding of the re-porter. If he or she considers the assignment dull and incomprehen-sible, that will be the inevitable result. If he or she remains vigilant to the possibilities, more assignments will be less "hum" and more "drum."

THEY'RE LEARNING TO DEAL
WITH REPORTERS

Most religion writers would probably agree that covering religion—particularly small local churches and religious groups—requires the utmost sensitivity. Many issues involving the subject are emotionally charged, and often the people written about are sensitive or defensive about what appears in the press or on the air.

The fact that religion is the subject matter doesn't imply that reporters won't have to apply their normal skepticism to sources, especially min-isters.

Mason believes that religious leaders involved in misconduct or controversy are just as likely as anyone else to cover up that misconduct. She has had to cover those types of stories, which usually require digging and persistence.

In addition to individual religious leaders who have learned to deal with reporters, every major denomination—and, in fact, some of the nation's very large individual churches—has public relations arms. These are no different from their counterparts in other fields. They can be very helpful, both as suppliers of information and as initiators of story ideas. They can open doors. They are subject to the same limitations of any PR outfit, so reporters are wise not to depend on them exclusively.

Two Popes Comment on Reporters and the Media

The expanding relationship between journalism and religion is underscored by comments made early in their tenures by the two most recent popes. The popes stress that the times dictate working together, and they emphasize the need for responsibility and the importance of the task:

Pope John Paul I: "This pleasing meeting gives us a chance to thank you for the sacrifices and toil to which you have faced during the month of August in serving world public opinion—yours, too, is a very important service— by offering to your readers, listeners and television viewers, with the rapid and immediate delivery required of your responsible and sensitive profession, the possibility of participating in these historical events, in their religious dimension, with their deep connection to human values and the expectation of today's society. . . .

"When major events happen and when the Holy See publishes important documents, you will often have to present the church, speak of the church, and sometimes comment on our humble ministry. We are sure that you will do it with love of truth and respect for human dignity because such is the goal of all social communications. We ask you to help safeguard in today's society a deep regard for the things of God and for the mysterious relationships between God and each of us, which constitutes the sacred dimension of human reality."[7]

Pope John Paul II: "My dear friends of the communications media: It would hardly be possible for me to depart from the United Nations without saying 'thank you' from my heart to those who have reported, not only the day's events, but all the activities of this worthy organization. In this international assembly, you can truly be instruments of peace by being messengers of the truth. You are indeed servants of truth; you are its tireless transmitters, diffusers, defenders. You are dedicated communicators, promoting unity among all nations by sharing truth among all peoples.

"If your reporting does not always command the attention you would desire, or if it does not always conclude with the success that you would wish, do not grow discouraged. Be faithful to the truth and to its transmission, for truth endures; truth will not go away. Truth will not pass or change.

"And I say to you—take it as my parting words to you—that the service of truth, the service of humanity through the medium of the truth is something worthy of your best years, your finest talents, your most dedicated efforts. As transmitters of truth, you are instruments of understanding among people and of peace among nations."[8]

But the two popes are not the only religious leaders to have some encouraging and kind words for the press. New York City's John Cardinal O'Connor called journalism a "terribly difficult profession" and one that requires reporters to "demand" the truth. He compared the printed page to the stone used by Moses to carve the Ten Commandments. "We tend to blame the press for everything from Original Sin to the flood survived by Noah in his ark to the condition of the Williamsburg Bridge."[9]

Evangelist Falwell, too, said the coverage of financial irregularities and scandal at the PTL ministry has actually helped Christianity. Christian leaders, he said, had been "arrogant, independent, (and) hiding behind the First Amendment" before that story broke.

He added that the *Charlotte Observer,* which broke the PTL story, and other media outlets should be congratulated for their coverage of it. The stories, Falwell said, led to a "personal religious awakening" by members of the media.[10]

RESOURCES FOR THE RELIGION REPORTER

Religion is not static. Reporters find themselves dealing with new ideas and new approaches. Keeping track of these ideas and approaches is possible. Even the local religion reporter has resources available and can read the major religious periodicals. Following are some that should be helpful.

Reference Materials:

Yearbook of American Churches, published annually by the National Council of Churches. Good for statistical information and for personnel lists of virtually every religious body in the country.

National Catholic Directory, published annually by P. J. Kenedy & Sons.

A *Bible,* of which several good translations are available. The most frequently used probably is the Revised Standard Version.

Concordance of the Bible, to provide ready answers to where a particular passage came from.

AP or *UPI Stylebook,* which contains relatively detailed background information on structure, officials, and beliefs of most major denominations.

Periodicals:

Christian Century, published in Chicago, an ecumenical publication which does a good job of digesting current thought.

Christianity Today, published in Wheaton, Illinois, a leading conservative evangelical publication.

National Catholic Reporter, Kansas City, Missouri, the best source of Catholic thought.

NOTES

1. Ronald I. Goble, "Church Pages and Religion: An Introduction," *Report of the APME Modern Living Committee,* 1979, pp. 2–3. Reprinted with permission from The Associated Press.

2. Leslie Brown, "The 'Cult' Beat," *Columbia Journalism Review,* November/December 1985, p. 46.

3. "The 'Cult' Beat," p. 47.

4. Sondra Chesky, remarks made during "Destructive Cults and How They Work," Society of Professional Journalists, October 21, 1989, Houston, Texas.

5. Karen Thorsen, "Destructive Cults and How They Work."

6. Cal Thomas, "Not Ready for Prime Time Prayers," *The Quill,* October 1986, p. 15.

7. "The Journalists Meet the Pope," *Origins, NC Documentary Service,* September 14, 1978, pp. 199–200.

8. From remarks presented October 2, 1979, at the United Nations, quoted in "Something Worthy of Your Best Years," *The Quill,* December 1979, p. 12.

9. Keith Kelly, "New York Cardinal Praises the Press," *Editor & Publisher,* July 16, 1988, p. 24.

10. "No Fault from Falwell," *Editor & Publisher,* October 10, 1987, p. 17.

Appendix

How to Use the Federal FOI Act

The following was adapted from "The Freedom of Information Act: A User's Guide," produced by the Freedom of Information Clearinghouse. The clearinghouse, a project of Ralph Nader's Center for Study of Responsive Law, provides assistance to individuals, public interest groups, and the media.

HOW TO MAKE A REQUEST

The first step is to determine what you want, since the law requires that your request must "reasonably describe" the records you seek.

This means that you may not simply ask questions, but must request records describing or pertaining to a particular subject. You do not need to specify a document by name or title. What you must do is provide a reasonable enough description to allow a government employee who is familiar with the agencies' file to locate the records you seek.

For example, if you want information on nursing homes in your area, and know that the government requires some sort of annual surveys to be conducted of nursing homes, it is sufficient to ask that you want to see the surveys and all documents pertaining to the surveys for particular years and/or regions.

The second step is to decide which agency has the information you want and the address to write to within the agency. There is no central government FOIA office; each agency has its own office or public information staff. There is no special way of determining which agency has the information other than common sense and telephone calls to various agencies. When you have found the agency that has the information, ask for the address of the office that processes Freedom of Information requests.

To submit a request do the following:

▶ Your request should state that it is being made pursuant to the Freedom of Information Act (5 U.S.C. Sec. 552).

▶ You should write "Freedom of Information Request" on the en-
velope and on the letter.

▶ You do not have to explain the reasons for your request, and government employees generally do not have any right to ask (except
when it pertains to a waiver of fees).

Under the FOIA, an agency may deny your request only if the documents are specifically covered by one of the act's exemptions. Moreover,
agencies may, in their discretion, release records even though they are
covered by an exemption.

HOW TO APPEAL

If your request is partially or entirely denied, you have the right to
appeal within the agency or department.

The denial form should inform you of appeal procedures and the
proper address to send your appeal letter. Your appeal letter should include a description of your request, a copy of your request, and a statement indicating that you are appealing the agency's initial decision.

If possible, you should try to explain why the denial was unwarranted,
either because the exemption does not apply or because the agency
should use its discretion to release the records anyway.

TIME DEADLINES

The law sets specific deadlines for replying to FOI requests: 10 working
days on the initial request and 20 working days on the administrative
appeal.

Nevertheless, delay is common. Even though the law says that an
agency may receive a time extension only in exceptional circumstances,
agencies extend these deadlines regularly. However, if an agency fails
to respond to your request within 10 days, you may treat the request as
denied and immediately appeal or go to court.

Remember, the more precise you make your request, the less likely
that an agency will delay its response to seek clarification. Also, following up written requests with phone calls can speed up your requests.
If agencies are aware that you know your rights, they will sometimes
move more quickly.

Agency Head (or Freedom of Information Officer)
Name of Agency
Address of Agency
City, State, Zip Code
Re: Freedom of Information Act Request

Dear (FOI Officer):

This is a request under the Freedom of Information Act.

I request that a copy of the following documents (or documents containing the following information) be provided to me: (identify the documents or information as specifically as possible).

In order to help to determine my status to assess fees, you should know that I am (insert a suitable description of the requester and the purpose of the request):

(Sample requester descriptions:

a representative of the news media affiliated with the newspaper (magazine, television station, etc.), and this request is made as part of news gathering and not for a commercial use.

affiliated with an educational or noncommercial scientific institution, and this request is made for a scholarly or scientific purpose and not for a commercial use.

an individual seeking information for personal use and not for a commercial use.

affiliated with a private corporation and am seeking information for use in the company's business.)

(Optional) I am willing to pay fees for this request up to a maximum of $_____. If you estimate that the fees will exceed this limit, please inform me first.

(Optional) I request a waiver of all fees for this request. Disclosure of the requested information to me is in the public interest because it is likely to contribute significantly to public understanding of the operations or activities of the government and is not primarily in my commercial interest. (Include a specific explanation.)

Thank you for your consideration of this request.

Sincerely,

Name
Address
City, State, Zip Code
Telephone number (Optional)

COSTS

The act provides that agencies may charge different fees depending upon who is requesting the information.

Commercial users pay reasonable standard charges for document search, review, and duplication. Educational or noncommercial scientific institutions and representatives of the news media may only be charged for reasonable duplication costs.

All other users may be charged for document search and duplication; however, except for commercial users, the first two hours of search time and the first 100 pages of copying are free. To save money on reproduction expenses, you can ask to see the documents themselves instead of having copies sent.

Regardless of the above categories, you may be entitled to a waiver or reduction of fees if, according to the act, "disclosure of the information is in the public interest because it is likely to contribute significantly to public understanding of the operations or activities of the government and is not primarily in the commercial interest of the requester."

In requesting a fee waiver, you should explain why you are seeking the information and how your access to it will further public understanding or awareness of government.

GOING TO COURT

The act is designed to make litigation as simple as possible. In some instances, taking an FOIA case to court is not overly complicated and requesters can do it themselves without a lawyer. However, it is more helpful to have a lawyer if you litigate in court.

After your appeal is denied, you may sue in the United States District Court, where you live, where the documents are located, or in the District of Columbia. If the government cannot prove that the requested documents fall within one of nine exemptions from the act's disclosure requirement, then the court will order the agency to give the documents to you.

THE NINE EXEMPTIONS

If the agency withholds some or all of the records you seek it must do so under one or more of the nine exemptions listed below:

(1) National Security: The documents exempt under this section are those that are properly classified pursuant to a Presidential Executive

Order. However, courts will not necessarily take an official's word on the propriety of the classification, and may look at the information itself to see if it is properly classified.

The fact that a document is classified may not justify its withholding if the information is old, or was classified merely to prevent domestic political repercussions.

(2) Internal Agency Rules: This exemption protects rules and practices of agency personnel that are "predominantly internal in nature and, where disclosure serves no substantial public interest and significantly risks circumvention of agency regulations or statutes."

Thus, minor employee matters such as employee parking and cafeteria regulations are exempt.

(3) Information Exempted by Another Federal Statute: This exemption honors mandatory nondisclosure provisions in other laws. There is a comprehensive list of all laws covered by exemption 3, but examples include income tax returns and completed census bureau forms.

(4) Trade Secrets: The agencies may withhold information under this section only if it is either a trade secret or commercial or financial information. Information that can be proven to be a trade secret is absolutely protected.

For commercial or financial information the government must prove that the information is confidential and that its disclosure would be likely to either impair the agency's ability to obtain necessary information in the future or to cause substantial competitive injury to the submitter.

(5) Internal Agency Memoranda: This exemption protects information about an agency's decision-making process. Thus advice and recommendations involving a "deliberative process" on legal and policy matters may be withheld but the factual portions of documents should be disclosed.

For instance, a memo from a staff person to a supervisor recommending that a particular policy be established would be exempt from disclosure. But the factual portions of this memo would not be exempt unless they reveal the deliberative decision-making process of the agency.

(6) Personal Privacy: This exemption involves a balancing of the public's interest in disclosure against the degree of invasion of privacy that would result from disclosure.

If your request involves this exemption, you should provide a brief explanation of the public benefits from disclosure so that it can be determined whether the invasion of privacy resulting from disclosure would be "clearly unwarranted."

(7) Investigatory Records: This exemption protects information compiled for law enforcement purposes that could reasonably be expected to interfere with enforcement proceedings, to identify a confidential source, to disclose techniques and procedures for law enforcement investigations, or to invade personal privacy.

(8) & (9) Other Exemptions: These are two special-interest exemptions relating to banking and oil-well information that are not relevant to most applications of the act.

Note: Under certain circumstances an agency may state that it has no records subject to your request, even though it does in fact have some relevant records.

For example, under exemption 1 (national security), the government can refuse to acknowledge the existence of classified records if the mere existence of records is classified. Under exemption 7 (investigatory records) where a subject is not aware of a criminal investigation and disclosure could interfere with law enforcement proceedings, the government can refuse to state whether such records exist.

Used by permission of the Freedom of Information Clearinghouse, P.O. Box 19367, Washington, D.C. 20036. Phone number: (202) 785–3704.

Index